STUDIES IN

Judaism and Pluralism

Honoring the 60th Anniversary of
THE ACADEMY FOR JEWISH RELIGION

Edited by Leonard Levin

Ben Yehuda Press
Teaneck, New Jersey

Published by Ben Yehuda Press
122 Ayers Court Suite 1B
Teaneck, NJ 07666

http://www.BenYehudaPress.com

paperback ISBN13 978-1-934730-60-7
hardcover ISBN13 978-1-934730-61-4

Grateful acknowledgement is made to reprint the following:

Joel Alter, "Documenting Core Values: A Pluralism Audit in a Day School," published in *Hayidion*, Fall, 2015. Reprinted with the permission of Ravsak: The Jewish Community Day School Network.

Shira Pasternak Beeri, "Texting Across the Jewish-Arab Divide" (October–November, 2014) and "A Ramadan Rorschach" (July, 2015), published as blogs in *The Times of Israel* (online). Reprinted with the permission of *The Times of Israel*.

Richard Claman, "A Philosophical Basis for Halakhic Pluralism," published in *Conservative Judaism* 54 (2001), 60–80. Reprinted with the permission of the Rabbinical Assembly.

David Greenstein, "By the Sweat of Your Brow: Approaching Kashrut from a Pluralistic Perspective," published in *Conservative Judaism* 56 (2003), 3–35. Reprinted with the permission of the Rabbinical Assembly.

Reuven Hammer, "Dilemmas of Democracy and Judaism in Israel." Portions of this were published in Reuven Hammer, "Jewish Political Ethics in Israel," in *The Oxford Handbook of Jewish Ethics and Morality*, edited by Dorff and Crane, 2013. Reprinted with the permission of Oxford University Press.

Beth Kissileff, "Where Denominations Lose Their Meaning," published in *The Tower* (online) 14 (May, 2014). Reprinted with the permission of The Tower.

Alan Mittleman, "Pluralism: Identity, Civility, and the Common Good," published in *Modern Judaism* 21 (May, 2001). Reprinted with the permission of Oxford University Press.

Susan L. Shevitz and Rahel Wasserfall, "Building Community in a Pluralist High School," published in *Jewish Day Schools, Jewish Communities*, edited by Alex Pomson and Howard Deitcher, 375–393. Reprinted with the permission of Littman Library of Jewish Civilization.

16 17 18 / 10 9 8 7 6 5 4 3 2 1   20161123

Table of Contents

Contents

Introduction   *Leonard Levin*   v

AJR and Pluralism

Living Pluralism at AJR   *Ora Horn Prouser*   1

Theories of Pluralism

Confessions of a Reluctant Pluralist   *Bruce Alpert*   11
On Epistemic Humility   *Leonard Levin*   19
A Reply to Leonard Levin   *Bruce Alpert*   29
Isaiah Berlin and Jewish Pluralism   *Leonard Levin*   31
Pluralism: Identity, Civility, and the Common Good   *Alan Mittleman*   41
Pluralism as Social Consensus and Personal Worldview   *Eliezer Schweid*   65

Pluralism in the Jewish Sources

Talking with Heretics: Pluralism in Rabbinic Judaism
and its Impact on Pedagogy   *Ruth N. Sandberg*   79
Rabbinic Pluralism — Then and Now   *Leonard Levin*   97

Diversity and Pluralism in Today's Jewish Communities

Pluralism: Making a Passionate Orthodox Judaism More Meaningful
Asher Lopatin   117
Pluralism in Action: Choosing a New Siddur in an Unaffiliated Synagogue
Ellen Lippmann and *Trisha Arlin*   123
Increasing Diversity in the American Jewish Community
Heidi Hoover   135
The Power of the Pluralist Rabbi   *Rabbi Rebecca W. Sirbu*   145

Pluralistic Approaches to Jewish Practice

A Philosophic Basis for Halakhic Pluralism *Richard L. Claman* 155
By the Sweat of Your Brow:
Approaching Kashrut from a Pluralistic Perspective *David Greenstein* 181
Magen Tzedek: A Memoir And Reflection *Morris Allen* 219

Pluralism in Jewish Education

Documenting Core Values:
A Pluralism Audit in a Jewish Day School *Joel Alter* 231
Documenting Core Values: Building Community in a Pluralist High School
Susan l. Shevitz and Rahel Wasserfall 235
CAJE into NewCAJE: Pluralistically Educating the Educators
Cherie Koller-Fox 255
Where Denominations Lose Their Meaning *Beth Kissileff* 277

Jews and Others in Today's World

Dilemmas of Judaism and Democracy in Israel *Reuven Hammer* 289
Texting Across the Arab-Jewish Divide *Shira Pasternak Be'eri* 301
From Burma to Brooklyn and Back Again:
How Mindfulness Captivated Jewish Spirituality *Michael Friedman* 307
Affiliation with and Abandonment of Judaism as
Acts of Spiritual Migration: A Theological Essay *Yehoyada Amir* 323

Teachings

Reflections on Gathering in Grief for Hope and Healing
2014 Israel/Gaza Conflict and Beyond *Katy Z. Allen* 349
Judaism as Ongoing Spiritual Evolution: Three Sermons
Kaya Stern-Kaufman 353
God and Gender *Dorothy Goldberg* 363
Kavanah Before Shofar-Blowing *Trisha Arlin* 367

Notes On Contributors 371
Pluralism and the Academy for Jewish Religion 375

Introduction

Leonard Levin

On behalf of the Academy for Jewish Religion (AJR), in celebrating the sixtieth anniversary of its founding, I am pleased to participate in offering this collection of studies and reflections on the meaning of pluralism for Jewish thought and practice, historically and in the current moment.

What is pluralism? And what does it have to do with Judaism?

When I teach the AJR course on pluralism, I offer the following succinct definition of pluralism:

"Pluralism is granting legitimacy to views and practices other than mine/ours."

Let me unpack the implications of this definition:

I start out with views and practices that I call "mine" or "ours." A view is a picture of the world that I take to be true. A practice is a way of behaving that I take to be right. I start with the naïve presupposition that my picture of the world is the one true picture, and that my way of behaving is the one right way. If that is the case, then a view or practice differing from mine may be presumed to be wrong.

I need go no further than my next of kin to challenge this presumption. Though belonging to the same family, each of us sees the world through different eyes and acts differently in the world. There is a temptation at this point to fall over into relativism. We may define relativism as the view that there is no objective right or wrong, but only your view and my view, without any possibility of deciding between them. Pluralism differs from relativism by striving for a golden mean between a dogmatic claim to objectivity and descent into pure subjectivity. It posits a triangle between my view; your view; and the objective world confronting us both, which we each try to capture in our subjective apperceptions. We need to negotiate the difference between your view and mine in order to arrive at a more comprehensive picture of reality. I need to appreciate the legitimate apperceptions in your view, and you need to do the same vis-à-vis mine, in order to arrive at a partial and it is hoped growing consensus of inter-subjectively validated apperceptions of the objective world. Pluralism is the ongoing give-and-take that seeks to achieve this dynamic partial consensus, while recognizing and respecting the differences that persist between us.

The dialectic that I describe between myself and my next-of-kin gets reproduced as I expand my purview to embrace the concentric circles describing the groups with which I identify—my immediate and extended family, my local face-to-face community, my tribe or city, my religious group, my nation, humanity, the biosphere, the planet, and the universe. At each level, we reproduce the dichotomy between our own views and practices and those of outsiders or dissenters. Orthodox Jews differ from Conservative, Reform, Reconstructionist, Renewal, and Humanistic Jews. Jews differ from Christians, Muslims, Buddhists, Hindus, etc. Americans differ from English, French, Russian, Chinese, Rwandan, and other peoples. Liberals differ from conservatives as do militarists from pacifists, etc. In each of these differentiated groupings, a pluralist approach is the same, conferring provisional legitimacy on those who differ from us, recognizing that despite our differences we each strive in good faith to perceive the reality of the objective world confronting us, and teaching us that we can learn from those who disagree with us, thus enriching our view of reality.

Another elastic term in the definition is "legitimacy." There are different degrees of legitimacy that I may confer on a differing view or practice. These have been analyzed perceptively by Donniel Hartman in the introduction to his book, *The Boundaries of Judaism*, where he speaks of pluralism, tolerance, tolerable deviance, and intolerable deviance. For example, Ashkenazic Jews confer complete legitimacy to the Sephardic Jews' custom of eating legumes on Passover. A lesser degree of legitimacy is accorded (let us say) by Jews who read the entire Torah portion on the Sabbath to those who follow the triennial cycle, reading one-third of the traditional portion. Many Modern Orthodox Jews generally place Reform Jews in a category of "tolerated deviancy," recognizing their Jewish status while not approving of their deviations from standard Jewish practice. We still have need, too, of the category of "intolerable deviance" for practices such as "Jewish messianism," terrorism, slavery, and racial discrimination.

In contemporary American political discourse, part of the issue between liberals and conservatives revolves around the question of whether the proponents on one side of the debate merely dismissively tolerate the legal right of those on the other side to voice their opinion, or appreciatively listen to it as a possible contribution to wisdom on regarding societal governance in pursuit of the common good. Among groups within Jewry, the same question applies in discussions about formulating the outlook and practices of Judaism in our own time.

In the interpretation offered here, yoking "Judaism and pluralism" also implies that this pluralist dialectic is intrinsic to Judaism historically, and crucial to confronting the tasks of Judaism today. This affirmation must be squared with the idea that Judaism as Torah represents objective truth: God's instruction and commandment to the Jewish people and to humanity. The paradox of objective truth and pluralism is captured in the rabbinic maxim, *elu ve-elu divrei elohim ḥayyim*—"these and those are both the words of the living God." In other words, God's truth is broad enough to embrace the differing human apperceptions of that truth, and each should respect the other as potentially embodying God's truth.

Pluralism is not absolute and infinite; the concept has its limits in each context in which it finds application. Scientifically, the limit is imposed by the concept of an objective world that different theories try to describe. Socially, the limit is imposed by the definition of social groups with their respective boundaries—the concentric circles of individual, family, community, tribe, religion, and nation referred to earlier. Each group defines itself by its values and practices, adherence to which constitutes belonging in the group. Pluralism within the group often focuses on negotiation of different conceptions of those boundaries. Thus, different Jewish groupings have different specific articulations of common Jewish practices such as Shabbat, kashrut, prayer, and other religious rituals, as well as of Jewish cuisine, folk languages, literature, and lore. The problematic of Jewish pluralism includes squaring this diversity with the notion of a common Jewish identity overriding the diversity.

* * *

The essays in this collection reflect on different facets of this set of issues. We begin the collection, appropriately enough, with a statement by Ora Horn Prouser, Academic Dean of AJR, describing how pluralism is integral to the educational environment and experience at the AJR.

The first main section deals with the general theory of pluralism. I begin with an exchange between Bruce Alpert and myself on the competing claims of standing for what we believe is right and recognizing the legitimacy of those (persons, or persons' views?) with whom we disagree. On the one hand, there are times when we are so certain that we stand for the right—and the stakes are so high—that some penalization of the opposing party or view (starting with denial of respect) seems absolutely called for. On the other hand, pluralism implies stepping out of the circle of our own private perspective and getting a glimpse of other viewpoints, which call the exclusive rightness of our own into question. We have purposely left this exchange of contrasting viewpoints unresolved. Like many issues in this field, we do not presume to lay down a final answer or rule. Rather, we hope that the reader, sensitized to these issues, will weigh the competing claims in each situation and make a principled decision informed by the whole spectrum of values in play.

A similar moral can be drawn from my essay on Isaiah Berlin's teaching of pluralism. Berlin's articulation of the theory of pluralism is a classic statement in modern political philosophy. He started his discussion by juxtaposing the opposed ideals of Christian teaching and Machiavelli's theory of political craft. From a traditional moral perspective, this might seem to be a clear case of right versus wrong. Yet on closer examination, there is a proper use for the virtues of each teaching in fashioning a society that will not only foster benevolence within its borders but will also provide security from enemies outside. This is an extreme example of "value pluralism"—that differing values held by different people may be incommensurable, yet each contributes in its unique way to the full panoply of human values. There is a similar opposition and balance between communitarian monism—pursuit of the core values of a society in order to maintain that society's identity—and allowing diversity of expression and cultivation of distinctive visions so long as these do not contradict or undermine the society's goals. Balancing "negative liberty" and "positive liberty" offers yet another polarity where the "truth" is not to be identified simplistically with one side of the argument. The point is not to endorse one member of a dichotomous pair at the expense of the other, but to think through the issues between them and arrive at a personal synthesis appropriate to the unique situation in which one finds oneself.

The articles by Alan Mittleman and Eliezer Schweid give further development of these theoretical underpinnings, discussing pluralism and its limits with application to the societies of the United States and Israel. Regarding the first, Mittleman stresses that, far from being a hands-free anything-goes approach, the tradition of pluralism in the United States developed out of a specific set of positive values, namely, those of civil society as articulated by the classic thinkers of the European and American Enlightenment. These values require adherence to norms of civility whose purpose is to foster the harmonious interaction of citizens of a common polity with differences in their specific visions of the good. There is a common element between this set of positive values and the Jewish values associated with the idea of a covenanted community.

Eliezer Schweid similarly posits a dialectical relation between monism and pluralism. On the one hand, a pluralistic society is dogmatically committed to the value of pluralism as a required consensual value of all its members—and, to that extent, is monistic—whereas a monistic society, organized around traditional values, generally accepts in practice a modest amount of pluralism on secondary matters. Schweid sees the growth of pluralism in contemporary Israel as evolving from the grudging, practical tolerance among monistic parties, each representing a particular stripe of Zionist ideology, toward a more principled pluralism drawing on the positive teachings of human dignity and shared cultural and covenantal values culled from the Jewish tradition. This is parallel to the distinction Mittleman draws (citing John Courtney Murray) between pluralism as "an article of peace" and "an article of faith."

* * *

The second section of this book deals with the sources for addressing pluralism in the Jewish tradition. Ruth Sandberg studies the narratives of rabbis' encounters with heretics in the Talmudic period. She draws lessons from them concerning the canons of civilized debate, and applies these lessons to pedagogy and contemporary ecumenical dialogue.

In my own article on pluralism in Talmudic discourse, I probe the extent to which the authors of the Talmud made the topic of their own disagreements a subject for discussion and reflection in its own right. I also examine the studies that three modern scholars—Moshe Halbertal, Donniel Hartman, and Avi Sagi—have made of the systematic importance of diversity of opinion in shaping the character of the Jewish tradition. Far more than merely documenting pluralistic tendencies in the Jewish tradition, each of the books discussed here makes substantive contributions to the theoretical understanding of pluralism as such, with the Jewish sources providing pertinent examples of the working out of monistic and pluralistic tendencies in the development of a religious tradition. All three are staples of the syllabus of the pluralism course taught at AJR.

* * *

The third section of this collection includes papers discussing the currents of pluralism in today's Jewish communities. This section begins with an essay by Asher Lopatin, one of the exponents of today's "Open Orthodoxy." Lopatin defends a pluralistic understanding of the Jewish tradition by citing examples of intellectual openness in many layers of the tradition, from the Talmud through the medieval philosophical commentators (Maimonides, Ibn Ezra, and Nachmanides) to the leaders of nineteenth century Orthodoxy (particularly Rabbi Naphtali Zvi Berlin, the "Netziv"). In his account, this pluralistic attitude manifested itself both internally (welcoming debate among different views within the Jewish tradition) and externally (opening oneself to truth from any source, even outside the tradition). Though Judaism has a strong commitment to the truth of Torah, this truth is multifaceted and is inclusive of many paths and differing interpretations.

Ellen Lippmann and Trisha Arlin describe the dynamics within a contemporary Jewish community with elements drawn from all the modern Jewish denominations, and, in particular, how these differences were expressed in the process of negotiating the selection of a prayer book for the congregation.

Heidi Hoover describes a different dimension of diversity: the subtleties and challenges of integrating families with mixed Jewish and non-Jewish origins, including participation of non-Jewish family members and the appropriate education for children growing up in mixed households. One of the lessons of her experience is how respecting differences and fostering Jewish values can be mutually reinforcing.

In "The Power of a Pluralist Rabbi," Rebecca Sirbu gives vignettes from her experience in the leadership of Rabbis Without Borders, facilitating dialogue and communication across all sorts of lines—between Jews of various denominations, Jews of different ethnic and racial backgrounds, ethnic Jews and Jews-by-choice, affiliated and unaffiliated Jews, and Jews and Palestinians in Israel in search of peaceful coexistence. It opens our eyes to the many ways that pluralistic conversations can energize today's Jewish community.

* * *

The fourth section discusses how pluralism is manifested in Jewish practice, especially in halakha, Jewish "law" or norms. Halakha addresses the very fabric of Jewish life even for those movements that take a liberal approach to it. Judaism is a religion of deeds, and so pluralism in Judaism must address diversity of patterns of practice as seriously as it addresses diversity of belief and outlook.

Richard Claman gives us a deep theoretical analysis, which considers many levels on which pluralism is manifested both within general American society ("above the line") and within private religious fellowships, such as Judaism, that operate by different sets of rules ("below the line"). He wrestles with many theoretical approaches that have been offered by Jewish thinkers and general legal theorists. In the end, he argues that different halakhic positions reflect different values among their advocates, and that these differences are irreducible for the reasons that Isaiah Berlin maintained in his theory of value pluralism.

Kashrut standards are potentially a powerful unifying factor or a powerful divisive factor in shaping Jewish communities. The choice of eating with someone or regarding eating with them as off-limits is one of the most powerful means we have of legitimating or delegitimizing the "other." David Greenstein was Rosh Yeshiva of AJR for many years and designed the AJR course in Pluralism that remains, with modifications, a standard part of the curriculum. His long article here ("By the Sweat of Your Brow: Approaching Kashrut from a Pluralistic Perspective") is an ambitious attempt to explore the principles of pluralism that start with the problem of what rules should govern the use of a microwave oven used in common by a diverse Jewish student community.

Morris Allen concludes this section with a memoir of his varied experiences in the administration of kashrut, particularly in advocating for Hekhsher Tzedek, a program to certify humane and ethical standards observed in food preparation, especially from animals. The successes and failures that he relates raise ongoing questions about the relations of sectors within the larger Jewish community.

We move on to another section with profound practical application, namely, the practice of pluralism as it affects the methods and pedagogic approaches in Jewish educational institutions serving diverse populations. We begin with two articles on the theory and practice of pluralism in Jewish day schools. Joel Alter writes of what it means to assert pluralism as a core value of a Jewish school, and proposes that even though there are obstacles to defining it operationally, it is still worthwhile to study the existing practices of a school in the form of an "audit" to assess whether this value is being achieved.

The next article, by Susan Shevitz and Rahel Wasserfall, gives us a detailed and sophisticated, methodologically-informed study of fostering pluralism in a communal Jewish day high school. This essay analyzes the pedagogical assumptions and practical interventions in which pluralistic principles are implemented in the many dimensions of school life, including academic studies, prayer services, and integrative discussions, among faculty and students of diverse backgrounds and commitments, aimed at moving everyone toward integrity, mutual respect, acceptance and understanding.

Cherie Koller-Fox distills the lessons learned from over 30 years of experience as director of the now-defunct CAJE (Coalition for/Conference of Advancement of Jewish Education) and its successor, NewCAJE. In both its incarnations, CAJE has not only been a forum for Jewish educators, ranging from Orthodox to the most liberal, to exchange insights and methods, but also has provided the occasion for people from those diverse backgrounds to live a Jewish life together for the week of the conference, complete with Shabbat observance and prayer services. Koller-Fox organizes the vignettes and feedback of that body of experience around the themes of inclusion, moving between boundaries, *Klal Yisrael*, creating safe space, curiosity about the other, and self-respect.

Finally, Beth Kissileff shares her journalistic observations of the broadening effects of Bible classes for Israeli soldiers, in which young citizens of religious and nonreligious backgrounds study together. From that experience, Kissileff shows, the participants learn to appreciate the value of viewpoints other than those with which they were raised.

* * *

The final section of studies provides a look at the relations of different kinds of Jews and non-Jews within today's State of Israel, as well as the interaction of today's Jews with other faith communities.

Reuven Hammer, who has worked for denominational pluralism in Israel for many years, gives a detailed and thoughtful narrative and analysis of the issues and dilemmas that the State of Israel has faced since its inception in trying to reconcile its two contrasting missions—as a state for all its citizens, and as the one Jewish state in the world that can give political expression to Jewish peoplehood. The reader who has digested the previous essays in this volume will see that this dilemma embodies the polarity of "pluralism" and "boundaries" in a special and critical way. As Eliezer Schweid pointed out, the pluralism toward which Israel has striven throughout its history is a pluralism based on some shared consensus of Jewish values. But different groups of Jews bring different understandings of "Jewish values" to the table, as well as the values of modernity and democracy implicit in the mission of the secular state. The struggles Hammer relates thus revolve around the boundary questions: How much democratic? How much Jewish? And who gets to determine what is "Jewish"?

Shira Pasternak Beeri shares two stories that highlight the ambiguities and angst of relations between Jews and Palestinians in Israel—enemies in one light, yet in another, human beings trying to relate to each other in a purely human plane. Michael Friedman studies those Jews who have tried to arrive at an accommodation between their Jewish background and their interest in Buddhism. And Yehoyada Amir, an Israeli, Jewish theologian and educator, offers a provocative and novel way of framing the process by which members of the Jewish and non-Jewish communities undergo spiritual migration across the boundary between them into the community of the other, and the way they are perceived by the members of those communities.

In the final section, we present four contributions that cross the line of teaching and liturgy. In "Gathering in Grief for Hope and Healing," Katy Allen describes an interfaith liturgical event in which Jews, Christians, and Muslims were able to come together on the plane of shared emotions and experiences, despite sharp political differences, after the 2014 Gaza conflict. Kaya Stern-Kaufman contributes three sermons with a range of lessons with pluralistic relevance. Dorothy Goldberg reflects on the way that gender ambiguity expands our sense of the potential not only of human beings, but also of God. We close with a meditation before shofar-blowing by Trisha Arlin. I imagine this as being followed by the sound of the shofar-blast itself—wordless, open to an infinite variety of understandings.

* * *

What do all these studies have in common? To paraphrase Hillel: "If being delegitimized for being different is hateful to you, do not do likewise to your fellow human being." And: "Who is wise? One who learns from everyone."

This is the whole Torah of pluralism; the rest is commentary.

Go and learn!

Acknowledgements

I am ever so grateful to Ora Horn Prouser, Academic Dean and Executive Vice-President of AJR, for inviting me in the first place to teach pluralism at AJR (a course originally conceived and developed by Rabbi David Greenstein) since Spring 2011, and more recently for inviting me to spearhead and edit this volume on Judaism and Pluralism for AJR's sixtieth anniversary. I am grateful to all my colleagues and students at AJR, whose example and discussion have enriched my understanding of the interplay of diverse views in an atmosphere of mutual respect. I am grateful to the members of the editorial committee—Ora Prouser, Jeff Hoffman, Caren Levine, and Peg Kershenbaum—who helped brainstorm the names of potential contributors and who helped in the evaluation and editing of contributed pieces. I am grateful to all the authors who contributed their scholarship and thinking to make this volume what it is. I am grateful to Larry Yudelson of Ben Yehuda Press and Rhonda Rosenheck of *Re: Work Editing* for all their work in assembling, reworking, and refining the contributed material, and bringing it to its final form. Lastly, I am grateful to my wife, Margie, for being a true *ezer k'negdi*, being supportive yet challenging me to respond to her otherness in pursuit of a higher harmony.

AJR and Pluralism

Living Pluralism at AJR

Ora Horn Prouser

Publishing a book on pluralism has been a goal at AJR for many years. It is, thus, with particular pleasure and pride that we see the realization of this dream. The term "pluralism" has become a buzzword in contemporary Jewish culture, with a variety of denominational, post-denominational, and other communities describing themselves as pluralistic. Each of these communities has a different definition of pluralism, and every organization tries to emphasize their pluralism as a positive attribute.

It is understandable why each of these communities tries to identify as pluralistic, as much of the larger Jewish world now sees pluralism as a key approach to Jewish life in particular, and to the larger world in general. At the Academy for Jewish Religion, we have a very distinct approach to pluralism: one that goes beyond what most of these communities describe. After all, AJR has been a living laboratory of pluralism for the past sixty years. At AJR, students study together, pray together, and function as a community despite (or perhaps because of) their great variety of backgrounds, approaches, and understandings of Jewish life. It is therefore instructive to share AJR's understanding of pluralism.

Fundamentally, the question has been asked how pluralism compares to diversity, non-denominationalism, post-denominationalism, et cetera. This is a very difficult question, and one that we have thought about quite a bit at AJR. Non-denominationalism and post-denominationalism assume that denominations are no longer relevant or viable. That is not the view at AJR. We have some students and alumni in our community who are very much part of denominations. Some in our community feel that they belong in denominations. They choose to be a part of AJR because they recognize that the Jewish world is larger than any one denomination, and they want to be comfortably engaged with all facets of the Jewish community, and truly to understand and to appreciate all areas. They themselves, however, identify within a specific movement. Thus, AJR's pluralism is not non-denominational or post-denominational.

AJR's approach to pluralism is an appreciation of diversity; but it is much more than that. There are communities claiming to be pluralistic whose members talk about respect for the other and tolerance of other viewpoints. Again, this does not adequately define the AJR approach to pluralism. Tolerance is necessary, but it is a very low bar for a pluralistic community. Respect is very important, but, it too, is not enough for true pluralism to flourish. AJR's approach to pluralism expects members of our community to cherish one another.

"Cherishing" means finding value in ideas other than your own and truly believing that you can learn from them. "Cherishing" means not only that you respect others, but that you know that your perspective, your life, and your approach to Jewish life are richer and deeper because of your interaction with other views and approaches. In a community that cherishes the other, individuals know that each of us benefits from being a part of a pluralistic community: not only by learning about others, but by becoming who we want and need to be.

This all sounds positive, dynamic, and enriching, so why wouldn't all communities choose to be pluralistic? The answer is that true pluralism is very difficult. The pluralistic community needs to be aware of many issues, and to be extremely sensitive to individuals and their needs and struggles in a way that is different from communities that are more homogeneous. This leads to another lesson we have learned at AJR about living pluralism. In a community of individuals with many different approaches, there is a tendency for individuals either to feel alone in their views, or to be concerned that their approach is being ignored. One refrain often heard when meeting with students is that "everyone in the community is (fill in the blank) but me." That is, everyone knows more Hebrew, everyone is more comfortable with prayer, everyone understands what it means to meditate, everyone has studied Talmud, et cetera. Because students come from so many different backgrounds, there is often an unwarranted sense of inadequacy or concern that comes from the worry that students from other backgrounds and approaches are better prepared for their studies. While it is true that some students are more prepared for high level Jewish study than others, our experience is that students bring to the table different strengths and weaknesses; and that, in general, students with one or another denominational background are not thereby more suited for rabbinic or cantorial education. The feeling of concern in the face of great diversity is real and needs to be respected and confronted directly. Therefore, there is a need to engage in serious and honest communication; a need to be willing to speak about ideas and concerns that are seemingly minor, as well as those that are hot-button issues. At AJR, we engage in this conversation as a community in a variety of ways. We encourage group conversations, large and small, formal and informal. Students know that they can go to faculty and administrators to work through their own ideas and practices, and to express concerns about larger communal issues. Students have spent real time in individual conversation with faculty, for example, to discuss issues of *Tefillah*, to struggle with their own Shabbat observance, and to express their feelings that their views were not given proper respect in a course. These individual conversations sometimes lead to small group meetings or large communal ones. Our approach is an absolute willingness to engage issues with honesty, sensitivity, and integrity.

Serious communication lodged in a warm and nurturing communal atmosphere allows us at AJR to negotiate a strong communal feeling together with a cherishing of differences. The importance of our community's being so loving and warm cannot be emphasized enough. That nurturing and sensitive communal atmosphere provides the perfect backdrop for complicated conversations. The AJR community is known for its warm and caring environment. This is evident in how each student is welcomed by fellow students and by faculty and administrators. It is clear in the way administrative tasks are carried out. It is reflected in the way in which teachers are there for students, in and out of class. This, too, is one of AJR's core values, and is made clear to all individuals who work at the school, who teach there, or who study there. Students are made to feel that they are being treated as individuals from the beginning of their education. They know that they are seen not only as members of a class, but as full individuals with families, jobs, interests, fears, struggles, and joys. While, on the one hand, this is simply how people should be treated in the world, at AJR we know that creating this environment is essential to achieving the goals of our school. It is this environment that makes it possible for students to achieve academically, grow spiritually, and become the spiritual leaders they have the potential to be. In addition, it is this environment that makes it possible for our pluralistic conversations and engagements to occur as smoothly as they do.

Despite this atmosphere, there are real areas of concern among members of a pluralistic community. There are misgivings among many that their viewpoint is not being adequately represented and expressed. As an example, during one semester I received the following expressions of concern from students and alumni:

"There are not sufficient members of the faculty who are Reform."

"Orthodox viewpoints are ignored and belittled in communal conversations."

"AJR's policy on not accepting students of patrilineal descent is not befitting a pluralistic institution."

"There is a lack of understanding among the community about the idea of feeling bound by *halakhah*."

What is evident in this brief list is that students and alumni were concerned that their viewpoints were not adequately expressed or represented. Some felt the need to push for their approaches. However, they often did not see that others on very different sides of the spectrum, those the complainants presumed to hold dominant or majority views, were feeling precisely the same concern. They did not see the parts of our policies that supported their views; they saw only the sides that they thought were not representing their own perspectives. Again, the key is strong communication within communal connection. Because our community is built on strong interpersonal connections, it is easy for students to approach teachers and administrators with their concerns. In addition, the pluralistic environment has made communal members open to hearing and thinking.

Living in a pluralistic community means being aware of these difficulties and addressing them. It is easy to say that individuals should not feel that way, but that is simply to fail to understand human nature. The reality is that pluralistic communities need to be willing to address issues like these head-on, continuously, in order to help individuals to see the larger picture. Recently, an alumna shared a concern with me about an AJR policy. She felt that her approach was not being adequately respected. She came to me directly to discuss the issue, and as we pursued her feelings of concern, and my explanation of how this policy fit in a pluralistic environment, we had a beautiful moment of understanding and appreciation. This happened only because the atmosphere is such that she knew she could come and ask for explanation, and knew that the explanation would include appreciation of her approach. In addition, there are times when it is necessary to step in and be the voice of the truly unvoiced. We have found that as students continue in the program they feel less defensive and more comfortable, and recognize the tremendous benefits of this structure. The AJR community makes that happen in both the overt and the subtle methods described. Being aware of the process of growth, however, is necessary.

Pluralism also means listening, as members of the community can make real contributions to addressing these issues. A good example is the observance of kashrut at AJR. The AJR policy on kashrut used to be that all public events, and all food meant to be shared, needed to be certified kosher. Food that individuals brought for themselves, however, did not need to be certified kosher. It could not include shellfish, it could not mix milk and meat, and all meat needed to be kosher. This worked as a whole, but, students felt frustrated that they could not bring in food to share with their friends and classmates. A student, therefore, suggested a new policy, which has since been instituted at AJR. Food at all public events still needs to be certified kosher. However, students are welcome to bring in food to share in the student lounge. Food that is brought in to be shared still needs to follow the rules of being kosher meat, not mixing milk and meat, and not including shellfish. Other food, however, does not need to be certified kosher. The person bringing in the food fills out a form that explains where the food came from. Is it store bought or homemade? If store bought, what kind of store? If homemade, what is the kashrut practice where it was prepared? Are meat and milk dishes kept separate? Is non-kosher food brought into the home? Are dishes washed together? Questions such as these are answered, and the form is left next to the food. It is then up to each member of the community to decide whether to partake of the items.

While this may seem like a lot of work to put out a plate of cookies, there is something much deeper going on here. This policy shows deep respect for members of the community, making it clear that communal eating can be a part of communal life, even while members of the community have different ways of observing kashrut. It makes it clear that the answer is not always to follow the most stringent level of observance; but, rather, that there are ways to allow for a variety of approaches to feel accepted. Furthermore, it challenges students to consider how their own personal decisions about religious observance affect fellow Jews. Quite as importantly, it also leads to important and valuable conversation. Once forms are filled out, members of the community can ask each other, why do they observe the way they do? How does it work for them? These conversations are a beautiful and necessary part of a pluralistic community. These conversations make it clear that individuals with different patterns of practice come to those decisions with deep thought, sincere appreciation for Jewish life, and honest desire to live a godly life. That understanding is not easy to come by in heterogeneous communities, but is of immense value in understanding the larger Jewish world and in cherishing others.

While some may find any specific practice or idea uncomfortable, we have found that true pluralism means that everyone is somewhat uncomfortable. An individual may be comfortable with our policy on Jewish identity but uncomfortable with our kashrut policy. A second person may be perfectly comfortable with our policy on kashrut but uncomfortable with our public prayer. The goal is not to make every person comfortable with each decision. Rather, the goal is to make the discomfort a generative discomfort: one that leads us to think, struggle, push ourselves, and ask important questions.

While we work to make our community extremely inclusive and accepting, we also recognize that pluralism cannot exist without boundaries. Every pluralistic community needs also to have core values which create boundaries to that pluralism. AJR, for example, has core values saying that we are egalitarian and gay-friendly. If someone believes that for religious reasons he should not hear a woman's voice in song, then he will not feel comfortable being a part of the AJR community, as women's voices are raised in song every day. If someone does not believe that rabbis and cantors should be openly gay, then they may not feel comfortable at AJR. We accept that, and don't claim otherwise. And if someone does not believe that rabbinical students need to engage in years of serious study of Talmud and Codes, then they may not feel comfortable at AJR.

A good example of the need for boundaries on pluralism was made very clear in a program we ran on patrilineal descent in pluralistic communities. We had some students who expressed the opinion that communities should be open and welcoming to everyone, and that Jews of patrilineal descent should be accepted as part of any community. They felt that there was no reason that a community should not accept patrilineal Jews. Some who felt that they could not accept patrilineal descent because of their understanding of Jewish law were concerned that their viewpoint was presented as cold and rejecting of important members of our community. In other words, people on both sides felt concern, rejection, and lack of understanding of the other side. It was our job as a community to make clear that while we appreciate all members of our community, and cherish all ideas, each Jewish community, including each pluralistic community, still needs to make a decision for itself whether and, perhaps, under what terms they accept patrilineal descent in their community – precisely as they must decide a variety of defining issues of practice, identity, and belief. That is setting the boundaries of the pluralism for that community. There is no way to have a pluralistic community without making those decisions. It is a fallacy to say that a Jewish community can accept all ideas or practices for that community. These decisions need to be made. They can be reviewed and amended, but the difficult issues must be addressed.

Given that these conversations were so complex, and addressed issues of identity, which are among the most difficult, in this and other similar events we brought in resources to help our community. For example, one very useful method has been to address the issues through the arts. We have brought in music therapists, with whose training small groups wrote songs that addressed their feelings. We have engaged in role-playing and dramatic recreations. We have used the visual arts and writing as modes of expression. These have all helped the members of the community to process their own feelings, and those of others, often leading to greater sensitivity and understanding.

One of the issues that we have seen in the current state of affairs in pluralism arose during this discussion of patrilineal descent. A member of our faculty said that she could not imagine any non-Orthodox Jew being upset if their son or daughter married a Jew of patrilineal descent. It was explained to her that for some Jews who consider Jewish law binding, a Jew of patrilineal descent is not considered Jewish. That was not part of her world view, though she considered herself pluralistic. In too many communities, pluralism has come to be synonymous with "left wing." Communities call themselves pluralistic and accepting, but some really do not include more traditional Jewish approaches in their mix. At AJR this is an issue we think about often. While there are certain areas that are liberal in the boundaries we have chosen for ourselves, beyond those, we absolutely see our community as open to those from all parts of the Jewish world. We try always to have a true variety of opinions presented in our programs and in our courses; yet we do acknowledge that the majority of our community is liberal in thought and practice.

An interesting case was made to us, however, by a traditional Conservative Jew. He told us that he was actually more comfortable at AJR at this point than at Conservative institutions that have become exceedingly liberal. The point he made was that given that we are pluralistic, there is room for many different viewpoints. He was less comfortable, however, with Conservative institutions that were not making room for traditional approaches. Thus, at least to some people, our pluralistic community feels more welcoming to traditional Jews than some denominational environments.

A difficult and essential area of decision making for every pluralistic community is how to engage in communal prayer. Some communities express their pluralism by having multiple *minyanim* whenever they engage in prayer, thus making room for many different types of prayer services to occur simultaneously. Often communities separate for all or part of prayer services and then join together for part of the service or for learning or socializing afterwards.

AJR has an approach to *tefillah* that we have not seen elsewhere in the Jewish community. Yet. When we pray together we make a covenant as a community to all follow whatever is decided by the prayer leader. The prayer leader decides which prayer book will be used (an assortment is available at all times), and decides what kind of prayer experience we will have. This can be traditional, meditative, musical, primarily movement, or anything else. The liturgy can be more or less traditional, for example, including or excluding matriarchs in the *Amidah*, using language of the classical liturgy, the Reform *siddur*, the Reconstructionist *siddur*, etc. The only non-negotiable rules for our services are that each service needs to include a mourner's *kaddish*, and that parts of the service that traditionally require a *minyan* cannot be included unless a *minyan* is present. This is not to say that everyone finds every service equally enjoyable or spiritually meaningful. There are prayer services that some consider as halachically fulfilling their requirement to pray, and others they do not consider as halachically fulfilling their requirement to pray. There are some prayer services that various members of the community find uncomfortable. Yet, we *daven* as a community. We share our experience as a community. We learn from each other. We find elements that are meaningful and fulfilling which, if we prayed only with those like us, we would never have experienced. As a community, we find this approach to be fitting, conducive to spiritual growth, and advantageous to all involved. Speaking personally, I find it to be one of the most beautiful parts of our pluralistic institution.

While this all works well, when an Orthodox faculty member needed to say *kaddish* for observance of a *yahrzeit*, he asked if he could lead and if we would have separate but equal seating for that *minyan*. The community readily agreed, and there, too, we felt the warmth and comfort of a unified community.

AJR is not only a community who "lives" together, dealing with prayer, food, and communal life. We are primarily a community that studies together. Pluralism makes its way into our courses as well. For example, in our liturgy classes, it is important that students learn the traditional liturgy, and then understand how each movement has worked with that liturgy, responded to it, and modified it to suit their theological approaches. In our professional skills classes, students learn how to perform ritual ceremonies for all parts of the Jewish community. They need to understand traditional life cycle events, and at the same time, how they are adapted by various parts of the Jewish community. At the same time, while becoming well versed in understanding how life cycle events are performed in all segments of the Jewish community, they need to work to determine their own personal practice and ritual parameters and standards in performing life cycle events.

Studying Bible in a pluralistic setting brings its own challenges. In the introductory class we spend time discussing our understandings of revelation. Students can have a variety of approaches to revelation ranging from believing that God wrote the Torah to an understanding that the Torah is the product of purely human hands, and everything in between. Students are given license to maintain their own beliefs in this area, but, at the same time, they need to understand the variety of approaches and the implications and reasons behind them.

As in all areas, studying Bible at AJR includes attention to the Bible as a pluralistic document. While that is not the focus of this paper, this approach emphasizes that traditional Bible study through the *Miqraot Gedolot* assumes that we study many and conflicting approaches at once. It makes the point that the biblical text itself includes conflicting approaches. Our understanding of *peshat* (contextual interpretation) and *derash* (interpretive reading as well as ethical, homiletical, mystical interpretation, etc.) also supports AJR's pluralistic approach. We emphasize that not only can we have multiple *derash* meanings to the text, we can also have multiple *peshat* readings of the text. In class we emphasize that we can agree or disagree about our reading of text, but that there is not only one legitimate reading. The fact that someone else has a different approach does not negate one's own reading. This approach to reading parallels the approach to AJR's pluralistic living. We can agree or disagree, knowing that we can learn from each other, but that a difference of opinion does not negate either view or either person. It is the text itself that unites us, as well as our shared commitment to that text and to one another as a community of learners. It is the text itself, together with our ability to interact with it and within a diverse community, which is one true test of our individual "readings."

AJR has been a living laboratory of pluralism for sixty years. As with all experiments, the validity of the findings is determined by the ability of others to replicate the results. The exponential growth of pluralistic communities, and of interest in the principles of pluralism among organizations and institutions heretofore more narrowly defined, indicates that AJR's sixty-year experiment has been a resounding success. It is now our privilege and our mission to offer our experience to an increasingly diverse Jewish community which can grow immeasurably by building upon our findings over the next sixty years. That is a mission of biblical proportions: to reach "120 years ... vision undiminished, vigor unabated" (Deuteronomy 34:7).

Theory of Pluralism

Confessions of a Reluctant Pluralist

Bruce Alpert

"Can you respect an idea that you think is wrong?"

It was the second time the committee had posed this question to me at my admissions interview for the Academy for Jewish Religion's rabbinical school. It reflected the dynamic of the session: had I the commitment to pluralism needed to be a member of AJR's community? I had never thought much about pluralism. Though the word dominated AJR literature, I was applying solely because its program worked for commuters and second career students like me. To the extent I had thought about it, I associated it with post-denominationalism — a phenomenon with which I was comfortable, as it reflected my own beliefs and practices.

Yet to the committee, pluralism meant something more. It meant creating an environment in which people would feel safe to explore their differences in theology, in ritual observance, in politics, in sexual orientation and in a host of other facets of life and experience. My application was insensitive to this intention, and it reflected just enough edginess to cast doubt on my ability to live in such an environment. Hence, the question.

For me, however, the question implied one thing: moral relativism.

I developed an abhorrence to moral relativism in my mid-twenties when I started reexamining many of the beliefs with which I had grown up. Leaving college and entering the working world, with its ever multiplying demands and expectations, I suddenly found the notion that there might not be principles and ideas that are true in all times and all places unacceptable. This view was reinforced when I read the Bible for the first time and discovered that this ancient text contained insights into human nature that were startlingly modern. In time, I would learn to appreciate the human quest to find truth as the essential spur to speculation, criticism, doubt and discovery. It would guide my discovery of my own religion and lead me, eventually, to this very interview.

I knew the answer I gave would be problematic when I offered it the first time. But I could not think of what else to say and remain true to the path that led me here. The wording of the question to me was decisive. Had I been asked if I could respect an idea with which I disagreed, I would certainly have answered yes. But the word "disagree" to me conveys a sense of individual analysis that reflects a person's subjective values, experiences and sensibilities. As such, these differences do not turn on issues of right and truth, but on perception and assessment.

The question I was asked – now for a second time – was whether I could respect an idea I thought was wrong. Perhaps it was the pressure of the moment, facing five intelligent people who were looking at me and my application so critically, but the word "wrong" for me went straight to the heart of my problem with relativism. This word *did* imply issues of right and truth and thus carried much more weight than a mere "disagreement." To answer the question in the affirmative implied that I accorded respect to ideas that I believed were factually or logically or historically or morally or in some other way erroneous, perhaps egregiously so. This made no sense to me. It still does not. I proceeded to answer the question word-for-word as I had answered it the first time:

"I can respect the person who holds the idea I think is wrong. And I hope I can have enough humility to realize that I might be wrong. But no, I cannot respect an idea I think is wrong."

I received the same head shakes and pursed lips I got the first time around. That I was offered admission anyway is probably a better testament to AJR's commitment to pluralism than any advertising claim. Yet the essence of my response – that one can respect a person while believing his or her ideas wrong – would ultimately become the way I managed to distinguish pluralism from relativism.

* * *

My first inklings of the nature of pluralism at AJR came at the *minchah* service on the first full day of my first fall retreat, a four-day program devoted to prayer, community and study. Prayer services I had attended so far that school year tended to be standard, Conservative Judaism practice. Though the prayer book cart had Reform and Orthodox books on its shelves, we tended to always use the Conservative *Siddur Sim Shalom*. That morning's service was also standard Conservative: most students and teachers in *tefillin* and *tallitot*, rifling through an over-stuffed service at breakneck speed.

Minchah, though, was different. It was led by a student I had come to regard as a model of "small 'c' conservative leadership," quiet, calm, intellectual, deliberate. Whether I reached for a *Sim Shalom* when I entered the room, I do not remember. It would not have mattered, because we did not use a prayer book at that service. Instead, my staid classmate led us on a guided meditation in which we were encouraged to "breathe," "find our center," and "visualize a place from our childhood where we felt safe." It was my first experience of meditation as prayer. It would not be the last.

In the half dozen services that followed that *minchah*, I would be treated to quite the variety of styles: a folksy, singing service; a nature-walk service; a creative liturgy service; a Classical Reform service in which the leaders wore black robes and used barely a word of Hebrew. And in subsequent fall retreats throughout my student career, the variety of services would proliferate: yoga as prayer, drum circles as prayer, dance as prayer, and many, many more guided meditations.

My reactions to all these experiments were mixed. I am no traditionalist when it comes to praying. Still, a deep respect for the theological concepts and ritual habits that traditional prayer inculcates informs my view of how prayer practices should be innovated. I embraced those innovations I witnessed that furthered those concepts and rituals and rejected those I believed ignored or even replaced them.

Prayer, however, is only the most visible front on which the wide diversity of practice and belief among both AJR's students and teachers is expressed. Different prayer practices often indicate deep theological differences that range from a kind of egalitarian Orthodoxy to New Age Spiritualism.

While my AJR education opened me to a broad spectrum of Jewish belief and practice that time and history has granted legitimacy, that spectrum is not infinitely wide. Like Maimonides's generation of Enosh, whose worship of the stars as God's creation quickly degenerates into the worship of them as deities, Jewish theology can at times be stretched beyond its breaking point. Such has happened many times already. Many of the congregants I serve have scant understanding of theology, and what they do have is often imbued with notions caught from the predominantly Christian culture we share. In such circumstances, the need for theological clarity about what lies inside and what outside Judaism's spectrum strikes me as being of paramount importance to a rabbi. Most of the students I knew understood and respected those boundaries. But a few struck me as holding theological ideas akin to those of Enosh.

And beyond prayer and theology there is always politics. The differences here are less about the politics themselves than about the importance they should play in one's rabbinate. I firmly believe that, while issues like social welfare and Israel make a rabbi's venture into political debate inevitable, he or she should tread very lightly there. A number of my colleagues strongly disagreed, seeing in their Judaism a clarion call to political advocacy.

So within three months of entering AJR, I found myself face to face with precisely the question posed at my interview: could I respect an idea that I thought was wrong? And if I could not, what would that mean for me as a member of the AJR community? For all the reasons detailed above, my AJR experience brought me into contact with many ideas that I thought wrong and unworthy of respect. And in doing so, I learned pluralism. Let me explain.

* * *

The fifty or so rabbinical students who are studying at AJR at any one time take as many as 80 courses across their student careers. A required class offered but once every two years might have upwards of twenty students. Most classes are considerably smaller, and the two hours of one-on-one *hevruta* study that precede each Talmud lesson are as intimate as learning can be. Even in large classes the tendency to break into ten-minute sessions of one-on-one study is quite common, in which case you find yourself in close dialogue with the person who just happened to sit next to you. I well remember the class in which we were asked to turn to our neighboring student and relate to him or her a highly personal story using only hand gestures. With the exception of those students who are ordained the year that one begins, rabbinical students at AJR get to know each other very well; students who enter the school within a year of each other form particularly close bonds as they work through the most rigorous parts of the curriculum together.

Moreover, the experience itself brings students to a certain intimacy with one another. The curriculum is long and hard. For those who have been outside an academic environment for 20 or 30 years, the challenge of presenting in class, or writing a paper, or taking a test can be quite discomfiting. Yet the idea that a would-be Jewish leader should stretch him- or herself emotionally and intellectually is a commonplace. In this intense and transformational experience, students tend naturally to unburden themselves with one another. Self-doubt is an undercurrent of many student conversations, particularly in the first year or two of study.

In my student years at AJR, I got to know every other student in the school. Many I came to know quite well, and a few have become good friends. Among those with whom I formed bonds were those whose ideas on prayer, theology and politics I believed wrong. For the most part I found them to be very much like the students with whom I agreed: kind, thoughtful, solicitous of others and highly self-reflective and self-critical. Their ideas were often intimately tied to their experiences and their identity. And while I thought those ideas wrong, I could not – knowing the whole person – desire to change them.

This, I believe, is the essence of pluralism. Diversity by itself is not pluralism, nor is it a non-judgmental openness to all comers. Rather, pluralism is founded on the respect offered to the other: to one whose ideas you believe are wrong. Such respect guarantees a civil public square in which a variety of ideas can be aired and evaluated without impairing the right of individuals or groups to decide matters of right and wrong for themselves.

* * *

Beyond that which is taught through interaction, AJR students are required to study pluralism itself – both as it has been understood in traditional rabbinic sources, and as it has been practiced in various civic and religious institutions. At the heart of our study, and dominating our class discussion for several weeks, was the modern-day theory of pluralism, particularly as articulated by Isaiah Berlin in his essay, *Two Concepts of Liberty*. Written in 1958, the essay is essentially an effort to understand the mass depredations of humanity committed both under Nazism and under communism as the natural consequence of either of those two concepts.

Berlin terms the two concepts of liberty positive and negative. The preposition they take most easily distinguishes them. Negative liberty is freedom *from*, as in freedom from interference in the way I live my life. Positive liberty is freedom *to*, as in the freedom to become a doctor, a lawyer, a rabbi, all of which require sacrifices of one's negative liberty to achieve the desired goal. Much of the essay is devoted to tracing how the positive concept of freedom can give way to monism: the idea that all proper ends should be reconcilable with one another. Some philosophers, for instance, argue that irrational acts are not truly free as they are governed by passions rather than reason. Therefore, any use of mental or physical force necessary to compel a person to act rationally actually makes him or her more free. Whatever the single criterion that animates a monism—the rule of reason, the quest for peace, the triumph of race, to name a few possibilities—it will ultimately run into some irreconcilable end, and then it will be used to justify virtually any level of tyranny to achieve its aim. For this reason, Berlin likens monism to a final solution.

But if within the concept of positive liberty lies the abusive potential of monism, the antidote can be found in the concept of negative liberty and its possibility of pluralism. Pluralism rests on the notion that ultimate ends can be many and are rarely reconcilable with one another. Values like liberty and equality, for example, are often in conflict; an increase in one being purchased only at the expense of the other. "To assume," Berlin asserts, "that all values can be graded on one scale, so that it is a mere matter of inspection to determine the highest, seems to me to falsify our knowledge that men are free agents, to represent moral decision as an operation which a slide-rule could, in principle, perform." This single statement captures what I believe is both the possibility and the danger of pluralism. The possibility lies in the assertion that people are free agents, afforded the negative liberty of non-interference in the choices they make. The danger lies in the assertion that there can be no single scale upon which moral decisions can be based; for while that statement is certainly true, it is open to dangerous misinterpretation. Here is where pluralism can be perverted into moral relativism.

Berlin saw in pluralism both an antidote to the grave dangers of monism and the horrific depredations that had been wrought in its pursuit, and a truer understanding and appreciation of moral complexity, where perfect knowledge is impossible. Carving out a zone of inviolable liberty in which a person is free from interference by others is a bulwark against the abuses of monism and a guarantee that individuals can and will pursue the variety of ends to which their reason or passion or religion or tastes takes them. I believe, however, that a distinction needs to be made between asserting the right of a person to pursue his or her ends and the validity of the ends themselves. This is where my AJR interviewer and I parted company.

I have, over the years, replayed that colloquy in my mind over and over. I remain satisfied with my answer that I could respect the person who held an idea I thought to be wrong, but not the idea itself. Still, I wonder how I might have put things differently. It never occurred to me to comment on the importance I placed on the word "wrong," implying, as it did for me, matters of truth and right and fact. By the same token, it never occurred to me to provide examples. "Racism," I could have said, "is an idea. Antisemitism is an idea. Must I respect those?" While these are extreme examples, I believe they illuminate an error into which many pluralists fall: they seek from pluralism not merely the respect that is due them as free agents, but a validation—which is a form of agreement—of their ideas themselves. This is more than I can give and more than I believe pluralism requires.

* * *

Modern writers on pluralism are usually at pains to deny the connection between it and moral relativism. Donniel Hartman, in his book, *The Boundaries of Judaism*, states that pluralism "does not necessitate the acceptance of all positions, and is not to be equated with relativism." Diana Eck, director of Harvard's pluralism project, writes that "pluralism is not relativism but *the encounter of commitments*" (emphasis in the original). Neither of these writers – nor, for that matter, Berlin himself – goes to any lengths to detail the distinctions they are making.

Yet the meaning of terms can evolve over time, and the pressures on the term "pluralism" to evolve are many. One source of pressure is definitional. Pluralism implies, if not relativism itself, then something close to it. In *Two Concepts of Liberty*, Berlin associates pluralism with "the ideal of freedom to choose ends without claiming eternal validity for them." If pluralism can choose ends that might not prove valid over *time*, why must they be valid over place or circumstance?

Another source of pressure on the term is societal. Moral relativism is one of the most prevalent notions of our time. Thirty years ago, Allan Bloom began his book *The Closing of the American Mind* with the claim that virtually every student he taught, whether liberal or conservative, rich or poor, religious or secular, believed that truth was relative. His summary of their defense of relativism sounds precisely the same themes that animate Berlin's writings: "The study of history and of culture teaches that all the world was mad in the past; men always thought they were right, and that led to wars, persecutions, slavery, xenophobia, racism and chauvinism. The point is not to correct the mistakes and really be right; rather it is not to think you are right at all." As the father of one college student and one recent graduate, I can attest that little has changed since Bloom wrote those words.

But moral relativism has acquired a bad name as it implies a kind of slipperiness. Pluralism, so akin to relativism, has no such connotations, and indeed seems to imply thoughtfulness, acceptance and a certain generosity of spirit. The pressure, then, for the term to evolve is great indeed. Hence, advocates of pluralism need to be much clearer and more forceful in reclaiming its distinct meaning.

That distinction, I believe, rests with applying pluralism where it properly belongs. If the need for pluralism is to protect the *individual* against coercion, and if pluralism itself derives from an *individual's* negative liberty, then the subject of pluralism must be the *individual* him or herself. This strikes me as the just demand we can make of someone. It is also in keeping with that noble sentiment we were taught in grade school, widely attributed to Voltaire: "I do not agree with what you say, but I will defend to the death your right to say it." We can and should demand of all citizens a generous acceptance of someone to hold views we think are wrong, perhaps even reprehensible. We must not demand that they validate such views with even so much as respect. Respect attaches to the person, not necessarily his or her ideas.

At AJR I learned not merely to respect those with whom I disagreed; I learned to cherish them as well. And while I never heard anyone express an idea I would term hateful, there were many that struck me as so far outside what I considered the boundaries of Judaism as to be unworthy of respect. But the intimacy of my relationship with students who held such ideas forced me to look beyond the idea itself and to the person. There was where my respect belonged, and there is where I gave it. From such an understanding, it is a relatively short leap to conclude that I owe the same measure of respect to people whose ideas I also consider wrong but whom I do not know well, if at all. This is how I understand pluralism.

For this essay, I have referred to myself as a reluctant pluralist. The reluctance does not reflect any hesitancy toward pluralism, but rather with the way it is understood. For such an important term there has been, I believe, little thought to its definition. In particular, pluralism needs to be defined not merely to distinguish it from relativism, but also from such important concepts as diversity and tolerance. It needs also to be understood as it applies on both an individual and a communal level. Without such definitions and understandings, the term pluralism may well lose its distinct and noble meaning. The idea is too important for such a fate.

On Epistemic Humility

Leonard Levin

> I am wiser than this man, for neither of us appears to know anything great and good; but he fancies he knows something, although he knows nothing; whereas I, as I do not know anything, so I do not fancy I do. In this trifling particular, then, I appear to be wiser than he, because I do not fancy I know what I do not know. (Plato, *Apology of Socrates*)

Dear Bruce,

I was moved by your confession of your struggling with the challenge of pluralism and evolving toward the stance of what you call that of a "reluctant pluralist." By your example, you invite the process of which Buber spoke in *The Knowledge of Man:*

> The chief presupposition for the rise of genuine dialogue is that each should regard his partner as the very one he is. I become aware of him, aware that he is different, essentially different from myself, in the definite, unique way which is peculiar to him, and I accept whom I thus see, so that in full earnestness I can direct what I say to him as the person he is. Perhaps from time to time I must offer strict opposition to his view about the subject of our conversation. But I accept this person the personal bearer of a conviction, in his definite being out of which his conviction has grown—even though I must try to show, bit by bit, the wrongness of this very conviction. I affirm the person I struggle with: I struggle with him as his partner, I confirm him as creature and as creation, I confirm him who is opposed to me as him who is over against me. ... If I thus give to the other who confronts me his legitimate standing as a man with whom I am ready to enter into dialogue, then I may trust him and suppose him to be also ready to deal with me as his partner. (Buber, *The Knowledge of Man*, 79–80)

The part of your essay that gave me pause was where you made what seemed to me a sharp distinction between respecting the person with whom you were engaged in disagreement while refusing respect to the idea with which you disagreed. It seems to me that it is not only possible but desirable that in the majority of our disagreements—even strong disagreements of principle—we may extend respect not only to the person with whom we disagree but to the idea as well. While exploring this possibility, I also want to affirm with you the important difference between pluralism and relativism, and to show that this respect for the idea that we disagree with need not necessarily lead us down the "slippery slope" to relativism.

This is a plea for epistemic humility. Perhaps instead of humility I should call it "humbition"—a neologism that Walter Kaufmann coined, which is a conflation of humility and ambition—the assertiveness to advance the claims I hold to be just, together with the wisdom to know my limitations. I see the world through these eyes of mine, and I must affirm this vision for it is my primary grasp of the world. At the same time, I must come to grips with the fact that you, seeing the world through your eyes, see it somewhat differently. And we are all of us, furthermore, dependent on a synthetic view of reality that has evolved by conflating and combining the insights of thousands and millions of our fellow humans into disciplines like science, history, and philosophy, which greatly enlarge our grasp of physical and spiritual reality far beyond what you or I would have come to through our own unaided resources. My epistemic humility is at bottom my honest acknowledgement and deep awareness that when the vision of the world that I get through my own eyes clashes with the report that you or others give, I may be wrong. It is a confession of my fallibility. And it implies the deepest respect for the view that differs from mine, the view with which I disagree.

Let us see how this translates to specific instances. Our disagreements with our peers focus on several kinds of assertions: assertions about facts past and present, about anticipations of the future, about value assertions, and about commitments of faith and action. We disagree among Jews about who is a Jew, about what God commanded, about what to eat, how to pray and celebrate, about our social and political visions for Israel and America, and about the proper balance of Jewish and modern democratic values in the ideal Jewish life. We disagree between Jews and non-Jews about the evidential and evaluative considerations for judging the best religion. We disagree between liberals and conservatives about the practical and evaluative considerations for choosing the ideal society. In none of these disagreements can we affirm with certainty that we stand on superior epistemic ground than our opponents: that our vision of the good and true is so much superior to our opponent's that if we could only convey to our opponent the vision of the world as seen through our own eyes, our opponent would yield up his own vision as seen through his eyes as inferior to ours and adopt our vision. I have tried innumerable times to proceed in discussion on the assumption that I could achieve this feat of persuasion, and I have almost invariably failed. I would be surprised if you have not had the same experience. Clearly, then, there is something about the vision of the world that our opponent sees through her eyes that has something to commend it, that is plausible and convincing from her point of view. I have even from time to time glimpsed the persuasive aspect of the view of the world with which I disagree, even to the point of identifying with it momentarily or even for a prolonged period of time. My ability to see things through another's eyes has enlarged my sense of my own humanity and occasionally opened me to develop possibilities in my own favored position that I had not seen before. To call this "respect" for the opposing view is, I hope, the barest understatement.

The Iran Nuclear Treaty

Let us consider the recent nuclear pact with Iran. The pros and cons of this pact have been debated bitterly within the Jewish community for over a year. Both the proponents and the opponents of the pact base their conclusions on arguments of fact and arguments of value that have to be taken with the utmost seriousness. The more perceptive proponents of each side have been broadminded enough to accord legitimacy to their opponents' views and to recognize that each viewpoint is defensible.

As in many such controversies, disagreement in policy does not necessarily (though it may) derive from difference in fundamental values or the basic facts of the matter. Many of the supporters and the skeptics of the deal both value peace as well as security. Perhaps they differ in their respective weighting of these competing goods, and perhaps the supporters are willing to entertain a somewhat higher risk of security in the interests of increasing the chances of peace.

Again, both the supporters and the skeptics perceive that the leaders of Iran are divided between bellicose authoritarian reactionaries and moderate liberals, and that the former have had the upper hand in the history of the theocratic regime since 1979. The pact supporters are hopeful that a show of reconciliation and concrete concessions can strengthen the hand of the moderates, hopefully to the point that they will prevail in the long run. The pact skeptics dismiss such a prospect as wishful thinking. Neither side has a crystal ball to know with certainty what the future will bring. Each potential decision carries risk.

Supporters of the pact ask its critics, "What alternative action do you suggest?" This argument rests on the utilitarian consideration that one should always adopt the course of action that will lead to the best good (if this could be known). But philosophers of ethics know that utilitarianism is only one of many competing ethical approaches. The opponents of the deal can take refuge in the moral absolutist stance of "Never collaborate with evil." In this view, rewarding Iran with increased assets while it is in the process of pursuing its bellicose aims is morally unacceptable and makes us complicit in those evil deeds. The counterargument to this is that the earlier assets (frozen during the period of sanctions) legitimately belong to Iran, and that future oil revenues will be forthcoming anyway because the European negotiating partners will not maintain sanctions any longer. The counter-counterargument is that the frozen assets should not be released as long as Iran proclaims the US and Israel to be the Great Satan and the Lesser Satan, and that just because the Europeans do business with Iran does not mean we should compound the sin and share the guilt. And so on.

Yes, we each must act and choose a position. But if we are wise, we will do so modestly, in fear and trembling, aware of the valid potency of the factual and evaluative arguments on both sides of the issue, and with respect for those who opt for the alternative position.

Kosherer Than Thou, And The Mutability Of Torah

I invite a cousin to my son's engagement party. I perceive he is reluctant to come because he, a black-hat Orthodox Jew, doesn't trust the kashrut of my caterer, who is supervised by a Conservative rabbi. If my wife and I attended his child's wedding, I might or might not join in the Mincha minyan before the wedding ceremony, but my wife would definitely not because the men and women do not pray together under Orthodox auspices. When an Orthodox family attended a Conservative Bat Mitzvah of our friends, the Orthodox men had their own private prayer-service before the main service.

I attend a nonobservant Jewish friend's wedding. I eat only the dairy and parve items of the buffet, because the meat entrees make no pretense at being kosher. My black-hat cousin would probably not have attended this wedding even if he were invited.

What are all these groups of Jews—Orthodox, Conservative, and Reform, disagreeing about? Does any of them have a superior epistemic claim—a more privileged access to the truth? In what sense is one set of views more respectable than another?

Though I do not share the view that the Oral and Written Law is directly mandated by God and essentially immutable, I accord it the deepest respect, if for no other reason than that it has been the most prevalent view for most of the history of rabbinic Judaism, and has had profound influence on core traditional Jewish values and lore. I also recognize that for a person brought up in that belief system, it provides the foundation of his/her core religious and ethical values. I would not initiate any discussion with a devout Jew aiming at calling those beliefs into question. If the person asked me what I believed about matters of Torah, revelation, and the authority of Jewish law, I would give honest expression to my views, but would couch my answers in a way so as not to subvert but to reinforce — insofar as possible — the authority of that belief structure for that person, though possibly suggesting modifications in a liberalizing direction that still maintained the legitimacy of the overall system.

However, if a person of Orthodox persuasion entered into discussion with me with a view to denying the legitimacy of my non-Orthodox belief structure, I would have no hesitancy about articulating my grounds for disbelieving in the Sinaitic origin of the Oral Law and even the written Torah. I would, however, couch my convictions in terms of "it is more convincing to me to believe," without seeking to dislodge the more traditional convictions in the mind of my interlocutor. I would also argue vociferously that the traditional sources of rabbinic Judaism allowed for more diversity of opinion on these matters than recent Orthodoxy permits, and would cite scholarly views, from Heschel's *Heavenly Torah* to Sagi's *The Open Canon* to support the legitimacy of pluralistic discourse within traditional Judaism. I would respect my interlocutor's personal belief in the divine origin of Torah and halakha but would have no respect for his attempt to impose those views on me.

Ultimately, in such a situation, I would argue for an epistemic truce. I would argue that historic evidence is insufficient to establish either the traditional account of Sinaitic revelation or the modern critical account of the historic development of Jewish religion over many centuries, thus leaving room for the believer to adopt either the one or the other view. I would also point out that (as Heschel wrote) revelation is not a chronological issue, that one may simultaneously maintain that the tradition evolved historically but also that it was divinely revealed or inspired no matter when it came about (as for instance, the institution of Kabbalat Shabbat in the sixteenth century in Safed does not diminish its sanctity).

I would have a different argument with the ultraliberal or nonobservant Jew if he or she were to question me on why I, who do not believe that the Jewish dietary laws and festival observances were specifically commanded by the creator of the universe, continue to observe them, at some inconvenience to myself and those around me. Here the argument would revolve not around whether a historic act of revelation of law occurred centuries ago, but whether the observances are intrinsically valuable to the person who practices them, and whether it is a good thing to perpetuate a rich Jewish cultural-religious identity through continuation of these observances. But the two arguments have a common denominator. Each is by its nature undecidable. In each case, the arguments that are convincing to the one who holds them will be unconvincing to the opponent.

Should I decline to respect the ultraliberal or nonobservant Jew for not maintaining traditional Jewish practice? I may deplore the overall decline of commitment to Jewish practice and group continuity. But even if I believed in the divine origin of the rules of the Torah (which I do not), there is no compelling evidence that I could offer that would prove it to this person's satisfaction. Moreover, I recognize that in today's society we, all of us, form our identities out of diverse cultural backgrounds. This person is (at the very least) a Jew, an American, a member of the X-generation, a New Yorker (or other local designation), an artist (or scientist or lawyer, etc.), and so forth. I may wish that this person set Jewishness higher in the scale of personal priorities. But it is for this person to choose. I have exercised that freedom in my own personal choices, and so I respect it in others. And if I have something to say on the matter to them, they will be respectful of me only if I am respectful of them.

The application of this argument to the differences among Jews, Christians, Muslims, Buddhists, Hindus, and other religionists is fairly straightforward, and I think you can extrapolate it without much difficulty.

Undecidable? Paradigms And Paradigm Shift

You may ask: Are all these questions truly undecidable? Don't we sometimes make decisions, including the decision to embrace or renounce a religious, ethical, or political worldview? Mightn't the arguments we have with each other over smaller matters influence these global decisions?

Yes, sometimes, and maybe so. Our religious, ethical, and political worldviews may fruitfully be analyzed on the model of "paradigms" as Thomas

Kuhn developed this model in his book, *The Structure of Scientific Revolutions.1*
Whether or not the Torah was literally revealed by God at Sinai, whether the
balancing of self-interests or group-identification or altruistic concern should
be the primary motivating force in our social relationships—these and similar guiding principles are not something that we are likely to decide on the
basis of a casual conversation or debate. We are educated into these principles
and outlooks from an early age. We reevaluate them gradually on the basis
of our accumulated experience in the course of a lifetime. Occasionally we
modify them on the basis of experience; even more rarely, we may undergo
a conversion or inner revolution in which we abandon an outlook that had
been the bedrock of our existence until then and adopt a different outlook.
The millions of non-traditional Jews in the world today mostly had ancestors who were more traditional Jews (or Christians or Muslims) at some prior
time—and even vice versa—so some changes in outlook must have occurred
along the way.

If the unexamined life is not worth living, then we may stipulate as a corol-
lary that the unexamined outlook is not honestly come by. Maimonides said
(in Chapter 50 of Part I of the *Guide for the Perplexed*) that whoever mouths a
dogma with his lips but does not think it through in his mind does not truly
believe it. To give sincere adherence to our own views, we must measure them
honestly against alternative views when these become available to us through
give-and-take with people who hold them. Such honest measurement presupposes an ideal discourse, in which each participant listens respectfully to all
arguments and decides honestly which is most persuasive to him or her. Even
under these ideal conditions, conversion from one's basic principles is rare, because the individual has adopted those basic principles as a working paradigm
and has managed more or less successfully to view and interpret a lifetime of
experience through their lens. But incremental change is possible, and over
the course of time repeated incremental changes may lead to a paradigm shift.

If I say that the basic principles are undecidable, I mean that no body of evidence is sufficient by itself to *compel* adoption of certain premises or rejection
of alternate premises. Enough individuals are still alive and well, living by
each of these sets of principles, to show that each can be viable.[2] An individual

---

[1] Thomas Kuhn, *The Structure of Scientific Revolutions* (third edition), Chicago: University of Chicago Press, 1996.

[2] Kuhn notes that in scientific paradigm change, too, conversion to the new paradigm is an uncertain process that may take a generation or more to be adopted, often
with much resistance. "All historical theories have agreed with the facts, but only
more or less. ...It makes a great deal of sense to ask which of two actual and compet-

may decide, in the course of living and learning, to reject one paradigm and adopt another. But that is the free choice of that individual, made in light of the totality of his or her life experience. I may facilitate such a decision by my interaction with that person, but I can never compel it. Recognizing my possible role and its limitations in such a process is part and parcel of my respect for that individual and of his or her beliefs and values. And my openness to learning and growing from such encounters is equally an index of that respect.

The Question of Relativism

So if there is no absolutely certain ground of knowledge to determine who is right or wrong in any of these issues, must we succumb to relativism?

Let us consider the question of abortion. The traditional Catholic, the liberal Jew, and the secular humanist differ in their assertions of matters of fact (none of which can be proved)—whether the immortal soul is present from conception onward, or the fetus during the first forty days is "mere fluid" (*maya b'alma*) and the organism achieves full human status precisely at birth, or whether the achievement of true human status is a progressive, continual process at which the crucial definitive boundaries are arbitrary and conventional.

Still, we all (at least, the vast majority, the "mainstream," in contemporary Western culture, confirmed by the basic laws and norms of our society) live in the same moral universe. We all agree that valuing human life as sacred is a necessary condition of our living together as human beings. We all agree that some degree of sanctity (we differ on how much) is to be accorded to human life in its potential stages, and that every prospective abortion raises a moral dilemma between the rights of the mother and the rights of the developing fetus. We are none of us living in the world of the ancient Greeks and Romans who considered infanticide the prerogative of the paterfamilias.[3]

---

ing theories fits the facts *better.*" (p. 147) "Both are looking at the world, and what they look at has not changed. But in some areas they see different things, and they see them in different relations one to the other." (p. 150) "The transfer of allegiance from paradigm to paradigm is a conversion experience that cannot be forced." (p. 151)

[3] If some denizens of the ancient Greco-Roman world were resurrected tomorrow and joined our society, we would be having a different conversation than the current one. And with moral skeptics, whether of the Pyrrhonian or deconstructionist variety, the conversation would be *very* different—more about epistemology than about ethics. At the opposite end of the spectrum, fundamentalist dogmatism in a position of power also puts an end to pluralistic conversation. But every conversation must have its boundaries. See the articles by Alan Mittleman and Eliezer Schweid in this sec-

Nor do we regard our moral stance on this complex of issues to be our mere subjective preference or a matter of taste, of equal standing with alternative possible views. Wherever we stand on this issue, we consider our position grounded in objective values—the value of human life and the value of human liberty (which may tug in different directions here as in other moral debates). Our situation may be compared to that of aviators approaching a continent that we perceive indistinctly through the haze. We may differ in our estimates of its exact contours and characteristics. None of us is close enough to be able to pin it down reliably and in detail. But the continent is there, and we are united in the common task of finding a secure landing place on it.

It may be helpful in this connection to adopt a principle of complementarity of perspectives, on the analogy of the principle of complementarity in modern physics. Is light a wave or a stream of particles? The wave and particle paradigms each reveal something about the reality of light. An experiment designed to exhibit one side of that reality often conceals the contrary facet of that reality that a different experiment will illuminate. So, too, in social-ethical and religious matters, alternative paradigms may each have something crucial to teach us about our own reality. Today's debates often revolve around the differences between the traditionalist and progressive, the libertarian and egalitarian, the rational and intuitive, the individualist and communitarian perspectives. If we find ourselves habitually on one side of any of these dichotomies, we probably have something to learn from the illumination that the contrary perspective has to offer—a reality just as real, and just as important for fulfilling our human potential.

In short, we agree that there is such a thing as moral and religious truth, and that we are aiming at it. We even agree broadly on many of its characteristics. But we disagree on its applications. And none of us is epistemically privileged to be able to assert with certainty that we are in sure possession of all of it. In this state of uncertainty, we must concede that our opponent is possibly right, and therefore deserving of respect even now in our state of uncertainty and incompleteness.

This, I believe, is the deeper meaning of the Talmudic saying, *Eilu v'eilu divrei elohim chayyim*—"these and those are both the words of the living God."

In appreciation and friendship,

Lenny Levin

---

tion, affirming the necessity of some prior consensus for every pluralistic conversation.

A Reply to Leonard Levin

Bruce Alpert

Dear Lenny,

Thank you for *On Epistemic Humility*. Whether from your interest in the subject, or your generosity and indulgence, I am honored to spar with you over our differing views of pluralism. As usual, engaging your ideas compels me to reexamine my own and sharpen my thinking.

Reflecting back on my interview, what really stuck me about the question posed – whether I could respect an idea I thought wrong – was that last word. For me, to say something is "wrong," goes beyond disagreement. It implies that the idea in question is factually, logically, morally, or in some other way erroneous. I believe that all of us are, by our nature, seekers after the truth – no matter how imperfectly and stumblingly we do so. To say, then, that one should respect an idea one thinks erroneous goes against our nature. It is, in essence, to ask one to sacrifice one's self-respect for what I believe can at most be the simulacrum of respect for an idea.

In your essay, you raised the issue of abortion. I want to pursue this because I think it illustrates my point.

Like many of us, my own feelings on abortion are a compromise between a woman's rights and a growing concern for the developing fetus. I draw that compromise in one place, but accord that judgment no epistemic superiority to those who draw theirs to the right or left. I respect both those differing views and the people who hold them. I do not, however, accord any respect to the extremes: either the belief that full personhood is owed to a zygote, or that society can have no say in how a woman treats a near-term fetus. To me, both these positions are wrong. I do, however, respect the people who hold these extreme views and appreciate the sincerity and fervor with which they do so.

So what does one say to a person who believes that any restriction on abortion rights constitutes a grave threat to women's rights in general? Do we tell that person, "You must respect the idea that abortion is murder?" This strikes me as an impossible demand: a demand that puts respect for an idea ahead of the self-respect a moral being requires.

I believe similar arguments can be made with regard to the other examples you cite. The Iran nuclear deal, in particular, has a kind of "Pascal's wager" quality to it in which one is being asked to respect, not the possibility that the other side is right, but the consequences of their being wrong. Again, this strikes me as an unsupportable intrusion into a person's autonomy and the self-respect that derives from it.

In this less-than-civil society of ours, I realize how provocative it is to suggest that others' ideas are unworthy of respect. Like most of us, I seek approval and validation for my ideas, particularly from those whom I admire. Given this, it is always challenging for me to disagree with you, an admired teacher whose knowledge on this subject so outstrips my own. I do believe, however, that respecting oneself is what allows us to give respect where it is due. That self-respect will almost invariably engender respect for other people, which I believe will increase our civility toward one another – regardless of how we view their ideas.

In appreciation and friendship,
Bruce

Isaiah Berlin and Jewish Pluralism

Leonard Levin

Why discuss Isaiah Berlin and Jewish pluralism? Why, for that matter, cultivate symbiosis between Judaism and pluralism?

One answer might be: Tradition. For as long as we can remember, Isaiah Berlin's essays—"Two Ideas of Liberty"[1] and "Pursuit of the Ideal"[2]—have been key required texts on the syllabus of the Academy of Jewish Religion (AJR) course in pluralism. But for anyone who was not there, or has not received this tradition, this answer must not suffice.

A deeper answer is rooted in the history of AJR. The Academy was founded to occupy a niche in American Jewish life previously occupied by the Jewish Institute of Religion, namely that of an institution of higher Jewish education not formally affiliated with any of the major American Jewish religious movements. The logic for maintaining such a niche might be explained along these lines: "We are committed to cultivation of the Jewish religious tradition, and open to truth from whatever sources bring it forth, be they ancient or modern. Modern Judaism has assumed multiple versions, forming from the many metamorphoses of Jewish wisdom and lifestyle that arise from the protean fecundity of Jewish tradition itself and from the variety of dispositions of creative Jewish minds. Nothing Jewish is alien to us. *Mikkol melammedai hiskalti*—we are open to learning from all these, and to claim them all as our teachers."

This has been AJR's vision throughout its history, and it is a pluralistic vision. Now, it is commonly accepted among connoisseurs of political philosophy that "value pluralism," as a general philosophical doctrine, received one of its classic formulations by Isaiah Berlin. For these reasons, when Rabbi David Greenstein designed the curriculum of his course in pluralism, he decided to make the study of Isaiah Berlin's statement of pluralism a staple ingredient. So the tradition was established, and so it continues.

There is a difference between Jewish pluralism and pluralism pure-and-simple. General pluralism asserts that there is great variety in the ideals that

---

[1] Isaiah Berlin, "Two Concepts of Liberty," in Isaiah Berlin, *Liberty* (ed. Henry Hardy), Oxford: Oxford University Press, 2004, pp. 166–217.

[2] Isaiah Berlin, "The Pursuit of the Ideal," in Isaiah Berlin, *The Crooked Timber of Humanity: Chapters in the History of Ideas* (ed. Henry Hardy), Princeton: Princeton University Press, 1990, pp. 1–19.

human beings pursue, a variety that can be glimpsed by surveying the many cultures that human beings have produced. The variety of cultural ideals described by the eighteenth-century cultural historians Giambattista Vico and Johann Gottfried von Herder was one of the factors inspiring Berlin to develop the idea of value pluralism.[3] Jewish pluralism does not extend to the range of values of all human cultures, but rather it restricts itself to those ideals that have a Jewish provenance and include as part of their content the commitment to maintaining Jewish religion and/or Jewish culture. Still, the working principles that underlie Berlin's (general) value pluralism can be readily applied to Jewish pluralism.

Jewish pluralism also affirms that there are elements of pluralism at the core of the Jewish tradition itself. The Jewish texts enunciating pluralistic perspectives run for many pages in the curriculum of the pluralism course, and there are citations and echoes of them throughout the current volume. *Elu ve-elu divrei elohim hayyim*, "These and those are both the words of the living God."[4] "For any given case, the words of Torah include 49 reasons to pronounce clean and 49 reasons to pronounce unclean."[5] "So open your ears to take them all in."[6] "The words of the lone dissenter were preserved so that a later court may have the discretion to rule according to them."[7] These rabbinic dictums, and many more like them, express the view that there are many sides to the truth, and that we should always be open to learn from positions that differ from our own position.

The Core of Berlin's Pluralistic Outlook

Two dichotomies underlie Berlin's pluralistic vision: monism vs. pluralism, and negative liberty vs. positive liberty. To appreciate the whole of his vision, both need to be articulated.

Berlin's pluralism began as a protest against what he perceived as the monism of the Western ethical tradition, from Plato through Hegel and Marx.[8] Throughout Western thought, philosophers have pursued the dream that there is a unitary ideal of "the good" that can be pursued in thought and deed.

---

[3] Berlin, "Pursuit of the Ideal," 8–10.

[4] BT *Eruvin* 13b; H. N. Bialik and Y. H. Ravnitzky, eds., *The Book of Legends* (trans. William G. Braude), New York: Schocken, 1992, p. 208 § 32.

[5] PT *Sanhedrin* 4:2, 22a; Bialik *Book of Legends* p. 442, § 380.

[6] BT *Hagigah* 3a–b; Bialik *Book of Legends* p. 441, § 378.

[7] Mishnah *Eduyot* 1:5.

[8] Berlin, "Pursuit of the Ideal," 5–7.

It was thought that if people thought and worked hard enough to attain it, they could move human society in the direction of this comprehensive ideal state. In modern times, many political movements and revolutions have been undertaken in order to achieve this ideal state. In the twentieth century, most of these attempts led to disasters, especially the disaster of totalitarianism brought about in the name of achieving perfect human fulfillment.

Berlin conceived of the pluralistic alternative to this vision when reading Machiavelli.[9] Though Machiavelli's specific recommendations to the tyrant-ruler are repugnant to many adherents of the Western religious-ethical tradition, the core of his thought revolves around a striking insight, namely that in the totality of human existence, different and incompatible ideals have a valid place. The ideal of the successful ruler embodies values that are different and incompatible with those of a Christian monk. Starting from this insight, Berlin went on to take in the historical survey of cultural ideals of Vico and Herder, ranging from ancient Judea, Greece, and Rome, through medieval Christendom and Islam, and up to the monarchies and republics of modern Europe. It would be utter distortion to reduce their variety to mere facets of one, all-encompassing, human ideal. On the other hand, each in its own way, with its own creative vision, draws on an objective common core of perennial human values—the need to embody love, justice, beauty, reason, creativity, imagination, and social solidarity. Each culture does this in its own unique way; each has its own distinctive ranking of common human values; no one of them could be confused with any other. Each is a unique expression of the inexhaustible potential of human achievement and adds value to the totality of human experience.

Liberty and equality are among the perennial human ideals of which Berlin speaks. Like any similar pair of values, they are incommensurable and not wholly compatible. Total liberty includes the liberty of the powerful to exploit the powerless. Complete equality can be achieved only by quashing liberty.[10]

Berlin speaks of two types of liberty. "Negative liberty" is freedom from external compulsion by one's fellow humans or by the state. To the extent that it exists, it gives one the space to do whatever one wants—but presumably not to quash the liberty of one's fellow-citizen. It is not to be confused with sovereignty; negative liberty exists for the individual irrespective of who rules

---

[9] *Ibid.*, 7–8.

[10] For example, Berlin writes: "The extent of a man's, or a people's, liberty to choose to live as he or they desire must be weighed against the claims of many other values, of which equality, or justice, or happiness, or security, or public order are perhaps the most obvious examples" ("On Liberty," 215).

society. Negative liberty is primarily an individual affair: the liberty to think, to create, and to fashion one's individual lifestyle.[11]

Positive liberty is the liberty to pursue specific ends, often ends that can only be achieved through individual discipline or collective action. Democracy—the sovereignty of the people—is one form of positive liberty, and entails the obligation to participate in the political activity of self-government—to meet in assembly, to discuss public affairs, to vote, etc., as well as to comply with decisions by the majority when these have been made in accordance with the democratic process. How far the majority can go in constraining the liberty of the individual is a matter to be decided by the constitution of each political state. Ethnic solidarity is another form of positive liberty and entails identification with one's ethnic group and engaging in structured activities to promote one's culture and collective way of life.[12]

The evil of totalitarianism comes about when the idea of "positive liberty" is combined with a narrow, monistic conception of the ideal; if there is only one all-embracing human good, then it is considered "rational" to create a society that forces the realization of this one good on everyone. Pluralism can be a corrective to this error. When one realizes that there are many incommensurable human goods, it becomes imperative to structure society with sufficient "negative liberty" to allow everyone to pursue his or her own vision of the ideal good.

Out of this quartet of terms, it can be inferred that Berlin's social ideal consists not in absolutizing any one or two of them, but in achieving a healthy balance among all four. Absolutizing pluralism and negative liberty can lead to an atomized, anarchic society, one in which everyone is absolutely free to do whatever he or she wants, but in which social solidarity is reduced to the vanishing point, and thus in which any goods requiring prolonged discipline, or collective endeavor, will never be achieved, because no one will accept any limitations on their absolute freedom. At the other extreme, if one abolishes negative liberty, there are no autonomous individuals, and those activities requiring individual autonomy (such as rational thought and cultural creativity) languish. The balance may be achieved when there is a broad but flexible consensus on overall social values, with a wide range of latitude, permitting individuals and subgroups to cultivate distinctive lifestyles and cultural patterns.

In a Jewish pluralistic society, that broad consensus must include a general commitment to certain Jewish values, however defined.[13] If Jews are going to

---

[11] Berlin, "On Liberty," 169–178.

[12] *Ibid.*, 178–181, 200–212.

[13] See Michael Walzer, "A Note on Positive Freedom in Jewish Thought," *Svara* 1

have a common Shabbat experience, there must be a common denominator of agreement as to what is Shabbat-appropriate behavior. If Jews are going to eat together at table, there must be agreed-on rules of what kinds of food are permitted for the common meal. If they are going to produce a common literature, there must be a language or languages (Hebrew, Yiddish, Ladino, English, etc.) that they share in common. If there is going to be an ongoing group prayer experience, there must be an ongoing commitment of enough members of the group to insure that there are always ten present (however one defines "ten"). But within these parameters, a great deal of freedom ("negative liberty") still obtains. Still, the balance between consensus and freedom must be more or less consensually agreed upon as one of the meta-rules by which the group operates. This internal balance will vary from one local Jewish group to another, so that there is also a higher-order pluralism among groups.

* * *

The balance and interplay of these factors can be made vivid by considering a recent controversy in Jewish, and specifically American-Jewish life: the debate over the position American Jews should take vis-à-vis the American-Iran nuclear deal.[14] It will be recalled that the prominence of the issue of Iran's nuclear-weapons development was raised to top priority in large measure because of Israeli Prime Minister Benjamin Netanyahu's insistence on the world stage that this was a mortal threat to Israel's survival, and it could not be safely ignored. By the spring and summer of 2015, the emergence of the agreement, with its submission to the US Congress for consideration, was the focus of a polarized debate among American politicians, among American Jews, and among Israelis. Israeli political opinion was overwhelmingly against ratification of the deal, while opinion in the United States was sharply divided, with many Republicans strongly criticizing it and the majority of Democrats following the line of the administration in supporting the deal.

In this context, two approaches dominated the debate within the American-Jewish community: (1) On the merit of the issues themselves, did the deal as presented provide the best achievable guarantee of peace and security or not? (2) In approaching the international constellation of powers, should

---

(1990), 7–12.

[14] I am indebted to Julius Rabinowitz for suggesting this issue as a fitting example to explore the dilemmas raised by Berlin's ideal of pluralism. The reader is free to sketch out a similar application of these concepts based on any contemporary controversial issue.

an American Jew prioritize America's interests or Israel's interests in making his/her personal decision?

A third underlying issue arises from the context of Berlin's theory of liberty: Should an individual participating in the debate on these issues do so primarily as a member of a group (whether American or Jewish), bound to expressing loyalty to the group in one's thoughts and actions, or as an individual with independent mind and judgment, seeking to arrive at the best intellectual comprehension and conclusion on the matter? And if both, what is the relative priority of these two factors?

The first matter (the intrinsic merits of the deal) is beyond the scope of the present inquiry. Let us address the second question then, the intersection of loyalties of an American Jew to the two societies—the United States and Israel—to which he or she in some manner belongs. In the nineteenth and early twentieth centuries, Jews debated whether it was consistent with citizenship in a modern nation-state to affirm the national dimension of one's Jewish identity altogether. Prayers for the return to Zion were even deleted from some prayer books on the grounds that a Jew loyal to Germany, England, or the United States could not legitimately voice the aspiration to return to a Jewish homeland that was outside the borders of one's current country of residence and citizenship. The Jewish anti-Zionists of that age would have looked to the controversy over the Iran deal as a case in point, where one would have conflicting loyalties to consider. It is therefore of interest that during the debate over the Iran nuclear deal, no one within the broad American political mainstream reproached American Jews with taking positions that cast aspersions on their American loyalty. The party from whom such accusations might have been expected to come in the early twentieth century—the Republican party—was most insistent in maintaining that the true support of American interests demanded unyielding support of Israel's position in this matter. Moreover, across the political spectrum it was taken for granted that it was perfectly legitimate for any American of any ethnic background to be in sympathy with the political interests of his or her country of origin, so long as that country was not actually at war with the United States (a consideration that weighs most heavily, in contemporary times, against Americans or potential immigrants from Muslim-Arab countries). This is testimony to the high esteem in which the value of ethnic pluralism is held in the United States today, as a value at the core of the prevailing vision of American democracy. Thus, the American endorsement of pluralistic values relieves present-day American Jews of the dilemma in which their recent ancestors often found themselves: trapped between voting their American interests and their Jewish interests.

Still, the question may legitimately be posed: Should an American Jew seriously weigh the call made by the political leaders of Israel to join in supporting Israel's political interests, regardless of one's private opinion of the issue at hand? The analogous consideration in parliamentary politics is "party discipline." Benjamin Franklin articulated it in his famous words, "We must all hang together, or else assuredly we will all hang separately!" Especially when one is a member of a small group struggling for survival in a hostile world, the value of survival as a member of one's cherished group with its special traditions can require that one forgo the indulgence of one's selfish desires (including expression of one's opinions for the sake of self-expression) in order for everyone's energies to be enlisted on behalf of the group's vital needs.

Here, then, is a cogent example of the case that can be made for what Isaiah Berlin called "positive liberty." The basis of this idea is found in Rousseau's notion of the "social contract." There is a mythical aspect to the notion of social contract, for the reason that most of us do not have the option to be present at the ground floor of creation of a social entity such as a nation. Maybe the Americans of 1776 and 1787 had a choice to send representatives to Philadelphia to vote on the founding documents of the United States. But most of us are born into an existing society with its laws and conventions, and though we do assent in the long run to be loyal members of our respective societies, this is at least as much a function of circumstance and existing sanctions as of our own free choice. Nevertheless, at bottom we are mostly willing citizens of the societies to which we belong. As such, we agree to the following tradeoff: that we will enjoy the benefits of being members of such societies, but we will agree to be bound by the will of the majority even when we are in the minority. If the majority passes a law with which I am not in agreement (let us say, to pay taxes to support such-and-such a venture), I will nevertheless comply with what the majority dictates so that I may enjoy the larger benefits which the existence of this society affords. My willing compliance with and endorsement of this arrangement is what Berlin calls "positive liberty."

So in the case at issue, with Israel's survival in the balance, should I, as an American Jew, vote the position advanced by Israel's leaders?

The standard countervailing libertarian argument—famously articulated by John Stuart Mill—argues for reserving the right to vote my opinion, on the grounds of freedom of discussion in a democratic society (and for this purpose, I invoke my membership in two democratic societies—the United States and Israel).[15] The factors in evaluating the Iran nuclear deal were quite

---

[15] "Why is it, then, that there is on the whole a preponderance among mankind of rational opinions and rational conduct? ...It is owing to a quality of the human mind,

complex. All agreed that the deal achieved certain limited goals but also had definite limitations. Much of the discussion revolved around evaluating the relative force of these positive and negative factors. As long as no decision has been made, freedom of discussion is crucially important to enable the broadest possible examination of all factors, so that the decision, when finally made, will be made on the basis of the best information available. I therefore have a positive duty, as a member of two democratic societies, to contribute whatever insight I may have to offer, so that the best possible decision can be made. If every individual makes a similar effort, then the debate will presumably have the benefit of the maximum of collective thought and insight, and the decision arrived at will be the best possible one.

On another level, I would like to argue that the entire discussion over the Iran deal—and of the legitimate role that American Jews can play in that discussion—points to the relevance of Berlin's other concept-pair, especially the issue of value pluralism itself that he gleaned from his study of Machiavelli, Vico, and Herder. Like many such controversies, the debate over the best policy vis-à-vis Iran was at bottom a debate over the relative priority of two fundamental ethical values (for instance, security and cooperation, though other dichotomies are possible), each legitimate in itself, both of them essential to maintaining a healthy society. One saw here the competition of two approaches to international affairs—military confrontation relying on armed strength, and diplomatic negotiations working toward cooperation and relations of trust. In the course of the protracted negotiations, the weighing of competing values has been taking place in at least three societies—the United States, Iran, and Israel. Part of the difficulty of the negotiations and of the discussions of ratification that followed (both in the United States and Iran) stems from the fact that each of the competing values is a core value whose cogency cannot be denied. At the same time, one might even argue that the international situation had come to an impasse because one of these values—security—was being exclusively stressed, to the point that it was undermining itself. Cooperation and trust must be woven into the fabric of international relations in order for security itself to be feasible in the long run.

---

the source of everything respectable in man either as an intellectual or as a moral being, namely that his errors are corrigible. He is capable of rectifying his mistakes by discussion and experience. Not by experience alone. There must be discussion to show how experience is to be interpreted. Wrong opinions and practices gradually yield to fact and argument; but facts and arguments, to produce any effect on the mind, must be brought before it" (John Stuart Mill, *On Liberty*, Indianapolis: Liberal Arts Press, 1956, pp. 24–25).

As an American Jew loyal to Israel, I may legitimately feel that a pluralism of values in Israeli society—balancing the ongoing need for security with the ongoing search for avenues of peaceful negotiation and international cooperation—is essential for the health of that society. I therefore would not construe "loyalty to Israel" as obedient endorsement of Israel's declared position, whatever it may be, but as being a party to the ongoing dialogue within Israeli society, for that society to have the benefit of the strengths of the many competing visions that have been nurtured within mainstream Zionism for its entire history. And as a loyal American, I wish to participate in the parallel interplay of competing visions that has nurtured and strengthened American society.

The conclusion of the present argument should not endorse either outcome—yea or nay—as the "correct" decision, but should note that each of the positions—supporting the treaty and opposing it—had valid arguments from the constellation of Jewish, American, and universal values to bolster its claim. In Talmudic parlance, the one and the other are both the words of the living God. The Talmud then goes on to say that the halakha needs to be decided according to the will of the majority. Yet even after that decision, the view that was outvoted retains its status as a facet of the eternal truth.

Pluralism: Identity, Civility, and the Common Good

Alan Mittleman

The problem of pluralism has become a significant datum for contemporary Jewish theology. Theologians such as Harold Shulweis, Eugene Borowitz, Irving Greenberg, Elliot Dorff, and David Hartman, although they differ on particulars, seek to ground a civil affirmation of profound interreligious and intra-Jewish differences on the deepest structures of the phenomenology of Judaism: the covenant, the Talmudic culture of argumentation, and monotheism itself.[1] Popular Jewish theology is full of praise for what Shulweis calls "the blessings of pluralism." It is full of testimony to the morally and intellectually uplifting consequences of embracing this blessing. Greenberg, for example writes:

> In appreciation of an open society and of the equality and uniqueness of others, I come to affirm the value of living and of teaching in the presence of other truths and systems. Other approaches teach me the limitations of my own views—preventing an imperialist extension of my truth/faith beyond its legitimate sphere into realms where it becomes a lie or is wrongly applied.[2]

It is clear from such a statement, and many more could easily be adduced, that for these writers, pluralism goes beyond what John Courtney Murray called an "article of peace" and has become an "article of faith". For its advocates, pluralism is deeply expressive of a moral and epistemological worldview. To threaten pluralism is to threaten a moral foundation; that is, to threaten an implicit sense of the proper order of society, to threaten the connection of that

---

[1] See, for example, Elliot N. Dorff, "A Jewish Theology of Jewish Relations to Other Peoples," in Elliot N.Dorff and Louis E. Newman, *Contemporary Jewish Theology: A Reader* (New York: Oxford University Press, 1999); Harold Shulweis, "The Pragmatics of Pluralism," Eugene Borowitz, "Respecting Limits in Pluralism," and Irving Greenberg, "The Principles of Pluralism," in *Sh ma*, Vol. 29, Number 561 (April 1999); David Hartman, *Conflicting Visions* (New York: Schocken Books, 1990), pp. 243-56. For a Jewish theological critique of pluralism, see Menachem Kellner, *Must a Jew Believe Anything?* (London: The Littman Library of Jewish Civilization, 1999), p. 111.

[2] Irving Greenberg, "The Principles of Pluralism," *Sh'ma*, Vol. 29, Number 561 (April 1999), p. 5

order with a central system of values. Pluralism has come to represent a significant social good. Its advocacy has come to be bound up with what William James called the "democratic temperament."[3]

Raising questions about pluralism is, in this day and age, seen to be anti-democratic, and to be anti-democratic in a democratic society is a harsh thing. Yet, as Leo Strauss reminds us, "We are not permitted to be flatterers of democracy precisely because we are friends and allies of democracy."[4] We might then properly ask how pluralism came to have this expansive significance for both democracy and theology. How did it come to have such dignity and scope? What are its intellectual origins, its logic and commitments? Does it require limits? By what is it ordered and constrained? What is the relationship between pluralism, with its affirmation of expansive difference, and the common good, with its postulation of likeness, convergence, and a public normativeness? And as to Judaism, is pluralism, in fact, as rooted in the Jewish tradition as its proponents claim? Should it be?

To answer these questions, I shall first discuss what I take to be the modern, uninhibitedly positive concept of pluralism. I shall then turn to a more sober, early-modern approach to pluralism. Finally, I will consider Judaism's ideal-typical construction of the covenantal community and its relationship to the problem of pluralism. My method is to recast the theological question into a political question or, more precisely, to expose the theological-political problem on which the theological question rests. By *theological-political problem*, I refer to the tendency over the past two hundred and more years to construct Judaism according to the patterns provided by the Enlightenment. The problem arises when confidence in the Judaism shaped by reference to the Enlightenment is undermined by a loss of confidence in the Enlightenment. I shall argue that the affirmation of pluralism in Judaism derives from an affirmation of the Enlightenment tradition of civil society but that today civil society has been rendered incoherent by a loss of its supporting philosophical architecture. To uncritically adopt the norm of pluralism for Judaism therefore perpetuates the present incoherence of the civil society tradition without any prospect of repairing its incoherence. What is needed is what Madison referred to as "republican remedies for republican diseases." I shall argue that Judaism needs to return to its model of itself as a covenantal society and that

---

[3] Joshua L. Miller, *Democratic Temperament: The Legacy of William James* (Lawrence, KN: The University Press of Kansas, 1997), p. xv

[4] Leo Strauss, *Liberalism Ancient and Modern* (Ithaca: Cornell University Press, 1989), p. 24

this model needs to be presented to civil society in order for civil society to renew itself.

Pluralism in the Context of Modern American Social Theory

The warrant for shifting a theological issue into a social and political key is that pluralism is first and foremost a social concept, an idea whose plausibility rests on its descriptive and prescriptive role in the discourse of a certain kind of society. The kind of society to which I refer is what Western political theorists have called, since the seventeenth century, a civil society. Pluralism is a characteristic of civil society. It is one of the ways in which society represents itself to itself as civil society. Let us focus first on the concept of civil society.

The concept of civil society is extremely malleable. The term was first used in opposition to the term "state of nature" to designate the political condition of humans who had emerged, according to the social contract theories of the Enlightenment, from the *status naturalis*.[5] But quickly, the idea of civil society came to designate not just human society as such, but a particular form of human society; namely, one where individual humans were originally free and equal moral agents, who, as rational beings, consent to share a common life with one another. Individuality, rationality, freedom, and natural right are the bases of the theory of civil society. The concept of civil society, however, is not the only claimant to these posits. Societies founded by covenant or by compact also lay claim to being constituted by originally free and equal moral agents who operate under a set of shared moral norms provided by either God or natural law or both. Indeed, the term *civil society*, which becomes dominant in the political theory of the eighteenth century, represents a secularization of earlier, biblically influenced conceptions of society as founded by covenant or compact. We find these conceptions primarily in the Reformed Protestant countries and in the Puritan settlements of New England. The practical experiences of Reformed Protestants in founding societies based on oath, promise, agreement and consent nurtured a *"federal" theology* derived from their reading of Scripture. With the breakdown of these integral Protestant covenantal communities, the term *compact* came to replace the explicitly biblical term *covenant*. Compact was further secularized, under the influence of the Enlightenment, into civil society.[6]

---

[5] This discussion follows that of Adam Seligman in Adam B. Seligman, *The Idea of Civil Society* (Princeton University Press, 1992), p. 22

[6] Daniel J. Elazar, *Covenant and Constitutionalism: The Great Frontier and the Matrix of Federal Democracy* (New Brunswick: Transaction, 1998), Introduction and Ela-

Civil society was an attempt to reconceptualize societies that were no longer ordered by the imperatives of inherited status. By the concept of civil society the founders of the new political science sought to reconfigure the relationship of individuals and groups to the institutions of governance under conditions where the status of individuals and groups were no longer predetermined by class, caste, estate, or corporation, nor, for that matter, by a shared Protestant faith. Since people began to speak of civil society, they sought to articulate the basis on which persons, who did not belong to the same corporation, primordial group, or church could nonetheless be bound to each other in a common social and political project. That is to say, they sought to constitute a new concept of *citizenship* and to endow it with the means to make sense both of issues of personal identity and civic relatedness.

The issue of identity came to the fore. Identity had been, in the medieval world, a matter of primordiality. Society was made up of a federation of primordial groups, including estates, guilds, *Bürger*, clerics, and serfs, all of whom participated—if only at a distance—in the central value system of their societies. The central value system was divinely legitimated and the various orders and subgroups of society found their just place according to a transcendent, cosmological scheme. Even groups that dissented from the central value system and its cosmology, such as the Jews, had their own cosmological scheme by which they reconciled themselves to their peripheral status vis-à-vis the authoritative Christian center. With the breakdown of this cosmologically ordered social universe, the need arose for an immanent, non-transcendent discourse of social order. One way of fulfilling this need was through covenant and compact. Society arises as an immanent human good, a product of the "deliberation and choice" of free consenting humans, but it arises under the cosmological umbrella of divine providence. When John Winthrop spoke to the passengers of the *Arabella* of their covenantal mission in the wilderness, where they would build a city on a hill, he spoke of an immanent human project. The project was a radical, risky departure from the old societies based on inherited status legitimated by cosmological claims. Nonetheless, it was not yet a purely this-worldly project in the Enlightenment sense of social contract theory and its vision of civil society. God was a guarantor of or partner to the project. The Christians on the deck of the *Arabella* entered into covenant with each other and with God. A generation or two later, the town constitutions of Puritan New England back away from such robust biblical covenantal language and speak more inclusively of compact rather than covenant. As the

zar, *Covenant and Civil Society: The Constitutional Matrix of Modern Democracy* (New Brunswick: Transaction, 1998), chap. 1.

rigors of the Puritan utopia became less compelling and society expanded to include the unregenerate in a "half-way covenant," compactual language replaced covenantal language. Shared moral norms somewhat eclipsed shared experiences of grace as the binding foundation of society. Civil society represents yet a further phase in the immanentization of this new kind of society.

In its philosophical origins, civil society drew on ancient and medieval theories of natural law to account for the basically social and political character of man and his natural rights and duties. We see this primarily in Locke. But by the eighteenth century natural law teaching was transformed by the Scottish Enlightenment into an even more immanent anthropology of human sentiments. Natural sympathy and the need for conviviality replaced Locke's more or less Christian natural law grounding of social mutuality, moral responsibility, and political obligation. Although the concept of civil society originated under a religious umbrella, it underwent radical secularization. Unlike the earlier concepts of covenantal or compactual society, civil society rested on interest rather than virtue. Humans left the state of nature to enter into civil society not to seek the good life in common, but to survive. They were driven by the fear of violent death, not by the aspiration for perfection. In a covenantal society, the members owe one another and the society as such their fidelity because they have jointly taken an oath to God. God is a partner in, and a guarantor of, the covenantal society. In a society founded on compact, the members take an oath under God and are pledged to one another on the moral ground of solemn promise, as can be seen in the Mayflower Compact (or as it was originally called, the "Plymouth Combination"). In a civil society, however, the ground of obligation, although it may gesture toward these older forms, is more explicitly "self-interest rightly understood." In civil society, the linkage of free and equal private persons in a just association rested on an ever more conventional or consensual notion of justice. Another way of putting this is to say that civil society is based on natural liberty while covenantal or compactual society is based on federal liberty. This distinction goes back to the federal theology of the Puritans. Natural liberty is governed by the rule that one's right to do as one wishes is limited only by the corresponding right of others. Federal liberty, by contrast, is a right to pursue, both singly and collectively, the realization of the covenant (*foedus*). It is, in Isaiah Berlin's language, the distinction between negative and positive freedom. On the account of natural liberty (or negative freedom), justice consists of non-interference in the lives of others as all pursue their individual projects of life. The agents work out what constitutes non-interference and what constitutes legitimate interference, as for example in the range and limits of the power of the state.

On the account of federal liberty, justice consists of public fidelity to the terms of the covenant. The covenant reveals the transcendent norms that constitute the just way of life.

Civil society, in opting away from its earlier covenantal origins, spurred the secularization of society. The effect of this process of disenchantment was that by the nineteenth century, the very term *civil society*, with its lingering natural law resonance, became suspect. The discourse shifted to the concept of citizenship, and its range and limits.[7] It is at this point that the term *pluralism* enters the picture. The concept of pluralism is nested in the idea of civil society. Pluralism speaks to the identity of persons and groups in their relations to one another and to the central political institutions.[8] Pluralism also bears a normative weight. It speaks to the way disparate individuals and groups relate to the public, or in the older phrase, to the common good. Pluralism, in its ideological deployment, is a supporting element of a theory of citizenship. It is a claim made in favor of primordial groups and their continuing salience as identity-endowing forces. A pluralist is one who argues that the connective tissue of civil society is sufficiently elastic so as to include groups that have not entirely identified themselves with the central value system. A pluralist

---

[7] The concept of civil society has experienced a comeback recently in the U.S. and in the post-communist states of Eastern Europe. In its current form, civil society is held to be crucially distinct from the state. The institutions of the state are limited and complemented by the institutions of civil society. Much of the work of civility, of building social trust and nurturing shared norms through shared public engagement is carried on within civil society. Civil society is also distinct from the sphere of the private, from a primordial group such as the family. In these usages, some of the root ideas of civil society reassert themselves. Civil society has always been primarily a way of addressing the problem of the relationship between individuals, primordial groups, free associations, and the central institutions of the political sphere. Civil society assigned a public yet non-governmental role to these sorts of institution.

[8] Pluralism concerns both the claims of individuals who define themselves by reference to primordial or elective groups and to the groups themselves. In its present extremity—multiculturalism—pluralism claims that society is made up of constituent groups, of truly divergent cultures, in a kind of contract with one another. In a sense, the idea of society as a combination of societies harks back to the earliest theorists of the civil society tradition such as Johannes Althusius (1557-1638). One of the advantages of Althusius's theory as over and against the more well-known Enlightenment theories of Hobbes, Spinoza, and Locke is that the parties to the original social covenant or compact are groups, such as families, rather than isolated individuals. Althusius, like Aristotle, has a more realistic grip on the actual conditions of sociality in which humans find themselves. Modern pluralists, to this extent, do a service in calling attention to the continuing significance of primordial groups in the composition of political society.

argues that such groups have a natural liberty to maintain themselves within civil society. At the end of the day, they demonstrate a *minimal consensus*, a requisite minimal level of identification with the sacred central values of the society, and that, in a civil society, this minimal consensus is enough. Indeed, a civil society—as a free society in the negative or natural sense—ought not to require too great an identification with its central *sancta*. A pluralist affirms difference: difference in culture, in substantive religious and philosophical views of the good life, in ethnicity, and in race. But a pluralist conditions this affirmation on the gains that inclusiveness is supposed to provide for civil society. An expansive concept of citizenship is justified by the contribution it is to make to the common or public good. In accord with the civil society tradition out of which it grows, pluralism validates a richly inflected social realm *with reference to* its potential contribution to the public good. While the connection between private and public is much weaker than would be the case for a covenantal or compactual society, a discourse about the connection is still important to the tradition.

If this is the general lineage of the concept, it is worth lingering for a moment on the specific path by which the concept made its way into the history of ideas. Pluralism appears as a theory of citizenship—that is, as a modern theory of civil society—in the writings of Horace Kallen. Kallen took the term from the work of his teacher, William James. James's interest in pluralism was explicitly metaphysical and epistemological rather than social or political. Nonetheless, it is reasonable to believe that the dynamic, segmented, and open-ended quality of American society provided the implicit life-context in which a pluralist metaphysics gained plausibility.

In his 1908 Hibbert lectures, William James argued against the lingering presence of Hegelian absolute idealism in contemporary philosophy. His target was a monistic conception of a closed universe. In opposition to this, James argued for an open, dynamic universe characterized by chance, creativity, and novelty. "What really exists," he writes, "is not things made but things in the making."[9] Reality consists of "active pulses" of pure experience. In "pure experience" the traditional dichotomy between consciousness and reality, between subject and object, is broken down. Reality consists of a stream of pure experience which each of us takes in many discrepant yet related ways. "Aboriginal forms of manyness" are knit together in the "oneness" of lived experience.[10] In such a universe, embodiment, the primacy of lived experience, and irreduc-

---

[9]William James, *A Pluralistic Universe* (Cambridge: Harvard University Press, 1977), p. xxiv
[10]Ibid., p. xxvi

ibly plural perspectives predominate. The Cartesian subject is dethroned. Its place is taken by an embedded subject, continuous with its field of experiential objects.[11] Although James's chief concern was not with civil society, he was actively engaged in civic life and thought that his metaphysical doctrine could inform a civic ethos appropriate to a developing American society. Gesturing toward the social theoretical employment of his metaphysics, he used the term *federal universe* as a synonym for *pluralistic universe*.

It was left to James's Jewish student, Horace Kallen, however, to develop this perspective into a theory of citizenship for the rapidly changing American republic.[12] Americans were increasingly confused by the significance of the massive expansion of the immigrant population. In works such as "Democracy *versus* the Melting Pot" (1915), Kallen articulated a social vision of a multi-ethnic, multi-cultural society in which the object—Americanism—is understood in "aboriginally many" and equally fruitful ways by a continuously evolving, diverse citizenry. Kallen contrasts a static, fixed concept of American ideas and values with a dynamic one, embodied in the perspectives of successive waves of hyphenated Americans. He rejects the denunciation of the hyphenated by contemporaries such as Woodrow Wilson as so much metaphysical and moral arrogance. The older custodians of the American idea, the British-descended New England elite, are simply living off inherited wealth. They no longer speak for the American mind, nor can they save it from its present incoherence. With the inevitable decline of the New England elite and its hegemony over the American mind, we are left with a cacophony. "What must, what can, what shall this cacophony become," Kallen asks, "a unison or a harmony?"[13] America is an unfinished project. Americans must take a risk and show a will to believe in America's unrealized potentialities.

---

[11] James also dethrones the transcendent god of traditional theism. God's place is taken by a limited god, who is enfolded into an evolving cosmos of spiritual and moral possibility. Perspectivalism and pantheism notwithstanding, James's well-known inclination toward pan-psychism and his extensive speculations on the metaphysical basis of religious experience redeem him, at least in his own eyes, from relativism. Insofar as critics of pluralism, such as Menachem Kellner, fault it for its alleged implicit relativism, it is worth recalling that in its philosophical cradle, so to speak, pluralism promised humility, discovery, risk, and faith, rather than indifference, withdrawal, and irresponsibility.

[12] For the translation of James's way of thinking into a social and political mode, see Ross Posnock, "The Influence of William James on American Culture," in Ruth Anna Putnam, ed., *The Cambridge Companion to William James* (Cambridge: Cambridge University Press, 1997), pp. 335-36

[13] Horace Kallen, *Culture and Democracy in the United States: Studies in the Group Psychology of the American Peoples* (New York: Boni & Liveright, 1924), p. 104

If the song that they choose to sing is a "unison," then they opt for "singing the old British theme," and betray both their own dynamic experience and the open, pluralistic universe with which it is continuous. The alternative is to achieve a "harmony" where the British theme is "one among many."[14] Rather than force the melting away of differences and coerce into existence an ersatz American race imitative of the older British stock, sound public policy should:

> ...Provide conditions under which each [existing ethnic and cultural group] might attain the cultural perfection that is *proper to its kind*. The provision of such conditions has been said to be the primary intent of American fundamental law and the function of American institutions. And all of the various nationalities which compose the American nation must be taught first of all this fact, which used perhaps to be, to patriotic minds, the outstanding ideal content of "Americanism"—that democracy means self-realization through self-control, self-discipline, and that one is impossible without the other.[15]

In Kallen's vision, the founders constituted America on the basis of the idea of self-government. Political institutions rest on a culturally pluralistic civil society formed out of overlapping and interacting primordial groups. What the political founders and their heirs at the center of the polity ask of the citizenry is participation in the process of self-rule, enlivened by patriotic affirmation of the republican project. To participate in a republic, that is, to be capable of ruling oneself, entails being true to oneself. The public that is to rule itself must not fool itself about who it is: it may be "aboriginally many" but it is on its way, in a pluralistic fashion, to becoming "one." Kallen adduces the example of Switzerland, the classic, multi-national, federal republic, as a model for the U.S. to emulate. Switzerland, he points out, "has the most loyal citizens in Europe" and is "the most successful democracy in the world."[16] Kallen's defense of the enduring existence and civic participation of primordial groups is premised on the belief that they will add to the public good. His confidence was not shared by the political elite who, a few years after the publication of Kallen's essay, passed restrictive immigration laws that expressed a quite different concept of civil society and citizenship.

---

[14] Ibid., p. 118
[15] Ibid., p. 121
[16] Ibid., p. 122

While we might decry, from our present vantage point, the restrictive im-migration policies of the 1920s and 1930s, we must also acknowledge the anxiety out of which those policies arose: that is, an anxiety about social cohe-sion. An advocate of pluralism, within the classic matrix of the civil society tradition, must have concern about that which orders pluralism. For Kallen's concept of pluralism to work, he must clarify what links the individuals and groups despite their primordial "manyness." What constitutes the unifying core of their citizenship? Kallen's view was that America is mainly constituted by its sacred core of ideas. Ideas are in principle universally available. Particu-lar groups can appreciate and assimilate universal ideas, albeit with their own particular inflections. Universal and particular, the private and the public are related to one another in a dialectical tension. The resolution of this tension is found when the periphery affirms the ideational content of the center. The affirmation of ideas such as the rule of law and the limitation of government by law; the liberty and dignity of the individual; and the right, under freedom, to develop one's potential are the ordering norms of America. Affirming these norms provides the content of citizenship.

Kallen, like many thinkers in the civil society tradition, sees freedom—in this case the freedom to define one's own identity by reference to a primordial group—as serving a republican end. Freedom implies self-governance. That is, freedom is the power to engage with others in the project of ordered liberty. The affirmation of pluralistic difference is very much tied, for Kallen, to civic engagement. The terms "free persons" and "public good" are necessarily relat-ed. But how are they related? The basic problem that a pluralistic society faces is how to sustain civility, the solicitude that citizens qua citizens have a right to expect from one another. Civility is distinct from conviviality. Conviviality is the friendship that like feels for like; it is the property of mutuality that en-ables community within primordial groups.[17] Civility is the attitude of respect based on a feeling of mutuality that citizens ought to have for one another in civil society. It is the ability to subordinate one's private interests and goals to the common good of civil society. It is the capacity to acquire a second nature, the nature of the citizen who has the ability to harmonize private interest with public good. Precisely because this kind of society takes private interests and goals seriously, civility is imperative. Unlike the primordial likeness linking members of subgroups, the relatedness of members of civil society is more at-tenuated, more in need of constant evocation, articulation, and nurture. The

---

[17] Edward Shils, *Center & Periphery: Essays in Macro-Sociology*, Vol. II (Chicago: University of Chicago Press, 1975), p. 7. On civility, see Edward Shils, *The Virtue of Civility* (Indianapolis: Liberty Fund, 1997), passim

requisite likeness of citizens in civil society, without which there can be no civility, is based on their shared participation in the central value system at the expense of their participation in the values of the periphery. Kallen believed that the values of the center, the "democratic faith of America," were sufficiently powerful to constrain a hyphenated Americanism and to provide for a rich citizen identity. Pluralism works only if civility prevails.

Postmodern theorists of pluralism—multiculturalists—would argue against Kallen's conviction that difference must, in the end, be ordered by likeness, by a shared profession of civic faith. Multiculturalists would no doubt find Kallen's postulation of an American democratic faith every bit as hegemonic as Kallen found the cultural preeminence of the older New England elite. Multiculturalism champions identity—however protean identity may be on the multiculturalist account—over civility. Nonetheless, contemporary multiculturalists share with Kallen a common assumption, namely that the fundamental political institutions within which civil society affirms difference may be taken for granted. The constitutional order is sound and stable enough such that the work of extending and enhancing pluralism or implementing multiculturalism can go on without reference to the fundamental stability of political institutions. This is, in a way, the gambit of all social criticism: that our institutions, despite the flaws that critics find in them, are basically sound enough to withstand their criticism. Things look different, of course, from the perspective of the early modern American thought that created the institutions in the first place. Statesmen such as Madison could not presume the stable future of American liberty. Arguably, we should not either. With this in mind, let us return to the founders' consideration of the—if not precisely identical, then at least analogous—issue.

Madison and the Problem of Faction

The modern pluralist, despite a concern for an ordering civility in the face of difference, has a relatively benign view of the public consequences of difference. Unlike the founders, the modern pluralist does not need to worry about the constitution of fundamental institutions, about the creation of political structures durable enough to accommodate the burgeoning differences within civil society and yet to provide order for the whole. There is thus a relative superficiality of the modern project vis-à-vis the early modern project. In Madison's treatment of the endemic problem of republican rule—faction—we find a deeper, more dialectical evaluation of the significance of difference in a free society than Kallen—let alone the contemporary enthusiasts of multiculturalism— has to offer.

The problem of faction, of the irrational dominance of—to use Rousseau's language—the "will of all" over the "general will," was a principal concern of the American founders. The republican form of government had historically been unstable. It lacked mechanisms to secure the common good over and against its propensity to splinter into competing interests. Given popular rule, faction was endemic to republicanism. Madison argues in *Federalist* No. 10 that men are endowed with different capacities for acquiring property. Their different aptitudes for acquisition of wealth shape their outlook and opinions. So disposed by different material interests, citizens will be unable to rise to a dispassionate devotion to the public good insofar as their reason remains connected to their self-love. Passion for their private advantage will infect all that they do. Factions of individuals who place their private or aggregate good ahead of the public good have been the historic bane of republics. Indeed, in direct democracies a faction is likely to become a majority that acts in passionate disregard of the "permanent and aggregate interests," that is, of the public good of the community. Since human nature will not change, the causes of faction cannot be removed without the removal of liberty. The tendency toward faction must therefore be moderated at the level of effect rather than of cause. A "republican remedy" must be brought for the republican problem.

Madison's prescription in *Federalist* No. 10 was to advocate an extended republic in which size and diversity would work naturally to undercut collusion and "factious combinations." Factions would be set against one another, achieving at best an unstable and temporary coalition unable to affect a tyranny of the majority. Under such circumstances they would have to learn to work together. As Michael Novak, interpreting Madison, puts it:

> Under a regime of majority rule, a large diversity of minor factions will oblige partisans of each to place themselves in one another's shoes, to learn each other's interests, and to seek compromises that will permit the formation of shifting, coalitional majorities. In this way, minor factions will be obliged to learn to appreciate the reach of views and interests other than their own. Shifting majorities will thus come nearer to a sense of the public good, never perfectly perceived, always only approximate, "at least of the greater, not the perfect good."[18]

---

[18] Michael Novak, *Free Persons and the Common Good* (Lanham, MD: Madison Books, 1989), p. 52

In this way, Madison takes the evil of faction and redeems it for the public good. He tries to find in self-interested difference a possibility for civility to take root. But Madison did not entrust civility to chance and the exhortation to virtue alone. His principal aim was to construct the frame of government in such a way as to minimize the possibility of a factious tyranny of the majority. Popular passions would be refined through a representative and deliberative body better able than the people as a mass to discern the permanent political interests—the central, constitutive ideas—and to act in accord with them. Referring to the Senate, he calls for a chosen body of citizens,

> ...Whose wisdom may best discern the true interests of their country and whose patriotism and love of justice will be least likely to sacrifice it to temporary or partial considerations. Under such a regulation it may well happen that the public voice, pronounced by the representatives of the people, will be more consonant to the public good than if pronounced by the people themselves, convened for the purpose.[19]

Madison is calling for the cultivation of a political wisdom capable of discerning the abiding principles of the public good and for their institutionalization in an effective frame of government.

Unlike Kallen, who seems naïve by comparison, Madison was under no illusions about the precariousness of difference for the project of the public good. Indeed, difference is natural. But Madison is not a follower of Rousseau—the natural is not per se a source of political good. Citizenship is a second nature, not an unmediated expression of our primal nature. Madison is enough of a Christian to see our primal nature as tainted by self-love. Civil society allows us the chance to restrain and refine our given nature. In *Federalist* No. 10 he does no more than allude to the possibility of virtuous and judicious citizens. His focus is on the frame of government more than on the spiritual conditions required for the nurture of prudent citizens. Indeed, Madison, unlike the anti-Federalists, had a great deal of suspicion of the idea of civic virtue and preferred to plant the Constitution on the hard soil of self-interest.[20] Nonetheless, he does not neglect the theme of the "habits of the heart" entirely, for without what Ernest Barker called "the traditions of

---

[19] Federalist No. 10 available at: http://www.constitution.org/fed/federa10.htm accessed 9/27/16

[20] Elazar, *Covenant and Constitutionalism*, p. 79

civility," no frame of government could withstand the disintegrative forces of human evil.[21] Although discernment of the abiding interests of the community requires a level of dispassion and insight that the people as a mass may be incapable of, the people as a mass nonetheless require some dispassion and insight in order to choose the best among them. Appealing to the older political science of virtue, Madison wrote:

> Is there no virtue among us? If there be not, we are in a wretched situation. No theoretical checks, no form of government, can render us secure. To suppose any form of government will secure liberty or happiness without any virtue in the people is a chimerical idea.[22]

Madison's achievement was not only to analyze the problem of potentially invidious differences but to neutralize them by an effective political apparatus. Conscious of the necessary evil of human self-love, he sought to harness the evil inclination and make it serve a public good. Impressed by the near anarchy of American life under the Articles of Confederation, he envisioned a more ordered liberty. Self-interest would be rightly channeled by the cooperative possibilities of civil society and constrained by carefully balanced political institutions. Traditions of civility—shared convictions and public virtues—would guide the consciences of the best of Americans and give them the discernment to curb the excesses of the worst.

Madison's Christian emphasis on the fallen nature of man, on his need for redemption through (civic) grace from the state of nature propounds a realism poles apart from Kallen's incipient "politics of recognition." The pluralist project, on Kallen's account, assumes the natural goodness of difference. While not neglecting the problem of ordering difference through civility, Kallen is overly sanguine—at least by Madisonian standards—about the implications of natural identity for the public good. Kallen does want to order difference by virtue, by the affirmation of moral ideas, but he lacks Madison's realism about the fragility of virtue as the guarantee for the public good. Madison ultimately sees the security of the republic in the multiplication of factions. None

---

[21] Ernest Barker, *Traditions of Civility: Eight Essays* (Archon Books, 1967). Barker takes civility very broadly in its older meaning as the quality of being civilized. He sees civility as consisting of holding on to Greek and Hebraic elements that have been continuously present in the western tradition.

[22] Novak, p. 50

will be strong enough to dominate the whole. But this is not to romanticize or to prize them for what they are in themselves. Liberty must permit difference, but difference is a problem for the ordering of liberty.

Judaism and Pluralism

Having considered the career of pluralism as a social and political concept, as well as different assessments of it, let us return to the theological-political problem of modern Judaism. Given the gains for modern Jews that pluralism as a theory of citizenship has brought, it is difficult if not impossible not to extend pluralism into the construction of modern Judaism per se. Pluralism is deeply rooted in the central ideas of the political system. How can it not carry over into the core of religious ideas? While pluralism, so conceived, brings an expansion of freedom into Judaism, it also tacitly recasts the Jewish polity into a civil society. How does Judaism *qua* civil society relate to the prior self-conception of Judaism as a covenantal polity?

It is well to begin with a midrash. As the Israelites advance toward Mt. Sinai to receive the Torah, the text tells us:

> Having journeyed from Rephidim, they entered the wilderness of Sinai and encamped in the wilderness. Israel encamped there in front of the mountain...." (Exodus 19:2)

In the sequence of verbs, the first three verbs are—as we might expect—proper plurals. The last verb, *va-yehan* (encamped), however, is a singular. Observing this sudden shift, the *Mekhilta* comments that whenever they journeyed (plural) or encamped (plural) they did so as a divided and dissenting people. When Israel, however, encamped (singular) before the mountain they made their hearts into one.[23] Drawing on this midrash, Rashi comments memorably that they were "as one man with one heart."

As understood by its traditional commentators, the biblical text shows both an anti-pluralist, utopian aspiration toward an ideal of national unity and a sober assessment of the constraints on that ideal. For one brief shining moment, Israel experienced a sublime *maximal* consensus. The usual rivalries between Moses and the people or between the tribes were suspended, only to be resumed in the aftermath of the theophany. Taken from a religious point of view, this brief achievement of unity (*ahdut*) is a minor miracle, proleptically

---

[23] *Mekilta de-Rabbi Ishmael*, Vol. II, Jacob Z. Lauterbach, trans. (Philadelphia: Jewish Publication Society, 1961), p. 200

pointing toward that eschatological moment when all Israel, indeed, when the whole world will submit to the kingdom of heaven. Miracles aside, from a political point of view the people had to be of "one heart" at the moment of founding in order for the Torah, *qua* constitution, to establish a binding, historically effective rule of law. For a constitution to fulfill its purpose (that is, the establishment of an effective frame of government under just laws) it must secure the broadest possible consent of those who would be governed by it. In the same spirit, the Preamble to the United States Constitution begins, "We the People of the United States, in order to form a more perfect union." "The People" to whom the Preamble refers is not merely the sum of enfranchised voters or members of ratifying conventions in 1788. Rather "the People" is a corporate entity stretching across time; a partnership, as Edmund Burke put it, "not only between those who are living" but also with "those who are dead, and those who are to be born."[24] Constitutions typically invoke a people in this transcendent sense. In the American case, the Constitution invokes the people founded by the national covenant of the Declaration of Independence eleven years earlier.

If a constitution succeeds in founding a viable political order it is because the people, who agree to it and who are in turn further formed by it, imagine that it represents their highest political interests or, as Madison put it, "the permanent and aggregate interests of the community." Constitutions are basic laws held to transcend the normal process of legislative enactment. Unlike ordinary bills or statutes, constitutions are not the product of legislatures and other law making entities. They cannot be, for these entities are themselves established only on the basis of the constitution. The logical and axiological priority of the constitution requires that it descend, so to speak, from a higher realm than that of ordinary legislation; that it represent that which is timeless and abiding. The source and recipient of that which is timeless and abiding can only be an ideal or symbolic collectivity, an entity that is itself removed from the ebb and flow of any given empirical aggregate of individuals. While there is an element of invention here, there is also an element of truth. An effective constitution, although it emerges from an empirical people rather than a transcendent collectivity, in a sense founds its own people. The nation that accepts a constitution witnesses a new birth. It becomes a trans-historical collectivity with a distinctive character shaped by its fidelity to the abiding norms of the constitution. A constitution produces coherence between the civic experience of "those who are dead" and "those who are to be born."

---

[24] Cited in Walter Lippmann, *Essays in the Public Philosophy* (Boston: Little, Brown and Co., 1955), p. 35

It is fitting then that prior to the ratification of the Torah-constitution, the people were of one heart. Thus was the necessary condition for their national consent secured, and their pledge of fidelity to the rule of law signified. Like other documents of political founding, the Torah is sensible about the morning after—the rapid slide into dissent and faction that follows upon the passing of the unitive moment. The Torah portrays repeated dissent from Mosaic governance, sometimes erupting into outright rebellion. It portrays whole tribes who seek to opt out of the national enterprise and pursue their sectional interests. It depicts the rise of anarchy—"every man did what was right in his own eyes"—in the absence of effective government, as well as repeated experiments in government such as prophetic leadership, tribal confederation, federal monarchy, despotism, and priestly hierocracy, each with its own fatal flaws. In all of these, social unity remains an elusive, eschatological ideal, projected onto the utopian future where a Davidic monarch will reign over a messianic kingdom. In the here and now, the social reality is one of faction.

The Torah seeks to constrain faction by what we might call Jewish traditions of civility or the Jewish public virtues. It is not only a matter of law but a matter of intent and mentality. The covenantal order is founded on *hesed*, on the force of loyalty and mutuality that animates religious duty. Leviticus chapter 19 might be read as a compendium of laws that, when coupled with *hesed*, become civility-sustaining practices. The section begins with a divine address to the entirety of the Israelite people, that is, all who are capable of responsible participation in the covenantal community (*kol adat bnei yisrael*). The entire sacred community is called upon to emulate God, to be holy just as their God is holy. Here is a clear marker of the distance between a community formed through covenant and a civil society. The text moves seamlessly between duties owed to the divine partner in the covenant and duties owed to the human partners (in the language of Jewish tradition, between commandments *beyn adam l'makom* and *beyn adam l'havero*). The proper conduct of sacrifice stands on the same plane as discharge of duties to parents and to the poor. On the intra-human or horizontal dimension of action, the text proscribes stealing and dealing deceitfully with one's covenant partner (19:11); insulting the deaf or impeding the blind—later understood as taking advantage of anyone in a situation of ignorance—(19:14); perverting judgment by deference to the poor or the rich (19:15); taking vengeance against one's covenant partner; or even harboring hatred against him (19:17). The text demands that one revere mother and father (19:3); leave various fruits and grains unharvested for the indigent of the community (19:9-10); and ultimately love one's covenant partner (*re'a*) as oneself (19:18). The latter is operationalized by the Jewish tradition in terms of visiting the sick, arranging for the burial of the dead, comforting the bereaved, providing dowries for poor brides, and protecting another's possessions as if they were one's own.[25] The members of the covenant community have a right to expect that these shared moral and religious norms be observed. They have a duty to perform them. Indeed, despite all of the vicissitudes of Jewish history, the Jewish "traditions of civility" have sustained a political and moral culture where Jewish communities have always sought public implementation of the covenantal norms. Even under circumstances of extreme secularization, Jewish communities maintain institutions to facilitate mutual assistance and covenantal solidarity. Civility, indeed, covenantal love (*ahavat yisrael*) has constrained the disintegrative potential of pluralism precisely because the Jews have not considered their society to be a civil society. Despite the embarrassment of explicitly religious and archaic motifs for secularized modern Jews, they have continued to understand Jewish life in covenantal or compactual terms, rather than purely civil ones. If Judaism were to be recast entirely along civil society lines, as the proponents of open-ended pluralism seem to advocate, would the sense of covenantal solidarity endure?

The American experience does not give us much guidance here. The "new order of the ages" at its inception was very much a civil society, not a covenantal one. The founders early on opted for an extended republic based on commerce rather than a small republic based on virtue. The states, rather than the national polity, were to be the small republics where the shared convictions and public virtues rooted in the older strata of the civil society tradition could shape public life. Yet the moral life of the states soon became as secularized and disenchanted as that of the national polity. While some states, such as Pennsylvania or Massachusetts, continue to call themselves *commonwealths* rather than states, this usage is merely a distinction without a difference. The moral specificity and thickness of a commonwealth bears no relation to life in the anonymous mass society of a modern American state.

While the American experience does not give us much insight into the career of civility against the reality of pluralism, neither can we neglect it. Judaism is indissolubly wedded to the American circumstance for American Jews. The problems of American political culture become the theological-political problem of American Judaism. Accordingly, reinvigorating American civility and reclaiming Jewish covenantalism are linked tasks.

---

[25] Abraham Chill, *Ha-Mitzvot v'Ta'ameihen* (Jerusalem: Keter Publishing, 1988), p. 154

Reconstituting Civility

At the end of the twentieth and the beginning of the twenty-first century, the "blessings of pluralism" are solidly anchored in our common life. We are, however, uncertain about the prospects for civility. The dreadful decline of civility in our politics, indeed, in our society as a whole, is an indication of the thinness of our relatedness. Citizenship no longer provides either a conceptually or a psychologically satisfying aspect of personal identity. Identity is cultivated almost exclusively in the private realm or the realm of the primordial or of that which is voluntarily chosen by an autonomous self. Our situation is paradoxical. Owing to modern communication and a dynamic market economy, more people than ever are participants in society; that is, more people than ever participate in a broad consensus about the central value system. Except, perhaps, for the Amish, participation in the modern web of social interaction and its underlying values is pervasive. The social distance between center and periphery has been virtually erased. Despite widespread cynicism and discontent with the central institutions of government, radical dissenters and revolutionaries are an insignificant fringe. They form, perhaps, the last distinct periphery. This was to be the promise of the modern age: that society would not be the possession of the few; that the nation would be constituted by all the people who live on a bounded territory; that politics would be the participatory domain of the many. All of these goals have been achieved, yet disaffection with the achievement seems to prevail. The concept of citizenship, and with it the basis for constituting social likeness in the face of the reality of deep difference, is in trouble. If pluralism is to continue to function as a rhetorical trope in the language of American politics and society, it must regain its bipolarity, that is, its original significance as a way of linking the private and the public, the primordial and the civil. It must return to its original setting in the idea of civil society where the virtue of civility had a crucial role to play. We must reconstitute civility as a counterweight to pluralism.

Civility, we recall, is civil society's alternative to conviviality. It is to the modern republic what *philia* and *eunoia* were to the ancient one.[26] The place

---

[26] There is a considerable debate on how friendship is to be understood in the ancient Greek and Roman contexts. Since the Enlightenment, it has been argued that since friendship was crucial to the political and economic relations of the ancient world, disinterested and affectionate friendship was not truly possible. See David Konstan, *Friendship in the Classical World* (Cambridge: Cambridge University Press, 1996), p. 6. For a modern "classic," see Hannah Arendt, "On Humanity in Dark Times: Thought about Lessing" in Hannah Arendt, *Men in Dark Times* (New York: Harcourt, Brace & World, 1968), p. 24. Aristotle's view was that *eunoia* (goodwill) was the proper

of friendship, of reciprocated mutuality, between citizens of a republic is not easy to determine either as an historical matter or as a normative one. Plato, with his cosmological analysis of *eros* and *philia,* saw intense mutuality as basic to the good polity. Against Plato's maximal version of social unity, Aristotle entertained the possibility of a less integrated society, held together by less intense forms of friendship. Unity was desirable, but it was to be effectuated through education and the cultivation of fellow feeling:

> The error of Socrates must be attributed to the false sup-
> position from which he starts. Unity there should be, both
> of the family and of the state, but in some respects only. For
> there is a point at which a state may attain such a degree of
> unity as no longer to be a state, or at which, without actually
> ceasing to exist, it will become an inferior state, like harmo-
> ny passing into unison or rhythm which has been reduced to
> a single foot. The state, as I was saying, is a plurality, which
> should be united and made into a community by education.[27]

What education must produce is a sense of goodwill (*eunoia*) or solicitude among the citizens for one another. As Lenn Goodman puts it, "People do not need to love each other as best friends do in order to live together harmo-niously in a city. 'Goodwill is a friendly sort of relation, but not identical with friendship.'"[28] Virtue friendship, the highest type or degree of friendship in Aristotle's analysis, cannot be cultivated except among the few and the best. The friendship available for the mass of citizens in their capacity as citizens is at best of the sort that arises naturally between men in a common situation, such as shipmates. Aristotle sees such friendship as deriving from a compact.

> Every form of friendship, then, involves association, as
> has been said. One might, however, mark off from the rest
> both the friendship of kindred and that of comrades. Those
> of fellow citizens, fellow tribesmen, fellow voyagers, and

---

relationship of citizens. *Philia* was reserved for close friends.

[27] *Politics* II 5, 1263b 27-37. Cited in Lenn E. Goodman, "Friendship in Aristotle, Miskawayh, and al-Ghazali," in Oliver Leaman, ed. *Friendship East and West: Philo-sophical Perspectives* (London: Curzon Press, 1996), p. 168
[28] Goodman, ibid., p. 169

the like are more like mere friendships of association; for they seem to rest on a sort of compact.[29]

When citizens are equal to one another, as in a democracy, they can have a diffuse friendship with or goodwill toward one another as a consequence of their equality. What Aristotle has in mind here is not a subjective feeling of affection, although that is not ruled out, but a mutual relation of helpfulness. Each form of polity, each constitution, entails a possibility for a justly scaled mutuality. A good king shows friendship toward his people by providing them with the benefits they deserve, so too a good father toward his children. Since subjects and children are not equal to kings and fathers, however, the genuine mutuality of friendship is constrained. Under a democratic constitution where citizens are equal, however, friendship and justice "exist more fully; for where the citizens are equal they have much in common."[30]

Although the Greek *philia*, in Aristotle's rather sober sense, could be used to describe the relations between ancient citizens, our *friendship* cannot be so used in the context of the modern civil society. I have suggested civility in the sense of solicitude for one another's welfare as the modern republican equivalent of ancient friendship or goodwill. Is even this too much to ask? Aristotle suggests that friendship develops through association by persons who have something in common. If we have nothing in common—pluralism taken to its end point—then we would be incapable of fellow feeling. He also suggests that it is the goal of education to produce commonalities or to produce the discernment to notice commonalities so that citizens can respond appropriately to them.

At the roots of the civil society tradition lie the older, biblically tinged forms of covenant and compact. In societies formed through covenant or compact, the oaths, promises and agreements requisite to covenanting and compacting provided commonality between persons. Their agreement to be in society together, continuously reenacted and reinvigorated in public rituals and public life, produced the common situation necessary for civility. As civil society frees itself from its covenantal origins, it rejects such bonds. Persons revert to a situation of natural liberty where nothing more is expected of them than that they leave one another alone. Without recapturing in some measure a sense of mutual involvement, common purpose, common participation in self-rule or enterprise, civil society cannot be sustained. t is at this point that Judaism, with its memory of covenantal association, might have something to

---

[29] *Nichomachean Ethics* VIII: 12 1161b 19
[30] *Nichomachean Ethics* VIII:11

contribute to modern civil society. By modeling the more intensive mutuality of a covenantal society, Jews might help civil society to become more aware of its early covenantal roots.

To do this, of course, Jews must free themselves of their uncritical infatuation with the limitless openness of modern civil society. What rankles about Jewish pluralism for those with a Madisonian, dialectical assessment of its blessings is that it entails the transformation of a covenantal polity into a modern contractual association. To the extent that Judaism resists this transformation, it is because its central value system continues to rely on a thick public web of religious and moral convictions that Western societies rejected in early modernity when they turned from commonwealths into civil societies. To the extent that the Jewish polity could ever be described along civil society-lines, it would be closer to the Christian commonwealths of seventeenth century theorists, such as Althusius or the Puritan thinkers, than to the secularized humanists of the eighteenth and nineteenth centuries. By imagining itself along the lines of a civil society, Judaism gains in freedom but loses in mutuality, in the *re'ut* or *ahavat yisrael* that is covenantal Judaism's equivalent of ancient republican *philia*. If the transformation to civil society were accompanied by a commensurate realization of civility then all would be well. But in fact, the Jews are experiencing the same decline in civility within their own civil societies, both in Israel and in the American Jewish community that Americans at large now experience. Particularly in Israel, where a genuine modern civil society exists, estrangement between religious and secular Jews deepens as pluralism expands. With the expansion of pluralism and the ever more strident calls for greater recognition of the rights of factions comes an erosion of the *tovat ha-klal*, of the common good, an erosion of the ability to conceive of a common good.[31] Common institutions, based on ancient covenantal habits, are more difficult to maintain both practically and intellectually when commonalities among Jews are no longer felt. Without a reawakening of a covenantal consciousness, of the expectation of more intense mutuality, Judaism will follow civil society into incoherence. Jews need to emphasize Jewish traditions of civility (*gemilut hasadim*) in their dealings with one another and so hold up to civil society a recollection of its covenantal origins. Jews should give civil society its due, but should not lose

---

[31] Note for example a call by the rabbinic arm of Reform Judaism for Reform Jews to redirect their charitable giving away from communal institutions such as the United Jewish Communities and toward institutions that "actively support religious pluralism." JTA Bulletin, June 14, 2000

their own form of life within it. Rather, they should practice and speak of that form of life in the American public conversation. Finding the proper language in which to speak of that form of life in the public conversation ought to be a desideratum for Jewish education. Jews need not only educate for pluralism, as liberal Jews constantly opine. They must also educate in the traditions of civility and in care for the public good.

Pluralism as Social Consensus and Personal Worldview[1]

Eliezer Schweid

Pluralism within the Jewish people and Israeli society is a complex matter. How does one define "pluralism" as a worldview? It seems simple enough: It is an affirmative attitude toward a variety of worldviews and lifestyles within a single society or culture. How shall we persuade skeptics that the people of Israel and Israeli society cannot preserve unity without a pluralistic consensus? This also seems simple: Even the most energetic opponents to pluralism have been compelled to accept it, because they are not ready or able to withdraw from the group. But a philosophy should not be forced on others. How can we negotiate a pluralistic consensus in such a way that proponents of various views accept it as being somehow aligned with their specific beliefs, faith or lifestyle? Many pens have been broken in the attempt to address this.

Fortunate are those individualistic liberals, for whom pluralism is part and parcel of their worldview! They will be able to live comfortably in the earthly paradise of pluralism without changing an iota of themselves, their outlook or their lifestyle. But there is no paradise without a snake lurking in the bushes, next to the tree of knowledge of good and evil.

Even the most fervent pluralists can run into conflict when they are driven to take a stand, seemingly based on their impeccably pluralistic principles, on political, social, and cultural issues affecting the community. Yet, what happens when they meet with a headwind of opposition from others, whose contrary position seems to them not merely different but mistaken and malicious, and worst of all, "anti-pluralistic"? What does true pluralism dictate in such a situation? We have already seen that the "pluralism" of well-meaning people is liable to beget Jacobin monsters, or that its spokesmen are likely to be forced to admit that pluralism is a dream incapable of fulfillment by mortal human beings in this world. But that is small comfort.

Both pluralists and their opponents will quickly run into the fact that human beings are unable to establish a perfect society in this world; no individual can fashion his own outlook and live in accord with it as a free person without

---

[1] Originally published as *Pluralism ke-muskama ḥevratit ukhe-hashkafat olam ishit*, *Gesher* 42:5754 (1994), 29–37. Republished in Schweid, *Ḥinukh humanisti yehudi be-Yisrael* (Tel Aviv: Hotza'at ha-kibbutz ha-meuḥad, 2000). Translated by Leonard Levin for this volume.

compromising it to some extent to adapt pragmatically to the fact of social difference. It seems, then, that it is impossible to escape the pluralism dilemma
without practical compromise between pure principles and the constraints of
their realization in a social order and lifestyle of an entire society with all its
diversity. But if pluralism starts as a grudging concession to practical necessity,
it can only succeed as an ideal if it is anchored in a comprehensive social outlook, based on assumptions whose source is in the experience of socialization
among human beings.

We may start from the observation that a certain measure of pluralism is
necessarily manifest in every human society, including the societies that strive
for a high degree of monistic uniformity. Even a religious sect, church, or
totalitarian state must compromise by allowing some measure of pluralism in
certain areas of their social, cultural, and political activity—at the very least,
a pluralism of rankings of values, of preferences in people's interests, of styles,
and of political judgments, deeds, or principles. Furthermore, they are forced
to acknowledge that a certain measure of pluralism is positive from their perspective, since it is a prerequisite for successfully managing the complexity of
the tasks of survival and social governance, and the richness of culture. It is
therefore incumbent on them to make the distinction between the highest
values, which govern the overall orientation, and lower-order values that condition each other relatively, among which it is possible to maintain a certain
limited pluralism without encroaching on essentials.

This forced choice follows, of course, from the fact that human nature is
not uniform. It is possible to bless this situation with the words of the rabbis: "God created all human beings from a single individual to demonstrate
God's greatness. For a person mints multiple coins from a single die and they
are all identical. But the King of Kings, the Holy and Blessed One, minted
all human beings from the die of Adam, and not one is identical to another.
Therefore every person is entitled to say, 'The world was created for my sake.'"[2]
One may regret this fact, as did Maimonides, who was interested in achieving
social and political discipline, which is frustrated by personal individualism
and libidinal egoism. He yearned for a monistic society in order to achieve
what appeared to him to be the single all-embracing purpose of rational human existence (namely, intellectual perfection). But precisely for this reason,
he could not ignore the obstacle in this path: Society must change human
nature if it desires to strive for a common social destiny.

Maimonides pitted two basic assumptions against each other in his politi-

---

[2] Mishnah Sanhedrin 4:2.

cal theory. The first was that man is political by his nature, in the Aristotelian sense. That is to say, a person cannot unfurl, develop and maintain his rational, human, distinctive qualities except within an ordered society. The second assumption was that man is *not* political by his nature, because of the special, individual difference of every person, not only in his physical appearance but, more importantly, in his temperament, his qualities, his views, and his beliefs.[3] The practical conclusion that Maimonides derived followed from his unequivocal and sharp preference for the first proposition over the second: In order to preserve the quality of reason that distinguishes human beings from the other animals in our world, we need a strong, authoritative rule that imposes unity based on a single religio-philosophical truth that governs both deeds and beliefs.

It is obvious that for this to succeed, it was necessary for Maimonides to leave sufficient space in his theory for the legitimate expression of differences between persons, so that it could facilitate—and not interfere with—achieving the common goal. Of course, Maimonides did not arrive at recognizing the equal value of all ethical qualities, opinions, and beliefs that are distributed among various individuals. Rather, he established a hierarchy, whereby each of these was either closer or more distant from the truth, the proper and the obligatory; a hierarchy of contributions that individuals contribute to each other and to the maintenance of the society.

The consistent pluralists of our time, who subscribe to the theory of individualistic liberalism, categorically choose the opposite preference: a positive valuation of wide variation among individual persons. But these pluralists also strive to achieve a common social goal: to preserve the individuality of society's members, in keeping with the principle of equality of human rights. They thus cannot free themselves of the necessity of Maimonides's first assumption: the fact that man *is* political by his nature forces them to propose a single goal of individual happiness for all, and to apply uniformly those values and norms that tend to the very existence of a perfect society, (in their view) one that preserves all its members' rights equally.

The criterion is, indeed, external: expression of the values and norms of the law as applied to deeds, and not to opinions. But if we are not to be taken in by the formalistic fiction separating desirable deeds from values and opinions, we shall have to agree that enforcing the law of pluralistic tolerance compels not only people's actions but also the ethical traits, values, and opinions and beliefs that underlie them.

---

[3] Maimonides, *Guide for the Perplexed*, book II, ch. 40.

What, then, is the difference in principle between a monistic society and a pluralistic one? To give a simplistic answer (though this will paradoxically have complex implications): the difference lies in the fact that the monistic society does not include pluralism among the values and outlooks that are absolutely obligatory, but only among its subordinate values, while the pluralistic society requires pluralism as its fundamental value. But the pluralistic society must limit its application of that fundamental value in order to maintain it; it must establish boundaries, which will differ from society to society and from nation to nation. For the principle of pluralism applies not only to individuals within their communities, and not only to communities within broader societies, but also among nations and states.

This fact requires a deeper examination of the relation between the two antithetical assertions: namely, that man is political by nature but also *not* political by nature. We saw that when we came to translate this "tension" to the language of values and norms, the question of priority first arises with respect to the historical and biographical process of socialization, and with respect to the definition of the common social goal. If so, what precedes what? Does the community precede the individual, or does the individual precede the community or society?[4] If we seek to answer this question on the basis of factual experience, it will become clear to us that it is possible to maintain each theory of priority in certain respects, in parallel arguments.

When we observe a society in its present functioning, it appears as an established form of cooperation of many individuals. Our eyes see only a collection of individuals, each one behaving according to his or her inclination or choice. The notion of "community" as a collective entity existing over and above the individuals comprising it, and the notion of "general will" as the will of a collective organism, will seem from this point of view as arbitrary fictions or as a myth. The actual community exists only as an organized institution brought into existence by individuals, and in this respect it is clear that

---

[4] Translator's note: It is clear from the next two paragraphs (and from some of Schweid's other writings) that he favors the answer: "The community has priority over the individual." He is thus a communitarian at heart. He values what Isaiah Berlin calls "positive liberty" in the form of fostering Jewish culture within Israel. He is also a liberal and pluralist within his commitment to this overall goal; he favors the coexistence of many different sub-groups that advance Jewish culture in different ways. That requires affirmation of "negative liberty." But since positive liberty and negative liberty pull in different directions, neither can be absolute, but each must be pursued in tandem with the other and limited by the other. This in itself is a special case of Berlin's "value pluralism"—namely, that negative liberty and positive liberty are two competing values, each with a measure of validity.

individuals create the community for their good and happiness.

But when we observe a society from the temporal developmental perspective, whether historically or biographically, the society as a collective entity, as expressed in its culture, has priority both temporally and in rank of value. No society has ever come into existence by virtue of a present decision of a group of individuals, unless a previous society existed from which it had already developed in the past. Furthermore, every individual belongs to a particular society into which he was born—a family, a community, a folk, a state—before he had the opportunity to choose his affiliation. Only as a result of belonging to the society into which he was born does the individual develop his independent personality, which then allows him, on reaching maturity, to go back and choose of his own free will the family, community, folk, and state in whose context he wants to live the rest of his life—of course, on the basis of the then-existing options, which are not defined by him. The possibility of choice thus exists, and it is sometimes necessary. But it is guided by external and internal given factors that were determined in advance, for the individual's personality develops by internalizing cultural resources that determine his horizon of choice and obligate him vis-à-vis the various circles of his society of origin—his family, community, national culture, and state. Even when one exchanges all these frameworks for others, he cannot change the role that they played in his original socialization and personality formation, an effect that is largely permanent.

If so, it is clear that a radically monistic social conception must give preference to the biographical-historical aspect of social development, deriving the goal of social existence from it, while ignoring the perspective that gives individuals precedence over the collective. Conversely, the radically pluralistic conception gives preference to the interests of the present moment, while ignoring almost entirely the biographical-historical perspective. It is easy to see that pushing either of these conceptions to the extreme turns them into fictions or myths: the myth of the "general will," as if it were a separate entity transcending the individuals, or the myth of "self-actualization" of the individual out of his or her own resources. The absurdity of each becomes clear, because it is impossible to conduct social life, or to realize collective or individual ideals, while taking only one of these aspects of the human condition into account.

The same kind of theoretical and practical absurdity is evident if one tries to define values and norms by which one intends to realize the goals of a radically monistic or a radically pluralistic society. The monistic social conception is based on the sweeping assumption that all values and norms are decided by and follow from a single authority, whether it is a superhuman religious authority or a human authority of society or state. On the other hand, the extreme pluralist conception is based on the sweeping assumption of ethical relativism and subjectivism, based on the sovereign free will of the individual. Each of these conceptions is self-refuting when presented as all-inclusive.

By definition, every individual moral assertion, insofar as it is moral, implies a claim to validity that transcends individual, subjective judgment, which is rooted in recognition of an obligating authority. The individual who demands justice from his fellow or from the group does not present his demand as relative and subjective, but as an objective value to which others should submit. On the other hand, values on which the lives, liberties, and happiness of all individuals depend, or on which the very functioning of the society depends, are viewed as absolutely binding from the perspective of the group.

But on the other hand, it is impossible to impose values on the totality of complex and changing relationships, and on the totality of actions of the members of a society, without recognizing the reciprocal interaction of different values and thus, of a relativity requiring subjective preferences, preferences whose source is found in that very confluence of values, and among their joint and interacting application to specific personal or collective situations.

This conclusion is trivial. In order to apply values in a complex and changing reality, we are called on, at all times and in every situation, to balance the priority of the group over the individual against the priority of the individual over the group, and similarly to balance the absolute aspect of value application against its relative and conditional aspect. Without this constant rebalancing, it is impossible to maintain either a monistic or a pluralistic society.[5] Even a monistic society must accommodate itself to the relative preferences and subjective truths that arise from the life situations and private feelings of individuals. And even a pluralistic society—one that is based on the relativity of values—regards pluralism and the value-set that comes with it as absolute values that shape the social relation itself: Or can extreme pluralism even tol-

---

[5] Translator's Note: Here, too, Schweid's argument is congruent with Berlin's. It will help if we understand "the priority of the group" in a monistic society as the pursuit of "positive liberty" and "the priority of the individual" in a pluralistic society as the pursuit of "negative liberty." As we said, Berlin does not affirm either of these absolutely, but recommends a just balance between the two as characteristic of a healthy society. Schweid follows Berlin in this recommendation of balance. At the same time, Schweid makes the paradoxical point that in Berlin's world of pluralism, all values are up for debate except the value of pluralism itself, which is absolutely maintained. Thus, a wholly pluralistic society, committed absolutely to the value of pluralism, may be said to be "monistic" in that very commitment.

erate anti-pluralistic outlooks and values within its precincts?

It follows from these considerations that we must free the kind of pluralism that we are discussing from the constraint of one-sided discussion that gives preference to one point of view and ignores entirely the contrary point of view. Extreme liberal supporters of pluralism present it only from the standpoint of the rights of the individual in the present. The opponents of pluralism examine it only from the standpoint of supreme authority (especially divine command or halakha) incumbent on the group. The valid arguments of both sides never meet on the same playing field, and so they never encounter a persuasive rejoinder. Substantive discussion will begin only when both sides recognize that pluralism is, first of all, the necessary foundation of a highly inclusive society—of a folk, a national society, or the totality of citizens in a state comprising many individuals—and therefore, it must be a position espoused by every individual and sub-group by virtue of their desire to belong to that society and to act in accordance with the values and norms of the entire society that comprises them.[6]

It is self-evident that the assent or dissent of individuals to the values and norms of the collectivity has an influence on the social consensus, which is always in the process of development, consolidation, qualification, and change. But one must again emphasize that there will always be agreements in accordance with which people act in any given present moment, in the guise of premises that were established in the past as the general legacy. This is the reason why it is so difficult to develop a pluralistic consensus in Israeli society: the point of origin of most of the social currents that, to date, shaped its collective present was monistic in nature, though each party, movement, and organization had its own, distinct monistic ideology. Only a quasi-pluralistic agreement permitted them to operate together in the framework of a single nation and state, for the sake of achieving common existential goals; but the compromises of that agreement were accepted until now as mutual compulsion on the basis of the balance of power called the "status quo." It was clear that as long as no other social consensus was formed to replace the prior factionalism around competing monistic positions, pluralism would appear as yet one more monistic ideology of self-righteous people seeking to impose it on everyone else.

---

[6] Translator's note: Schweid implies here (and spells out in detail toward the end of the essay) that the social consensus must include not only the affirmation of inclusive pluralism, but also a broad commitment to those cultural values that constitute the nation or folk as a social group with a certain positive character and common history. In the case of Israel, this common denominator is "Jewishness" broadly defined. All this is in the realm of Berlin's "positive liberty."

This is the place to address the difference between "tolerance" and "pluralism" as concepts that have a relation of similar application but not identical meaning. Tolerance is a mode of relation between individuals in the same society who hold different views, or among contending groups and movements within a single nation; thus, it starts out as a stance that individuals adopt when relating to each other or to the collectivity. But the reverse is the case with pluralism, which starts out as a general social agreement, albeit based on tolerance, and not as a view of individuals or groups. If the will to unity and partnership among the majority of individuals and groups in a single society, or of parties and movements in a single nation, holds greater sway than the disagreements and factional splits that exist among them, then they will arrive at an institutionalized consensus that all the worldviews and lifestyles of the various parties, movements, communities, families and individuals in the society are equally legitimate. Of course, this legitimacy is granted on condition that they do not contradict the fundamental values and legal and judicial norms that are assumed as the basis of human socialization.

Such a decision does not eliminate, abrogate, or efface the theoretical disagreements and differences of opposed lifestyles; it confirms them. Moreover, the parties to the disagreements and differences are not required to give explicit legitimation or assent to worldviews that are, in their view, incorrect or to the lifestyles that express those views. Legitimation is granted by the overall social consensus; all components of that society are required only to give direct legitimation to the overall agreement, by virtue of their desire to belong to the society and to participate in building it. From this point onward, it is up to the parties to the disagreements to conduct their debates and reconcile their differences of lifestyle on the basis of mutual understanding and respect, on the assumption that their society accorded legitimacy to all of them on a fully equal basis.

Such an agreement is, of course, a substantive change in their mutual relations, not only in outward behavior but also in feeling. The debate will have to shift over from the track of mutual vanquishing/forcing to a track of dialogue that implies a willingness in principle for reciprocal changes in position. This implies that the parties will draw closer and forge new agreements (though they will also discover new points of disagreement). It is self-evident that the agreement to enter into this kind of social arrangement expresses intellectual and emotional readiness for change, and that such readiness is itself a kind of change of position, especially on the part of those whose worldview tended to monism from the outset.

How can these parties, movements, organizations, and individuals adapt their worldviews, in order to accommodate the change in the direction of pluralism, to their prior worldview, which they still hold? There is not, nor can there be, a single answer to this important question, and a pluralistic society would not permit itself to dictate such an answer as an official decision.

There are several ways, based on tolerance, to adapt and translate the pluralistic agreement of the collective into the language of the particular outlooks of each group and individual. Each group and individual will find, in their own way, the most appropriate opening on the basis of the reason that moved them—in the depth of their worldview and scale of values—to the desire for unity and the commitment to it. Thus it will turn out that in every pluralistic society there will be a broad spectrum of definitions of pluralism and many different interpretations of its values. Moreover, pluralism and the ways of applying it will continue to be a topic of perpetual debate among proponents of different conceptions of its meaning and ways of implementation: for in its essence, pluralism is a complex process of relations that change in accord with certain rules, not a uniform social position that was decided once and for all and then imposed on all individuals and groups according to a single standard.

The final question calling for clarification is: What are the common values that, if consensually agreed upon, would constitute a basis for the will to unity and the maintenance of a pluralistic society?

The first condition follows from what we have already said: there must be agreed-on laws and standards of justice; ethical norms that define mutual responsibility for maintaining the rights of members of the society. We should emphasize in this context that we are speaking of fairness in social relations, including the economic sphere and not just the judicial, because this fairness is a precondition for not letting differences between worldviews and lifestyles to become marks of preferential or lowly status, or to be taken as symbols of elevation or degradation, and thus foci of hostility and alienation.

It is self-evident that this condition applies not only to social ethics but also to the very form of government. A pluralistic society can be maintained only through a democratic regime based on it, applying it, and defending it. But we should also emphasize in this context that a "democratic regime" is not a single fixed pattern. Democracy is a pluralistic process conducted through continual struggle over the interpretation of its values and the ways of applying them. Democratic regimes (of every people, every nation and state) adapt themselves to different cultural characteristics and different historical situations. Allowing for this cultural variation of political democratic structures is also substantively relevant to the application of a comprehensive and consistent pluralistic outlook.

Law and order, constitution and regime are not legislated and maintained only by legislators and judiciaries. Prior to them in time and importance are the primal socialization processes of the family, communities, and folk, all based on common language, cultural values and symbols, faith, and religion. It is proper, here, to emphasize that this is a historical truth that applies equally to secular and even anti-religious societies as to religious ones. The foundation of the social ethos from which the processes of tolerance and pluralism developed was religious, and this fact cannot be denied or altered on the layer of cultural existence and consensus. A shared language—both in the sense of the straightforward function of communication and in the sense of the deepest and most comprehensive creative, behavioral, moral, and experiential expression—is a prior condition without which no society could unite or exist. The same applies to tradition, which is a condition for the existence of a common fabric of life.

A pluralistic society that strives to avoid compulsion as much as possible is in need of a common cultural language and tradition. Moreover, a society with a richly layered and varied cultural memory and a cultural language rich in meanings and subtle nuances—an expressive language whose stores of memory nourish a spectrum of views—could support pluralism and develop it while preserving a sense of shared connection to a common root. To the extent that the culture is richer, more varied, more subtle and discerning, and more open to dialogue with its surroundings, it is better able to nourish a broader, more profound, and better-grounded pluralism. For the unity of a multi-hued society is based not so much on actual agreement in values and practices, but rather, on the ability of the proponents of different views to understand each other thoroughly and face-to-face, to have consideration for each other on the basis of this understanding, and to arrive at the necessary compromises, which are effectually agreements that arise from, and acknowledge, disagreement.

Finally, we come to the deepest, primal substratum of the society and culture, from which values, ideologies, worldviews, and religions are nourished, but which stands prior even to them as the fundamental experience of positive humanity. We can get our bearings here by distinguishing between intellectually articulated values and those moral-emotional values and fundamental experiences that shape human existence, such as a sense of belonging, familial relatedness, kinship, proximity, love, compassion, common participation, mutual responsibility, and shared destiny.

The unity of family, community, and folk is not based *a priori* on common intellectual values and worldview, but on emotion-based values stemming from proximity and from common responsibility. For this reason, this unity will persist even when members of the family and community, or between different groups in the community and folk, manifest oppositions in worldview and lifestyle. Of course, it is impossible to sever the connection between the emotional substrate of existential belonging, which connects people to each other, and those people's outlooks. As we said, existential emotions and experiences are the wellsprings for the development of worldviews, scales of values, ideologies, and religions. If so, it is clear that without preserving the consensual moral boundaries that maintain togetherness, even the deepest feelings of love and kinship will not stand the test. This applies even in the intimate family and between parents and children, and all the more so on the level of community and folk. But the emotional values that flow from the existential substratum are able to nourish a cultural spectrum of outlooks and lifestyles that are not only different from each other but may stand in conflict with each other, while still preserving a sense of relatedness to a common source.

The difference between extreme monism and a pluralistic approach will thus be revealed, at its root, to be the difference between a worldview that exalts its own ideologies, or the dogmatic elements of its religion, more than it values the living persons who hold those views or religion and a worldview that values the people themselves and their human qualities and feelings of brotherly love more than it values overarching ideologies or religious dogmas, which may be regarded as true or false when they stand as independent values. For individuals who subscribe to a worldview always have the potential for more than one outlook or practice, and as people they are far more than the outlooks that they hold or the practices that express those outlooks, and it is for this "something more" that they are beloved and respected.

Of course, in characterizing pluralism as a worldview, we include also this positive affirmation of the pro-social emotional and existential values of the tradition as an intellectually-articulated value in its own right. Call this "the value of pluralism itself"; consider it as included within the constellation of values and having its own weight. One must therefore go back and define the place of this value in relation to the other values within the same worldview, ideology, or religion to which the members of the pluralistic community subscribe. In any case, it is clear that only those worldviews, ideologies, or religious outlooks in which these pro-social emotional and existential values hold a high status relative to other values can adapt themselves to a pluralistic consensus. As long as this component is present,, there is no doubt that their proponents will be able to find a way to tailor their position to allow full integration, despite all the difficulties.

For the Jewish people, for the Jewish religion in all its variants and fac-tions, and even for the national-cultural movements that developed within the Jewish people in modern times, the feelings of brotherly love, mutual responsibility, and recognition of a "covenant of fate" that unites us are among the supreme values. These that can be made the basis for a will to unity that can withstand difficult tests. Pluralism follows logically from this will to uni-ty, despite the nay-sayers (including proponents of both religious outlooks and of secular nationalist persuasions). It follows that pluralism will never be guaranteed as smooth sailing over the calm waters of preexisting ideological consensus. Nonetheless, the way is open for us to arrive at a stormy, con-frontational pluralism, rich in tensions and conflicts, and yet still sufficiently stable to elicit innovation and creativity.

Pluralism in the Jewish Sources

Talking with Heretics:
Pluralism in Rabbinic Judaism and its Impact on Pedagogy

Ruth N. Sandberg

The Pluralistic Nature of Rabbinic Judaism

Gratz College, where I teach, has a mission statement that is dedicated to pluralism: "Gratz College provides a pluralistic education rooted in Jewish values and engages students in active study for personal and professional enrichment." This emphasis upon pluralism parallels the mission statement of the Academy for Jewish Religion: "The Academy for Jewish Religion serves the needs of the Jewish community by ordaining rabbis and cantors and training Jewish leaders who combine their mastery of the intellectual and spiritual richness of our tradition with openness to its application in the pluralistic, contemporary Jewish community."

The concept of pluralism is far from just a contemporary one, however. Pluralism has its roots in ancient rabbinic Judaism, which developed from the first through the six centuries CE in both Israel and Babylonia.[1] There any many well-known passages in rabbinic literature which support a belief in the validity of more than one voice or more than one point of view. In fact, in many ways the very nature of rabbinic Judaism is based on the notion that we can move toward finding the truth only if we investigate every point of view on a given subject. The popular phrase, "two Jews, three opinions," really grows out of the rabbinic tradition, where multiplicity of viewpoints is encouraged and normative. Argumentation and debate are at the very core of the Mishnah, the earliest rabbinic compilation focused primarily on Jewish law. Furthermore, in this ancient system, once a person becomes a rabbi, he is given the authority to argue and disagree with all of his fellow rabbis.

So, in a system that is so open, so fluid, so accepting of divergent opinions, so *pluralistic*, how can any definitive decisions be reached or any order be

---

[1] For a detailed discussion supporting the evidence of pluralism in tannaitic literature and its development in later rabbinic sources, see Steven Fraade, "Rabbinic Polysemy and Pluralism Revisited: Between Praxis and Thematization," *AJS Review*, vol. 31, no. 1 (2007), pp. 1-40.

maintained? At one time, before the dissolution of the Sanhedrin in the fifth century, rabbinic Judaism determined that debates over Jewish law would be decided by majority. If the majority of rabbinic authorities voted a certain way, that would become the accepted halakhah; however, the minority opinion would be recorded as well.[2] This practice of recording both sides to an argument underscores the desire of the rabbis to demonstrate that the majority vote is not necessarily the *right* one, nor that the minority view is the *wrong* one. The well-known talmudic statement in BT Eruvin 13b that *"these* as well as *these* are both the words of the living God," insists that both sides have equal validity, even if one opinion becomes the view that is followed in halakhah.[3] David Golinkin also points out that once the Sanhedrin was disbanded, "there was no longer one group of rabbis who could decide by majority vote. As a result, Jewish law became much more pluralistic."[4] One could argue that the United States Supreme Court has a similar procedure: once a decision is reached, both the majority and minority opinions are recorded in order to demonstrate the diversity of thought on any particular aspect of law.

Pluralism is even more pronounced in the realm of aggadah, where a wide variety of beliefs are expressed side by side with no attempt whatsoever to award the majority opinion with any status above that of the minority. For instance, in Genesis Rabbah 1:3, Rabbi Yohanan states that the angels were created on the second day, while Rabbi Hanina says that they were created on the fifth day. The audience members listening to such debates, or later reading them, would be free to pick whichever opinion suited them. Going back even further in Jewish history, the debates between the Pharisees and the Sadducees are evidence that pluralistic views on theology existed well before the rabbinic period. According to ancient sources, the Pharisees insisted that the human soul was immortal and would be judged after death, while the Saddu-

---

[2] On the issue of majority rule, see BT *Berakhot* 9a and *Bava Metzia* 59a; on recording the minority opinion, see M *Eduyot* 1:5 and Tosefta *Eduyot* 1:4.

[3] On the phrase "both are the words of the living God" and the notion of the "rejected" view in halakhah as maintaining theoretical or practical value, see Avi Sagi, *The Open Canon: On the Meaning of Halakhic Discourse* (Bloomsbury Academic, 2008), p. 18. However, in the interests of true pluralism, note that Joel Roth disagrees that the statement "both are the words of the living God" supports unlimited pluralism and insists that the rabbis tolerate pluralism only if both parties have a basic commitment to observance of the halakhah; see Joel Roth, "Pluralism in the Rabbinic Period: What are its Limits?" in *Shofar*, vol. 6, no. 2 (1988), pp. 26-28.

[4] David Golinkin, "Does Judaism really favor pluralism?" in *The Times of Israel*, July 16, 2015, http://blogs.timesofisrael.com/does-judaism-really-favor-pluralism.

cees argued that the soul ends with the physical death of the body;[5] the Pharisees also believed in resurrection of the dead, while the Sadducees did not.[6]

Granted, these two groups could get into rather heated and nasty debates, and eventually the Pharisees became the predominant view expressed in rabbinic Judaism, but their debates are kept alive in rabbinic sources for a purpose – not just to tout the victory of the Pharisaic "winners," but to show that theology is not a simple, one-sided game in which opposing voices are suppressed.

While Judaism has certain theological beliefs that are essential to its monotheistic foundation and form a small core of dogmatic beliefs, a pluralistic patchwork of dissent is spread over the whole of Jewish tradition. This lack of strictly dogmatic teaching in rabbinic Judaism has been noted by Louis Jacobs, who points out that the ability of rabbinic Judaism to consider points of view that are mutually oppositional stands in contrast to early Christianity:

> The various councils of the Church met in order to define Christian doctrine, any departure from which was seen as heresy. In Judaism, on the other hand, while there are Jewish dogmas, there has never been any officially accepted formulation of these, no meeting, say, of authoritative rabbis, to decide what it is that Judaism teaches in matters of faith.[7]

So too has Shaye Cohen noted that "Rabbinic Judaism is dominated by pluralism, the ideology which allows the existence of conflicting truths. The truth is many, not one."[8]

Rabbinic Debates with Sectarians

This pluralism is best exemplified in the rabbinic sources that involve a rabbi speaking with a sectarian or heretic. A sectarian or heretic, a *min* in Hebrew, is someone who rejects the beliefs or teachings of the rabbis. Much scholarly debate has taken place over the exact meaning of the term *"min,"* but what is significant is the fact that this term can apply to Jews, Jewish-

---

[5] See Josephus, *The Jewish War* 2:14; *Avot de Rabbi Nathan* Chapter 5.

[6] See the *Acts of the Apostles* 23:8. [Note: the work in question is variously known; it is called in some Christian communions *The Acts of the Apostles*.]

[7] Louis Jacobs, *The Jewish Religion: A Companion* (Oxford University Press, 1995), p. 235.

[8] Shaye D. Cohen, "The Significance of Yavneh: Pharisees, Rabbis, and the End of Jewish Sectarianism," *Hebrew Union College Annual* 55 (1984), p. 47.

Christians, or gentile Christians.[9] The rabbis were so open to the notion of pluralistic thought that they did not shun conversations even with those who utterly rejected them and their authority, whether they were Jews or not.

What is so surprising is that these rabbinic debates with *minim* contradict a firm ruling found in BT Avodah Zarah 27b: "No one should have any dealings with *minim,* nor is it allowed to be healed by them even if one has only a short time to live."[10] It is also stated that "heresy can be attractive, and one can be attracted to it." Tosafot has a similar interpretation of what it means to "have dealings" with *minim*: "One should not speak at length with them, lest one be attracted to them." In other words, both the Talmud and Tosafot are acknowledging that interactions with *minim* can result in a faithful Jew being persuaded to join them. Their arguments and discussions are not seen as trivial or insignificant, but just the opposite; their thinking is powerful enough to appeal to those who attempt to oppose them.[11]

Based on the prohibition against interaction with heretics, we should not expect to see rabbis engaged in conversations with *minim,* yet rabbinic literature has recorded a variety of these encounters. Admittedly, many of these exchanges can be quite hostile and certainly cannot serve as exemplars of polite interreligious dialogue, but the fact that the rabbis want nevertheless to engage in discussions with people they classify as "*minim*" is significant. As long as the conversation can be kept going, there is the chance that the straying Jewish sectarian may find his way back to the Jewish community, or that the hostile gentile may realize that the Jews cannot be uniformly classified as devoid of any value or human qualities.

It can also be argued that passages in rabbinic literature containing lively discussions with *minim* are not necessarily meant to arouse hostility or hatred against the heretical opponent. The rabbis engage in rather heated debate and disagreement with their fellow rabbis, but this does not imply any personal animus against their opponent. So too do the rabbis engage with *minim* in

---

[9] Ruth Langer, *Cursing the Christians? A History of the Birkat HaMinim* (Oxford University Press, 2011), p. 25-26; see also Reuven Kimelman, "*Birkat HaMinim* and the Lack of Evidence for an Anti-Christian Jewish Prayer in Late Antiquity," in *Jewish and Christian Self-Definition*, vol. 2, ed. E. P. Sanders et al. (Philadelphia: Fortress Press, 1981), pp. 228-32.

[10] It has been argued recently that the *minim* mentioned in this text refer specifically to Jewish Christians, based on archaeological evidence. See Eric Meyers and Mark Chancey, *Alexander to Constantine: Archaeology of the Land of the Bible*, vol. 3 (Yale University Press, 2012), p. 185.

[11] In fact, Rabbi Eliezer regretfully admits that at one time he had found Christian heretical teachings to be attractive and had accepted them; see *Qohelet Rabbah* to 1:8

discourse that can get testy or impassioned, but in this case as well the opposing heretical party is not necessarily meant to be vilified or despised. Defeating an opponent in a theological gambit can be motivated simply by the pleasure of flexing one's intellectual muscles or showing one's mental superiority, not for the purpose of denigrating or deriding another's beliefs.

There are several examples of these intellectual exchanges in rabbinic sources that involve debates with *minim* over the meaning and interpretation of Scripture. For instance, the Talmud contains a discussion about proving the resurrection of the dead:

> Some *minim* asked Rabban Gamliel: How do we know that the Holy One, blessed be He, will resurrect the dead? He answered them by quoting from the Torah, from the Prophets, and from the Writings, but they did not accept his proofs. Rabban Gamliel first quoted from the Torah—as it is written: "The Lord said to Moses: Behold, you are about to sleep with your fathers, and then rise up..." (Deut. 31:16) They responded to him: But doesn't the verse really say, "The Lord said to Moses: Behold, you are about to sleep with your fathers, and this people will rise up and go astray?" Rabban Gamliel then quoted from the Prophets —as it is written: "Your dead will live, corpses shall rise. Wake up and rejoice, you who sleep in the dust..." (Isaiah 26:19) The *minim* objected and said: Doesn't this refer to the dead whom Ezekiel resurrected (in Ezekiel 37)? Rabban Gamliel then quoted from the Writings —as it is written: "Your mouth is like fine wine, flowing to my beloved like new wine, causing the lips of those asleep to speak." (Song of Songs 7:9) The *minim* responded: Doesn't this mean that their mouths will merely whisper? ...Finally, Rabban Gamliel quoted from Deuteronomy 11:21: "In order that your days and the days of your children will be long on the land, which the Lord swore to give to your fathers." It does not say "to you," but "to them (your fathers)." Thus, resurrection can be proven from the Torah.[12]

This text is an excellent example of the intellectual challenge which Rab-

---

[12] BT *Sanhedrin* 90b.

ban Gamliel accepts in order to persuade the *minim* that resurrection can be proven from the Tanakh. What occurs here is a midrashic duel in which both sides show their prowess in biblical interpretation, with the *minim* being the ones to seek out the rabbi in order to engage in a debate with him.

Rabban Gamliel first tries to utilize Deuteronomy 31:16, by cleverly reading the Hebrew text as if it were saying that Moses will die and then "rise up" resurrected again. However, the *minim* also know the Tanakh well and point out that the word "*ve-kam*," "rise up," does not apply to Moses, but to the following phrase, which describes how the Israelite people will "rise up" after Moses dies and will go astray into idolatrous worship. Rabban Gamliel then quotes Isaiah 26:19, which describes how the dead "will live" again and will wake up from "sleeping in the dust." Not persuaded, the *minim* respond by insisting that Isaiah is simply referring to Ezekiel 37, in which the prophet witnesses the resurrection of specific individuals only, those who were buried in "the valley of the dry bones." Rabban Gamliel tries yet a third time by quoting Song of Songs 7:9, in which resurrection is allegorically referenced in an obscure verse imaging "sleepers" who are able to speak again. Still not persuaded, the *minim* argue that this verse merely describes how the effects of wine can cause the inebriated to babble in whispers. After attempting to prove resurrection in all three parts of the Tanakh, Rabban Gamliel tries one last time, using Deuteronomy 11:21, in which Moses informs the Israelites that God had promised to give the land of Israel to their "fathers." Since these ancestors are no longer alive, the only way that this promise can be fulfilled is through their resurrection. This last verse seems to be persuasive, since there is finally no challenge from the *minim*. In spite of the ruling that one is not to engage in conversations with *minim*, this text clearly shows that even an important personage such as Rabban Gamliel found it worthwhile to have a dialogue with the *minim* and to exchange differing scriptural interpretations. There are no nasty invectives thrown at each other or disparaging remarks about the "other," only a lively debate over the meaning of Scripture. While it is true that Rabban Gamliel appears to have "won" the debate, the conclusion is not about the individuals involved and who is the winner or loser, but about the question of finding a way for a religious belief to be derived from the Torah. Both parties are part of this effort and spur each other on to reach the important conclusion.

Another example of *minim* seeking out a rabbi to debate Scripture concerns the interpretation of Genesis 1:

Some *minim* asked Rabbi Simlai: How many Powers created the world? He replied: You and I, let us inquire about the six days of creation. They said to him: Is it written in the Torah, 'In the beginning God (*Eloha* in Hebrew in the singular) created?' No! It is written, "In the beginning Gods (*Elohim*, the Hebrew term for God, which appears to be a plural word here) created' (Gen. 1:1). Rabbi Simlai replied: But is the verb in the plural, 'they created' (*baru*)? No! It is written, "He created" (*bara*, a singular verb, indicating that the word *Elohim* is also singular although appearing as if it were plural). The *minim* replied: But further is it written, "And Gods (*Elohim*) said: Let there be a firmament; let the waters be collected; let there be lights." Rabbi Simlai responded: But it is written: "and He said" (*Va-yomer*, a singular verb again with the word *Elohim*).

When they came to the account of the sixth day, the *minim* exultantly said to Rabbi Simlai: Look, it is written, "Let us make humanity in our image!" (Genesis 1:26). He replied: It is not written here, 'And they created humanity in their image,' but it says, "And God created humanity in His image' (Genesis 1:27). They said to him: But isn't it written, "For what great nation has gods close (*Elohim kerovim*, in the plural) to it?" (Deut. 4:7) He replied: But does the full verse say, 'For what great nation has gods as close to it as the Lord our God, whenever we call on them?' No! It is written, "whenever we call on Him."[13]

This particular conversation is initiated by the *minim*: they want Rabbi Simlai to answer the question of how many "Powers," or deities, created the world. His response is quite welcoming and gracious: "You and I, let us inquire about the six days ofcreation." It is as if he is inviting the *minim* to engage in *hevruta*-style learning with him. They sit together and review the language of the opening verses of Genesis. The *minim*, who want to try to prove that more than one God was involved in creation, point out that the word for God in Hebrew, *Elohim*, appears to be a plural word. Rabbi Simlai then shows them that wherever the word *Elohim* appears in Genesis 1, it is always with a singular verb, proving that only one deity created the world.

---

[13] *Devarim Rabbah* to 4:7; comp. *Bereshit Rabbah* 8:9.

Undeterred, then the *minim* become exultant (*s'meychim*) when they discover what they believe is the perfect proof text for their point of view: Genesis 1:26 indicates that one deity is speaking to another deity about creating humanity in their image! Nevertheless, the Rabbis points out that the very next verse refers to God creating humanity in "His image," clearly in the singular.

Defeated in the creation story, the *minim* move on to Deuteronomy 4:7. They claim that this verse proves that more than one God exists, for Israel has "gods close to it." The *minim* have a strong linguistic argument, because the Hebrew is clear: the word *Elohim* has a plural adjective *kerovim* and thus means "gods who are close." Rabbi Simlai counters by quoting the rest of the verse, in which it is clear that Israel calls upon "Him," not upon "Them." The phrase *Elohim kerovim* applies to other nations who believe in more than one deity, but only Israel has a God who is truly close and who responds when Israel calls on Him.

This conversation has no vituperative language or epithets cast on either party; it is simply a give-and-take debate over whether or not the Torah reflects a belief in more than one God. It gives the impression that the *minim* and the rabbis are sitting together with a Torah scroll between them, reading and discussing and debating the text just as Rabbis do with one another.

A similar exchange can be found in the following text:

> It is written: "Has any other people heard the voice of God speaking from the midst of fire and survived as you have?" (Deut. 4:33). Some *minim* asked Rabbi Simlai: Are there not many deities in the world? He replied: How so? They said: Look, it is written, "Has any other people heard the voice of gods speaking..." (i.e., the word for God is *Elohim*, in the plural.).[14] He said to them: But the verb "speaking" is not written "*m'dabberim*" (in the plural), but rather "*m'dabber*" (in the singular).[15]

Again, the *minim* make their case that the Bible refers to multiple deities, but Rabbi Simlai responds without rancor by simply pointing out the singular verb used in the text.

In the following example from BT *Sanhedrin* 106b, a *min* also seeks out a

---

[14] It is possible that the *minim* are arguing here that other people have had a revelation of God similar to that of Israel, by interpreting Deut. 4:35 as saying: "Haven't other people heard the voice of gods speaking from the fire, as you have, and lived?"

[15] *Shemot Rabbah* 29:1 to Exodus 20:1

rabbi with whom to engage in a debate:

> A certain *min* said to Rabbi Hanina: Do you know how
> old Balaam was? He replied: His age is not written in the
> Torah, but it is written, "Violent and deceitful men shall
> not live out half their days" (Psalm 55:24). Therefore, he
> was thirty-three or thirty-four years old. The *min* replied:
> You have spoken well! I myself have seen the Account of
> Balaam, where it is written: Balaam the lame was thirty
> years old when Phinehas the robber killed him.

In this text, Rabbi Hanina takes the time to find a verse that will answer
the *min*'s question, and the *min* in turn acknowledges that the Rabbi's citation
of Psalm 55 agrees with the Account of Balaam, an apocryphal text[16] which
the *min* apparently considers authoritative. There is a certain mutuality in
their conversation that does not appear to exhibit any hostility in their providing textual information to each other. In fact, Jenny Labendz suggests that
this text actually sees the *min* in a favorable light: "One might say that the
reason this passage is included in the Talmud is that it displays the cleverness
of the rabbis; even without a rabbinic tradition, a rabbi can deduce the answer
from a biblical verse. But it is worth considering that the passage might be
valuable for the sake of the *confirmation* the *min* provides for this rabbinic
suggestion. In that case, the *min* is portrayed actively and independently contributing to rabbinic knowledge."[17]

Another account tells us about a group of rabbis who conversed with *minim*
while visiting the city of Rome:

> Rabban Gamliel, Rabbi Joshua, Rabbi Eliezer ben Aza-
> riah, and Rabbi Akiba went to Rome and taught there: The
> ways of the Holy One blessed be He are not like as those
> of a human being, who makes a decree and tells others to
> observe it, while he does nothing. The Holy One blessed be
> He is not like that.
>
> After they had left, a *min* followed them. He said: Your
> words are only lies. Didn't you say that God does what He
> says? Why does He not observe the Sabbath? (i.e., God uses

---

[16] See *Encyclopedia Judaica*, second edition, "Jesus," vol. 11, p, 250.

[17] Jenny Labendz, *Socratic Torah: Non-Jews in Rabbinic Intellectual Culture* (Oxford
University Press, 2013), p. 182.

the wind and storms on the Sabbath, which are forms of
"carrying," and carrying is not permitted on the Sabbath.)
They replied: Wicked one! In this world, isn't a person permitted to carry in his own courtyard on the Sabbath? He
replied: Yes. They then said to him: The higher (heavenly)
realms and the lower (earthly) realms are the courtyard of
the Holy One, blessed be He, as it is said: "The whole earth
is full of His glory" (Isa. 6:3). And even if a person carries a
distance equal to his own height, he commits no transgression? He said: Yes. They replied: As it is written: "Do not I
fill the heavens and the earth?" (Jer. 23: 24).[18]

This particular *min* set out to challenge the rabbis' theological conten-
tions in a hostile manner, and they respond equally hostilely by calling him
"wicked." Nevertheless, the *min* ends up agreeing with their point of view, but
only because the rabbis still choose to take the time to explain to him that
his understanding of God was flawed. Rather than simply dismiss him, the
rabbis choose to intervene and engage in a dialogue, resulting in the *min* now
understanding how God in fact does not violate the Sabbath.

Here is another example of sectarians being instructed in biblical interpretation by rabbis:

"Enoch walked with God, and he was no more, because
God had taken him." (Gen. 5:24)
Some *apikorsim* (i.e., those who reject rabbinic authority)
said to Rabbi Abbahu: We do not find the death of Enoch
in the Torah. He asked them: How so? They replied: In
Genesis 5:24 the word "taking" is used in relation to Enoch,
and in II Kings 2:1 the word "taking" is also used (in connection with Elijah being taken up to heaven) – "For today
the Lord is taking your lord away from you." He said to
them: If you want to interpret the word "taking," the word
"taking" also appears in Ezekiel 24: 16: "Indeed, I am taking
away from you the delight of your eyes" (i.e., your wife is
about to die). Rabbi Tanhuma said: He responded to them
well.[19]

---

[18] *Shemot Rabbah* 30:9 to Exodus 21:1
[19] *Bereshit Rabbah* 25:1

In this conversation, the *apikorsim* challenge Rabbi Abbahu to disprove their contention that Enoch never died, just as Elijah never died. Abbahu chooses to use their own proof to show them that the word "taking" can refer to a person's death, not just to being taken up to heaven and not experiencing death. Rabbi Tanhuma, who was present at this exchange or who heard about it later, congratulates Abbahu for his excellent response. Jenny Labendz notes the respectful tone of the exchange: "In this dialogue, Rabbi Abahu takes the time to find out exactly what bothers the *minim* so that he can answer them appropriately and satisfactorily... it serves to highlight the deliberate, thoughtful approach with which Rabbi Abahu is portrayed responding to *his* questions question from outsiders. He makes a point of answering them in a way that will satisfy them in particular..."[20]

There are also examples of rabbinic exchanges with sectarians that do not involve any scriptural discussion. In a passage from the Talmud, a *min* has a conversation with Rabbi Ishmael, in which he asks the rabbi to explain the meaning of eleven dreams he has had. In each case, the rabbi interprets the dream imagery as referring to the *min's* sexual immorality or thievery – not very flattering to the *min* and most likely revealing the rabbi's disdain for the man. Nevertheless, the *min* presents the rabbi with a twelfth dream:

> I had a dream in which people said to me: Your father has bequeathed you money in Cappadocia. Rabbi Ishmael said to him: Do you have money in Cappadocia? He replied: No. The Rabbi asked: Did your father go to Cappadocia? He replied: No. The Rabbi said: If so, then the word Cappadocia (does not refer to a city) and really means "beam" and "ten."[21] Go and look at the beam (in your house) which is at the head of ten other beams, for it is full of coins. He went, and found that it was full of coins.[22]

The text does not explain Rabbi Ishmael's motivation. He could have chosen to interpret this last dream in an equally negative way, but he makes the choice to interpret the dream so that the *min* ends up finding a treasure of coins. While not all the rabbis believe in the accuracy of dream interpreta-

---

[20] Jenny Labendz, op. cit., p. 178

[21] Rabbi Ishmael is making a pun on the name Cappadocia, associating "Cappa" with the Aramaic word *keshora*, a wooden pole or beam, and "docia" with the Greek word *deka*, which means "ten."

[22] BT *Berakhot* 56b

tion, and some texts point out how dream interpretations can be manipulative and fabricated,[23] if Rabbi Ishmael really believes in the truth of dream interpretation, this last dream just happens to contain the key to finding a secret treasure, and the rabbi feels compelled to be honest with the *min* about it. In a circumstance where he could have justified hiding important information from a *min*, Rabbi Ishmael chooses to be generous and bring about the man's good fortune.

In BT *Sanhedrin* 91a, Rabbi Ammi is confronted with a *min* who appears to reject resurrection based on the rational and scientific laws of nature:

> A *min* said to Rabbi Ammi: You say that the dead will live again, but they are dust, and can dust live again? He replied: I will make a parable for you. To what is this like? Like a king of flesh and blood who said to his servants: Go and build me a great palace where there is no water or earth. So they went and built it (without benefit of water or earth). Some days past, and it fell down (due to its flimsiness). The king said to them: Go again and build it in a place where there is water and earth. They said to him: We can't. The king got angry with them and said: You built it in a place without water or earth, but now that there is water and earth, all the more so you should be able to build it! (i.e., if God created humanity from nothing, all the more so can God can resurrect human beings from dust.)
>
> Rabbi Ammi said: If you don't believe this, go to a valley and look at the mouse which is only partially formed, made half of flesh and half of earth, but tomorrow it will grow larger and be made entirely of flesh.

At first, Rabbi Ammi resorts to proving resurrection by discussing God's divine abilities. However, he realizes that the *min* is thinking scientifically, so he decides to utilize the natural world as his proof. In this case, he refers to a particular type of mouse that was (supposedly) created from a combination of flesh and earth but which can become entirely flesh the next day. So, this natural phenomenon proves that resurrection is possible: like the mouse, the partially decomposed flesh of a corpse that is combined with earth can become entirely flesh again through the resurrection process.

---

[23] See, for instance, BT *Berakhot* 56a, in which a man named Bar Hedya interprets dreams favorably only if he is paid, and unfavorably if he is not paid.

One author suggests that this story is meant to be a philosophical debate, in which the rabbi is refuting the Aristotelian notion that matter is eternal and unchanging: "Aristotle's unchanging universe has always existed in the state in which it exists today. Hence, mice have always been born from earlier mice, stretching back in time forever. Aristotle's unchanging universe left no room for God being a dynamically involved Creator. A creator that is born from inanimate matter refutes such a theory, and indicates that the universe can indeed spring into existence ex nihilo."[24]

In either case, whether this particular *min* is scientifically or philosophically minded, Rabbi Ammi is willing to prove his point by using the man's own categories of truth. The rabbi does not mind going outside of Scripture and divine revelation in order to talk to someone who does not hold his beliefs. He is willing to speak to the *min* on his own terms, whether this involves a scientific discussion or a philosophical one.

It is admittedly true that in each of these texts, it is the rabbi who gets the last word. This is not surprising, since rabbinic literature serves to uphold and reinforce rabbinic teachings. Nevertheless, the rabbis' willingness to talk with heretics and sectarians is a far more open and compassionate strategy than refusing to speak with their opponents or simply ignoring or vilifying them.

However, even when there is hostility between the rabbis and the *minim*, we see how the rabbis' own sense of morality can guide them into a more compassionate attitude:

> There was a *min*[25] in the neighborhood of Rabbi Joshua ben Levi who used to aggravate him very much with his interpretations of Scripture. One day, the rabbi took a rooster and placed it between the legs of his bed and kept an eye on it. He thought: When the time comes, I will curse him (i.e., the rooster would crow at dawn, and that would presumably be the time for reciting the curse). When the time came, he was asleep. After waking up, he said: We learn from this that it is not proper behavior to do such a thing. It is written: "His mercy is upon all His works." (Ps. 145:9) And it

---

[24] Nosson Slifkin, *Sacred Monsters: Mysterious and Mythical Creatures of Scripture, Talmud and Midrash* (Zoo Torah, 2007), p. 331.

[25] Some manuscripts read "Sadducee."

is also written: "It is not good for the righteous to bring punishment."[26] (Proverbs 17:26)[27]

Even though Rabbi Joshua ben Levi was clearly upset over how the *min* was misinterpreting the Bible, he overcomes his desire to place a curse on him. He recalls the biblical teachings that God is merciful to all creatures, and so he should be merciful to the offending *min*. Furthermore, he remembers Proverbs 17:26, which instructs the righteous not to be quick to bring punishment against others. What could have resulted in an ugly confrontation ends with forgiveness and compassion.

The Impact of Rabbinic Pluralism on Pedagogy

After studying and teaching rabbinic sources for so many years, it was inevitable that their pluralistic nature would have a profound impact on my personal pedagogy. I have learned from these texts how important it is to engage in a dialogue with every student, no matter how skeptical or cynical or doubting that person might be, or how much they disagree with rabbinic Judaism or the Torah or any other Jewish text. It is our responsibility as educators, and especially those of us who are Jewish educators, to emulate the rabbinic quality of openness to multiple points of view.

Two of the most famous passages in the Talmud concern Hillel's encounter with two hostile men. In the first story, one man had made a bet with another individual that whoever was the first to make Hillel angry would win four hundred *zuzim*, quite a significant amount of money for that time. This man tries to get Hillel irritated by asking a series of impertinent questions, but Hillel never loses his temper and patiently answers each question respectfully and with seriousness. The man finally gives up, exclaiming in exasperation that he lost four hundred *zuzim* because of Hillel's patience. Hillel responds: "Watch out how you are feeling, because it is due to Hillel that you are losing four hundred *zuzim* and will lose another four hundred, because I will not become angry!"[28] This account is followed by a second story, in which a gentile taunts Shammai by saying that he will convert to Judaism if he teaches him the whole Torah while standing on one leg. After Shammai angrily dismisses

---

[26] This verse could also be read as: "It is not good to bring punishment to the righteous," implying that even though the *min* was wrong about his biblical interpretations, he was still ultimately a righteous person who did not deserve to be cursed.

[27] BT *Berakhot* 7a.

[28] BT *Shabbat* 31a.

him, the man then goes to Hillel and makes the same request. Instead of becoming annoyed, Hillel simply says: "Do not do to someone what you would not want him to do to you – that is the whole Torah. Now go, and study it."[29]

The Talmud then notes that Hillel's kindness toward the hostile gentile resulted in the man actually converting to Judaism.

While the men in these accounts are not identified as *minim*, their hostile behavior is similar to what we see in some of the *minim* stories. Nevertheless, Hillel keeps showing respect to the men, no matter how outrageous they become. When I encounter a student with a similarly hostile attitude, I try to keep Hillel's patience in mind, and try to respond to the student with the same respect as I would toward the most courteous student.

In addition, the rabbis teach us that we need to develop the ability to see the world through someone else's eyes. In a debate, I may not agree with my adversary, but if I want to engage in a dialogue with that person, I need, at least, to understand why that person has that particular point of view. In my rabbinics courses, it is not uncommon to have traditional Jews and non-traditional Jews studying in the same class. Part of what I see as my responsibility is to get these students to listen to and understand each other; not to agree, but to be open to a point of view that is far different from their own.

This openness is equally vital in teaching courses in Jewish-Christian studies. Not only do I have to have a pluralistic acceptance toward my Jewish students, but I must have the same pluralistic acceptance for the beliefs of my Christian students. These courses are even more challenging, because I have the added task of making sure that the Jewish and Christian students, coming from different religious traditions, learn to respect each other's beliefs. I have dual pedagogic duties in these courses: I have the responsibility of ensuring that Christian belief is understood and appreciated while making sure that the Jewish concerns of Christian anti-Semitism and Christian intolerance are equally validated. One of the happiest days was when I began co-teaching a class with Phil Cunningham and Joe Davis in the summer institute.

Sister Mary Boys, professor of Practical Theology at Union Theological Seminary and a leading scholar in Jewish-Catholic dialogue, has similar goals when teaching Catholic students about Judaism:

> ... Serious and sustained encounter with another religious tradition is critical to fostering intelligent participation in religious pluralism. It forms commitments that are at once

---

[29] *Ibid.*

clear and ambiguous, rooted and adaptive, even as it animates a more vital understanding and practice of one's own
tradition of faith... But our efforts to convey Christian life
in clear and compelling ways must be grounded in truth
– and that means attentiveness to a God beyond imagining and thus to a God beyond the bounds of the Christian
imagination. Those of us who believe, with Rabbi Greenberg, that "pluralism is God's will" must incarnate that
claim in the way we live and teach our faith... it would obligate us to at least two commitments: engagement with the
"other" and employment of pedagogical practices that enable
persons to engage in "border crossing".... We must model
our engagement in our teaching. That is, we must teach in a
dialogical way if we hope to open people not simply to the
significance of other traditions but also to an understanding
of differences. In most cases, this entails a radical revision
of our pedagogy, one characterized less by providing persons with givens and more by opening possibilities for them
to pursue their own questions, needs, and purposes."[30]

I think that the "radical revision of our pedagogy" that Boys addresses has
its roots in the rabbinic world. It is important to note that the ancient rabbis do
not necessarily succeed in persuading the *minim* to accept their way of thinking.
Most often, these rabbinic sources lack a final statement from the *minim* admitting defeat. This silence could be interpreted as showing us that ultimately,
the dialogue is not about who "wins." In my personal pedagogy, I do not want
to have the goal of "converting" my challengers to my way of thinking. In fact,
I try to "convert" myself into understanding the opposing position better. After
all, the word "educate" comes from the Latin, which means "to lead or bring
out". I want to "bring out" what a student thinks, rather than "indoctrinate" by
forcing my way of thinking into their minds. It is also not my responsibility
to "convince" a traditional Jew that she or he is incorrect in their thinking and
needs to change their beliefs to be more in line with modernity, just as it is
not my job to convince a non-traditional Jew that he or she must become more
traditional in their beliefs or practices. On the other hand, it is my responsibility to assist Christian and Jewish students to understand each other's religious
perspectives, not to declare one side "right" and the other "wrong."

---

[30] Mary C. Boys, *Jewish-Christian Dialogue: One Woman's Experience* (Paulist Press,
1997), pp. 86-88.

My true pedagogical purpose is to let the rabbinic or Christian texts speak for themselves, for my students to appreciate the depths of these religious writings and their varying theologies, and, regardless of whether they embrace or reject the encounter, to be enriched by it.

Rabbinic Pluralism —Then and Now

Leonard Levin

How indigenous is pluralism to Judaism? Is pluralism a modern intellectual fashion to which we defer reluctantly, at risk of compromising our commitment to Jewish values? Or does pluralism have roots in the Jewish tradition, so that we can be pluralistic and true to Jewish teaching at the same time?

In this paper, I will first make some broad, programmatic generalizations about the part that I believe pluralism has played historically in the rabbinic tradition. Next, I will examine two key passages in the Talmud that comment on the fabled controversy between the rabbinic schools of Shammai and Hillel, and try to draw out the implications they have for this picture. Finally, I will briefly review three contemporary books that study different aspects of the Jewish tradition—mostly though not exclusively the rabbinic tradition—through a pluralistic lens.

The Dynamic of Monism and Pluralism in the Rabbinic Tradition

Judaism is a religious way of life, organized by a common framework of beliefs and practices. For it to cohere as a unity, there must be common ground. But as it has evolved in practice, it has exhibited a high degree of diversity, both in beliefs and in practices, locally and globally.

Next to the Hebrew Bible, the Talmud is the key foundational document of rabbinic Judaism. It is a wide-ranging discussion of the Mishnah, the code of Jewish law dating from the second century BCE. The Mishnah itself presents the law in the form of common bases of agreement together with divergent opinions as to the details of implementation of the law. The Talmud is even broader in its range of viewpoints than the Mishnah, bringing in for discussion sources of legal opinion that the editor of the Mishnah omitted or passed over, for whatever reason.

Debate is central to the Talmudic method. Anyone plunging into the Talmud at random is likely to encounter disagreement and discussion among conflicting views of rabbis on topics ranging from the received law itself, the exegetical methods for deriving a particular rabbinic tradition from the Torah text, different versions of a legal tradition from a particular rabbi, the validity of general legal or argumentative principles, as well as questions of theology and outlook. Disagreement and debate on all these matters are endemic to the Talmud.

The Talmud served at least two distinct purposes in later Jewish life. One was to engage in the academic study of the law. The other was to establish settled law to regulate the collective life of historic Jewish communities.

From these two purposes, one can readily explain both the pluralistic and the monistic tendencies in the later growth and development of the traditions of rabbinic Judaism. For the purposes of academic study, the more possible views of seeing a matter, the better. But for the purposes of a law to live by, there have to be consensually agreed methods for distilling a single legal conclusion from this multiplicity of options. The British drive on the left and the Americans on the right, but in any given country we must choose one or the other and establish a clear rule regarding which side of the street to drive on, if we are to avoid accidents. For similar reasons, people seeking to engage in business ventures, or in observing Shabbat and holidays together, or in maintaining a common eating community or prayer community, must look to established standards of behavior in order to advance common objectives, satisfy each other's expectations, and achieve social harmony. The very survival of a cohesive Jewish community has depended historically on having consensual norms in these areas.

In view of these two sets of needs, it is not surprising that the history of rabbinic literature exhibits a pendulum-like alternation between phases of pluralistic exploration and monistic accommodation. In a text like the Talmud, the pluralistic tendency is in the ascendancy. Every page exhibits debates, often left unresolved. It is an ideal text for study, for intellectual repartee, and for training the mind in thinking clearly about complex networks of possibilities.

To serve, however, as a source of settled law, its debates had to be subjected to modes of analysis including rules of precedence and tie breaking. "Rabbi Akiva's view outranks those of any of his colleagues, but is overruled by the majority; the halakha follows Rab's view in ritual cases, but Samuel's view in monetary cases; a later authority overrules an earlier authority"—these and similar rules became accepted over time to deduce definitive legal rulings from the Talmud's interminable discussions.[1] Furthermore, in the course of time, comprehensive codes were written deciding the preferred law across the whole spectrum of Jewish practice. Most notable of these were the *Sefer Halakhot* of Rabbi Isaac Alfasi (eleventh century), the *Mishneh Torah* of Maimonides (twelfth century), the *Arba'ah Turim* of Rabbi Jacob ben Asher (fourteenth century), and the *Shulhan Arukh* of Rabbi Joseph Caro (sixteenth

---

[1] See: "The rules for arriving at decisions in disputes..." from Rabbi Samuel Ha-Nagid's Introduction to the Talmud (11th century), in Aryeh Carmell, *Siya'ta Ligemara—Aiding Talmud Study* (Jerusalem: Feldheim, 1998), pp. 73–76.

century). Each of these authorities boiled down the multiplicity of legal options to a single preferred option. Characteristically, however, each of these texts came to be studied in the format of a central text surrounded by marginal commentaries, in which everything resolved by the central text became opened again for discussion by the commentaries.

This cyclical alternation between monism and pluralism has prevailed in the area of halakha—Jewish law and practice—over the centuries of Jewish existence. The situation is a lot less clear in the realm of *aggada*—Jewish belief, lore, and outlook. The interested reader is encouraged to explore the anthology of rabbinic lore compiled by the modern Hebrew poet Hayim Nahman Bialik and translated into English by Rabbi William Braude. Of special interest in this connection are the sections "The Deeds of the Sages" and "Torah."[2] In addition to illustrating the diversity of opinions of the Talmudic rabbis on a wide range of issues, these sections contain many texts where the issue of the proliferation and contention of legitimate views on matters of Torah is addressed, directly or indirectly.

A more disciplined attempt to analyze this diversity of rabbinic beliefs and opinions, especially on the matter of the nature and authority of Torah itself, was undertaken by Rabbi Abraham Joshua Heschel in his major work *Heavenly Torah: As Refracted through the Generations*.[3] In this work, Heschel categorized two main tendencies in the thought of the rabbinic sages of the second century, epitomized in the outlooks of the common-sense Rabbi Ishmael and the mystical Rabbi Akiva. He showed how their duality of approach is manifested in their dicta on such issues as textual exegesis, miracles, ritual, worldly concerns, suffering, and martyrdom. He also extended his research into the development of these tendencies into the medieval thought-worlds of Jewish philosophy and kabbalah. Heschel's work is a potential starting point for further researches into the diversity of outlook in the rabbinic and post-rabbinic thought worlds. At the very least, one can conclude from it that ever since its classic articulation in rabbinic times, Judaism has historically manifested a wide range of diversity of belief among its adherents.

Another way to view this diversity (though on a more philosophical plane) is through the study of the history of dogma in Judaism. It is noteworthy in this respect that the first formal articulation of dogmas in Judaism did not

---

[2] See H. N. Bialik and Y. H. Ravnitzky, eds., *The Book of Legends* (New York: Schocken, 1992), Part II, "The Deeds of the Sages" (pp. 201–331), and Part III, Chapter 7, "Torah" (pp. 403–468).

[3] Abraham Joshua Heschel, *Heavenly Torah: As Refracted through the Generations* (New York: Continuum, 2006).

occur until Maimonides, and that in the centuries between Maimonides and the Renaissance, by Menachem Kellner's count, no fewer than sixteen other thinkers offered lists of principles of belief, each different from the others. Yet Kellner notes: "When we consider theological debate within medieval Judaism against the canvas of medieval theological debate generally we cannot help but be struck by the absence of schisms and sects and by the absence of charges of heresy."[4]

Case Study in Rabbinic Pluralism:
The Controversies of the Schools of Hillel and Shammai

We have noted how debate (often unresolved) is endemic to the discussion of Jewish law within the pages of the Talmud. But it is one thing to exhibit disagreement and debate routinely as standard practices, and it is another thing to raise the plurality of positions to a theme for discussion in its own right. In arguing for the latter case, I hope to show that the rabbis were self-consciously aware that the plurality of positions was a central feature of their method and practice, and that they frequently gave attention to reflecting on it and raising the cultivation and acceptance of multiple views to the status of a principle.

There are at least two key passages in the Babylonian Talmud where the rabbis call attention to the famous disputes between the School of Shammai and the School of Hillel and comment on it. One of these passages is rather brief, stating the fact of the controversy of the schools and commenting on the virtues of the School of Hillel, among which the respect they showed for their opponents figures prominently. The other passage leads to a lengthy excursus in the Gemara that takes rabbinic disagreement in general as its theme and discusses its character and implications.

The first passage is from the Babylonian Talmud, *Eruvin* 13b:

> R. Abba stated in the name of Samuel: For three years there was a dispute between the schools of Shammai and Hillel, the one asserting, "The halakha is in agreement with our views" and the other contending, "The halakha is in agreement with our views." Then a heavenly voice issued

---

[4] Menachem Kellner, *Dogma in Medieval Jewish Thought from Maimonides to Abravanel* (Oxford: Littman Library, 1986), 207. See also Solomon Schechter, "The Dogmas of Judaism," in Solomon Schechter, *Studies in Judaism* (New York: Atheneum, 1958), 73–104.

announcing, "These and those are both the words of the living God, but the halakha is in agreement with the rulings of the School of Hillel." Since, however, both are the words of the living God, what was it that entitled the School of Hillel to have the halakha fixed in agreement with their rulings? Because they were kindly and modest, they studied their own rulings and those of the School of Shammai, and were even so [humble] as to mention the actions of the School of Shammai before theirs. ...This teaches you that whoever humbles himself, the Holy One, blessed be He, raises him up, and whoever exalts himself, the Holy One, blessed be He, humbles; whoever seeks greatness, greatness flees from him, but whoever flees from greatness, greatness pursues him.

This short passage teaches several pluralistic lessons that are all part and parcel of the rabbis' outlook:

1.   Multiple opinions, even those that contradict each other, can all have the blessing of God's approval ("the utterances of both are the words of the living God").

2.   Though social considerations require choosing one of the views for normative practice (halakha), this does not detract from the theoretical validity of the views not chosen.

3.   It is a virtue to study the views of one's opponents as well as one's own views.

4.   It is especially meritorious to defer to one's opponent and show them respect—for instance, by giving mention to the opponent's positions and actions prior to one's own.

The other passage starts with a famous Mishnah, then continues with an oft-neglected Gemara discussion, which I will make the focus of my analysis here. First, the Mishnah:

[In certain cases of potential levirate marriage to close relatives and the co-wives ("rivals") of those relatives], the

School of Shammai permit [marriage to the co-wives] and the School of Hillel forbid it....Though the one forbade what the other permitted, and the one regarded as ineligible what the other declared eligible, the School of Shammai, nevertheless, did not refrain from marrying women from [the families of] the School of Hillel, nor did the School of Hillel [refrain from marrying women] from [the families of] the School of Shammai. [Similarly, in respect of] all [questions of ritual] cleanness and uncleanness, which the one declared clean where the other declared unclean, neither of them abstained from using the utensils of the others for the preparation of food that was ritually clean.

The following is a paraphrase of the discussion in the Gemara of this passage, beginning on page *Yevamot* 13b (omitting a few brief introductory comments):

1. We learn elsewhere that the Scroll of Esther is read on the 11th, 12th, 13th, 14th, or 15th of Adar, depending on time, place, and circumstance. Is this not a violation of the principle *lo titgodedu* (Deut. 14:1)—do not break apart into separate sects? (The implied etymology of this phrase is from *gedud*, a troop.)

2. But does *lo titgodedu* really mean "do not break apart into separate sects"? This is a fanciful midrashic reading! Shouldn't we follow the plain sense of *lo titgodedu*, meaning "do not gash yourselves in mourning for the dead"?

3. A technical argument is advanced that the verse can carry both meanings simultaneously, and this argument is accepted.

4. Evidence for diversity of ritual practice is adduced from the difference of communities' customs whether to perform manual labor on the morning before Pesach. But can one cite evidence from a customary practice to one mandated by Scripture? Yet on one view, the prohibition of manual labor on the morning before Pesach is legally binding and not merely customary!

5.   It is suggested that Beit Shammai's dissent from
     Beit Hillel's views was merely theoretical, but they
     yielded in practice to Beit Hillel's ruling. But Rabbi
     Yohanan insists that Beit Shammai differed not only
     theoretically, but also in practice! Which of these
     views is right?

6.   It is proposed that the issuing of a heavenly voice
     [mentioned in our previous passage *Eruvin* 13b,
     endorsing Beit Hillel's position] marked a crucial
     milestone in the history of this controversy. But even
     granting this premise, the possibilities for disagree-
     ment proliferate further. Prior to the heavenly voice,
     some say that Beit Shammai yielded in practice to
     Beit Hillel because the latter were in the majority;
     others say that Beit Shammai did not yield, because
     Beit Shammai were intellectually keener and this
     outweighed the consideration of Beit Hillel being in
     the majority. After the heavenly voice, some say that
     Beit Shammai yielded in practice to Beit Hillel out
     of obedience to the heavenly voice; others say they
     still did not yield, because they followed the view of
     Rabbi Joshua in the "oven of Achnai" episode that
     scholars engaged in halakhic debate should not de-
     fer to a heavenly voice.

7.   If Beit Shammai persisted in their own view in prac-
     tice (whether after the heavenly voice or after the
     decisive vote of the Sages), were they then in viola-
     tion of the principle, "do not break apart into sepa-
     rate sects"? This depends. Abaye is of the opinion
     that this principle only forbids having two compet-
     ing courts of law with varying opinions within the
     same town, but competing courts of law in two dif-
     ferent towns may in fact differ in their views. Raba
     disagrees with Abaye. According to Raba, the dis-
     agreement of Beit Shammai and Beit Hillel is simi-
     lar to having two differing courts of law within the
     same town. This, however, is permitted according to
     Raba—the injunction "do not break apart into sepa-

> rate sects" only forbids having differences of opinion
> within the same court of law.
>
> 8. Other outlier opinions on different halakhic top-
> ics are mentioned: Rabbi Eliezer permitted cut-
> ting wood to produce charcoal to forge a knife for
> circumcision. Rabbi Yose the Galilean permitted
> eating fowl with milk. Rabbi Abbahu carried an
> extinguished lamp on the Sabbath in the locale of
> Rabbi Joshua ben Levi but not in the locale of Rabbi
> Yohanan.
>
> 9. How, finally, could Beit Shammai and Beit Hillel
> intermarry, if they disagreed on certain cases of the
> laws of permitted marriages? They informed each
> other of the cases that would offend each other's
> principles, and thus prevented their opponents from
> being in violation of their own principles.

I find this passage even more remarkable than the previous. On the view of
Eruvin 13b, there was a theoretical disagreement that was resolved in practice
by decree of the heavenly voice; thereafter, though the theoretical disagreement persisted, one unified practice prevailed. According to the account in
Yevamot 13b–14b, we are not even sure whether there actually was agreement
of practice after the heavenly voice. Moreover, the disagreements listed in this
passage proliferate to the point that we have trouble keeping track of them all:

> 1. The Schools of Shammai and Hillel disagree on the
> basic law, whether one is permitted levirate mar-
> riage of the "rivals" of the incestuous degrees or not.
>
> 2. There are differing practices regarding the day that
> the Scroll of Esther is to be read.
>
> 3. There is disagreement whether *lo titgodedu* is to be
> interpreted as "Do not break apart into separate
> sects" or not.
>
> 4. There is disagreement whether the parallel law of la-
> bor on the eve of Pesach is merely customary or legal,
> and whether it can be used as an analogy of the case
> of reading the Scroll of Esther or not.
>
> 5. There are multiple disagreements as to whether the
> dissent of Beit Shammai was only theoretical or also

practical, and as to whether this occurred prior to the heavenly voice or after it.

6. There is implied theoretical disagreement as to whether the rule of the majority is absolute, or whether the "keener intellect" of the minority party offers grounds for exception.

7. There is also implied theoretical disagreement as to whether the heavenly voice decided the issue between Beit Shammai and Beit Hillel, and as to whether indeed a heavenly voice can ever decide any halakhic controversy.

8. There is a constitutional disagreement as to whether it is ever permitted to have multiple courts of law in the same city with systematic differences in their legal opinions. (In other words: Does Judaism foster pluralism within the same locale, or among contiguous or distant locales?)

It seems to me that the editor of this passage of the Gemara paused to reflect on the Mishnah's statement of the differences of the School of Shammai and the School of Hillel in the technicalities of levirate marriage and said, "Wait a minute! The Mishnah raises the problem, how it was possible for factions who disagreed on the substance of the law to live together in community—which they did. But how widespread was this issue? Was it restricted to levirate marriage? Certainly not! What were its full ramifications?" Here the editor took a leap and started to brainstorm issue after issue, argument after argument. There were differences in customary practice. There were differences in interpreting a verse of the Torah. There were differences in theology: whether to listen to a heavenly voice or not. There were differences in legal philosophy and the structure of authority: is one allowed to extend one's disagreement into actual practice, or not? Is one allowed to maintain different methods of legal rulings within the same city, or not?

The passage ends on a positive note—though maintaining their disagreements, they were able to work out accommodations that permitted the preservation of Jewish community without stifling differences. Coming after the encyclopedic listing of differences in this passage, it is a powerful statement affirming pluralism as a value at the heart of the Talmudic tradition.

Three Contemporary Analyses of Pluralism in the Jewish Tradition

So far, I have argued that the primary texts of rabbinic Judaism, dating from the middle of the first millennium, were aware of the divergence of opinions in their ranks and celebrated it as a positive value. I will now submit for examination three contemporary scholars of Judaism who express a pluralistic outlook in their interpretation of the traditional Jewish canon. It is important for my purpose to argue that their contemporary Jewish pluralism is itself rooted in the pluralism of the traditional Jewish texts that they interpret. For the most part, I will let the argument of these scholars speak for itself as evidence for this point.

The three works analyzed here have been included in the syllabus of the course on "Pluralism" that has been taught at the Academy for Jewish Religion in recent years. All three scholars have been affiliated with the Shalom Hartman Institute in Jerusalem, founded by the Modern Orthodox rabbi David Hartman, and presided over currently by his son, Rabbi Donniel Hartman.

Halbertal: *People of the Book*

The first book, by Moshe Halbertal, is *People of the Book: Canon, Meaning, and Authority.*[5] Halbertal divides his attention among three periods within Jewish history: biblical, rabbinic (Talmudic-Midrashic), and medieval. His analysis of each of the three periods raises questions of the pluralistic interplay of different views and interpretations, but the method and expression of this pluralistic process is different in each period.

Halbertal finds a plurality of viewpoints first of all among the authors of the Bible. The creation of the biblical canon seems at first sight to suppress this plurality and impose a monistic uniformity: whatever is included in the canon is endorsed as true, while whatever is excluded from the canon is stigmatized as illegitimate. Furthermore, whatever the original viewpoints of its component authors, reading them together tends to smooth out their differences and encourage a harmonizing understanding of the collected works. But pluralism nevertheless asserts itself again in two ways. First, certain books within the canon—especially Job and Ecclesiastes—are outliers, expressing viewpoints that dissent from the mainstream views of most of the other books. The presence of these books assures the outlier individuals within the community that

---

[5] Moshe Halbertal, *People of the Book: Canon, Meaning, and Authority* (Cambridge, Massachusetts: Harvard University Press, 1997).

a broader than obvious latitude of views on certain issues is permitted. Second, once the canon is established, disagreement shifts from the status of the books to their interpretation. All agree that these canonized books represent the truth—but how should one read them? The same text can be understood in different ways. A variety of methods of reading and interpreting preserves the legitimacy of multiple opinions.

The rabbinic canon begins with the Mishnah. This book enshrines pluralism in a striking and unique way. Where else can one find a law code in which the stated law is not one opinion, but a listing of opinions as voiced by the School of Shammai and the School of Hillel, by Rabbi Eliezer and Rabbi Joshua, by Rabbi Meir, Rabbi Judah, Rabbi Akiva and their colleagues? The diversity of views presented here continues through the successor texts of the rabbinic tradition, especially the Babylonian Talmud. Multiple views are advanced on every page. Debate and controversy reign.

In the medieval period, Halbertal portrays the controversy and struggle for dominance among three principal traditions—Talmudism, philosophy, and kabbalah. All three are agreed on the canonicity of the Bible and the Talmud. But philosophy and kabbalah each add an additional crucial component, with the addition in each case radically changing the meaning of the whole. By insisting on philosophy as an essential component of the Jewish tradition, the Jewish philosophers required that the other core components—the Bible and the Talmud—be read through a philosophic lens. Similarly, the kabbalists insisted that these core components be understood kabbalistically.

The unanimity on keeping the Bible and the Talmud at the core of the Jewish canon continued to preserve the unity of the Jewish people and its tradition. At the same time, the controversies among the abovementioned parties ensured that there would be a plurality of options within Judaism. The tension between unity and diversity has thus marked the Jewish tradition through all the periods of its development.

Avi Sagi: *The Open Canon*

In *The Open Canon*,[6] Avi Sagi has achieved a *tour de force*, exploring the variety of interpretation of the core rabbinic texts embracing pluralism, some of which we have just examined. In addition to the two Talmudic texts we have just mentioned, another text, from Mishnah *Eduyot*, is also central:

---

[6] Avi Sagi, *The Open Canon: On the Meaning of Halakhic Discourse* (trans. Batya Stein, London and New York: Continuum, 2007).

Why do they record the opinions of Shammai and Hillel to set them aside? To teach the following generations that a man should not [always] persist in his opinion, for indeed the founding fathers did not persist in their opinion.

And why do they record the opinion of a lone dissenter among the many, when the halakha must be according to the opinion of the many? So that if a court prefers the opinion of the lone dissenter it may rely on him. For no court may set aside the decision of another court unless it is greater than it in wisdom and number....

Rabbi Judah said: If so, why do they record the opinion of a lone dissenter among the many to set it aside? So that if a man shall say, "Thus have I learned," they may say to him, "You heard the tradition according to the opinion of so-and-so." (Mishnah *Eduyot* 1:4–6)

Sagi's book presents a thousand years of widely contrasting, differing interpretations by various authorities regarding the Talmud's own statements concerning diversity of opinion among the rabbinic sages. Though I and my fellow-pluralists intuitively read these texts (such as the *Eduyot* text just cited) as loudly proclaiming pluralism, someone of a strongly monistic disposition, committed to the Jewish tradition, would read them differently, and this should not surprise us. This is yet another instance of human diversity rearing its head. We fall short of complete understanding of the Jewish tradition unless we take this diversity of readings into account.

At the risk of oversimplification, I offer the following thumbnail sketch of the journey that Sagi takes through the vast literature on rabbinic methodology:

1. Monism. Though only one of the Mishnaic views (that of Hillel) is true, the contrary view is presented by way of contrast for theoretical and practical reasons. Theoretically, the contrasting view offsets the "true" view and helps us understand it better. Practically, the view that is rejected in one situation may provide a valid reason for ruling in a different situation; what is invalid for one time and place may become valid for another time and place (Caro, Rashi).

2. Pluralism: The halakhic ruling is the human apprehension of divine revelation. Each human being receives a differ-

ent aspect of that revelation, whether one understands this difference mystically or rationally (Meir Ibn Gabbai, Solomon Luria).

3. The harmonic outlook: The different views in each valid controversy are reconciled in a higher unity within the all-encompassing divine perspective (Zadok of Lublin, Maharal, Kook).

4. The religious value of the quest for truth: Human beings are not in possession of the ultimate higher truth, but always on the road to it; all views in a controversy are equally valid as stepping stones on this never-ending quest (Reines, Hirschensohn, Hayyim of Volozhin).

Sagi concludes his survey with a discussion of the indispensability of dispute as a constitutive element in traditional halakhic Jewish culture.

Donniel Hartman: *The Boundaries of Judaism*

"Pluralism" and "boundaries" often figure as opposing terms in polarity. Pluralism permits and includes: boundaries define what is forbidden and excluded. Yet they are complementary, and a healthy community must exhibit both. The tension, balance, and accommodation between the two factors define the character of a community.

In this vein, Donniel Hartman's *The Boundaries of Judaism*[7] articulates a rich conceptual framework for characterizing the different stances that a society adopts toward individuals in its midst who conform with or dissent from its basic values. He then goes on to analyze traditional halakhic Judaism in the light of this framework and to assess whether today's (particularly Orthodox) leaders follow the wisdom of the Jewish tradition in this regard or have deviated from it.

Hartman's rubric defines the following basic categories:

1. Pluralism: the stance that "assigns equal value to certain differing positions." (Example: the differing practices of Ashkenazim and Sephardim regarding consumption of legumes during Pesach.)

2. Tolerance: Acceptance in practice of behaviors and attitudes

---

[7] Donniel Hartman, *The Boundaries of Judaism* (London and New York: Continuum, 2007).

that one deems to be wrong.

3. Tolerable deviance: Deviation from the group norms for which no effective sanctions are imposed. (In rabbinic parlance: *patur aval asur*—such an offense is forbidden but not subject to formal penalization.)

4. Intolerable deviance: "the intolerable deviant is one whose transgression is considered to so severely contravene communal standards that it constitutes a renunciation of core values and jeopardizes the integrity of shared cultural space." (p. 17)

Even within the category of "intolerable deviance," there is a gradation of penalties and forms of marginalization that can be imposed on the offender, from minor penalization to ostracism and expulsion from the group. Hartman stresses that "a community's ability to live with difference is enhanced in direct proportion to the rich variety of ways in which it is able to assess its diversity" (p. 20).

> Deviance, particularly intolerable deviance, sets the boundaries and creates the possibility of fellow members finding their commonality. Pluralism, tolerance, and tolerable deviance, on the other hand, create the possibility of collective life despite our differences and disagreements. The building of a healthy and viable community requires that each have [sic] their place. Where one is removed, or when one becomes too dominant, the bond between members is weakened and the social fabric begins to unravel. Where pluralism is applied too broadly, it makes it difficult to identify a shared cultural space....At the same time, intolerable deviance, while a critical feature of every social group, has to be limited in nature. When it is too extensive, it begins to encompass too many members of the society, making sectarianism and social bifurcation inevitable. (p. 30)

After this preamble, Hartman devotes the main part of the book to historical analysis of how these categories have operated in past and present Judaism. In the rabbinic period, we find that the Talmudic rabbis defined the various zones of deviance through specific categories:

- The *meshumad* (apostate): "A radical, far-reaching deviant who has separated himself completely from either or both the Jewish people and Judaism." (p. 37)

- The mere wicked of Israel (*poshei yisrael*): "those who violate commandments." (p. 38)
- The *min* (heretic): "He is not merely a heretic, but an individual who actively challenges rabbinic articles of faith; he is constantly on the attack." (p. 44)
- The *apikorus* (skeptic): "The term is primarily used as a category for heresy alone—deviance unaccompanied by delinquency....The [category of] *apikorus* is always tolerable in the sense that it is never subjected to legal or this-worldly sanctions." (p. 46)
- The *kofer* (denier): One who rejects or denies a particular belief or precept (p. 48).
- *Meshumad le-teiavon* vs. *meshumad le-hakhis* (one who rebels based on appetite vs. based on malice)—the latter is clearly more severe. Similarly the distinction between *meshumad le-davar ehad* (one who rebels specifically against one precept) and *meshumad lekhol ha-Torah kullah* (one who rebels against the entire Torah—see pp. 40, 51).

Hartman analyzes the practical sanctions applied in each of these cases and concludes that "great care and precision is exercised in the application of forms of marginalization, with the latter contingent on the nature of the deviance." (p. 37)

Turning to the medieval authorities, Hartman finds, first of all, that Maimonides has taken the various categories of deviance mentioned in the Talmud and developed them into a system of enforcement of belief, particularly those beliefs he considers crucial (including the belief in divine incorporeality) and those that serve as boundary markers between Judaism and other religions (such as the belief in an intermediary between God and humanity). But Hartman notes a difference between Maimonides's treatment of this problem in his code *Mishneh Torah* and in his responsa, particularly regarding the Karaites. Though belief in the Oral Torah is maintained as a mandatory marker of Jewishness in the codes, in the responsa Maimonides permits intermarriage between rabbinic Jews and Karaites. Thus, what appears to be "intolerable deviance" in theory turns out to be tolerated in practice.

Hartman uses the conceptual apparatus he has developed to launch a trenchant critique of two major thinkers of ultra-Orthodoxy in the modern period—namely, Moses Sofer and Moshe Feinstein. Hartman charges them with extending the deployment of the category of intolerable deviance far beyond what was contemplated in the earlier Jewish tradition, thus abetting the rifts that have divided the Jewish people in the modern period.

Conclusion

I wish to conclude by connecting Donniel Hartman's analysis of the concentric circles of tolerance and deviance with the polarity of monistic and pluralistic tendencies in historical Judaism with which I began this chapter.

Hartman points to some of the needs for monism when he speaks of the need for creating a sense of community. A community, by definition, is the group of those with whom we have things in common. The boundaries of the community need to be defined: Who is a member, and who is not? In addition, law and custom regulate the interactions of members of a community or society. Consensual standards need to be in place defining who is related to whom, who is married to whom, and (for instance in business transactions) what obligations are binding and in force.

The rules for social interaction need to be definite in order for us to know what we can expect from each other, in order for us to plan our lives accordingly. We spoke before of the rules necessary for social cohesion and order, such as choosing which side of the road to drive on. We drew the analogy there to Judaism, where the web of practices around Shabbat, kashrut, prayer, and holiday observances establish ground rules that foster the cohesiveness of Jewish communities on the local level and world-wide.

On the other hand, a large measure of pluralism is necessary for creativity and self-expression of individuals. This is not only a need of modern people. Rabbi Yannai is quoted as saying, "If the Torah was given in clear-cut decisions, we would have no leg to stand on."[8] Another midrash says, "When God gave the Torah to Israel, He gave it as wheat to make fine flour and flax to weave into cloth for garments."[9] There is a benefit for the social group as well, for it is the creative thought of individuals that leads to a robust variety of solutions to historical problems that aid in the survival of the group.

The crisis in Judaism today can be summarized in the question: Can the historical dynamic of monism and pluralism, as it evolved in the alternation of Talmudic discussion and consolidating codes, along with the development of philosophical and kabbalistic interpretations of Judaism alongside the Tal-

---

[8] PT *Sanhedrin* 4:2, Bialik *Book of Legends* p. 442, § 380.
[9] *Tanna devei Eliyahu Zuta* 2, Bialik *Book of Legends* p. 441, § 377.

mudic mainstream, continue into the future? Can the development of modern branches of Judaism (religious and secular) be contained alongside the body of traditionalist practitioners within the framework of a unified Jewish people? Or will the ultra-traditionalists consign the modernists to the ranks of "intolerable deviants"?

One of the rhetorical devices of the ultra-traditionalist anathametizers is their claim to speak in the name of the historic tradition of Judaism, especially of rabbinic Judaism. This presupposes an uncompromisingly monistic reading of that tradition. It is to the credit of Halbertal, Sagi, and Hartman that each shows that if such a reading is possible at all, it is at best only one among many possible readings, and not the most convincing. By revealing the pluralistic dimension of rabbinic Judaism, these authors enable all Jews, of whatever contemporary persuasion, to claim that heritage as their own.

Diversity and Pluralism
in Today's Jewish Communities

Pluralism: Making a Passionate Orthodox Judaism More Meaningful

Asher Lopatin

Is pluralism a Jewish concept? Is it an Orthodox Jewish concept? On the surface, the idea that there can be several truths or several correct paths in life would seem to contradict the strong language of the Torah: "Behold I set before you ... a blessing if you obey the commandments of the Lord your God ... and a curse, if you do not obey the commandments of the Lord your God...."[1] Or, "... and thou shalt do according to the sentence, which they ... shall tell thee, and thou shalt observe to do according to all that they inform thee...."[2] The Torah is filled with commandments and with punishments that come with not obeying the laws, let alone for having heretical beliefs. Our rabbis sometimes lessened the punishments (being 'cut off, karet' could occur later in life or could be forgiven)[3]; questioned the applicability of the most harsh ones (the rebellious son and capital punishment)[4]; and even re-interpreted the commandments (sacrifices and ablutions without a Temple); but they never questioned that there was a path that God wanted us to take, or that there were paths that God would not want us to take.

On the other hand, in sorting out the major disagreements of the rabbinic period, especially between Beit Hillel and Beit Shammai, our rabbis declared that rather than choosing sides of truth, we must accept the pluralistic concept of *elu v'elu divrei elokim ha'im*, both opinions, while contradictory, are the words of the living God. Sometimes the practical ruling had to be in favor of one side, but the other side was still recognized as equally valid, equally true; just not meant for the current situation. In other cases, especially in the laws of prayer, the Talmud tells us that you can choose whichever opinion you want, as long as you are consistent — and even there we are not always consistent (praying the evening prayer before sunset, for example). Based on a verse in Jeremiah, that the words of God are like "a hammer smashing a stone,"[5] our rabbis use the phrase "seventy faces/dimensions to Torah", that the words of God are so difficult to understand, that they can mean seventy different things. Of course,

---

[1] Deut. 11:26-28
[2] Deut. 17:10
[3] BT Yoma 85b
[4] BT Sanhedrin 71a, Mishnah Makot 1:10
[5] Jer. 23:29

through the ages, different customs developed as did different methodologies of halachic rulings. Certainly there were always parameters and limits to *elu v'elu*, but the concept that there can be 70 faces of Torah introduces pluralism as a Jewish truth and a Jewish value, equal in power to the idea that God has given us one truth. In fact, these ideas do not contradict each other: God has given us a truth that can be understood by mortals in many different ways. Pluralism in service of God's Torah started right from the moment of revelation at Sinai, if not from the days of Abraham and Sarah, who tried to figure out what God was asking them to do.

Let me be clear: pluralism, at least as I outlined it from the Jewish tradition, is not moral relativism. Pluralism holds that there is a truth, but that there are either multiple paths to that great truth, or there are multiple ways of understanding that truth. Or it may be possible that different people understand the truth—such as the Torah or a piece of Talmud—in different or even contradictory ways. In the broadest, most digestible way of understanding pluralism, we believe there is a truth, but that we are all struggling to find it out and we can never be sure that we are right. That enables us to have respect for all those who are seeking truth, and all those who value the journey toward truth. In fact, the very idea of a supernatural revelation, central to Orthodox Judaism, brings us to a respect for the need for pluralism: God gave us a divine truth, but we are spending an eternity to figure out what exactly God told us. Pluralism means that we accept that there is truth in the world (whether revealed by God or not), there is morality and an ethical standard for living, and, at the same time, we accept that we must respect those who are working to find that truth and that ethical standard.

Rav Yisrael Lipschitz, one of the great commentators on the Mishna, the Oral Tradition, wrote in the 19th century, that the rabbis in Pirkei Avot required the student of Torah to work with ideas and questions external to the revelatory process in order to understand the law and its underpinnings. "Know what to answer the Heretic"[6] is an imperative to challenge our understanding of revealed law in order strengthen our understanding of Revelation. In this way, pluralistic realization—that there can be many possibilities of understanding the truth—is a way of strengthening the Jew's belief and understanding of the tradition, rather than weakening it. In fact, from the Jews of the Levant and Iraq all the way to 18th and 19th century Ashkenazic Jewry, there is a long tradition that studying knowledge external to our tradition enhances our Torah knowledge, rather than diminishing it.

---

[6] Pirkei Avot 2:14

So once we recognize the legitimacy of pluralism in our tradition, and we understand that it is in service of truth rather than at war with truth, the key question is how, when, and to what extent we can apply pluralism. Can any person come up with his or her own understanding of what truth is and gain our full respect and admiration? Does any idea, no matter how outlandish, unsubstantiated or unconvincing, deserve our respect if we believe in being pluralistic?

There are several layers to answering these questions from a pluralistic perspective. First, it is important that we—the listeners, the learners—approach outside ideas with a positive, welcoming outlook. The great halachist, commentator, and *rosh yeshiva*, Naftali Tzvi Yehuda Berlin, the Netziv, says in many places in his commentary on the Torah (*Ha'amek Davar*) that one of the key elements to living Torah is *chiddush* (innovation); and for innovation to happen, we have to be open to external ideas and wisdom (*chochmot chitzoniyot*) (Exodus 27:20; 37:19). Thus, sustaining and growing Torah requires outside information, and we have to have an eager attitude toward such information. However, the Netziv elaborates that these outside wisdoms, while welcomed, are then debated and discussed in the free market of ideas, in the Beit Midrash, virtual or real. He calls this *pilpul*, the spice of Torah discussion. If they hold up to the scrutiny of the tradition and the sources, then they eventually become part of the tradition; if they do not do well when respectfully challenged, they are rejected. Step one of applying a pluralistic outlook is welcoming everyone's thoughts; step two is taking them seriously enough to consider them carefully. Yet a pluralistic attitude does not mean that we need to validate every idea. We need to allow ideas to be expressed; we need to show respect and be supportive of people's right to speak up. But then we need to subject the ideas to rigorous debate and examination.

The Netziv discusses elsewhere—in the introduction to his work on Midrash—that as new ideas are debated and discussed, the more resilient they are, the more they become part of the tradition. Eventually, if a new idea prevails and convinces everyone of its truth, it is declared *halacha l'moshe mi'sinai*, an integral part of the Mosaic, Torah tradition. This implies that the more tested an idea is, and the more precedents one can find for an idea, the more weight it will have, even in a pluralistic setting. So while every idea is welcomed for its potential to help us grow and become better Torah Jews, an idea which has withstood the rigors of time and debate will get more respect and more traction than will a new, untested, and unsupported idea. However, the

Talmud [7] says that the youngest judge on the Sanhedrin was always asked to speak up first because we never want to dismiss an idea even if it doesn't have the clout of being sagely and long-tested and studied. Those who study Torah and Jewish law need to balance a respect for time-proven ideas with an openness for fresh, brash, and potentially revolutionary ideas.

While pluralistic learning is deeply embedded in our tradition, and Rav Avi Weiss has argued that Open Orthodoxy is the best title that reflects this pluralistic approach, many may fear this openness to new ideas. Will these ideas poison the faith of the masses? In the opening chapters of Maimonides's *Guide for the Perplexed,* he discusses the limitations of sharing ideas with everyone. Sometimes things should only be taught by one teacher to one student. Yet, at the same time, it was Moses Maimonides who wrote the books that did discuss the ideas, controversial at the time, which had entered his Jewish philosophical outlook through the teachings of Aristotle and the medieval Arabic philosophers. The Torah tells us that when pursuing the truth we cannot be afraid of anyone. "Thou shall not fear any person...."[8] We should not be afraid of strange ideas, and we should not cower before people who demand that we ignore investigation because it will lead us astray. It is true that there is a strong stream within the Jewish tradition of not studying outside philosophy or theology and avoiding heretical ideas, specifically because they can be corrupting. As we have shown, there is an equally strong stream that argues we must not avoid all these rich ideas. Those who are more afraid, choose the stream that rejects pluralism; those who live by the verses that tell us not to be afraid will embrace pluralism much more enthusiastically.

Beyond the essential arguments for pluralism, I would advocate a pluralistic attitude out of a love for Jews and a respect for all of humanity. *Kevod habriot*, respect for humanity, is a fundamental principle in the Talmud and our rabbinic tradition, and in a sense, pluralism is really about taking people seriously.[9] As Jewish pluralists, a love for other Jews pushes us to engage with our fellow Jews of all types, and to listen in a loving and respectful way to their ideas. Of course, as I have argued, we stand to benefit by taking diverse ideas seriously, but we also solidify our connections with other Jews by taking a respectful, pluralistic attitude. One of our great commentators, Moshe Nachmanides, reveals this love in his attitude toward another great, but controversial, commentator, Avraham Ibn Ezra. In his commentary to the Torah, the Ramban openly criticizes Ibn Ezra; however, in his introduction,

---

[7] BT Sanhedrin 32a

[8] Deut. 1:17

[9] BT Brachot 19b, *et alia*

the Ramban says openly that he writes about Ibn Ezra with "open rebuke, but hidden love." In other words, the Ramban wants us to know how much he loves Ibn Ezra, and therefore, while he may rebuke him in disagreeing strongly with his explanations of various verses, he loves him and respects him as a great Jew. In fact, it is precisely because the Ramban takes a pluralistic attitude for his time and quotes Ibn Ezra extensively that the Ibn Ezra himself gained the legitimacy to become a central part of the traditional commentary on the Torah. The Ramban displayed the critical love for Jews and love for truth that enabled our Torah to be as rich as it is today, with commentary that is diverse and frequently spans the gamut of ideology.

A final argument for pluralism rests on the pillar of humility and awe of God. Our tradition goes back to the reverence that Abraham and Sarah have for God — they walk where God wants them to walk; they act completely contrary to their world because a belief in God calls for that. If we truly believe in the divinity of God's word and God's truth, the divinity in the Torah, then we have to believe this truth is something we as mere mortals can never fully understand. We have to believe that nothing is clear-cut: this is infinite truth and wisdom given to finite, mortal beings. It is no surprise that God chose the humblest of people, Moshe, to facilitate the revelation of the Torah and to be the transmitter of God's Torah to the Jewish people. Moshe understood that he would never figure God out, and that our understanding of the Torah would forever remain a work in progress. So how can we, the heirs of Avraham and Sarah and Moshe, ever dismiss an idea or a thought that expresses something new or different? Who are we to claim really to know the Divine mind? How are we to know for sure what is not Godly, so as to avoid it? Humility and an awe of the infinite nature of Torah should drive us to be committed pluralists. Every preconceived notion we have must be tested, as the Tiferet Yisrael tells us in our encounter with a heretic. We always need to feel that we are on a journey to learn more, to grow, to get closer to a truth that we will never fully understand. Nothing is clear; nothing is simple; nothing is open or shut. There is a truth, and God has set us on a path to get closer to that truth, but part of successfully traversing that path entails listening to encouraging a multiplicity of voices.

Pluralism in Judaism is about celebrating two of God's gifts to us: the Torah and the journey to understand that Torah. We can be afraid to be on that journey, fearing moving in the wrong direction or getting lost. But we cannot avoid this holy journey because we Jews are told from the start: "*Lech Lecha!*"

"Go—for your own sake!"[10] God would love for us to embrace the journey of thought and truth and changing the world because it will ultimately be good for us and make us the people we need to be. With God's help, and with the help of an open, welcoming attitude toward new and challenging ideas, we will succeed in this journey. God has confidence in us. With humility, joy, love for our fellow Jew and respect for humanity, we will move ahead and continue the Torah mission that God has given us.

---

[10] Rashi, Gen. 12:1

Pluralism in Action

Choosing a New Siddur in an Unaffiliated Synagogue

Ellen Lippmann and Trisha Arlin

In the first year or so of regular planning meetings for our new independent Park Slope Jewish community, we realized that "Ellen's shul" needed a real name. The first suggestions dealt with such concepts as "feasting" and "celebrating." Lisa B. Segal, a founding member but not yet an ordained cantor, suggested that we use the word Kol (voice), which had nice echoes of, but a different spelling from, the word for "all." The first name suggestions were things like Kol Simkha, Voice of Joy. Then early member Michael Forman, z"l, said, "You know, life is not all feasting and rejoicing; it also includes sorrow and anger and pain. Our name should reflect that." That moved to the idea of full life – Chayyim – and we played with names like Kol Chayyim, the voice of life. Someone else offered that we all had different voices. Thus, we arrived at Kolot—Voices (plural)—Chayeinu (our lives, plural)....all the voices of all our lives.[1]

Kolot Chayeinu was founded in 1993 by eight people sitting around Rabbi Ellen Lippmann's dining room table as what would probably now be called a havurah, but with a focus on food and community. Over the years, as we became more like a regular synagogue, we began to define ourselves to ourselves: in 2004 and 2005, in a careful and deliberative process, we wrote a mission statement, and a set of values by which to live our community life, which reflects the broad diversity of the congregation.[2] Around 2007, the question of affiliation with a denomination was raised and became a major issue within the

---

[1] In 2015, as of this writing, Kolot Chayeinu is a proudly independent, unaffiliated congregation in Park Slope, Brooklyn. We have 415 adult members, 200 children ages infant to 14 in our school, seven staff members, ten teachers, and two clergy members.

[2] Our Mission Statement: "Kolot Chayeinu/Voices of Our Lives is a Jewish congregation in Brooklyn, where doubt can be an act of faith and all hands are needed to build our community. We are creative, serious seekers who pray joyfully, wrestle with tradition, pursue justice and refuse to be satisfied with the world as it is. As individuals of varying sexual orientations, gender identities, races, family arrangements, and Jewish identities and backgrounds, we share a commitment to the search for meaningful expressions of our Judaism in today's uncertain world. http://kolotchayeinu.org/values

congregation. Then, in 2008, we decided it was time to purchase a hardbound siddur, a first for our young community. This article is about how our independent Brooklyn synagogue chose our new siddur.

Who We Are

Kolot's congregants, ranging in age from 20s to 86, come from many Jewish backgrounds, including Reform, Reconstructionist, Conservative, Renewal, a few from Orthodox families, and many with little or no formal Jewish background or education. Our membership includes many interfaith couples and many single people of all ages, both heterosexual and LGBTQ. Kolot counts members by individuals rather than by couples or family units. Many of us are political activists, artists, musicians, writers, social workers, rabbinic students, academics, and lawyers, though as the neighborhoods in which our members live change through gentrification, the make-up of our membership changes too. We have always embraced our diversity, though in the last few years we have come to understand that for the most part this diversity did not include Sephardic and Mizrachi Jews along with Ashkenazi Jews, nor did it often include the presence or engagement of Jews of color. For nearly four years we have been involved in a concerted effort to confront and educate ourselves about racism within and outside the Kolot community; and the number of people of color, including many Jews of color, has grown substantially.

The founding Rabbi, Ellen Lippmann, grew up Reform and in a family that included Mordecai Kaplan and many early Reconstructionists. She was ordained by the Reform seminary, HUC-JIR. Cantor Lisa B. Segal grew up Reform and also attending a Conservative synagogue. She was ordained by the Academy for Jewish Religion (AJR), a pluralistic seminary. Executive Director Scott Nogi grew up Conservative, as did Director of Learning and Action Franny Silverman, who attended Jewish day school as well as a public high school.

Kolot's History[3]

Originally conceived as more of a cafe and study group/havurah than a traditional synagogue, early on, Kolotniks met in living rooms to plan and study; within a few months we were holding Friday Shabbat dinners, with story and song, and Saturday morning Torah study with breakfast. Two decisions led

---

[3] http://kolotchayeinu.org/kolot_timeline

us away from the cafe idea. First, we had begun a small after-school program for children, with one teacher and five children in a member's basement, and this quickly grew and established an important place in the congregation's life.[4] Second, those who came to Shabbat morning Torah study began to want ritual acknowledgement of the events of their lives; so we started to include a Mourners' Kaddish and a *Mi She-Berakh* for those who were ill. It was not long before a morning service developed. While it would be some time before we established a formal Torah service, a Shabbat morning service became the norm. Between this and a weekly "Hebrew school," Kolot Chayeinu developed into a real congregation.[5]

Around 2007, leaders of the shul began to ask if perhaps it was time for us to consider affiliation with a denomination. Kolot members were proud— perhaps overly so—of what we perceived as our uniqueness as an unaffiliated, diverse, politically progressive, intentional community. (Many other such communities and minyanim now exist, but when Kolot began, independence from any denomination was unusual.) We engaged in a year and a half process of exploration, including meetings with representatives of the Reform and Reconstructionist Movements and of the large, unaffiliated New York City synagogue, B'nai Jeshurun. After reading, visits to other synagogues, and much discussion, there was a well-attended, lively, and somewhat contentious vote: first on whether to affiliate, and, second, if we voted to affiliate, whether to become Reform or Reconstructionist. While the majority voted to become Reconstructionist *if* we affiliated, most voted to stay independent.

Kolot's original "siddur" was a simple cut-and-paste handout; more song sheet than siddur. Though this was adequate for some, there was a growing number of members who wanted something different. Gradually, as we met for study and life-cycle events, enough of us wanted at least some elements of a more traditional service, such that we began to discuss acquiring a siddur. Sometime around 2000, Rabbi Lippmann got Kolot into the system of Reform congregations that were piloting early versions of Mishkan T'filah before publication in order to help the editors analyze and revise the book. We received free softbound copies of that siddur (and later a second, revised, softbound version) and we used those books for years. By that time, we were doing a regular Shabbat Shacharit service with a Torah service, and we had a regular hazzan (who was studying to become a cantor at AJR). We got used to

---

[4] Those five children have now become 200.

[5] The cafe dream lives on primarily in weekly breakfasts after Torah study and before services, and in Kabbalat Shabbat services with skilled professional and amateur musicians, often followed by dinner and sometimes a presentation or discussion.

following the structure of a regular siddur. But as the congregation's experience and knowledge grew, we began to be aware that certain Hebrew prayers were redacted in ways that didn't make sense to us (e.g., the deleted second paragraph of the Sh'ma, even though we understood it was usual for a Reform siddur) and that English translations were not always accurate or meaningful. Inertia might have kept things as they were but, by 2008, the softbound books were literally falling apart. Loose pages of the temporary siddurim littered the sanctuary floor after every service. We had no choice: It was time to get hardbound siddurim, so we needed a process of selection.

Pluralism and Siddur Selection at Kolot Chayeinu

Kolot Chayeinu has defined itself as a broadly welcoming congregation but never as a pluralistic Jewish community per se. We are diverse as people, and that aspect continues to grow in importance for us. We are diverse in our study, as well. Shabbat services are preceded by a well-attended Torah study session guided by the fabbi and our maggid hamakom (storyteller of this place), Arthur Strimling, in which modern and ancient commentaries spark wide-ranging conversation and deep reflection. Members have created self-run groups, such as a Shabbat morning chanting group led by students of Rabbi Shefa Gold, and a Jewish history reading group. An IJS-inspired course on Wise Aging led to the beginnings of a conscious and active group called HaHachammot (The Wise Women). Our anti-racism work has led to book and article discussions, panels on topical and Jewish issues, a Pesach seder for multi-racial families, a special Omer counter and more. A group is exploring ways for the community to speak together about Israel and Palestine. In a community whose members are otherwise largely aligned in political and social opinion, the range of opinion and emotion about Israel and Palestine is notable.

Shabbat morning services have a clear and regular structure, the keva (the set elements) that allows for wide-ranging kavannah (prompts for subjective meaning). They are an amalgam of traditional nusach (chanting and word choices), tunes (traditional as well as Friedman, Carlbach, Weisenberg, Jagoda, and other new Jewish music), poetry and kavannot (focusing intentions and poems, often from our members), discussion of current events, life-cycle rituals, chanting, hevruta (paired study), and drashot (Torah talks, delivered most weeks by a member). Our Torah service never has more than three aliyot, which are often Jewish Renewal-style aliyot based on a kavannah, usually drawn from the week's Torah portion. The rabbi and cantor always seek new ways to engage service goers, and lay leaders are frequent shlichei tzibbur (ritual leaders). Using any one denominational approach or prayer tradition would not work.

One of the most important lines in our mission statement is, "Kolot Chayeinu/Voices of Our Lives is a Jewish congregation in Brooklyn, where doubt can be an act of faith." Prospective and longtime members quote the line about doubt regularly; it is featured on congregational T-shirts, and has been a major factor in drawing the interest of new members. Broadly, it means (at least) two things: that Kolot cherishes and encourages questions on any and all assumptions about Jewish theology and practice; and that many—if not most—Kolotniks do not believe in God, though we may differ as to which God we don't believe in. For some, God is in our ethics, or in everything, or is, as Jewish poet Alicia Ostriker has said, the Fierce Mystery. For others, God is the force for good or the spark of life or simply something or someone we know is there but we don't need to define. Many members may engage in the holy conversation of prayer, but like many liberal Jews, we don't often talk about our theology. This de facto God-pluralism can be heard in the divrei Torah from adults and young people; b'nai mitzvah may express their doubts in ways that sometimes shock their guests, though not their fellow congregants.

As noted above, the Kolot "values statement"[6] about Israel is a reflection of our desire for a diversity which can be understood as pluralism. In the process of creating the values statement, we discovered that a core value was respect for the individual within the safety of community. Since there was much disagreement whether we could say where Kolot stood on the subject of Israel, including threats to leave the congregation if the final language was not in agreement with that individual's stance, we chose to respect individuals' right to hold diverse opinions, while ensuring the safety and viability of Kolot Chayeinu. It was suggested that we say that we were "mid-wrestle," and thus we arrived at the language that has now stood since 2005:

> We believe that Jews have an obligation to grapple with the many issues and emotions connected to our historic attachment to Israel and the current political situation in Israel and Palestine. While we join Jews everywhere in facing Jerusalem while we pray, we have no consensus on political solutions nor their philosophical underpinnings.

---

[6] http://kolotchayeinu.org/values

We understand that this sometimes puzzles or shocks other Jews, but this pluralistic statement allows for all opinions to co-exist while not insisting that the body as a whole choose any particular stance. This has allowed us to continue holding discussions and sponsoring speakers that run the gamut from the then-Ambassador from Israel, Michael Oren, to speakers from the pluralistic Shalom Hartman Institute, to liberal Jewish-American writer and activist, Peter Beinart, to representatives from Jewish Voice for Peace who were calling for a cultural boycott of Israel. These discussions continue, as does the lack of consensus among us. Especially when considering this way of looking at Israel, we refer to Kolot Chayeinu as an "open tent," thinking of Abraham's legendary hospitality and openness.

It was resonance with our pursuit of doubt, God-wrestling, social justice, and diversity that we sought in the new Kolot siddur.

The Siddur Selection Process

We had voted against affiliation, and without movement requirements or pressures, we were free to select a siddur that would suit our particular community.

The Siddur Committee began with the rabbi and seven self-selected, interested and knowledgeable members. We met regularly for about two years, our numbers eventually settling at three members and the Rabbi, until the final decision was made. Those three members represented the diversity of Jewish background in the congregation and the fault lines that would show up during the discussions.[7] The rabbi brought eight siddurim for us to consider and to get an idea of the choices before us. We brainstormed about what we wanted in the best of all possible worlds. Through our discussions, we realized that we didn't care about which denomination's siddur we chose, as long as it met our criteria. But what were our parameters? We developed a process to find out.

First, we chose five representative siddurim, Kol Rina from the Orthodox

---

[7] Those three members: 1) one from a traditional Reform background who tended to prefer a regular Reform service and a siddur that would accommodate people without much Jewish knowledge; 2) one who grew up in a Conservative non-egalitarian synagogue, with an interest in the Reconstructionist and Renewal movements and who desired more Hebrew; 3) one from a less religious, though very political, background who was open-minded and more concerned with the social justice values put forth by the English translations and readings.

world[8]; the Conservative Movement's Sim Shalom;[9] the Reform Movement's Mishkan T'filah; the Reconstructionist Kol HaNeshema; an independent Reconstructionist siddur, Hadeish Yameinu; and an independent siddur that had originated in the Havurah Movement, Eit Ratzon. The rabbi chose a particular prayer or section from each rubric in the service and copied those pages from each siddur so that we had six pamphlets consisting of each siddur's approach to that section. Each pamphlet went from the Orthodox siddur to the Conservative to the Reform to the official Reconstructionist to the independent Reconstructionist to the independent Havurah pages, so that we could track the traditional structure, use of Hebrew and translations from the most conservative to the most non-traditional. We met weekly and reviewed one or two rubrics per meeting. By the end of this process we all had a much better sense of the similarities and differences and of what each of us wanted in a siddur for Kolot.

The Siddur Committee made a list of criteria by which we could compare and judge the remaining five siddurim and then broke the criteria into two sections, which roughly corresponded to 1) Theology, Spirituality and Social Consciousness, and 2) Look and Feel of Book/Ease of Use. The Theology question primarily concerned: God language; inclusion of women/imahot (the matriarchs' names along with the traditionally named patriarchs); gender neutral translations; prayers that could be spoken by the broadest range of the community; and eventually, inclusion of poetry, kavannot and commentary. We also looked for a consciousness of Tikkun Olam (Repairing the World), as we were hoping, as much as the tradition would allow, to integrate our social justice lives with our prayer lives. The Look and Feel/Ease of Use section was concerned with how the book was laid out as a whole; where text was on the page; how heavy or large the book was to hold during a service; use of illustrations; beauty; where in relation to the Hebrew the translations were; and, if there was transliteration, where that was on the page in relation to the Hebrew.

We then created a multi-page table that listed the criteria in the left hand column. The top row headings comprised the name of each siddur. A point system was developed, from one to five, with five being the highest/best. We then went through this table, item by item, and decided on a rating for each entry. For example, on the question of non-gendered God language in the English translation, Kol HaNeshema scored a five and Sim Shalom scored a

---

[8] The Orthodox selection was present more as a traditional basis for comparison than as a likely choice for our congregation.

[9] This was long before Lev Shalem was a possibility.

two. This analytical process was time-consuming and well worth the effort.

It was during this discussion that we learned to transcend personal preferences; we each came to see that there were certain attributes that our siddur
simply had to have for our congregation. Kolot Chayeinu is deeply committed
to inclusion and egalitarianism, and we had to have a book that reflected this,
with gender neutral translations and God language. The most contentious,
but ultimately consensus-building criterion, was that of transliteration. Many
of our members do not read or understand Hebrew. The member who wanted
more Hebrew felt adamantly that a lack of transliteration should not get in
the way of picking a siddur that we otherwise liked, and that we should be
encouraging more Hebrew knowledge in our members. The member from the
traditional Reform background felt that a siddur without transliteration for
the most important prayers, at minimum, was elitist and exclusionary. In the
end we decided that the values of more Hebrew and adequate transliteration
were both necessary for our siddur.

After weeks and months of discussion and some contention, we added up
the points for each siddur and decided to do two-month tryouts for whichever
were the top three. Very broadly, we liked Mishkan T'filah for its layout and
look and feel, for the poetry, for its use of transliteration, and for the familiar-
ity. We liked Kol HaNeshema for the kavannot, God language, intellectual
asides, interesting alternative translations, and the assumption of progressive
social justice activism. We also chose Hadeish Yameinu because it was a beautiful book with a Reconstructionist outlook, but a less radical approach to the
translations than the movement's official choice. Just as we were trying one
siddur with less Hebrew than we wanted (Mishkan T'filah), we would also
try out one book that did not have much transliteration (Hadeish Yameinu),
to see how the congregation responded to each possibility.[10]

From outside the committee came requests to deliberate on some more
flexible solutions as well, such as an online siddur or a cut-and-paste siddur
that could change each week. We considered none of these possibilities seriously. At that time, the online presence of prayers was just starting and
wasn't adequate to what we needed (and we didn't even want to take on the
environmental issue of wasting paper to print a new siddur every week or the

---

[10] Though the rabbi was drawn to Sim Shalom for its inclusion of Hebrew prayers
that Mishkan T'filah left out as well as its meditative writings, its almost complete
lack of transliteration meant we could not even consider it. We all liked Eit Ratzon
very much but felt that the layout was distracting, with equal weight given to the
service and the learning. Additional note: We were deeply saddened to learn in spring
2016 of the death of Rabbi Ron Aigen, author of Hadeish Yameinu.

dissonance and distraction of having people bring their tablets to services on Shabbat!). We had started with a cut-and-paste sort of siddur, and found over time that it lacked the depth or breadth we desired; plus, this choice would take us back to the era of finding scattered pages on the floor. It was also suggested that we create and publish our own siddur, but this was not a viable option. At that time, we did not have enough members with the requisite Jewish knowledge, publishing skills and/or time to pull off such a big project and, more to the point, we didn't have the money it would take. (Online publishing was not then the option that it is now.)

So, we picked our three siddurim to present to the congregation and got permission to make copies from the publishers (and in the case of Mishkan T'filah, were loaned new softcover copies of the final version).[11] The rabbi and the (then-student) cantor led services using each book. After two months each, they asked the Shabbat morning regulars (and other interested members) to gather at Shabbat lunches to discuss what they felt worked or did not work in each siddur. Members also rated the siddurim by filling out hard-copy tables listing many of the same criteria we used to select the three finalists. The rabbi and the cantor also gave feedback to the committee on how it felt to lead a service from each book.

Feedback: Mishkan T'filah was already very familiar to us, as we had been using early versions of it in the softbound books, and some members of the siddur committee felt this would give it an unfair advantage. But there were many in the congregation who were concerned about what Hebrew prayers were omitted and by its interpretive rather than literal translations; and there were others who found the English translations to be too sweet and unchallenging for the times in which we lived. Kol Haneshema pleased those who loved commentary in a prayer book (among other reasons, some felt they could read commentaries when the service bored them), the many names for God in the translations, and the social justice subtext. Some felt it might position Kolot as the closest thing to a Reconstructionist shul in Brooklyn, which could be helpful in drawing members. Most felt the book was laid out awkwardly and the rabbi and cantor were concerned that a service with this siddur would involve a great deal of page turning. The rabbi and cantor loved leading the service from Hadeish Yameinu. It is beautifully laid out, but has very little transliteration. Its author created a companion booklet of transliteration but we found it awkward to hold a book and a booklet at the same time. Members also felt that it was limited in its appreciation of non-normative relationships;

---

[11] We promised to dispose of the loose copies in a geniza (ritual burial for Hebrew pages with God's name written on them) when the selection process was finished.

for some, this reached the point of being offensive. We therefore decided to take Hadeish Yameinu out of the running.

Around this time, we were introduced to Sha'ar Zahav, a siddur put together by the Reform LGBTQ synagogue of that name in San Francisco. We met twice with one of its primary editors. (We got a lesson on how complex and time-consuming it is to write your own siddur, which validated our decision not to take that path.) Believing that we had much in common with that synagogue, we decided to give their siddur a two-month tryout with a feedback Shabbat lunch. The Shabbat regulars loved the many original prayers and kavannot in English and the inclusive language, as well as some lovely graphic innovations. Ultimately, though, the feeling (first voiced by Kolot LGBTQ members) was that Sha'ar Zahav was too specifically oriented to its LGBTQ shul of origin; that it might exclude our many non-LGBTQ members; and that it excluded much of the Hebrew that was also missing from Mishkan T'filah: these factors convinced us to set it aside.

This narrowed the choices to Mishkan T'filah and Kol Haneshema. In a final meeting, the last three committee members each expressed an opinion. The committee decided that the ultimate decision should be left to the Rabbi and Cantor; the congregation's board concurred.

The Decision

The rabbi and (now ordained) cantor had initially loved Mishkan T'filah but came to feel it was a little light and a bit "pious" in a way that did not reflect accurately the hard and often painful world in which we live. Though they had initially found Kol Haneshemah difficult to work with, they both came to feel that it offered deeper spiritual and intellectual concepts and more room for community growth in prayer. It also provided more substantial holiday services and traditional prayers. For these reasons the rabbi and cantor chose Kol Haneshemah; the Board of Trustees concurred, and it was presented to members at a congregational meeting.

While we now use Kol Haneshamah, each book includes an explanation written by our cantor on the inside cover explaining that, though this is the Reconstructionist siddur, Kolot Chayeinu is an independent congregation. While we chose a Reconstructionist prayer book we do not use it as Reconstructionist shuls do. Our prayer is somewhere between Reform and Reconstructionst, with a bit of Jewish Renewal mixed in: what we sometimes call "Kolot-ish". We have been pleased to find that, as we had hoped, Kol Haneshamah allows the community to grow and deepen in prayer and knowledge, to acknowledge the sorrows and joys of the world around us ("life is not all feasting and rejoicing; it also includes sorrow and anger and pain"), to include all our voices in prayer and ritual celebration, and to continue to bring a plethora of other resources into our Shabbat and holiday services. Its many unique names for God seem a reflection of the many and unique voices gathered in prayer on any Shabbat or holiday, the many-faceted one God inspiring the many-faceted Brooklyn congregation that is also ultimately one community, Kolot Chayeinu/The Voices of Our Lives, where doubt can be an act of faith and all hands are needed.

Increasing Diversity in the American Jewish Community

Heidi Hoover

About one in six American Jews was not born Jewish, but rather, had converted, according to the Pew Research Center's 2014 U.S. Religious Landscape Study.[1] According to the same survey, there is some racial diversity among Jews: 90 percent are white,[2] four percent are Hispanic, two percent are Black, two percent are Asian, and two percent are Other. (It is important to remember that not all Jews of color have converted to Judaism—some are born Jewish.) Out of all U.S. Jews who are married or have a partner, 35 percent have a non-Jewish spouse or partner.[3] All of these statistics have increased over time: There is more conversion to Judaism in the U.S. than there used to be, more intermarriage, and more racial diversity. (Paul Golin, associate executive director of the Jewish Outreach Institute, points out at speaking engagements that the number of intermarriages increases at twice the rate of the number of in-marriages, because for every two Jews who marry each other, one marriage is created, while for every two Jews who marry non-Jews, two marriages are created.)

It is undeniable that the make-up of the United States Jewish population is shifting and changing. This has implications for our Jewish communal institutions and the skills rabbis need to serve our communities effectively. To illustrate this, I will share some of my experiences as rabbi of a small congregation in Brooklyn, NY. We are affiliated with the Reform Movement, the Union for Reform Judaism. We are located in a rapidly-gentrifying, popular neighborhood, to which many young families choose to move.

Like all Reform congregations in the United States, my congregation includes many interfaith families. In our religious school last year (2014-2015/5775), there were about 40 students from 26 families. Of those families, 15 of them had all Jewish members in the nuclear family. Eleven of the families

---

[1]   http://www.jta.org/2015/05/12/news-opinion/united-states/1-in-6-jews-are-new-to-the-faith-and-9-other-new-pew-findings

[2] Though some say that people born Jewish, even if they look white, are not really white, and historically Jews who look white were not always considered quite white in this country. http://www.pewforum.org/2015/05/12/chapter-2-religious-switching-and-intermarriage/

[3]   http://www.pewforum.org/2015/05/12/chapter-2-religious-switching-and-intermarriage/ use ibid.?

were interfaith families. Of the 15 all-Jewish families, I am aware of four that involved conversion of a member of the nuclear family. Even in the all-Jewish families, the likelihood that there are extended family members who aren't Jewish is very high. Also, among the families without children in religious school (those with grown-up children, or couples and singles without children), there are many interfaith partnerships, though it is more difficult to determine those numbers because our records are less clear.

We pride ourselves on being very open and welcoming to anyone who wishes to be part of our synagogue community. Openness can have its pitfalls, though, and sometimes we struggle to find our boundaries, the limits of what variations off our norms we will accept. Mostly, though, we choose to err on the side of inclusiveness.

When we discuss interfaith marriage in the Jewish community, we are usually concerned with what will happen with the children. Will they be raised Jewish? Will they have a Jewish identity? Will they raise their own children as Jews? Those who participate in these discussions generally consider intermarriage between Jews and non-Jews to be terrible for the future of the Jewish community. I do not hold this view.

In my congregation, almost half of the families with children in religious school are interfaith families. They are committed to raising Jewish children. When the non-Jewish parent is the mother, she is often the one who brings the children to synagogue for school week after week and participates with them, while we rarely see the Jewish father. I joke that Christian congregants are the best, because they think it is important to show up every week, on time, while Jewish congregants are more lax about that. (Of course, this tongue in cheek generalization is not applicable in every case.) The faculty and I try to honor this commitment by making religious school fun and interesting, and by aiming to build community among the students and parents. We want them to have social connections that encourage participation at religious school and synagogue: it becomes a way to enjoy seeing one other regularly.

True, many interfaith families are not raising Jewish children, are raising their children without any religion while sharing with them a mixed cultural heritage. The term "half-Jewish," which I hear frequently, may apply in a cultural sense, but not in a religious one. I believe strongly that a person cannot follow two of the monotheistic religions simultaneously—the theological differences require a choice. One cannot believe both that Jesus is divine (Christian) and that he isn't (Jewish). One cannot believe both that Mohammed is Allah's (God's) prophet (Muslim), and that he is not (Jewish, because Jews believe that prophecy ended before Mohammed's time).

The practices, if not all the beliefs, of a religion like Buddhism can easily coexist with the practices of Judaism, as the many "Jewbus" (Jewish-Buddhists) will attest. At a cultural level, the more secular celebrations of Christmas and Hanukkah can also be enjoyed together. Easter eggs hunts can be accompanied by matzah and a dinner that includes gefilte fish. (My own feelings about where the meaning is when these celebrations are denuded of religion are beside the point.)

Popular wisdom in the Jewish community blames the loss of Jewish religious practice and Jewish identity in interfaith families on the fact that they are interfaith. I have a different position. I don't think interfaith marriage is, itself, the issue. If Jewish families and the Jewish community raise their children to love Judaism, to make the practice of Judaism integral to their lives, it does not matter whom they marry: They will want to have Jewish homes and Jewish children. They will not be able to imagine living any other way. Intermarriage is not the problem. The problem, where one exists, is sub-par religious education that kids hate, a lukewarm or resentful attitude toward Judaism on the part of parents, and the insistence that the reason to stay Jewish and marry a Jew is "so that Hitler doesn't win." Jews who crave a Jewish life for themselves and their children were instilled early with positive, joyful experiences of, and reasons for, being Jewish and practicing Judaism.

I do believe that each family should choose one religion in which to raise its children. If one parent is a devout and active Christian and the other is a Jew who does not much care about Judaism, except perhaps culturally, then it seems likely that Christianity is the path for that family. If it is the opposite is true, then Judaism makes more sense. If, though, each parent is actively involved with a different religion, then a whole lot of tough conversations may be necessary until they settle on one of the faith traditions, as is my husband's and my story. Preferably, these conversations would take place before there are children to raise, but often they do not. The role of the rabbi is to encourage these conversations and facilitate them where possible.

In my experience, many parents initially assume that the simple and easy solution is to raise children with exposure to both religions and then, let them choose. Sometimes this is accompanied by the rationale that parents should not make such a decision for their children. I find that pushing this thinking can be helpful. First of all, parents must, and do, make important decisions for their children all the time, with far-reaching consequences: everything from deciding where the family should live to how to handle vaccinations to what schools their children attend. Small children are in no way equipped to make these kinds of decisions well for themselves. Furthermore, in order to thoroughly expose children to two religions, one would need to attend educational programming and celebrate holy days for both religions. This could be a scheduling nightmare. More significantly, it would be unfair to ask this of a child, especially since the educational messages the child would receive would inevitably contradict each other in fundamental ways.

Finally, I let people seeking my counsel know that, from what I have read and personally experienced, most children raised "as both" (usually I encounter Jewish-Christian intermarriage, as opposed to Jewish-Muslim, Buddhist, or Hindu) end up Christian or with no religious belief at all. (As always, there are exceptions.) Sometimes, this gives the Jewish parent pause, sometimes it doesn't. I do not see my role as convincing a family to make their decision the way I would wish, but rather, as giving them information to consider what they may not have thought about. My most helpful resource on this topic has been *Mixed Blessings: Overcoming the Stumbling Blocks in an Interfaith Marriage*, by Paul Cowan with Rachel Cowan. It was published in 1987 and, unfortunately, is out of print, though used copies can be found.

Meanwhile, many interfaith families choose Judaism. The Reform Movement in the United States has been welcoming these families officially since 1990, when Rabbi Alexander Schindler, then president of the Union of American Hebrew Congregations (the predecessor of the Union for Reform Judaism), advocated outreach to interfaith families and non-Jewish spouses.

When I first became involved with Judaism in the 1990s, it was through my boyfriend, Mike, who later became my husband. He was born Jewish, I was not. We were together for nine years before we married, and for about seven of them, it seemed that we would have an interfaith marriage with Jewish children. I did not believe I could convert to Judaism, yet it was clear from the time we started dating that Mike's children had to be Jewish. If they were going to be my children too, then I had to figure out how to become okay with that. Our story illustrates one of the situations rabbis must help navigate in the Jewish community of today.

I was raised in a religious, Lutheran home. Mike was raised in a Reform Jewish home in New York. He attended religious school, had a bar mitzvah and participated in youth group. Mike was close with his youth group rabbi, who called Mike when he moved back to New York City after college. The rabbi invited him to join the steering committee of a new group for young professionals at Central Synagogue in Manhattan, called the Central Issues Group. When I moved to New York two years later, Mike started taking me with him to meetings. I had been hearing about its activities from him for two years. I enjoyed the learning opportunities and the social aspect of the group, and became more and more involved. The rabbi who started the group, Rabbi Tom Weiner, became my first rabbi.

Rabbi Weiner was the person I turned to when experiencing a crisis of faith. Religion seemed to stand between me and the man I loved, and that felt wrong. I struggled with the idea of raising children who would not be the religion I grew up with. Judaism is a wonderful tradition, but it wasn't mine. I believed I understood the Jewish attitude of being a small, struggling people after the Holocaust, for whom it was important not to lose more members. That was one of the primary messages I received about why the children of Jews needed to be Jewish.

Rabbi Weiner presented ideas to me that were helpful, and that I had not heard before. Rather than telling me that intermarriage is bad, he told me it would certainly be possible for me to raise Jewish children as a non-Jew. He said they could learn about my tradition, but it would be as guests, not as their tradition. He acknowledged that it would be a great sacrifice for me to give up passing on my faith tradition to my children.

The latter point was immensely important for me. It was true, yet no one had acknowledged the sacrifice to me before. It was part of Rabbi Weiner's way of recognizing that non-Jews who participate in Jewish community and raise Jewish children are doing something extraordinary. Rabbis need to recognize the faith traditions of non-Jewish partners/parents as important and valid, appreciate that they are giving up something valuable to them, and honor them for the work they are doing for the future of a tradition that is not theirs.

Because I decided to convert to Judaism before having children, my immediate family is not an interfaith family. However, my experience as the partner of a Jew when I did not intend to become Jewish has helped to inform my interactions with interfaith families, whether or not they ever involve a conversion.

In the Reform synagogue where I serve as spiritual leader, each bar and bat mitzvah includes a ritual that I believe is common among Reform congregations. Near the beginning of the Torah service we invite the grandparents, parents, and bar or bat mitzvah to form a line on the bimah. The Torah scroll is passed down the line, from grandparents to parents to the young man or woman. It is a literal manifestation of passing the Torah from generation to generation.

The congregation's policy is to reserve the honor of holding a Torah scroll for Jews, along with certain blessings and readings. In our inclusive setting, though, it can feel awkward to tell anyone that there are rituals from which they are excluded. I try to handle this sensitively. In explaining that readings designated for Jews are the ones that refer to ourselves as Jews, or that describe us as being commanded to perform an action. It does not make sense for those who are not Jewish to read a blessing or statement that would lead them to refer to themselves as Jews, or to say that they are commanded to perform an action that, as non-Jews, they are not commanded to perform. When it comes to passing the Torah from generation to generation, non-Jewish parents and grandparents are called to the bimah along with the Jewish ones. I present the Jewish grandparents and parents as representing their generation in passing the Torah. Then the Jewish grandparents and parents pass the Torah to the bar or bat mitzvah. Usually the non-Jewish parents and grandparents understand this completely and have no expectation of holding the Torah scroll.

Rarely, I make exceptions to this policy. A few years ago, a Catholic mother in our congregation attended religious school with her daughter and learned to read Hebrew. She wanted to be able to help her daughter practice. Not only did I include this mother in passing the Torah scroll, I explained to the congregation during the service that we pass the scroll to those who have been directly involved in bequeathing Torah to this next generation, and that this mother very much did that.

Another extraordinary case is that of the member family in our congregation, consisting of two children with their father and stepmother. Neither adult is Jewish. The children's mother—not a member of our synagogue—is Jewish, and the divorce agreement stipulated that if the children were to be raised in a religion, that religion would be Judaism. While the mother does not feel strongly about raising the children with any religion, the stepmother, a devout Catholic, shared that she does not know how to live without faith, and cannot imagine raising children without religion. Since her stepchildren's religion must be Jewish if anything, then by gum, she is determined to raise them as Jews! The Catholic stepmother made it her business to learn how to celebrate Jewish holidays in her home. She brings the children to services and religious school on the weekends when they are with her and their father. She is the single driving force behind these children being raised and educated as Jews. When those children have their b'nei mitzvah, I will certainly be passing the Torah scroll to their stepmother. She cried when I told her. While she had no expectation of being given that honor, it is right for our community because of her role in teaching Torah to her stepchildren.

There are very few completely non-Jewish couples raising Jewish children. But being open and welcoming to them, and to the non-Jewish parents in interfaith families who are raising Jewish children, is how we encourage and increase the practice. With this family and others like them in mind, my congregation made a change to its membership form. The form used to read, "Being a member of the Jewish Faith, I/we hereby make this application for membership...." It now reads, "Being committed to the Jewish Faith...." Besides supporting interfaith families, this also enables those who are going through the process of conversion as individuals, but who are not yet Jewish, to join the synagogue.

Supporting interfaith families who want to have Jewish homes and lives requires more than occasional ritual changes and sensitivity on the bimah. We also need to pay attention to the language we use and the assumptions we make in all aspects of synagogue communication.

We speak frequently in religious school, and in programming for adults, too, of our Jewish ancestry. There are activities that encourage children or adults to think about their Jewish upbringing with grandparents, or of their parents' or grandparents' Jewish childhood. When planning these kinds of activities, we need to be aware that some participants did not have a Jewish upbringing, and that their parents and/or grandparents may not (all) be Jewish. Lesson plans of this nature must take diversity of background into account. Including those who have converted to Judaism, who are not Jewish, or who have parents and grandparents who are not Jewish, will also help us be more inclusive to those Jews with a secular upbringing, or whose grandparents were not involved in their childhood. We must similarly challenge the working assumption that all American Jews today descend from Eastern European Jews who came in one of the great waves of immigration around the beginning and middle of the 20th century. Not only does this not apply to many Jews in families with conversion or interfaith families, it is also inaccurate for many all-Jewish families, whether their ancestors were Sephardic Jews, who emigrated long before the 20th century, or came from other parts of the world.

When I speak of Jewish ancestry, I often speak of Jewish spiritual ancestry. All Jews claim descent from the Israelites of the Exodus, though we Jews who have converted believe that we are not descended from them by blood. Converts to Judaism get to claim that history as our own, and are thereby spiritual descendants of those Israelites, as are our children. The fact is that no Jews alive today can definitively trace their lineage back to the Israelites, and it is likely that many or even most Jews living today are not descended by blood from those Israelites. It is, for all of us, the spiritual ancestry that is most essential to our Judaism. In my sermons, messages I write for our newsletter, and other communications, I am wary of using words implying that everyone in my audience is Jewish. They certainly are not all Jewish, though I consider them all part of my community. I try to make sure that the non-Jews in the community understand why, sometimes, they may not be included in the specific language used. I consider the non-Jewish members as much my congregants as the Jewish ones, and want them to feel that I am talking to them, as well, when I preach and teach. That said, our synagogue environment is exclusively Jewish. Our community is for those who want to "do Jewish." Members don't have to *be* Jewish, they just have to choose to *do* Jewish.

As I said above, when we talk about interfaith families, we usually talk about what will happen with the children. The less talked-about challenge for rabbis of interfaith families to address is death, mourning practices and our responsibilities toward non-Jewish widows and widowers in our congregations.

My congregation changed its membership form so that non-Jews who are committed to Judaism may be members. For congregations that do not allow non-Jews to be members, yet welcome married interfaith couples: what happens if the Jewish spouse dies first? Is the non-Jewish widow or widower, who may have been a part of the community for many years, tossed out at the next membership cycle? In my opinion, that is unacceptable. The non-Jews in our congregations are part of our community too, and over time, we rabbis and cantors are likely to have become their spiritual leaders.

In a workshop about death and dying several years ago, a congregant asked if I would perform a funeral together with a priest. I said no, because I don't co-officiate life-cycle rituals with non-Jewish clergy. She called me later, upset, and we met to discuss my answer. Spurred by the recent death of a close friend, she had begun to think about what would happen if she and her husband died at the same time—in a car accident perhaps, or some other tragedy. As a Jew, he would be buried by a rabbi, but she is Catholic and would want a priest. How would this be possible, she wanted to know, if I refused to co-officiate? There is policy and then there is the case before you. My response to her specific situation was that we could do the funerals separately but back-to-back in the same room, or even that the two services could be intertwined, as long as it was clear that I was doing her husband's funeral and the priest was doing hers. It would be simultaneous or serial officiating, rather than co-officiating. I then encouraged her to attend church more often, because it was clear that she did not get the spiritual sustenance from Judaism that she did from Catholicism. She and her husband raised their children as Jews, but Judaism never became what spoke to her soul.

In another situation, I have a non-Jewish congregant whose wife died several years ago. She was Jewish. I performed her funeral. They had also raised Jewish children, though at the point I met them, they were attending synagogue primarily on the High Holidays. The man ushered in the sanctuary every year on the holidays, and continued to do so after his wife died. A couple of years ago, he called: He was getting married again, and wondered if I would officiate at the wedding. I did. It happened that he was marrying a Jewish woman this time also, but I suspect he might have called me even if he wasn't. After all, I'm his rabbi.

The increasing diversity of the American Jewish community is not only due to interfaith families. While our communities have always included people with disabilities, awareness of their needs has increased in recent years, raising their visibility in our communities. As it is said, there are those who are disabled, and there are those who are not disabled right now. It is likely that most of us will be disabled at some point in our lives, whether temporarily, as with a broken ankle or wrist, or permanently, due to age, illness, or traumatic event.

It can be difficult for those with disabilities to participate in synagogue life. For those with difficulty walking, stairs, cracked sidewalks, and toilets without grab bars or elevated seats present barriers. For those who do not hear well, poor sound systems and people not using microphones make it hard to understand what is happening. For those with autism or other issues that make it difficult to be still, services that require stillness and quiet can be impossible, while services that do not require quiet can be impossible for those with difficulty hearing or focusing.

My synagogue has a ramp to the door, and, fortunately, has no stairs to the sanctuary from the ground floor. There are, however, stairs to the bimah, so when those who cannot manage the steps receive an honor, we find ways for them to fulfill it from their seats. Our function room, on the lower level of our over-100-year-old building does not allow for handicapped accessibility. So, we hold all events possible in our ground-floor community room, though sometimes it is just not large enough.We endeavor to treat everyone with equal respect and to find ways for those with disabilities to participate as much as possible. For example, at one pot luck Shabbat dinner, I noticed that a congregant who walks with difficulty remained seated at her table while everyone else stood in the middle of the large room to recite the blessings over the candles, wine, and bread. Now, we put the candles on her table and recite the blessings with everyone standing around it; around her. Our Friday evening service starts on the late side, which makes it natural that primarily, adults attend; it tends to be a service where there is not much sound outside of prayer and song. Our Saturday morning service is our family service, with a frequently-stated policy that those who are able to sit still are expected to do so, while those who cannot may do what they must to stay and participate. We recognize that the ability to sit still and participate is not age dependent. Rather than judge each congregant's abilities, I leave it to them and their families to know what they can—and cannot—do.

Simply letting our congregants know that we pay attention to their difficulties, that we notice them, and that we strive to make participation easier, makes a difference. This applies to other types of diversity in our communities too. Jews of color or LGBTQ Jews (or non-Jews of color and LGBTQ non-Jews who are fellow travelers with us) have many of the same spiritual needs as heterosexual Jews and pale-skinned Jews (not all pale-skinned Jews consider themselves white), and often face challenges of prejudice within and outside the Jewish community. Acknowledging these challenges, both privately and publicly, as concerns of our whole community, is one way to let everyone in our congregation know that they are valued as full members.

The key to effectively engaging the increasing diversity of the American Jewish community is to meet all individuals where they are with love, compassion, and respect; to notice them and honor their experience. I try not to make assumptions about people, not even about who is or is not Jewish. Congregational leaders and members must become educated about and aware of the challenges to full participation faced by Jews, and fellow travelers with Jews, who are different from our assumed norms. The diversity of the Jewish community in the United States is bringing us more richness and wisdom, and in turn the wisdom and richness of our tradition can help all our different Jewish community members to flourish.

The Power of the Pluralist Rabbi

Rebecca W. Sirbu

"Mommy, what am I?" asks a young girl.

"What do you mean?' replies her mother.

"Am I black, white, Asian or Jewish?" she asks.

In the past, this would have been a ridiculous question. The vast majority of American children grew up in religious and ethnic enclaves and clearly knew "who they were," be they Irish, Italian, Jew, black, Chinese, etc. Identities were static and well defined.

Today, this is no longer the case. Just turn on the TV to see President Obama, Mariah Carey or Bruno Mars. Mixed racial, ethnic and religious identities are now the norm. According to the Pew Research Center, "About 15% of all new marriages in the United States in 2010 were between spouses of a different race or ethnicity from one another, more than double the share in 1980 (6.7%)."[1] Public perceptions regarding the mixing and marrying between races has also changed sharply. "More than one-third of Americans (35%) say that a member of their immediate family or a close relative is currently married to someone of a different race. Also, nearly two-thirds of Americans (63%) say it 'would be fine' with them if a member of their own family were to marry someone outside their own racial or ethnic group."[2] Barriers that used to separate people from one another are falling.

In addition to new ethnic mixes, Americans are now also switching their religious identities at a far higher rate than in the past. "If all Protestants were treated as a single religious group, then fully 34% of American adults currently have a religious identity different from the one in which they were raised …. If switching among the three Protestant traditions (e.g., from mainline Protestantism to the evangelical tradition, or from evangelicalism to a historically black Protestant denomination) is added to the total, then the share of Americans who currently have a different religion than they did in childhood rises to 42%."[3] We live in a new era, one in which people are switching religious affiliations, blending their families in new ways, and mixing different belief systems in order to bring meaning to their lives. Religious identities and communities are in flux.

Therefore, it should come as no surprise that the Jewish community in

---

[1] http://www.pewsocialtrends.org/2012/02/16/the-rise-of-intermarriage

[2] http://www.pewsocialtrends.org/2012/02/16/the-rise-of-intermarriage

[3] http://www.pewforum.org/2015/05/12/americas-changing-religious-landscape

America is also becoming more diverse: "Twenty percent of America's six million Jews, or 120,000 Jews, are African American, Latino/Hispanic, Asian, Sephardic, Mizrachi and mixed race."[4] The intermarriage rates among Jews are also rising: "Forty-four percent of all currently married Jewish respondents – and 58% of those who have married since 2005 – indicate they are married to a non-Jewish spouse."[5]

The face of the American Jewish community is literally changing right before our eyes. The question asked by the child above, "Am I black, white, Asian or Jewish?" could easily be answered by a mother saying, "You are all of the above."

In addition, the denominational lines that have long defined American Judaism are beginning to blur. According to the Pew Research Center's 2013 Jewish Population Study, Jewish denomination identity breaks down according to the following lines: 35% Reform; 30% No denomination; 18% Conservative; 10% Orthodox; and 6% other.[6] Note that "no denomination" is almost as big a group as Reform Jews. This is a marked change from the past. Many people no longer feel the need to claim a denominational identity. In addition, when people were asked if they were "Jews by religion" or "Jews of no religion," 22% identified as "Jews of no religion." The growth of "Jews of no religion" parallels the growth of "nones", people who do not affiliate with any religion in general. Today, 30% of the general American population does not identify with a particular religion, and this group is steadily growing.

There is a tremendous amount of change taking place today. Religious institutions and communities are not known for their ability to respond to change. If anything, religious communities often do their best to hold off change, instead clinging to traditional ways of doing things.

However, the Jewish community needs leaders — particularly rabbis — who understand these seismic demographic changes, and are well prepared to respond to the needs of the people who are living them. This is why Clal – The National Jewish Center for Learning a Leadership, a Jewish think tank, leadership training institute, and resource center, created Rabbis Without Borders in 2008. The goal of Rabbis Without Borders is to create a network of rabbis who can share Jewish wisdom and traditions in innovative, pluralistic ways,

---

[4] Racial Diversity and the American Jewish Community, Diane Tobin and Aryeh Weinberg in *Journal of Jewish Communal Service* Vol 89, 1 Fall 2014.

[5] http://www.pewforum.org/2013/10/01/chapter-2-intermarriage-and-other-demographics

[6] http://www.pewforum.org/2013/10/01/jewish-american-beliefs-attitudes-culture-survey

with anyone, anywhere.

Pluralism is the backbone of Rabbis Without Borders. Rabbis who have a pluralist outlook are uniquely capable of serving the diverse population of people who now make up the larger Jewish community, including those who are not Jews themselves, but who are interested in associating with, learning from, or being a part of the Jewish community for various reasons. Rabbis who are pluralist may be very grounded in their own particular belief system or movement. What makes them pluralists is their ability to meet each person where they are; to hear and recognize that person's individual needs, and respond in a way that is helpful to that individual. To be able to do this, rabbis must be able to see different perspectives, to understand that what is "right" or "true" for the person in front of them may not be right or true for themselves.

This kind of pluralist rabbi who knows how to use Jewish wisdom and traditions to speak to the needs of the black-white-Asian-Jewish child he or she encounters is the kind of rabbi the Jewish community needs today. For the Jewish community as a whole to thrive, rabbis need to be comfortable in diverse environments and with a diverse array of people, because, as the statistics show, that the Jewish community is comprised of that array. To hold together an increasingly diverse Jewish community, we need rabbis who are comfortable with diversity, and who are comfortable with open borders in religious, cultural, and political life.

Rabbis Without Borders (RWB) fosters this comfort with pluralism, with the changing and pushing of various borders in the one-year introductory fellowship program, which funnels trained rabbis into the RWB Network. Each year we convene a highly selective cohort of about twenty rabbis to participate in the RWB Fellowship. This group is purposely selected to be diverse. We select rabbis representing all of the denominations and those who consider themselves to be "post-denominational" or "non-denominational." We take rabbis from across the United States, from large and small communities with varying degrees of experience in the rabbinate, from working in the field only a year to those who have 40 years of experience. In addition, we take rabbis in all sorts of roles: those who are serving in pulpits, those who are in schools, Hillels, non-profit and those pursuing independent or entrepreneurial rabbinates, since we recognize that the role of rabbi itself is changing and growing into new venues.

When the fellows gather together, we ask them to leave their assumptions about one another at the door and get to know each other as individuals, not as labels. Doing so, we have discovered that there are socially liberal Orthodox rabbis and politically conservative Reform rabbis. There are Reconstructionist ordained rabbis who are on the right on Israel and Conservative ordained rabbis who are on the left. There are rabbis who are pro-gun and rabbis who are anti-gun, rabbis who are pro-life and rabbis who are pro-choice. We recognize that our tiny sample of 20 rabbis form a microcosm of the diverse community we service. We have people who represent almost every possible political viewpoint and span a variety of observance styles. We learn how not to have knee-jerk responses when people ask us questions, and we learn how to share our views in a way that invites dialogue and conversation. We recognize that there is not just one "right" way to do something; that an answer to a particular question might change depending on the context in which it is asked and who is doing the asking.

We use the time together to break through preconceived ideas about each other and the Jewish community as a whole. We open up each other's minds to new ways of seeing things and new ways of being and doing "Jewish." We ask ourselves what the ancient wisdom and practices of Judaism offer to help us, as individuals, and our diverse communities flourish.

The ideas and experiences shared in the RWB fellowship year open the rabbis to think, teach and share Judaism differently. They each come out of the experience with new ideas and projects to apply to their particular rabbinates. In evaluations, alumni of the program report on the impact of the Fellowship in their lives and work:

- 98% of RWB Fellows report that their participation in RWB has affected their thinking about Judaism.
- 96% of RWB Fellows have strengthened and increased their comfort crossing denominational and institutional boundaries.
- 94% of RWB Fellows report an increase in their audience (i.e., the people with whom they are in contact as a rabbi).
- 91% of RWB Fellows have created new programs or approaches to programming in their synagogue/organization.
- 81% of RWB Fellows have seen an increase in participation in programs and services in their synagogue or organization.
- 80% of RWB Fellows are appearing in/writing in/teaching in new venues since participating in the fellowship.

Collectively, RWB Fellows are reaching over 1.5 million people. It is work that the rabbis do out in the field that shows the true impact of the fellowship and the ongoing RWB Network, where the rabbis continue to challenge each other and grow together. Several programs large and small have resulted from the rabbis' increase in pluralist outlook, but three examples will show the depth and breadth of their work.

Roots/Judur/Shorashim: A local Palestinian and Israeli Initiative for Understanding, Nonviolence and Transformation was founded by a Rabbi Without Borders Fellow, Hanan Schlesinger, together with Shaul Judelman and Ali Abu Awwad, to form bonds among Israelis and Palestinians who are working toward peace yet are separated by fear of each other. After experiencing RWB, Rabbi Schlesinger realized that he has never taken the time to get to know his neighbors outside of Gush Etzion, a town in the West Bank of Israel where he settled many years ago. One day, he took the courageous step of reaching out to a group of Palestinian neighbors headed by Palestinian peace activist Ali Abu Awwad, who themselves had decided to take the courageous step of reaching out to the settler population. He was amazed to hear how afraid of him they were, when he was so afraid of them! Through several conversations and meetings, they got to know each other and decided to work to bring the two communities—Arabs and Israelis—together. Only once they began to talk to each other and understand each other's points of view, could they hope to work toward true peace and mutual understanding. The project has taken off. There are now monthly meetings between Palestinians and Israelis, family gatherings, a women's group, children's gatherings, cultural exchanges and language lessons. People are slowly getting to know each other as individuals, without preconceived notions and hostilities. Slowly, relationships are being built, and a path toward peace is being laid.

A completely different type of project, called "ISH", has been launched by two other RWBs, Rabbis Andrew and Cheryl Jacobs. Noting the changing demographics of religious identity in the US, and the growth of the unaffiliated, the Rabbis Jacobs wanted to create an opportunity for unaffiliated spiritual seekers to come together, discuss issues important to them, and learn from Jewish wisdom. ISH is both an online portal (https://www.findyourish.com/) and a real-world address. Online people can participate in classes, chat rooms, and different ways of learning. In person, they can ask the rabbis of ISH to provide lifecycle services, classes and other spiritual encounters and experiences. There is a full menu of services. ISH is an experiment. It is a new way to connect based on pluralist principles, which take into account the lives people live today. The core values are clearly stated on the website:

> We believe in unconditional love and respect.
> We believe in an enabling, empowering and evolving spirituality.
> We believe everyone has a right to a self-defined spiritual connection and community.

We believe that wisdom and generosity lead to fulfillment.

Being challenged to think outside the traditional borders of what it means
to serve people as a rabbi inspired the Rabbis Jacobs to open ISH. It was created with a pluralist mindset and the intent to serve a diverse population. For
the future health of Judaism, we need rabbis who are willing to experiment
and try new ways of reaching people; the old ways are just not working as they
once did.

Bechol Lashon (In Every Tongue) is an organization that "imagines a
new global Judaism that transcends differences in geography, ethnicity, race,
ritual practice, and beliefs. Discussions about 'who-is-a-real-Jew' will be replaced with celebration of the rich, multi-dimensional character of the Jewish
people."[7] Rabbis Without Borders Fellow, Ruth Abusch Magder, is the organization's Rabbi-in-Residence. In her role, Rabbi Abusch Magder connects
with Jews of color around the world, educates white Jews about diversity, and
strives to introduce the many different communities of Jews to each other. In
our increasingly connected world, this work is crucial to the continuity and
growth of the Jewish community. Jews have always been a multi-racial people,
and the numbers of black, Asian and multi-racial Jews are growing. Many
in the Jewish community need sensitivity training, so that they do not question the Jewish bona fides of Jews of color, and instead welcome with equal
warmth each Jewish person walking through their doors. Her experience in
RWB prepared Rabbi Abusch Magder for the challenges of her work. For
instance, it helped her to understand those who are shocked by the presence
of an African-American Jew, and to hone the skills needed to compassionately
work with them to broaden their viewpoints. This is pluralism at work in the
Jewish community.

A pluralist mindset empowers rabbis and other Jewish leaders to welcome
different ways of being a Jew. This is not an "anything goes" Judaism, but
rather, a Judaism that is open to questions, explorations and experimentation.
This very act of questioning is at the core of what has made Judaism such a
vibrant tradition for thousands of years. The tradition has never been static.
Our sacred texts record disagreements and philosophical debates, and show
how changes in outlook and practices have evolved over generations. Given
today's realities, we need pluralist rabbis who can meet people where they are,
whoever they are, and use Jewish wisdom and traditions to inspire them to

---

[7] http://www.bechollashon.org/about/mission.php

lead more whole and fulfilling lives. This is how Judaism will flourish in the next generation.

Pluralistic Approaches to Jewish Practice

A Philosophic Basis for Halakhic Pluralism

Richard L. Claman

A central tenet of Conservative halakhah is that two (or more) propositions may each be a valid statement of halakhah, notwithstanding that the propositions are inconsistent with each other. (For example, it is a valid proposition of halakhah that: (i) a woman may/may not have an *aliyah;* (ii) feeding tubes may/may not be withdrawn from a terminally ill patient; and (iii) weddings may/may not be celebrated on otherwise ordinary days preceding Lag Ba'Omer.)

From a philosophic viewpoint, this tenet is surprising: how can a single system incorporate mutually inconsistent elements?

Indeed, Elliot Dorff wrote recently that he "knows of no philosophic justification of [halakhic] pluralism, for that would entail the legitimization of accepting a position and its contrary or contradictory."[1]

There is one modern moral philosopher, however, who has argued that it is possible for a philosophic system to be non-relativistic and yet pluralistic: Isaiah Berlin (and he was Jewish).

This article shows how one might ground halakhic pluralism on the foundation arguments presented by Berlin for his "objective pluralism" in moral philosophy.

A. The Domain of Halakhah:
Distinguishing Between Cultural Pluralism and Halakhic Pluralism

As a first step, it is necessary to locate the sphere of halakhah on our philosophic map.

We often talk about the United States as being characterized by cultural pluralism. But we all understand that that does not mean that the U.S. legal system includes multiple and inconsistent propositions as to any legal issue.

We understand that law and society are in some sense operating in different areas of life.

Oversimplifying, we share the following picture:[2]

---

[1] Elliot Dorff, "Jewish Tradition and National Policy," in Frank, ed., *Commandment and Community* (State University of New York Press, 1995). Dorff makes this point also in his article, "Pluralism: Models for the Conservative Movement," *Conservative Judaism* 48:2 (Winter 1995) pp. 21-35.

[2] This picture is developed in, e.g., John Rawls, *A Theory of Justice* (Cambridge: Harvard University Press, 1971).

STATE (including institutions such as the legal system, the taxing system, the welfare/redistribution system, the legislature, etc.)
THE BORDER A/K/A CONSTITUTIONAL PRIVACY
SOCIETY (in which associations are free to make their own rules for their members)

Pluralism, in the U.S., means that we are generally free to march in the Steuben Day Parade, or the Salute to Israel Parade, or the St. Patrick's Day Parade. We understand, moreover, that while the "State" may not discriminate against homosexuals, the sponsors of the St. Patrick's Day Parade, as a private association, are permitted to do so.

Institutions within "Society" may thus have rules: but these should not be confused with the rules of the legal system, which operates at a different plane concerning a different sphere of human activity. Baseball, for example, has a system of rules, and even a system of appeals; recall, for example, the "Pine Tar Incident."[3] We understand, however, that the system of baseball rules does not necessarily share the characteristics and requirements of legal rules: baseball rules may take into account not just the "rights" of the litigants, but also prudential policy considerations of the "good of the game." By contrast, a court is supposed to follow the law, even if the outcome, as in, *eg.*, the desegregation cases, threatens a practical crisis.

Where, in this picture, is halakhah? I submit that halakhah constitutes—and traditionally conceived itself as constituting—a set of "rules of the game" for a particular association within Society generally. Halakhah is thus "below-the-line."

To illustrate this point: Suppose Connecticut had passed a law that a husband and wife may not have sexual relations during the daytime, except in a darkened room. And suppose Connecticut produced, in support of such a law, some sociology studies showing that married couples having sex in the light have a higher rate of divorce (and thus impose an increased burden on the State), because they are thus able to see physical defects in each other.

The Talmud indeed clearly prohibits sex in the daytime, for precisely this

---

[3] See generally, e.g., *In re Brett: The Sticky Problem of Statutory Construction*, 52 Fordham L. Rev. 430 (1983).

reason. B. Niddah 16b-17a states:[4]

> Rav Hisda said: A man may not have intercourse during the day, for it says *And you shall love your friend as yourself* [Lev. 19:18]. Said Abbaye: What is the meaning of this? Perhaps he will see in her something which is ugly, and she will become unattractive to him.
>
> Rav Huna said: Israelites are holy and they do not have intercourse by day.
>
> Said Rava: But if it was a dark room, it is permitted, and a scholar may darken the room with his garment and have intercourse. . .

Yet, I would hope that if Connecticut passed such a law, it would be held unconstitutional, and held to violate our right of constitutional privacy, for the reasons articulated by Justice Douglas in *Griswold v. Connecticut*, 381 U.S. 479 (1965). That case concerned a statute forbidding the use of contraceptives by, *inter alia*, married couples. Justice Douglas, for the Court, explained:

> [The] specific guarantees in the Bill of Rights have penumbras, formed by emanations from those guarantees that help give them life and substance. Various guarantees create zones of privacy. The right of association contained in the penumbra of the First Amendment is one, as we have seen. The Third Amendment in its prohibition against the quartering of soldiers 'in any house' in time of peace without the consent of the owner is another facet of that privacy. The Fourth Amendment explicitly affirms the 'right of the people to be secure in their persons, houses, papers, and effects, against unreasonable searches and seizures.' The Fifth Amendment in its Self-Incrimination Clause enables the citizen to create a zone of privacy which government may not force him to surrender to his detriment. The Ninth Amendment provides: 'The enumeration in the Constitution, of certain rights, shall not be construed to deny or disparage others retained by the people.'

---

[4] Translation from Daniel Boyarin, *Carnal Israel: Reading Sex in Talmudic Culture* (Berkeley: University of California Press, 1993), p. 127.

The Fourth and Fifth Amendments were described . . as protection against all governmental invasions 'of the sanctity of a man's home and the privacies of life' [and] as creating a 'right to privacy, no less important than any other right carefully and particularly reserved to the people.'

Would we allow the police to search the sacred precincts of marital bedrooms for telltale signs of the use of contraceptives? The very idea is repulsive to the notions of privacy surrounding the marriage relationship.

We deal with a right of privacy older than the Bill of Rights — older than our political parties, older than our school system. Marriage is a coming together for better or for worse, hopefully enduring, and intimate to the degree of being sacred. It is an association that promotes a way of life, not causes; a harmony in living, not political faiths; a bilateral loyalty, not commercial or social projects. Yet it is an association for as noble a purpose as any involved in our prior decisions.

If Connecticut could not permissibly ban daylight sex, then is there something fundamentally invalid about the Talmud's proscription? No. To the contrary: in the U.S. we expect that different groups within the Society, e.g., different churches, will set standards for their members as to how to best live "holy" or worthy lives. Indeed, one goal of the State is to be "neutral" as amongst different value systems, preferring none, but yet encouraging the flourishing of all, within some boundary of mutual toleration.

There is, accordingly, nothing wrong about the Talmud addressing "private" issues, because the "privacy" line (in the constitutional sense) is *between* the State and Society, but does *not* limit the rules of an association *within* Society. (A person who does not care for an association's rule can simply exit that association.)

Conversely, halakhah recognizes that restrictions of halakhah may not apply to the State. Thus, for example, halakhah recognizes that the State can execute persons as murderers even though, as a matter of halakhah, they could not be executed by the Rabbinic Court. Maimonides (Mishnah Torah, Book XI, *Homicide*, II, 4, 5) there summarizes:[5]

---

[5] Translation by Horowitz, *Spirit of Jewish Law* (New York: Bloch, 1963), p. 195. Maimonides further opines that "A regular court, also, may execute such persons as a temporary measure; for if the emergency requires it, they may do as they see fit."

> One who hires a killer to kill his neighbor, or sends his
> slave to kill him, or binds the victim and places him before a
> lion and the beast actually kills him; and also one who kills
> himself; every such person is a shedder of blood and is liable
> to death at the hands of heaven, but not to execution at the
> hands of the court . . . And all these and similar killers who
> are not liable to execution by sentence of a regular court, a
> king of Israel has lawful authority, if he so desire, to execute
> them in accordance with royal law for the sake of social
> order and stability.

When the Conservative movement talks about halakhic pluralism it is referring to pluralism *within* a single association of persons—Conservative Jews—who are seeking to order their lives within "Society." Accordingly, halakhic pluralism is fundamentally different from cultural pluralism, which concerns the relationship *between* different private associations, when viewed from the perspective of the State. Therefore, our bases for advocating—in the U.S.—the latter cannot be invoked uncritically to support—within the Conservative movement—the former.

It is sometimes argued that there is an analog within Judaism to cultural pluralism, namely, the existence of different traditions, i.e., Ashkenazic, Yemenite, Spanish-Portuguese, etc.; and further, that the existence of such pluralism proves the possibility of halakhic pluralism.

It is important to clear this confusion out of the way. Preliminarily, the fact that some sort of diversity has existed historically is not a philosophic justification: one cannot get an "ought to" from an "is." In any event, pushing on the analogy moves us in an undesirable direction.

Halakhah is a below-the-line institution, and so constitutes the "Rules of the Community." It follows that when there are halakhic differences between persons, those persons thereupon constitute, as a result, different communities. (The phrase "Rules of the Community" is intended to bring to mind the Qumran scroll "Serekh ha-Yahad," and the multiple "Judaisms" that flourished in the last days before the destruction of the Second Temple.)

In contrast, we all understand that, supplementing the halakhah, there is a body of custom. When we see a Torah scroll completely enclosed in a single cylindrical silver case, we recognize it as "Sephardic," but not as representing any different halakhic practice. Multiplicity of customs is recognized in the Talmud. See generally the discussion in *Encyclopedia Judaica* (Keter,

1971) of "Conflict of Laws," discussing principally the Talmud's treatment of conflicting customs. For example, there is a debate recorded in the Mishnah, between R. Akiva and R.. Johanan ben Nuri, M. Rosh Hashanah 4:5, as to the order and interplay of the blessings and the shofar blasts in the Rosh Hashanah *musaf* service. (The debate continued throughout the talmudic period. *Cf.* B. Rosh Hashanah 32a, where R. Judah Ha-Nasi disagrees with his own father.) The J. Rosh Hashanah 4:6, records:[6]

> In Judah they followed the custom *[nahagu]* of Rabbi Akiba, and in the Galilee that of Rabbi Yohanan ben Nuri. If one transgressed *[avar]* and did in Judah like the Galilee, or in the Galilee like Judah, he has fulfilled his responsibilities *[yatzah]*.

But tolerance for differences in customs within a single community does not imply any tolerance for multiple halakhic practices within a single community. While the line between custom and halakhah is not always clear, it nevertheless exists—and can be seen when communities once separated are now rejoined. Indeed, what we see today in Israel, as the many different communities of the Diaspora are reunited, is that all but the most superficial distinctions—matters that are plainly 'trivial customs,' and not matters of halakhah—are being erased in the name of uniformity.

What if however, we insist on pressing the analogy, and so assert that such diversity in practice *should* continue to exist even at the halakhic level?

In *Sacred Fragments* Neil Gillman concedes that, if halakhah is linked to community, then the recognition of halakhic diversity apparently requires one to recognize that we consist of a host of "mini-communities:"

> We should [he argues] view the community of caring, committed Jews as a series of overlapping mini-communities, each of which centers itself about a body of mitzvot that it accepts as binding. Institutionally, these mini-communities organize themselves into three major coalition movements, Orthodox, Conservative and Reform . . .[7]

---

[6] Translation from Neusner, ed., *J. Talmud: The Rosh Hashanah volume*, translated by Goldman.

[7] Neil Gillman, *Sacred Fragments: Recovering Theology for the Modern Jew* (Philadelphia: Jewish Publication Society, 1990), p. 56.

The Conservative movement, in this view, is like the Democratic (or Republican) party: it does not then itself stand for any values; rather, it is just a political alliance of convenience, for the particular moment, among different mini-communities with their own different agendas. Recall, for example, Clinton's indusion of welfare reform as part of the Democratic Party platform in 1992. It is meaningless to ask: was that consistent with traditional party values? What mattered was simply a pragmatic calculus: would inclusion of this platform bring more "moderate" resources (voters and money) into the tent than the party would lose in traditional "left/liberal" resources? Similarly, Nixon's "Southern Strategy" was hardly faithful to the legacy of Lincoln: but parties are pragmatic, temporary coalitions, not *communities* with values in themselves; again, the test is simply temporary success.

According to Gillman, then, pluralism in halakhic practice can only be saved by considering the Conservative movement as a political coalition, and, at the limit, *each* individual member thereof as a potential mini-community in his/herself. The decision to ordain women as rabbis, then, cannot be addressed as a matter of movement "values," for the movement itself has no inherent values. Rather, that decision should be seen simply as pragmatic politics: a hope that admitting women would bring more resources into the coalition than would be lost to new splinter parties.

Suppose that there are ten halakhic issues, each admitting two valid positions. Then, there would be 2^{10} possible alignments, or 1,024 mini-communities.

In other words, since halakhah is *already* a below-the-line institution, the application to it of the below-the-line concept of cultural pluralism, carrying the Sephardic/Ashkenazic analogy to its end-point, results in the fragmentation of any halakhic community into just a collection of individuals, *each* belonging to his or her own halakhic mini-community.

Perhaps we can do no better, and should just accept this "realistic" portrait. This portrait is *not* itself a philosophic justification, but rather an insistence that our search—for justification of halakhic pluralism within a single community—is meaningless. Perhaps, per Gillman, we should accordingly just admit that our decisions, e.g., to ordain women, are just politics, combined with the political rhetoric appropriate to campaign platforms.

I am not ready to so concede: and I would like the reader, too, to consider the arguments that follow, which try to explain how one can justify halakhic pluralism within a single *community*, where the community itself has inherent values, and is not just a political coalition.

B. Types of "Pluralism" Within A Single Community: Some Terminological Distinctions

It is also necessary to distinguish halakhic pluralism, in the sense advocated by the Conservative movement, from two other types of pluralism, which we will call (i) interpretive pluralism; and (ii) pre-halakhic pluralism.

1. *Interpretive* pluralism. Everyone agrees that there can be two or more mutually inconsistent interpretations of biblical verse, as a matter of *haggadah.* For example: we are told (Ex. 19:17) that the people of Israel, when they gathered to receive the Ten Commandments, stood *bitaḥit hahar.* That phrase would appear, literally, to mean that the people stood *under* the mountain. Rashi preserves one midrashic explanation: that God held the mountain-top over the heads of the people, and informed them that if they refused the Ten Commandments, He would drop the mountain-top, and they would perish; and that it was only under such duress that we accepted. The Mekhilta sets forth a different picture: that the mountain top was suspended like a *huppah,* a wedding canopy, marking the covenant/marriage between God and Israel.[8]

The co-existence within the tradition of such diametrically different interpretations does not generally trouble us. We understand that, for example, different directors can have dramatically opposed pictures of the character of Hamlet. (Whether we should be more troubled by this phenomenon is a question for another day, best left to our experts in hermeneutic theory.)

2. *Pre-halakhic pluralism.* We also understand that, prior to the time that "the halakhah" is determined with respect to any particular issue, it is appropriate for different persons to advocate different positions, and to act in accordance with those positions. Since there is no resolved halakhah on the question, how else *should* one act?

The paradigm of such pluralism is Beit Hillel and Beit Shammai before the *bat kol"* prodaimed (at Yavneh) that the *halakhah* was in accordance with Beit Hillel. So long as the halakhah was still being debated, we would expect Beit Shammai to act in accordance with its view. [Once the *"bat kol"* was heard, however, the Bavli cannot imagine how pluralism in practice could persist (except insofar as Beit Shammai was entitled to adopt the view that we do not attend to a *"bat kol"* to resolve a halakhic dispute). See Yevamot 13a and following.]

Likewise, the Bavli, Eruvin 6b-7a—a passage that Joel Roth cites (see *infra)—asserts* that participants in ongoing disputes in our own day should be

---

[8] See Reuven Hammer, *The Classic Midrash* (New York: Paulist Press, 1995), pp. 141-142 (commenting on Mekhilta, *Baḥodesh,* 3, II 217.)

entitled to—at least pending some resolution (by consensus or otherwise)—practice their own positions, just as did Beit Shammai prior to the *"bat kol."*

Again, such pre-decision pluralism does not seem troublesome. In the U.S. federal court system, it occasionally happens that the different trial and appellate level courts begin to split on the interpretation and application of, e.g., a federal statute regulating securities; and the U.S. Supreme Court, instead of stepping in immediately to resolve the split, chooses to *"deny cert."*—*i.e.,* to abstain from hearing cases presenting the disputed issues—in order to wait and see if a consensus develops amongst the lower courts. Accordingly, we may live through several years of diversity, until the U.S. Supreme Court, now able to see how the issue is addressed and resolved in a large number of cases, decides to hear and resolve the issue. In the interim, we expect different courts, in different states, to follow the different precedents set by the different local Federal Circuit Courts of Appeal.

Once interpretive and pre-halakhic pluralism are distinguished from halakhic pluralism, it can be see that the Talmudic texts cited by, e.g., Dorff, supra, support only interpretive and/or pre-halakhic pluralism. This point is well presented by H. ben Menaḥem:[9]

> But first, a word of caution. We must guard ourselves against a very common, indeed tempting fallacy. Everyone who is familiar with talmudic Law is well aware of the great variability and differentiation of legal opinions recorded in the Talmud with regard to almost every legal issue. Our sources record and discuss a multitude of diverse legal opinions and this is considered as a characteristic feature of the Talmud. Is this very fact not sufficient to establish the pluralistic nature of talmudic Law? To show the fallacy of this argument we must look briefly into the attitudes in the Talmud itself towards this celebrated phenomenon of dissension.
>
> One finds statements scattered throughout the Talmud to the effect that the various dissenting opinions were all "given by one and the same shepherd" or that "one leader

---

[9] H. ben Menaḥem, "Is There Always One Uniquely Correct Answer To A Legal Question In The Talmud?", *Jewish Law Annual* VI: 164 (1987). See also, by that author, *"Postscript:* The Judicial Process and the Nature of Jewish Law" in Hecht et al., *An Introduction to the History and Sources of Jewish Law* (Oxford: Clarendon Press, 1996).

uttered them all." And there is of course the famous saying that "these and these are the words of the living God,"
referring to the controversy between Bet Shammai and Bet
Hillel. On the basis of this last citation, B. Jackson claims
that Jewish Law denies that there is always one uniquely
correct answer—ascribing this view not to the deficiencies
of the human intellect but the superiority of the Divine who
can transcend the law of contradiction. However, a careful examination of these citations reveals that they do not
justify the dissension nor indeed do they deal with the jur-
isprudential status of dissenting opinions but are concerned
with a different problem altogether. The problem is this.
Given the dissension one might be puzzled by a theological
difficulty: how do we know that a particular opinion chosen from amongst many others as the legally binding one
actually represents the will of God? The answer given is
that all legal opinions by virtue of being sincere attempts
to discover the true will of God are qualified candidates
to be a model for the *Halakhah*. In other words, the will of
God will be accomplished by following any of them. On the
theological level the content of the binding law is immate-
rial; what is important is the form and manner in which the
law is determined. One might even say that these citations
support the claim that "Halakhic truth is not and need not
necessarily be identical with absolute or divine truth." But
from this it does not follow that "it is possible to have more
than one valid solution to a legal problem." On the legal
level, that is, the level of the binding (valid) law, there is according to these citations one uniquely correct answer. The
saying concerning the controversy between Bet Shammai
and Bet Hillel condudes after all: "But the law follows the
opinion of Beth Hillel."

Consider also, for example, the story of Akavyah ben Mehalalel (M.
Eduyot 5:6-7; cf. B. Sanhedrin 88a). One of my teachers reads this story as
an endorsement of the possibility of change: even though Akavyah will not
himself—to move forward in time—accept women as rabbis, he directs his
son to adopt the view of the new majority. I read the story with more concern:
I imagine Thurgood Marshall trying to convince his successor as to the need

to keep dissenting in every death penalty case, to keep alive a record for the day when capital punishment will be seen as unconstitutional; and the successor retorting: a majority has now ruled, I can no longer dissent.

In either event, one moral of the story is that only one view can be accepted in practice at any one time, at least once the majority has ruled. I see nothing in this story that permits pluralism in halakhic practice *after* the majority ruled.[10]

In considering the Talmudic texts, one further distinction is helpful: between what I will call (i) *sectarian* pluralism and (ii) *sharing* pluralism.

Consider the following: my synagogue rabbi's daughter is coming to my house for a play-date with my daughter. I intend to cook macaroni and cheese. My home is kosher. But I get to thinking: concerning cheese; there is a controversy going way back.[11] The Conservative movement has validated the so-called "lenient" position, that all cheeses subject to federal regulation are considered kosher, without the need for a *hekhsher*. But I suppose the more "stringent" position is also valid. I think, in fact, that when I have eaten at my rabbi's house, I have seen cheese with a *hekhsher*. Now, there are several things I can do: (a) I can take the position that pluralism means *sharing* pluralism— i.e., that he would respect my position, for conduct within my home, and eat my cheese, even if he knew I took the "lenient" view; (b) I can assume that he takes the stringent view, and further assume that he advocates only a *sectarian* pluralism: i.e., that I can do what I want for myself, but I should accommodate him (and his daughter) in taking their view, and so use cheese with a *hekhsher* for his daughter; (c) I can ask him—but he may be of the don't-ask-don't-tell school; i.e., he will respect "my" *kashrut*, as long as I *don't* confront him; and in fact he would rather that I *didn't* ask him, because he doesn't want to impose on me the extra expense and bother of going out and finding cheese

---

[10] How can Akavyah have learned from a majority, and yet his son have learned the opposite but also from a majority? I like to imagine the following context for this story. Hillel has come from Babylonia, with his own traditions. Akavyah grew up with some different Palestinian traditions. Hillel's first deputy was Menahem, who apparently left the academy after a few years for a more politically-involved career. Perhaps Menahem was chosen precisely because of his Palestinian political interests, to counterbalance the Babylonian influx. When Menahem resigned, the Sanhedrin looked for another deputy who would be both a strong adherent of the Palestinian tradition, but also willing to acknowledge the Babylonian ascendancy. Akavyeh would not. Shammai would. With the Babylonian influx, however, the majority tipped, and so Akavyah's son saw a different majority.

[11] See generally Isaac Klein, *A Guide To Jewish Religious Practice* (2d ed. 1992) (New York: Jewish Theological Seminary), p. 306.

with a *hekhsher;* but if asked, he will insist that I do so, based on a *sectarian* pluralism position.

The problem is not new—it is raised in the Talmud. The context is a debate over serving fish with a milk sauce on a "meat" plate. B. Hullin 111b. ("Separate dishes" is generally a post-Talmudic development.) The story is as follows (Soncino trans. at 614-615):

> It was stated: If (hot) fish was served on a (meat) plate: Rab says, It is forbidden to eat it with milk sauce; Samuel says, It is permitted to eat it with milk sauce. Tab says, It is forbidden, because it imparted a flavor to it. Samna says, It is permitted, because it imparted a flavor indirectly.
>
> R. Eleazar was once standing before Mar Samuel, who was being served with fish upon a (meat) plate and was eating it with milk sauce. He [Samuel] offered him some but he would not eat it. Samuel said to him, I once offered some to your Master [i.e., Rib] and he ate it, and you won't eat it. He [R. Eleazar] then came to Rab and asked him. Has my Master withdrawn his view? He replied, Heaven forfend that the son of Abba b. Abba [i.e., Samuel] should give me to eat that which I do not hold (to be permitted)!

Apparently, in the context of this pre-halakhic dispute, Samuel believed in *sharing* pluralism, while Rab was horrified at the concept, and could only conceive of a sectarian pluralism.

I would think that the Conservative movement, in advocating halakhic pluralism, means to adopt a *sharing* form of halakhic pluralism—i.e., that my rabbi's daughter will knowingly be eating non-*hekhsher* cheese in my house.

With the foregoing additional distinctions in mind, we can now address the text that perhaps goes furthest of any Talmudic text in considering the problem of pluralism: J. Yevamot 1:VII. (The base Mishnah is M. Yevamot 1:6 = M. Eduyot 4:8: the Bavli's discussion begins at Yevamot 13a.)

The Mishnah states:[12]

> Though these forbade what the others permitted, and these regarded as ineligible what the others declared eligible, Beth Shammai nevertheless did not refrain from marrying women from (the families of) Beth Hillel, nor

---

[12] Transalation from Soncino, B. Yevamot at 67-68.

did Beth Hillel (refrain from marrying women) from (the families of) Beth Shammai. (Similarly, in respect of) all (questions of ritual) cleanness and uncleanness, which these declared dean where the others declared unclean, neither of them abstained from using the utensils of the others for the preparation of food that was ritually dean.

J. Tal. then comments (Neusner, trans.):

> Yose b. R. Bun said, "Rab and Samuel differed. One of them said, 'These and those conducted themselves in accord with the law,' and the other one said, 'These conducted themselves in accord with their view of the law, and those conducted themselves in accord with their view of the law.'"
>
> (As to this latter view), there is the matter of the genealogically illegitimate status of children between them, and yet you say this (that they both intermarried and also followed diverse views of the law)? (Incredible!)
>
> The Omnipresent watched out for them, and a practical case (involving illegitimacy) never actually took place.

The context here is clearly *prior* to the *"bat kol"*—the Yerushalmi goes on, in the next lines, to state its view that the *"bat kol" was* heard in Yavneh, and that once the *bat kol* was heard, even Beit Shammai followed the halakhah as thus decided.

Nevertheless, if one could *justify* philosophically a *sharing* form of pluralism, even pre-halakhic, that might well give us a due as to how to justify halakhic pluralism. We see first another dispute attributed to Rab and Samuel about pluralism. We then see the Yerushalmi asking the key question: how can Samuel *justify* sharing pluralism?

One of my teachers argues that the Yerushalmi's conclusion, that God watched out for Beit Hillel and Beit Shammai, is an endorsement of sharing pluralism: i.e., I can follow Samuel, and serve you cheese that *I* consider kosher, *without* having to worry about your view.

But there is also a *deus ex machina* here that *avoids* the problem: no one ever had to really share someone else's view, because God shuffled everything so that a test never arose. (Note that the Yerushalmi talks only about the marriage context, and not the sharing-utensils context that is also presented in the Mishnah; it is perhaps harder to picture God shuffling all the pots and pans appropriately.) If I am a cheese-with-hekhsher adherent, will God protect me from my lenient neighbors as he protected Beit Hillel and Beit Shammai?

In any event, even if God has *endorsed* sharing pluralism, neither God nor the Yerushalmi has given us an answer to the philosophic question of how that can be *justified*.

C. Roth's Philosophic Argument

Dorff is incorrect in suggesting that no philosophic defense of halakhic pluralism has ever been advanced: Joel Roth[13] gives a clear argument. He (i) begins by arguing that halakhah is analogous to law; and (ii) then argues that just as a particular philosophy of law, known as Legal Positivism, can justify pluralism in practice, so too that philosophy can justify halakhic pluralism.

One problem with the foregoing is that Legal Positivism has been all but refuted by Ronald Dworkin, in various writings beginning with *Taking Rights Seriously*.[14] To illustrate Dworkin's point, consider the following example, drawn from the Talmud:

You are a rabbi, in a small town in the Galilee, in the year 300 C.E. You know your Mishnah; there is not yet any Talmud. The following case comes before you: Benjamin, the borrower, borrowed 100 shekels from Levi, the lender, in February 300, giving Levi a proper written note, promising to repay on demand at any time after 30 days. In May, Benjamin died. In August, Levi died. It is now October. Levi's son ("Levi Jr.") has now sued Benjamin's son ("Ben Jr.").

You know the following rules:

1.   In general, an oath is imposed upon only one side: otherwise, if there are competing oaths, someone may perjure himself

2.   If a Lender sues a Borrower, produces a written note, and takes the oath that the note has not been repaid, Lender wins.

3.   If Borrower dies, Lender can sue Borrower's heirs; and if Lender produces the note, and takes his oath, Lender wins.

4.   If Lender dies, Lender's heir can sue Borrower; and if son produces the note, and takes an oath that "my father left no instruction, in writing, that the note was repaid," son wins.

How would you argue now, if you were the lawyer for each side, in our case

---

[13] Joel Roth, *The Halakhic Process: A Systematic Analysis* (New York: Jewish Theological Seminary, 1986).

[14] Ronald Dworkin, *Taking Rights Seriously* (Cambridge: Harvard University Press, 1978).

of Levi, Jr. vs. Ben Jr.?

For Levi, Jr., you might argue that the *principle* underlying the existing precedents is that the writing controls, plus a minimal oath; and since Levi Jr. has the note, and is prepared to take the "son's oath," Levi Jr. should win. For Ben Jr., you might respond that something has changed here: so long as at least *one* of the original parties was present, the oath had a certain seriousness—the Lender's son would not be likely to swear falsely in the face of the Borrower. But with everyone dead, that essential element is now missing, and the written note is not enough. Levi Jr. might respond: but if you let Borrower's estate off the hook, based on the accident of Levi's death, you will discourage lending: the whole point of writing is to make notes readily transferable, and so encourage lending to those in need. Ben Jr. would respond that a common-law equitable principle of "laches" applies: that it was *unfair*, once his father died, for Lender not to sue immediately, and the delay on Lender's part is what caused the problem here. And so on.

The one thing no lawyer would ever say to the judge (or rabbi) is: "Your Honor, there is no precedent on point, and so you are free to do whatever you feel is just: there is nothing more to be said; it is a matter of judicial discretion."

Legal Positivism is the doctrine espoused in particular by British legal philosophers from around 1900 (e.g., John Salmond, whose treatise, subsequently updated and republished, is repeatedly cited by Roth) until around 1961, when H.L.A. Hart published his *The Concept of Law* (Oxford). (Hans Kelsen, writing in this period, was also a member of this school; and Roth cites also to Kelsen.) According to those Positivists, once the precedents, or statutes, have "run out," all that is left for a judge to do is to exercise his judicial discretion.

Dworkin's point is that when the precedents have run out, we don't stop arguing, but rather we look to the *principles* underlying the precedents, and try to construct the answer most consistent with the precedents and the principles. For, according to Dworkin, one side or the other has the *right* to prevail; and the judge is required to do his or her best to render the decision that is the best "fit" with the precedents and the underlying principles. There may be human error, due to human limitations in understanding, but that does not change the fact that we believe that there *is* one right answer, and we try to reason-out that one right answer.

The Talmud's answer to the above case is as follows (B. Shevu'ot 48b, Soncino trans. *at* 300):[15]

---

[15] Ben-Menahem, in his article supra, discusses this text as his best—if not only—example of this phenomenon in the Talmud. He does not advance any philosophic

[This case was disputed between Rab and Samuel on the one hand, who rule for Ben Jr.; and R. Eleazar, who ruled for Levi Jr.]

R. Hama said: Now, since the law has not been stated either in accordance with the view of Rab and Samuel or in accordance with the view of R. Eleazar, if a judge decides as Rab and Samuel, it is legal; if he decides as R. Eleazar, it is also legal.

R Papa said: This document of orphans we do not tear up, and we do not exact payment on it. We do not exact payment on it—in case we agree with Rab and Samuel; and we do not tear up—for if a judge decides as R. Eleazar, it is legal.

There was a judge who decided as R. Eleazar. There was a Rabbinic scholar in his town who said to him: I can bring a letter from the West that the law is not in accordance with R. Eleazar. He replied to him: When you bring it. He came before R. Hama. He said to him: If a judge decides as R. Eleazar, it is legal.

I have tried this "moot court" exercise in a couple of different classes. Each time, when I have presented the Talmud's answer, the class has been horrified: how can the law be that both views are valid? If Roth, and Legal Positivism, are correct, we should be satisfied with the Talmud's answer: that is what judicial discretion means; *i.e.,* there can be multiple, inconsistent results, all of which are valid halakhic decisions, because the precedents have run out. Thus Roth clearly states:

> One implication of the right of different arbiters to exercise judicial discretion as they see fit is that divergent behaviors, not only divergent theoretical positions, are systematically legitimate within the halakhic system.[16]

But Roth and the Legal Positivists are not correct: in the law, such pluralism cannot be justified, because it ignores the force of *principles*.

Incidentally, Maimonides cannot tolerate the Talmud's resolution, either.

---

account of how it can be justified: he presents it rather as an interesting problem for analysis.

[16] Roth, p. 61.

He writes:

> If the debtor died first and then the creditor died the creditor's heirs take nothing from the debtor's heirs. For at the time the debtor died the creditor became liable to an oath before he could collect the debt, as we have stated, and now that the creditor is dead the heirs cannot succeed him to the oath, because they cannot swear that their father had not been paid anything. If, however, the judge, in disregard of this rule, administered an oath to the creditor's heirs and they collected the debt, it may not be reclaimed from them.[17]

How is it, however, that I hope to justify halakhic pluralism, if I agree that Dworkin's "right answer" thesis is correct, as a matter of philosophy of law?

The key is to remember the proper *domain*. Law, according to Dworkin, yields a right answer because the courts are permitted—as part of the "division of labor" within the institutions of the State—to consider *only* arguments of *principle*, and not arguments of *policy*. Dworkin explains:

> Arguments of *policy* justify a political decision by showing that the decision advances or protects some collective goal of the community as a whole. The argument in favor of a subsidy for aircraft manufacturers, that the subsidy will protect national defense, is an argument of policy. Arguments of *principle* justify a political decision by showing that the decision respects or secures some individual or group right. The argument in favor of anti-discrimination statutes, that a minority has a right to equal respect and concern, is an argument of principle. These sorts of argument do not exhaust political argument. Sometimes, for example, a political decision, like the decision to allow extra income tax exemptions for the blind, may be defended as an act of public generosity or virtue rather than on grounds of either policy or principle. But principle and policy are the major grounds of political justification.
>
> But if the case at hand is a hard case, when no settled rule dictates a decision either way, then it might seem that a proper decision could be generated by either policy or

---

[17] *Mishneh Torah*, Book VII, Civil Laws, Debtor and Creditor (Yale Judaica Library trans.), ch. XVII, 3.

principle. Consider, for example, the problem of the recent *Spartan Steel* case. The defendant's employees had broken an electrical cable belonging to a power company that supplied power to the plaintiff, and the plaintiff's factory was shut down while the cable was repaired. The court had to decide whether to allow the plaintiff recovery for economic loss following negligent damage to someone else's property. It might have proceeded to its decision by asking either whether a firm in the position of the plaintiff had a right to a recovery, which is a matter of principle, or whether it would be economically wise to distribute liability for accidents in the way the plaintiff suggested, which is a matter of policy.

If judges are deputy legislators, then the court should be prepared to follow the latter argument as well as the former, and decide in favor of the plaintiff if that argument recommends. That is, I suppose, what is meant by the popular idea that a court must be free to decide a novel case like *Spartan Steel* on policy grounds; and indeed Lord Denning described his own opinion in that case in just that way. I do not suppose he meant to distinguish an argument of principle from an argument of policy in the technical way I have, but he in any event did not mean to rule out an argument of policy in that technical sense.

I propose, nevertheless, the thesis that judicial decisions in civil cases, even in hard cases like *Spartan Steel,* characteristically are and should be generated by principle not policy.[18]

In short, Dworkin argues that fairness, being a relatively limited concept, will at the end of the day produce, on analysis, one conclusion that is more fair than the competing conclusion. *Policy* disputes, by contrast, may be inherently indeterminate, because of the complexity and "richness" of the competing considerations. But in our "State," policy matters are left to other institutions, *eg.,* the legislature, or to the taxing and welfare/distribution systems.

Once, however, we move *below the line,* things change. There is nothing in halakhah analogous to the constitutional division of labor *within* the State:

---

[18] Dworkin, pp. 82-84.

indeed, the Sages exercised both quasi-legislative power, in the form of the *takkanah*, and what we might call judicial power. The "good of the game," a policy concern, is properly inherent in any rabbinic decision. Indeed, even in what would appear to be private disputes, a *bet din* is permitted to base its ruling on what it believes is good for the peace of the community.[19]

In sum, once we are below-the-line, we enter into a world of moral complexity and contradictions. This is the situation of interest to Isaiah Berlin.

D. Berlin's Objective Pluralism

Perhaps you might recall facing (yourself, or vicariously, through a child) the following dilemma: (a) you liked certain things about *big* colleges: their very bigness promised diversity, extra-curricular opportunities, a multitude of potential friends, etc.; but (b) you also liked certain things about *small* colleges, e.g., the collegiality, faculty contact, etc. You could choose one or the other, but you couldn't go to both at the same time. Within the category of big colleges, you preferred Wisconsin to Virginia, but you were undecided as between either of those, and a small school like William & Mary. Within the category of small schools, you preferred Wesleyan to William & Mary; but you were still undecided between Wesleyan and Wisconsin. (You have exduded a variety of other schools: we are concerned here only with your final choices—what an economist would call the choices at the "margin.")

This dilemma is a consequence *not* of the poverty of these options, and their underlying values, but rather of the overabundance, or richness, thereof.

At the end of the day, I will choose either the "better" big or small college, and I will think that I have made the better choice. But if, at the margin, *you* choose the other, I cannot say that you have made a mistake. (If you choose a college that is *not*, however, at least at the "margin," but rather is "within" the margin, and so is objectively 'inferior' in terms of your objectives and values, I can and will criticize you for not fully pursuing all your available horizons.)

In a "normal" system, preferences are transitive: if "A" equals "B," and "B" is greater than "C," then "A" is greater than "C."

Accordingly, if Wisconsin = William & Mary, and Wesleyan > William & Mary, how can Wesleyan *not* be preferred to Wisconsin?

The answer is that not everything in life is transitive and commensurable:

---

[19] See, e.g., *Meisels v. Uhr*, 79 N.Y.2d 526, 583 N.Y.S.2d 951 (1992) (upholding power of a *bet din* to issue, within its *peshera* jurisdiction, a compromise judgment, awarding defendant certain rights even though, as a matter of law, plaintiff *was* entitled to prevail).

not everything "trades" against everything else; not everything can be captured on a single utilitarian metric.

(For New Yorkers, consider also the debate over City versus suburb: I can prefer East Side to West Side, and Larchmont to New Rochelle, and still be uncertain as to *either* side vs. *either* suburb as the best place to raise my family.)

Conversely, there *are* choices that are "tragic," in the sense that *either* alternative leads to problems; and yet we must choose. Consider Hamlet. He has come up with a reasonable plan: he needs to develop more evidence, beyond the accusations of a ghost; to do so, he must stay at Elsinore; to do so, he needs an excuse; and the best excuse is to feign "melancholy." But what about Ophelia? If he tells Ophelia, she may leak the plan to Polonius, who will tell the King, and Hamlet will be executed; but if he does not, she may become mad from despair, and commit suicide, and her brother Laertes will demand revenge from Hamlet, and there will be a duel, etc. The tragedy is that Hamlet must choose as best he can, and play it out; neither choice leads to a happy ending; but neither choice can be considered wrong.

John Gray, in his analysis of Isaiah Berlin's position, summarizes as follows:[20]

> At the very beginnings of the Western intellectual tradition it is affirmed that all genuine goods are compatible. In the Platonic conception of the Form of the Good, yet more is affirmed: that all genuine goods are not only compatible with one another—that is to say, in ideal circumstances, conjointly realizable, achievable together—but that they somehow entail or imply one another. The same idea, more moderately expressed, is found in the Aristotelian ideas of the Mean and of the unity of the virtues—the idea, in this case, that no true excellence or mode of human flourishing can, at any rate in the best human life, compete with, or drive out, any other.
>
> To admit that genuine questions may not have a single right answer is to impeach a traditional conception of truth, according to which all truths are not merely compatible but in some sense mutually supportive. This is to say that, on this traditional view, not only does every genuine question have one right answer, but that all these answers are mutually compatible, or even entailed

---

[20] John Gray, *Isaiah Berlin* (Princeton: Princeton University Press, 1966), pp. 39-52. Gray quotes from Joseph Raz, *The Morality of Freedom*, (Oxford: Oxford University Press, 1988), p.334; see J. Raz, "Multiculturalism in a Liberal Perspective," in J. Raz, *Ethics in the Public Domain*, (Oxford: Clarendon Press, 1994), 179-180.

by one another. It seems to be this truly fantastic conception of reason that is embedded in the Platonic and Socratic, and even the pre-Socratic, foundations of the Western tradition.. .

Nor is this foundational view confined to the (Socratic) Greek roots of the Western tradition. It is a feature of the Christian tradition that, however tragic may be the moral and practical dilemmas we face in mortal life, they are all in principle soluble by reference to the will of God; and the ideas of deity and of perfection are conjoined. There cannot, in the Christian view at least, be an ultimate moral tragedy, an unredeemed loss of value or a conflict of right with right, since to allow this would be to subvert the providential order and so undermine the very possibility of theodicy. For a Christian, as perhaps for some Jews and all Muslims, the idea of the best of all possible worlds must be a meaningful one, since, if it is not, the monotheistic conception of divinity is destroyed....

Berlin rejects this foundational Western commitment. He denies that genuine goods, or authentic virtues, are, necessarily, or as a matter of fact, such that peaceful coexistence among them is a possible state of human life. It is true of many goods, according to Berlin, that they are rivalrous and conflictual. More, Berlin denies that, when such competition among goods occurs, it is always capable of resolution by the application of a rational standard. Human goods are not only often uncombinable; they are sometimes incommensurable. This is Berlin's celebrated doctrine of *value-pluralism*...

The deeper content of Berlin's value-pluralism is in the thesis that any complex morality recognizes goods that are in their very natures uncombinable—the goods of autonomous agency and of unreflective decency, perhaps—such that there is a conceptual or logical incoherence in the very idea that a single person at the same time could possess or exercise both. This aspect of Berlin's value-pluralism affirms that any morality which, like our own, is at all complex and developed, will generate for its practitioners moral dilemmas, and rivalries among the virtues, that reasoning cannot resolve. Or, to put the same point in "other terms, the perfections identified by any morality such as ours, or by any similar morality, are plural and competitive, and the idea of a perfection that encompasses them all without loss is incoherent...

Berlin's ethical theory is a species, not of relativism or scepticism, but of *objective pluralism,* and that the objective pluralist idea of value-incommensurability is central in giving content to what I have called his agonistic liberalism...

Incommensurability is not an incompleteness or an imperfection—in the criteria of value of an object or options, say. It does not arise because criteria of value are multiple and their rankings indeterminate, nor because the boundaries between different categories of objects or options are vague or shifting. There is incommensurability when all of these forms of incompleteness have been removed. As Raz puts it, "where there is incommensurability, it is the ultimate truth. There is nothing further behind it, nor is it a sign of imperfection." Nor does incommensurability denote indifference: as Raz puts it incisively, "Incomparability does not ensure equality of merit and demerit. It does not mean indifference. It marks the inability of reason to guide our action, not the insignificance of our choice."...

"On a reductive-monistic view (of values) when one trades the pleasures (and anxieties) of a family life for a career as a sailor one is getting, or hoping to get, the same thing one is giving up, be it happiness, pleasure, desire-satisfaction, or something else. So long as one plans correctly and succeeds in carrying out one's plans there is no loss of any kind. One gives up the lesser pleasure one would derive from family life for the greater pleasure of life at sea. If value-pluralism is correct this view is totally wrong. What one loses is of a different kind from what one gains. Even in success there is a loss, and quite commonly there is no meaning to the judgement that one gains more than one loses. When one was faced with valuable options and successfully chose one of them one simply chose one way of life rather than another, both being good and not susceptible to comparison of degree."

How does this apply to halakhah? Consider a guidance counselor advising various students. We would expect the guidance counselor to recognize the virtues of both big and small colleges, and to try to match the values thereof with the values of his or her different students. (A guidance counselor who preferred big schools, and so directed his or her advisees exclusively to big schools, is not, I think all would agree, doing his/her job.) Analogously, our halakhic decision-makers, speaking for the community, can and should recognize that, in certain cases, the virtue of uniformity is outweighed by the need to recognize that there are multiple ways to implement the complexity of our Jewish values as applied to particular questions, depending on how those different values fit with different persons' pursuit of Jewishly-valuable lives. And in those circumstances, the community can appropriately validate, and recognize the value of different, and even contradictory, positions.

The hard cases of halakhah are, I suggest, cases where our Jewish values come into conflict with each other. In some disputes, e.g., marriages during the ordinary days prior to Lag Ba' Omer, it may appear that there is simply a "stringent" and a "lenient" position, and that one can, by following the "stringent" position in a particular dispute, also encompass the "lenient" position: so why not just do the stringent?

But certainly there are disputes that plainly involve competing values, where there is no "stringent" vs. "lenient." Thus in the dispute in Yevamot, supra, Beit Shammai was seeking to fulfill, to the maximum, the mitzvah of marrying the childless brother's widow; while Beit Hillel was seeking to fulfill the conflicting value, in the scenario there, of equating the status of "rival" wives. Neither can be said to be more stringent or more lenient.

Similarly, many of the problems concerning the terminally ill present a conflict between the obligation to value life, and the obligation to minimize pain and preserve dignity.

And upon reflection, even the question of the *kashrut* of cheese involves a conflict between the value of keeping *kashrut* relatively simple and affordable, and the desire to build a fence around the law.

All of these conflicting values are Jewish values. Nor does the existence of conflicts prevent us from saying that some "solutions" are clearly inframarginal, and hence Jewishly wrong: e.g., active "mercy killing" of the terminally ill.

Furthermore, these competing values exemplify not just "principles," in the limited sense of that term discussed above, but also broader considerations of "policy," i.e., of our purpose as human beings, and the purpose and meaning of our covenant with God.

And these value conflicts emerge because of the *richness* of our tradition. See for example, the discussion in David Hartman's *A Living Covenant* as to how Maimonides and Nachmanides, basing themselves on two different conceptions of the covenant between God and Israel, and the role of miracles, came to two opposing views concerning medical treatment?[21] Maimonides

---

[21] David Hartman, *A Living Covenant* (New York: Free Press, 1985), ch. 10.

argued that medical intervention is as necessary as eating, and that just as it is man's role to generate and eat food, it is man's role to try to cure. Nachmanides, on the other hand, saw medicine as an accommodation for those unable to sufficiently trust in God and the ever-present reality of miracles. Both Maimonides and Nachmanides speak for authentically Jewish values; they just are in conflict, nor is there any deeper principle that can be invoked to reconcile them, or to rule in favor of one against the other.

One consequence of this value-pluralism is that one cannot "do" halakhah without doing theology—for, as the Maimonides/Nachmanides dispute noted above shows, our values emerge from our basic theologies.

Roth has fought vigorously for a separation between the two. But, as we have seen, to do so, Roth has to argue that sometimes precedents just run out, and judges then just exercise discretion. But that is not how we in fact *act*, either in the domain of law (as Dworkin has shown, see supra) or even in the domain of halakhah, as exemplified, e.g., in Dorff's discussion of how basic Jewish values can help us in resolving terminal-illness treatment matters.[22] It doesn't help, I suggest, to just say: there's a "black box" of discretion, and no reason and/or no way to open it up and look inside.

Plainly, there is *something* inside that our *posekim* are using to make their decisions in hard cases. And those "somethings" are, in the realm of halakhah, *values*. The more we try to articulate those values, and the value-conflicts that make cases hard, the better, I suggest, our decision-making is likely to be.

A related consequence of value-pluralism is that we need to change the way we *argue*. We need to stop arguing like lawyers, as if there is a right answer. Consider, for example, the debate over the ordination of women. The Conservative movement has proudly published a volume containing most of the competing responsa, intended as an exemplar of how our movement debates halakhic matters.[23] But *not one* of those responsa acknowledged that the opposing view was motivated by a competing but legitimate Jewish value! Consider matters from the viewpoint of one opposing ordination: Robert Gordis states that the entire concept that one can only act as an agent when one is herself obligated is completely nonsensical ("The original [premise] is dubi-

---

[22] See Elliot Dorf, Matters *of Life and Death* (Philadelphia: Jewish Publication Society, 1998). The weakness, to my mind, of Dorff's effort is his insistence on trying to shoe-horn halakhah into a legal framework. Doff tries, curiously, to maintain Roth's framework—even though to do so Dorff is forced to mischaracterize Dworkin. I suggest that if Dorff relocated his analysis *"below* the line," it would flow better, and be more compelling.

[23] Simon Greenberg, ed., On *the Ordination of Women as Rabbis* (New York: Jewish Theological Seminary, 1988).

ous"); Simon Greenberg argues that the opposition is relying on a sociological predicate that women should be kept barefoot and pregnant; Mayer Rabinowitz asserts that the entire concept of the *shaliah tzibbur*, and the restrictions relating thereto, are obsolete and irrelevant, now that we all have access to prayerbooks; and finally, even Roth argues that the key traditional text must be seen as at least somewhat ambiguous, and so we can and should apply the principle that "times have changed."[24] If I believe, however, that the traditional rule is clear, and alive, and meaningful, how am I supposed to react to these sorts of attacks?

I don't wish to get bogged down in the substance of this debate, which fortunately is now behind us. (And I wish to be dear that I *favor* ordination of women.) But, I do think that one can come to a pro-ordination position, via a variety of arguments, that would *recognize* that this was a "hard case" precisely because there were legitimate Jewish values being advocated on the other side, even if in the end I choose a pro-ordination position.

Value-pluralism in halakhah requires, I suggest, not just an acceptance of pluralism in *outcomes*, but also a pluralism in reasoning and discussion. Legal-style argumentation will produce at best only *sectarian* pluralism; only a different type of analysis can yield sharing pluralism.

Finally, notwithstanding that there is a broad range of values that are all legitimately Jewish, I do not believe that *all* values are legitimately Jewish. I do think that our characteristic shared concepts, like the "covenant," *constrain* our values, and force us into a realm of shared discourse. I recall reading, a couple years ago, in short succession, Eugene Borowitz, *Renewing the Covenant* UPS 1991); and Neil Gillman, *Sacred Fragments*, supra; and David Hartman, *A Living Covenant*, supra. What struck me most was the common ground towards which each seemed to be headed, and to which each felt *driven* by shared concepts such as "covenant."

E. Conclusion

Berlin's philosophy is, of course, not the last word in moral philosophy. He has had few followers to date, although the number may be growing.[25]

---

[24] Ibid., p. 54 (Gordis), p. 88 (Greenberg), p. 117 (Rabinowitz), pp. 143 and 146 (Roth).

[25] See, e.g., John Rawls, *Political Liberalism* (New York: Columbia University Press, 1993), p. 57 (citing to Berlin's arguments for pluralism). See also Ronald Dworkin et al., eds., *The Legacy of Isaiah Berlin* (New York: New York Review of Books, 2001). (I have tried to avoid here taking any side on the debate noted therein as to whether

Value-pluralism does, however, provide, I suggest, a coherent and reasonable philosophical basis for the sort of sharing halakhic pluralism that the Conservative movement is advocating. Moreover, the arguments developed here show that this sort of pluralism is not some add-on feature, adopted as a mere political flag by the Conservative movement, but is indeed deeply inherent in the nature of halakhah, given its domain and its place in our lives.

Berlin saw *all* of politics as characterized by moral incommensurables, or whether he believed that there was some neutral justification for a liberal state.)

By the Sweat of Your Brow

Approaching Kashrut from a Pluralistic Perspective[1]

David Greenstein

We begin with a series of snapshots taken across time, from earliest history to the present day:

Snapshot One—from the Torah

Adam and Eve have just transgressed their only mitzvah, a simple dietary law. They have violated their system of *kashrut* and are to be punished by God. See them tremble and perspire:

> And He said to Adam, "Because you listened to your wife and ate from the tree of which I specifically told you not to eat, the earth is cursed on your account. You will eat from it with pain for your whole life. [The earth] will grow thorns and this-tles for you and you will have to eat the grass of the fields. You will eat bread by the sweat of your brow, until you, yourself, return to the ground, for that is from whence you were taken. You are really just dust and you will go back to being dust. (Gen. 3:17–19)

From now on, the act of eating will not be automatic and thoughtless. It will be preceded by hard exertion. We will have to eat by our sweat (*zei'ah*).

Snapshot Two—from the Mishnah

A woman slaves over a hot cooking pot. She stands over the steaming caul-dron. We can almost see her sweat dripping into the food:

---

[1] An earlier version of this essay was presented to students at the Academy for Jewish Religion in spring 2002, when I served there as president and *rosh ha-yeshi-vah*.

[In the case of] a woman with hands that are ritually pure who stirs a pot that is ritually impure—her hands become ritually impure; if her hands were ritually impure and she was stirring a ritually pure pot—the pot becomes ritually impure. R. Yose says provided her hands dripped [sweat into the pot]. (Makhshirin 5:11)

The Mishnah teaches that if the woman is ritually impure, her sweat will defile the food in the pot because the steam rising from the pot creates enough of a contact with the food in the pot. Against R. Yose's opinion, we do not require that the sweat actually drops into the pot. Contact with the steam (*zei'ah*) is sufficient. As the Mishnah states earlier (*Ibid.*, 2:2), "*merḥatz teme'ah, zei'atah teme'ah*," (if the bath is impure, so is its steam).

Snapshot Three—14th Century Toledo, Spain

We see an older man and a younger man, father and son. The father, the Rosh, has made the difficult journey from the North, leaving his native German Jewish community to become a leading sage in the very different culture of Spanish Jewry. He has invested much time and sweat in teaching his sons to be great Torah sages as well. The Rosh's son asks him whether it is permissible to place a pan with milk below a pot of meat to cook them together in an oven. The Rosh replies:

> My son, may he live ... It seems to me that it is forbidden, and even in the case where it has already been done I would forbid the pot because the steam that rises from the pan is just the same as milk, as taught in the Mishnah in the second chapter of *Makhshirin* (2:2)—if the bath is ritually impure, its steam is ritually impure ... from all of this we learn that steam issuing from something is considered to be the same as that thing. It follows that the steam from a dairy pan is dairy ... (Responsa of Rabbenu Asher ben Yehiel [1250–1327], *K'lal* 20, par. 26)

In this responsum, the Rosh becomes the first authority to transfer the concept of *zei'ah* (steam, in this case) from the realm of ritual purity to the realm of *kashrut*. His view is accepted and elaborated upon by subsequent authorities.[1]

---

[2]   See *Shulḥan Arukh, Yoreh De'ah* 92:8.

Snapshot Four — Our Own Time

Students at the Academy for Jewish Religion, an independent rabbinical and cantorial seminary that draws its faculty from all streams of Judaism and whose student body spans a vast range of Judaic practitioners, receive the gift of a microwave oven. The microwave oven is more than a labor-saving device. It is the instrument heralding the beginning of our redemption. This device was invented to cancel the primeval curse placed on Adam and Eve. No longer will we have to sweat to eat our bread.

A Question

The students at the academy confronted a question: What is the proper *kashrut* policy to adopt regarding a microwave oven to be used by them in their own student lounge? The question could be taken in a number of ways. One way to frame it is to ask what the "normative *halakhah*" is in the case of a microwave oven. What rules govern its use? Are foods prepared in a microwave oven considered cooked foods in the same sense as foods prepared on a range or in a conventional oven? Is it possible to use the microwave oven for various foods, such as dairy *and* meat dishes, one after the other or simultaneously? Are there special procedures that must be followed for this? Is there a kashering process that must be followed? Can such a process be employed after the microwave oven has been used for heating a dish which is not kosher, in the opinion of this or the next user?

An Answer

Asked for a response to this problem, I offered the following: "Assuming the inside of the oven is kept clean, the main issue is the *zei'ah*. So you see, no matter how hard we have tried, the situation is that you can only eat '*be-zei'at apekha*' (playfully translated as, 'by the steam of your baking')."

Depending on the type of food, the heat level, and the duration of the heating, many foods will create steam in the microwave oven. If the food is dairy, the steam is considered dairy. If it is *parve*, the steam is *parve*. If it is a meat dish, the steam is considered meat. There is room to presume that the steam should impart this status to the inside walls of the microwave oven. (Although, it might still depend on how hot the steam really is.) In itself, the status of the oven is not a problem. But the problem arises with regard to the next food placed in the microwave oven. If a dairy food is heated after a meat dish, the steam from the dairy food may touch the walls of the oven, which may now be considered to have meat status. This contact contaminates the steam itself, so that, should this steam now fall back into the dairy dish, the food becomes a forbidden mixture of meat and milk.

Perhaps. Different people will weigh the significance of these concerns differently. In my view, if the microwave oven is kept clean — placing a plate or a napkin under the dish to be heated, lightly covering the top to prevent spattering, and cleaning the inside with a cleanser should it become dirty — there is sufficient basis to allow normal usage of a microwave oven for heating up foods without requiring that the oven be kashered after each time.

If someone wishes to kasher the microwave oven, for whatever reason, it is sufficient to place a cup of water in it and boil it long enough to fill the oven with steam.[3]

The Question, Again

This was my short answer. But, it was already apparent from the outset that more is at stake here than the clarification of a policy.

This question takes on a different complexion when we deal with a community comprised of individuals who have differing kashrut practices. Whose practice should be followed? Is the adoption of one standard of practice an implied rejection of the other standards? Is this a practical or political question only? Are the diverse opinions we hold the product of principle, tradition, temperament, convenience or some combination of these? Should such a combination of motives be accepted as legitimate for all, or is it to be considered treif, (unacceptable)? If our differing practices derive from different sets of principles — or different evaluations of the same principles — how can these differing viewpoints be brought into a dialogue with each other, and how may we succeed in adopting a standard faithful to that process?

In most settings that pursue pluralistic Jewish living, these questions are approached from a primarily practical perspective. What is to be gained by trying to think beyond the usual solutions? What might emerge from an attempt at

---

[3] For contemporary discussions about *kashrut* issues related to microwave ovens see, among others:

Ya'akov David Ulekh, *Sefer Sha'are David 'al Hil. Basar be-Ḥalav ve-Ta'arovet* (Bene Beraq: 1992), p. 80.

R. Moshe Morgan, *A Guide to the Laws of Kashrus—Sefer Re'aḥ Ha-Bosem*, vol. 2 (Lakewood, NJ: C.I.S. Publishers, 1989), pp. 68–74, 142–143.

Rabbi Binyomin Forst, *The Laws of Kashrus—Pitḥei Halakhah* (Brooklyn, NY: Mesorah Publications, 1993), *passim*.

Keeping Kosher: A Diet for the Soul (A Newly Revised Edition of The Jewish Dietary Laws by Samuel H. Dresner; *A revised guide based on* A Guide to Observance *by Seymour Siegel, David M. Pollack*), Robert Abramson, editor (New York: The Rabbinical Assembly/USCJ Commission on Jewish Education, 2000), pp. 55–56, 72.

thinking through these issues with a commitment to a pluralistic approach as the initial starting point?

The Usual Solution

The usual solution adopted in contexts in which Jews of various approaches to kashrut interact has been to accept a set of rules that can satisfy the Orthodox adherents involved. Even if some participants may not require these standards, or may view them with discomfort, or even disdain, the operative assumption is that everyone can certainly eat the food prepared and served under these rules, while any other rules would effectively exclude the Orthodox group from participation.

The practical advantage of this solution is clear. But the success of the solution depends on a significant asymmetry of response to the pluralistic range of kashrut observances and interpretations. It demands that all parties — other than the Orthodox — relinquish their principles regarding kashrut observance. In effect, it posits only one standard of kashrut.

This policy can be justified in a number of ways. Sometimes, it is true that non-Orthodox participants will state that they simply do not keep kosher. Then it is usually understood that there should be some deference shown to those who adhere to this traditional practice. But what if those non-Orthodox participants do claim to adhere to the laws of kashrut, but differ in their interpretation of what this means? Often enough, the numbers decide the issue. Since the Orthodox are more evident as observers of kashrut, with other adherents constituting a minority, the Orthodox standard may be adopted in the name of democracy. But this policy is adopted in other cases, in which non-Orthodox groups or institutions of some size are involved. In such cases, the way to explain this policy of deferring to Orthodox standards is that it indeed recognizes that there are various approaches to *kashrut*, but that these approaches may be graded according to ascending levels of stringency. It accepts a hierarchy of standards in which the Orthodox standard is the strictest and therefore, the highest, with all others considered inferior. Therefore, from a traditional perspective, all that is being asked of everyone else is to be a little stricter than usual, to be a *mahmir*, under these particular circumstances. But such a justification does not acknowledge that this very perspective already accepts the Orthodox approach as solely determinative.[4] It does not acknowledge the possibility that

---

[4] Recently the New York State statute regulating the sale of kosher products has been challenged by partners who own a kosher meat store under the supervision of a Conservative rabbi *(Yarmeisch v. Rubin)*. This is not the place to consider this case. But it is relevant to note that the law, formulated in 1915, identifies kosher food as that food "sanctioned by the orthodox *(sic)* Hebrew requirements." A supporter of the statute,

other approaches may not accept this hierarchical evaluation and may view Orthodox standards as unnecessary burdens of no halakhic or spiritual significance, or even as misstatements of Torah teachings. It recognizes that only the Orthodox have firm, immutable principles, while all others have values that can be compromised if necessary. More often than not, this ends up being the case, and it is decided that it is better to swallow one's own claims to authenticity in the face of a more intransigent claim for the sake of unity. This approach, however, is usually accompanied by some hurt feelings and resentment.

So is that the only way? Is it possible to develop an approach that respects the authenticity of all the various viewpoints? What follows is a preliminary investigation into this question.

Another Attempt at an Answer

We shall begin by outlining the basic elements of the traditional system of *kashrut* as they are taught in the Written and the Oral Torah. These teachings will give us some indications of possible meanings to be found in this system. It will emerge that besides the specific laws that are the subject of much learning and discussion in the sources, there is a constellation of values, concerns and tendencies that are rooted, as the Torah states, in pre-Sinaitic traditions and both can manifest themselves through the legal process and also influence the legal process. We will suggest that the approaches to *kashrut* developed by the various movements are each important and that each should be taken seriously because they're all sensitive to particular values or elements of the total constellation and because they all function as an important source of critique vis-à-vis the other approaches.

Basic Elements of Kashrut Before Sinai

The Torah is replete with laws regulating what, when and how food may be eaten. As mentioned already, the very beginning of the Torah teaches that the human condition as we know it derives from the inability of humans to abide by a simple dietary law. Adam and Eve are expelled from the Garden after violating the one law God commanded them: to refrain from eating of the Tree of

---

Assembly Speaker Sheldon Silver, is quoted as explaining that "the meaning of kosher has become synonymous with being according to Orthodox standards" ("State Kosher Laws: It's Up to the High Court," *The Jewish Week*, August 16, 2002, p. 16). The lawyer for the State, Nathan Lewin, argues further: "If you want to […] go by a Conservative standard, then don't call your product kosher" (Katherine Marsh, "Busting Chops," *legalaffairs*, Sept./Oct. 2002, online at www.legalaffairs.org).

Knowledge (Gen. 2:16–17).

There seem to be tantalizing allusions to a system of dietary laws at the beginning of the Noah story where God tells Noah to collect certain foods and edible animals (Gen. 6:21 and 7:2,8). When the Torah says that some animals are edible, is it referring to food taboos or to other criteria? In addition, while the concept of purity is introduced (some animals are *tahor* and some are not), the Torah does not explain what this means.

There is no ambiguity, however, at the story's end. The covenant renewed with Noah is centered on the prohibition against eating blood, a prohibition connected to the prohibition against murder itself (Gen. 9:4–6).

Later, the covenant with the ancestors of the Jewish people is made. The introduction of the name Israel, which will become the name of the people as a whole, occurs when Jacob struggles with a divine being who blesses him. This turning point in our sacred history has been marked by the Jewish people, the Torah tells us, through the adoption of a food taboo, the *gid ha – nasheh*, variously translated as the thigh or sciatic muscle, sinew or nerve (Gen. 32:32–33).

We see that, for the Torah, the adoption of food taboos is an expression of sacred consciousness, appropriate for marking our reverence for life or for commemorating pivotal beginnings in our histories as human beings and as Jews. Thus, the dietary laws operate on two planes of meaning: the universal/existential and the particular/national. The universal message endeavors to mediate between our elemental drive to consume other living beings for the sake of our continued vitality and survival, on the one hand, and the uniquely human recognition that our lives participate in a greater, even cosmic, ecology of life on the other, that we take our places in this world in the midst of others who also take their places in it. Therefore, Adam and Eve, by transgressing their law of *kashrut* (through undue assertion of self), literally lose their place in the world. The satisfaction of their, and our, need and drive to eat will be henceforth fraught with difficulty (requiring the utmost exertion of the self ("by the sweat of your brow"). *Kashrut* is the basic reminder that we are not alone in this world of needs and drives. *Kashrut* is a means of preparing human consciousness for the recognition of the Other, a recognition that is foundational to our very humanity.

The second level of meaning operates as an affirmation and consolidation of Jewish identity. Dietary laws played a role, from the outset, in our nation building, and then in national definition. The nationalist aspect of dietary laws is apparent at the very start of the history of the Jewish people as a liberated people under God's care. The liberation from Egypt is marked, while the Israelites are still in that land, by the introduction of positive and negative dietary commandments, the laws mandating the eating of the paschal foods and prohibiting *hametz* (Ex. 12:5–10, 15–20).

A bit later, after the miraculous redemption of Israel at the Red Sea, God cares for His newly acquired people by showering Israel with heavenly bread. Predictably, this gift of food is accompanied by restrictions. Furthermore, even before arriving at Sinai, when God introduces the sacred discipline of Shabbat, it too is accompanied by food restrictions specific to that holy day (Ex. 16:16–27). The food restriction reinforces the sanctity of the day.[5]

The fact that food restrictions may serve as national definers for other nations as well as for Israel is recognized by the Torah in the Joseph story, where dietary laws are used by the Egyptians as a reinforcement of their own national uniqueness:

> And they served him separately and them separately and the Egyptians eating with him separately, because the Egyptians could not eat bread with the Hebrews because it is an abomination to the Egyptians. (Gen. 43:32)

An aspect important to this nationalistic significance is clearly present here. This is the element of exclusion. Eating is not merely a survival strategy of the individual. It is a social activity. The forming of social groups is done, to some extent, by means of exclusion of outsiders. Thus, the mandated eating of the paschal lamb is a group activity of celebration and definition that entails the exclusion of the foreigner and the uncircumcised (Ex. 12:43–49).

We see that there is some tension between these two levels of meaning. The universal/existential message puts a limit on the individual and encourages recognition of the claims to life of others. The particularistic level of meaning reinforces a sense of identity by affirming one group while excluding all others. This tension is relevant to the development of the laws and practices of *kashrut* and the various attitudes toward it to this very day.

By examining all these instances that are mentioned in the Torah even before the legislation of the *kashrut* laws themselves, we have already encountered the basic themes, usages and meanings of these laws. We have seen absolute prohibitions on certain foods (blood and thigh sinew), regulations for preparation of foods and their consumption (paschal lamb, manna), circumstantial prohibitions of certain foods (leaven on Passover; the fruit of the Tree of Knowledge, perhaps), and regulations about the fitness of certain people to eat or not to eat certain foods. We have seen that these laws serve to regulate our most basic drives, as well as our desire to create moments of remembrance, celebration or

---

[5] The combination of national identity and Divine providence is found later in the book of Daniel, where Daniel and his three friends refuse to eat Babylonian food and insist on eating only vegetarian food, so as not to defile themselves. God helps them to thrive despite their paltry diet (Dan. 1:8–21).

sanctification in our lives or in our history, and to establish our sense of identity. The extensive treatment of dietary laws found in the rest of the Torah, in the part predominantly devoted to legal teachings, is an elaborate working out of a system that continues to embody these elements, already enunciated.

Pots and Pans and Holiness

What, then, is added by the Torah in its legal sections? The Torah's collection of laws (or, rather, collection of collections of laws) comprises much new detail, some new emphases and a new orientation. This new orientation is effected through the clear and explicit embedding of *kashrut* laws within the system of values that constitute Israel's way of holiness. Israel is commanded to follow laws of *kashrut* in order to be holy, as God is holy (Ex. 22:30).[6]

To be holy like God means at least this much: to take control of one's physical needs, drives and environment; to be able to see one's world and make appropriate distinctions; and to be able to accept limitations. These three elements enable the Israelite to serve God faithfully, thus drawing him or her closer to God. And, in some ways, to be like God.[7]

This emphasis on holiness is independent of the *kashrut* aspects of the cultic system and of the dietary laws relating to living in the land of Israel, arenas where holiness is an obvious factor. In going beyond those arenas of sacred behavior, the Torah further claims that the *kashrut* system is to be observed by every one of the people of Israel, everywhere, and at all times, as one component in the array of mitzvot that sanctify Israel.

As far as the details go, the Torah elaborates on which foods are kosher, that is, fit to eat, and which are not (Lev. 11; Deut. 14). It adds the prohibition against cooking a kid in its mother's milk (Ex. 23:19, 34:26; Deut. 14:21). But then there are vast areas of *kashrut* that are not at all explicit in the Torah—the slaughter and salting of meat, the mixing of milk and meat, and the general question of mixtures of forbidden and kosher foods together. These areas had to be developed by the Oral Torah.

The Sweat of the Oral Torah

The process whereby the Oral Torah develops these new areas is characterized by the insistence of the tradition that all gaps in the Torah's legal system be filled. Those gaps may exist because the Torah is silent concerning a particular matter (e.g., kosher slaughtering). But it may also exist because the Oral Law

---

[6] See also Lev. 11:43–47 and Lev. 20:25–26.

[7] God exhibits these qualities in the first two chapters of Genesis. But see note 19 below.

has a new worry that's not present in the Written Torah — and that new worry is worry itself. The Oral Tradition worries about the already existing concerns — the commandments and the prohibitions — of the Written Torah. Will they really be fulfilled? Will they be ignored or transgressed? What can be done to protect the Torah?

The human's self-generated propensity to sin is also acknowledged by the Written Torah. Indeed, the Written Torah sometimes voices concern that Israel may be led astray by foreign influences or by human nature itself. Such influences are to be considered pernicious. They should be avoided or eliminated. Its prophylactic solution is to have one look at *tzitzit* (Num. 15:39–40). But, in general, the Torah seems to assume that declaring something commanded or forbidden will suffice to produce acceptable compliance among the faithful.

The Oral Law, however, goes much further in its worry. It worries that the forbidden may somehow fall into the area of the permitted. And it worries that the faithful will not really maintain, execute and protect the commandments with sufficient care.

Herein lies a basic difference between the Written Torah and the Oral Torah. The Written Torah posits a clear dichotomy between the faithful and the faithless, between those who choose the Torah, thereby choosing blessing and life, and those who reject the Torah, thus choosing accursedness and death (Deut. 30:15,19). But the Oral Law sees things as being more complexly interconnected. The Written Torah believes that good and evil can be distinguished and kept separate. The great problem for the Oral Law is that in real life, these ingredients refuse to stay apart. Thus, the Oral Law's main worry is that the Torah will be violated not by its sworn enemies, but by ourselves, her sworn adherents — not necessarily out of rebelliousness and evil — but out of laziness, ignorance and forgetfulness. The life-ingredients of mitzvah (commandment) and 'aveyrah (transgression) refuse to stay apart. This is the problem of ta'arovet (the mixture of the prohibited with the permitted). The Oral Torah will try to prevent such intermingling of faithfulness and disobedience. It will seek to protect the Written Torah. This is the tradition's defining charge "va'asu seyag la-torah (make a fence around the Torah)" (Avot 1:1).[8]

---

[8]Sometimes the Oral Law teaches that expressions of this protective, expansive propensity are found in the Torah itself. The expansive prohibitions regarding meat and milk are justified by the Oral Law as being the Torah's own expression of utmost avoidance of anything related to the cooking of a kid in its mother's milk. Another possible example is the Torah's prohibition against eating leaven on the afternoon preceding Passover. (See *Sefer Ha-Hinnukh*, ed. Chavel, §487—"For the Torah makes a fence around it for us.") This follows Rambam's opinion. But Ramban (Gloss to *Sefer Ha-Mitzvot* Neg. #199) disagrees and does not enumerate this prohibition as a separate *mitzvah*. The Ramban seems uncomfortable with the idea that the Written Torah makes fences. (See also their dispute at Neg. #353, and see R. Yosef Engel's *Lekah*

We see this, as well, in the difference between the level of concern for mixtures in the Written Torah and in the Oral Torah. For the Written Torah it is sufficient to prohibit certain mixtures. These are the laws of *kil'ayim* (Lev. 19:19). But these laws apply to objects that are, like meat and milk, themselves permissible. The Torah simply outlaws the mixing of these two permissible items. But it does not concern itself with handling cases in which prohibited items, or these self-same prohibited mixtures, become mixed with other, permissible items. The presumption seems to be that such a mixture can be either prevented or rectified, or that they are of no concern at all. But such is not the approach of the Oral Torah. The problem of mixtures — mixtures of the permitted with the prohibited — occupies a large proportion of *hilkhot issur veheter* (laws of the forbidden and the permitted).

There is another instance in which the interplay between the Written Torah's and the Oral Torah's stated concerns create a new area of halakhic concern, an area directly relevant to our initial *kashrut* question, and that may be seen as paradigmatic of this very interplay and relationship. The area is the Torah's guidance regarding purging cooking utensils of impurity:

> And Eleazar the priest said to the army-men going to the war, "This is the set law of the Torah that God commanded to Moses. Only regarding the gold, silver, bronze, iron, tin and lead — anything that goes into fire — you shall pass through fire to become purified, provided it is purged through special waters, while anything that does not go into fire you should pass through water." (Num. 31:21–23)

It is noteworthy that the connection between taking a human life and keeping kosher, first made apparent at the covenant with Noah, unexpectedly reappears here, by the way the Tradition reads these verses — substituting the second issue for the first. Rather than reading these laws as mandating purification for soldiers returning from battle with their booty, and who are impure from coming in contact with the dead, the Oral Law reads these verses as having to

---

Tov, Klal 8, pp. 45b–48d, on this topic, from which it is possible to adduce additional examples of Ramban's refusal to see fences in the Written Torah.) This may be related to Ramban's mystical understanding of Torah, in which every precept has a theosophical and theurgical significance, and so, cannot be viewed as being engaged in human psychological issues. For Rambam, on the other hand, manipulation of the human and consideration of what the Torah can realistically mandate is a genuine concern for God, requiring Divine cunning. (See also, Josef Stern, *Problems and Parables of Law: Maimonides and Nah.manides on the Reasons for the Commandments* [New York: SUNY Press, 1998].) For an aggadic discussion of this, see *Avot dR. Natan*, A, Ch. 2 (Schechter, ed., p. 8), B, Ch. 1 (Schechter ed., p. 3).

do with making the pots and pans of the Midianites kosher (M. Avodah Zarah 5:12, B. Avodah Zarah 75b).

The Torah itself had already used the terms for ritual purity and impurity to refer to kosher and non-kosher foods. Just as ritually impure objects could infect other objects and persons through proximity and touch, so, too, forbidden food becomes more than an object of prohibition. The object is seen to have the power to influence other objects as well. But this power does not principally reside in the tactile dimension. This power will persist even after the object itself is no longer present. Since the object prohibited is food, its power must reside in its taste. In advancing this reading, the Oral Law established one of the basic principles of *kashrut*: "*ta'am ke-'ikkar,* (the taste of a food is like its essence)" (B. Pesaḥim 44b).

The process through which the Oral Torah accomplished this new teaching — and so many others — is both creative and constraining, expansive and exclusionary. What is the motive behind this great effort to enlarge the Torah's purview, to encompass ever widening experiential horizons, while simultaneously filling these newly ramified spaces with restrictions, prohibitions and demands? In the best cases, the motivation is the pursuit of *kedushah,* as explained by Ramban in Lev. 19:1, and as Rava says (B. Yeva – mot 20a), "*kadesh 'atzmekha ba-muttar lekha* (sanctify yourself through what is permitted to you)." The Oral Torah is not merely a baroque legalistic system, it is the faithful, continued expression of the Written Torah's essential contribution to its pre-Sinaitic traditions — the development of a way of holiness through which one may become holy like God. To make sure that one is doing this, one must worry.

Worrying about a Microwave Oven

Returning to the cases of the pots and pans, we see that the Oral Torah created an entirely new realm for worry: The realm of mixtures. This includes not only mixtures of objects but of things more abstract — of the essences or derivatives of these objects (i.e., their tastes).

How might taste be transferred? The basic method is through cooking. Just as heat is transferred from the fire to the pot to the food, so is the taste. It is released and transferred from the food into the pot. This taste will persist in the pot, so that the next time the pot is sufficiently heated the taste will transfer to another food. Kashering a pot is simply the application of heat to the pot such that it releases the taste it has absorbed from the forbidden source, *ke-vol'o kakh polto* (B. Pesaḥim 30a, 74a–b). (We will ignore the case of *noteyn ta'am lifgam* [giving a spoiled taste].)

We have reached the first set of principles in traditional *kashrut* that has bearing on our case of the microwave oven. What is the status of the microwave oven in which a certain food is heated? If, for example, a cup of milk is heated in the microwave oven, is it now dairy, and therefore, precluded from use for the heating of meat foods?

The answer, so far, should be "No." The microwave oven is not the vessel in which the milk is being cooked. It is merely the container in which the glass of milk sits. Furthermore, the milk is not heating up by virtue of being in contact with the surface of the microwave oven, or with the heat within it. On the contrary, whatever heat is generated in the oven is emanating from the milk, which has been heated through the waves focused on it.

However, this answer does not worry enough. There is more to worry about. What if there is spattering or spillage? What if the taste could be transmitted by the vapor of the food? We have seen that Rabbenu Asher took these worries to heart, establishing the concept of *zei'ah* in *kashrut*. Others took these worries still further, so that, in all honesty, I must say that the guidelines I laid out before are unacceptable to most authorities of *halakhah*. Some consider the transfer from the food to the oven through steam to be a certainty (since the oven is closed).[9] Some forbid using a microwave oven for more than one kind of food. Some require a longer, more complicated process of kashering. Some do not believe a microwave oven can be kashered at all.[10] All would agree that I have not worried enough about these things.[11]

Rejection or Critique?

Of course, I am not alone in this. There is by now a long history of dissatisfaction with traditional determinations of *kashrut*, including outright rebellion against the entire system. I suggested before that these alternative approaches and commitments should be taken seriously, and not be dismissed as mere rejections of the tradition. If we examine Reform, Conservative and Reconstructionist statements about *kashrut* we should find that they uphold certain values important in *kashrut* while opposing or ignoring others. In addition, by taking those positions seriously as critiques, rather than as rejections of *kashrut*, we allow ourselves to entertain the possibility that *kashrut* is not a self-sufficient concept, but is a complex of values brought into dynamic interaction. As noted before, these values can be summarized as follows:

---

[9] See R. Akiva Eiger to *S.A. Y.D.* 92:8.

[10] See sources cited in note 3, above.

[11] The RaBaD issues a striking attack against a legitimate lenient ruling, accusing those who hold that opinion of failing to value worry: "How ugly it is that the worry about eating forbidden foods has left them because of its nullification in the majority substance." (Quoted by *Maggid Mishnah* and *Kesef Mishneh* to Rambam *Yad, Hil. Ma'akhalot 'Asurot* 3;16. Cited in Elliot Dorff, "The Use of All Wines," in *Proceedings of the Committee on Jewish Law and Standards of the Conservative Movement 1986–1990* [New York: The Rabbinical Assembly, 2001], p. 212.)

The laws of *kashrut* serve to regulate and channel our most basic drives, as well as our desire to create — in our lives or in our history — moments of remembrance, celebration or sanctification; they also establish our sense of identity. These values are commanded by God because they are important for the realization of our covenantal relationship with God.

When formulated in these general terms, the constellation of values outlined above is pretty much held in common by all denominations. It is the particular ratio of one value's weight to another's that may be determined differently through the different approaches identified with the various contemporary denominations. But will this commonality of discourse hold as the discussion deepens? As the conversation proceeds, it will emerge that there are many important issues of contention and critique. However, we must allow the flow of critique to travel in every direction. It is important to realize that, if these approaches are seen as critiques, then the prevalent Orthodox practice must be allowed to stand in critique of the other approaches as well. Thus, all positions should be seen as existing in conversation with each other.

Still, the starting point for such a conversation would seem to entail the acceptance of the Torah's insistence on a number of *kashrut* laws, rather than by assuming that there is no warrant for any such set of laws. It would require a radical critique, indeed, to advocate dispensing with *kashrut* altogether. Yet, such a radical critique was advanced by classical Reform. The Pittsburgh Platform (1885) boldly states:

> We hold that all such Mosaic and Rabbinical laws as regulate diet, priestly purity and dress originated in ages and under the influence of ideas altogether foreign to our present mental and spiritual state. They fail to impress the modern Jew with a spirit of priestly holiness; their observance in our days is apt rather to obstruct than to further modern spiritual elevation.[12]

The Reform critique is not merely a rejection based on charging *kashrut* with irrelevant anachronism. Rather, the claim is that *kashrut* does not work to promote holiness for the modern Jew, though it may have served that purpose in the past. In effect, though, this claim to modernity is really an acknowledgment that we must finally accept the validity of Jesus' critique of the Judaism of his time:

---

[12] W. Gunther Plaut, *The Growth of Reform Judaism* (World Union for Progressive Synagogues, 1965), p. 34. Plaut records (p. 36) that this paragraph was adopted unanimously.

> On another occasion he called the people and said to them,
> "Listen to me, all of you, and understand this: nothing that
> goes into a person from the outside can defile him; no, it is
> the things that come out of a person that defile him." When
> he had left the people and gone indoors, his disciples ques-
> tioned him about the parable. He said to them, "Are you as
> dull as the rest? Do you not see that nothing that goes into
> a person from the outside can defile him, because it does not
> go into the heart but into the stomach, and so goes out into
> the drain?" By saying this he declared all foods clean. (Mark
> 7:14–19)[13]

Such a radical statement does not allow any validity at all to the concept
of *kashrut*. Its concept of holiness shares no common ground with the ancient
dietary system. Many contemporary Reform thinkers have backed away from
such radicalism, but have not found a clear alternative. Thus the discussion
about *kashrut* in the *ḥumash* of the Reform movement struggles with this issue:

> The spokesmen of Reform Judaism … do not regard such
> provisions as the literal word of God; they hold that they are
> no longer religiously meaningful and therefore need not be
> followed. But they have no quarrel with those who chose to
> observe the dietary laws. Yet conscientious Reform Jews can-
> not disregard the subject altogether … In a larger sense, we
> must rethink the whole question of eating, in view of our
> frequent statements that Judaism deals with every aspect of
> human life … This is not to argue that we should revert to
> the laws of Leviticus, chapter 11; it means only that there are
> many religious aspects to the question of what we eat and
> how much, and of what there is for others to eat.[14]

The sense of unease is palpable. The idea that the realm of eating should be
left alone by Judaism is untenable to Rabbi Plaut. But it is also impossible to
"revert" to the biblical system. One suspects that this term does not merely sig-
nify a return to a previously held practice. It seems rather to convey a conviction
that to practice this system would be to betray the essentially progressive char-

---

[13] As translated in *The Oxford Study Bible*, edited by M. Jack Suggs, Katherine
Doob Sackenfeld and James R. Mueller (New York: Oxford University Press, 1992),
p. 1313.

[14] *The Torah: A Modern Commentary*, edited by W. Gunther Plaut (New York: Union
of American Hebrew Congregations, 1981), p. 813.

acter of Judaism. But if that system cannot be saved, what purchase is available on sanctifying eating? Rabbi Plaut speculates about issues of vegetarianism, the world food supply, and eating disorders. He also finally admits that "adherence to *kashrut* meant for many people, not merely self-discipline, but real sacrifice." But it is not clear whether this sacrifice is being valorized as an act of moral grandeur or of religious devotion.

A discussion more hospitable to *kashrut* observance is found in the Reform guide, *Gates of Mitzvah*. Various options are offered to any person who might freely choose to adopt elements of traditional *kashrut*. Various reasons are offered for why such a choice might make sense, most of them centering on Jewish identification. It is also acknowledged that *kashrut* may be a means of attaining *kedushah* (holiness). Finally, the guide concludes:

> One or more of these reasons as well as others might influence certain Reform Jews to adopt some of the dietary restrictions as a mitzvah, while others may remain satisfied with the position articulated in the Pittsburgh Platform. However, the fact that kashrut was for so many centuries an essential part of Judaism, and that so many Jews gave their lives for it, should move Reform Jews to study it and to consider carefully whether or not it would add *kedushah* to their homes and lives.[15]

Earlier, the essay explains that "The range of options available to the Reform Jew is from full observance of the biblical and rabbinic regulations to total nonobservance. Reform Judaism does not take an 'all or nothing' approach."[16] It should be pointed out that this range of options is certainly not limited to Reform Jews. Everyone has this range of options. What the statement really means is that, from a Reform perspective, any of these options is equally legitimate. But then one would have to wonder why anyone should choose to practice *kashrut*. The final answer of this guide is that the historical allegiance of the Jewish people to *kashrut* should be felt by everyone as a factor forcing them to consider adopting "some of the dietary restrictions as a mitzvah" because they may "add *kedushah* to their homes and lives." The range of options has been narrowed. No longer is acceptance of the entire *kashrut* system included as an option. Why is this? Apparently, the problem is not with *kashrut* itself, since it

---

[15] *Gates of Mitzvah: A Guide to the Jewish Life Cycle,* edited by Simeon J. Maslin, Illustrated by Ismar David (New York: CCAR, 1979), p. 133. It may be noted that the guide to home observance, *Gates of the House,* does not include any discussion on *kashrut.*

[16] *Ibid.,* p. 132.

is acknowledged, against the claims of the Pittsburgh Platform, that practicing *kashrut* can bring holiness into one's life. The problem with adopting the entire system must be that this would violate a cardinal value of Reform Judaism: personal autonomy.

Any commitment to systematic observance is a ceding of autonomy to the authority and integrity of the system itself. Such an abdication of autonomy is unacceptable for this Reform guide. To select "all" is not to exercise one's power of selection. But, as explained by Rabbi Arthur J. Lelyveld, once the Bible is seen as a human document, "we necessarily become selective, for there are points in Scripture at which man has broken through to an understanding of the highest, while there are also points that preserve primitive practices, anachronisms, or injunctions that long ago became obsolete."[17] Thus, in the elevation of the principle of personal autonomy, we can discern an implicit critique of *kashrut*. We can hear the echoes of the Pittsburgh Platform in its charges of primitivism, anachronism and obsolescence.

In the last few years a noticeable shift toward acceptance of ritual has become pronounced in Reform circles. So it is not surprising that a prominent Reform rabbi recently urged the possibility of complete observance of *kashrut*. Still, the abdication of one's own autonomy is justified not for the sake of greater holiness, but in the name of Jewish continuity. Thus, Rabbi David Forman writes:

> By maintaining a respect for kashrut and incorporating some, if not all, of the rules governing a kosher home into our life, we have a good chance of holding on to our Judaism and contributing to the perpetuation of the Jewish people.[18]

Kashrut America

While such an argument does not advance any new critique or appreciation of the practice of *kashrut*, a different line of thinking is expressed by another important Reform figure. Rabbi Lawrence Kushner attempts to rethink *kashrut* from another angle. In an interview some years back, Rabbi Kushner mentioned his personal experimentation with traditional observance and his subsequent abandonment of it:

> I remain very respectful of traditional observance, but I no longer think it's the way for me, and I suspect it's not going

---

[17] Ibid, "*Mitzvah:* The Larger Context," p. 111.
[18] "How *Kashrut* Can Help With Continuity Crisis," *Forward,* Aug. 17, 2001, p. 15.

to be the way for many other Jews. *Kashrut* as it's currently practiced is putting itself out of business.

Because it's so extreme?

Yes, because no matter how kosher you are, there's always someone who won't eat in your kitchen. I'd like to see a reasonable standard of *kashrut* defined for liberal Jews. There is more than one way to be a serious and observant Jew. [...] We need a vocabulary to describe, not varying levels—that implies better and worse—but different ways of expressing the sacred in our lives. Because there is no name for this mode of *kashrut*, it exists in a sort of black market. What we ought to do is take ourselves seriously enough to give it a name.

What name would you give it?

Kashrut America, say. If we put this out there and give it a name, I think a lot of people who would like to keep kosher would. There's an obsessive-compulsive aspect to traditional *kashrut* that doesn't seem to have anything to do with what God wants, it's just obsessive behavior. How beautiful it would be if someone could say, I observe *kashrut* America.[19]

Rabbi Kushner's critique has a number of components. He denies that holiness can be attained only through a stringent traditional practice of *kashrut*. His critique can be analyzed conceptually, but its main thrust seems to operate, rather, on the behavioral plane. He notices two problems with the traditional practice of keeping kosher. One is the communal tension created by the fragmentation that results from exclusivist claims to *kashrut* standards. The result is that people will not eat in each other's homes. Those who will not eat in another's house are said to abide by a higher level of *kashrut*. This phenomenon is the subject of much humor in Orthodox and traditionalist circles, humor that betrays a considerable degree of unease among some, but by no means all, of the members of the community.

What is the source of this unease? After all, argue those who adopt this approach without qualms, is it not accepted that one should take precautions to avoid any possibility of eating forbidden foods? The problem is that more and more people feel that such a possibility in the *kashrut*-observing community is overly exaggerated. Instead, the phenomenon seems based on a different fundamental proposition: that it is holier *not* to eat in someone's house than to eat there. Such a conception of the sacred does violence to our sense of the meaning

---

[19] William Novak, "A Conversation with Lawrence Kushner," *Kerem* 6, 5759/1999, pp. 24–25.

of *kedushah* in two ways. It accepts self-limitation as the defining characteristic of *kedushah*. Hence, more self-limitation is more holy. Self-limitation is a problematic value in today's world. Still, it can be advocated as a real value of the tradition. The problem is exacerbated, however, because paradoxically, while using a justification that appeals to the value of self-negation, the current stringent practice also appropriates the value-charge of *kedushah* — the fact that this value is weighted heavily in our scale of values — for elitist purposes of self-promotion.[20] For whatever reasons, modern sensibilities are acutely attuned to, and revolted by, this kind of self-serving paradox.

Another powerful observation of Rabbi Kushner is that the emphasis on stringency in *kashrut* observance has a damaging effect on those most genuinely committed to it. He describes this effect as "an obsessive-compulsive aspect to traditional *kashrut* that doesn't seem to have anything to do with what God wants, it's just obsessive behavior." However, we may wish to formulate what it is that God really wants,[21] and despite Freud's contention that all ritual is akin to obsessive-compulsive behavior,[22] we would agree that God does not want us to turn into obsessive-compulsives.

Thus, Rabbi Kushner's critique rejects the traditional practice of *kashrut* as destructive of the very value that we understand *kashrut* should promote, holiness, and of the context in which this value should be lived, holy community.

---

[20] Maimonides, in *Hil. Tum'at Okhlin* 16:12, has a forceful expression of the concept of *Kedushah* as elitist separation. I. Twersky (*Introduction to the Code of Maimonides* [*Mishneh Torah*], New Haven and London: Yale University Press, 1980), p. 435 points out that such an appreciation of piety is absent from the *Guide*. A different conception of the essence of *kedushah* is taught by Shimon Shkop, in his introduction to his magnum opus of talmudic analysis, *Sha'are Yosher* (Warsaw, 1928): "If we say that the essential meaning of holiness that God demands of us in this commandment of 'You shall be holy [for I, God your Almighty, am Holy]' (Lev. 19:2) is to distance ourselves from permitted enjoyments *(motarot)*, such holiness has no relationship at all with God, may He be blessed. Therefore it appears, in my humble opinion, that within this commandment is included the very basis and root of the purposeful goal of our lives, which is that all our service and toil should always be dedicated to the good of the collectivity *(le-tovat ha-klal)*, that we not avail ourselves of any act or motion, benefit or enjoyment unless it have some aspect that is for the good of those other than ourselves *(le-tovat zulatenu)*... . In this manner the notion of this holiness does imitate the holiness of the Blessed Creator to a small degree. For as with the act of the Holy Blessed One in the entire Creation, as well as in each and every second that He sustains the world, all His actions are dedicated to the good of that which is other than Himself, so it is His will, may He be blessed, that our actions should always be dedicated to the good of the collectivity and not to one's own benefit."

[21] See B. Makkot 23b–24a for the various citations to Micah 6:8 and others.

[22] See his 1907 essay, "Obsessive Acts and Religious Practice," printed in (among other places) *Character and Culture*, edited by Philip Reiff (New York: Collier Books, 1963), pp. 17–26.

What, then, would count as a healthy approach to *kashrut*, in particular, and to holiness in general?

It is significant that the name Rabbi Kushner chooses for his suggested solution — echoing Rabbi Stephen S. Wise's phrase, *Minhag* America — is *Kashrut* America. Rabbi Kushner's approach implies that the reinforcement of community identity that is basic to *kashrut* is a more congenial foundation for the modern pursuit of the sacred. Because today's community is so variegated, any practice meant to promote group identity would have to be inclusive of group variations. It would have to accept and respect freedom. He does not develop fully what this approach would really entail, but it is clear that he recognizes that it is in America that such an approach has become possible. The influence of America on contemporary thinking about *kashrut* is explicit and marked in the literature emanating from the Conservative and Reconstructionist movements, as well.

Holiness and the Good Life

Despite its European, German-Jewish background, the Conservative movement is essentially an American Jewish phenomenon, greatly influenced by the American experience and by American values.[23][22] This has informed Conservative discussions about Judaism in general and *kashrut* observance in particular. Conservative scholars and halakhic authorities have grappled with many questions relating to *kashrut*. On a number of issues, the Conservative stance has been more lenient than the stances adopted by the Orthodox community. One example of this can be seen regarding the status of wines not having a *hekhsher* (rabbinic certification of *kashrut*). Whatever the practice may be among individual Orthodox Jews, Orthodox authorities are unanimous in regarding such wines as forbidden because of the long-standing rabbinic prohibition against all wines of non-Jewish provenance *(stam yeynam)*. In the latest Conservative responsum about this question, however, Rabbi Elliot Dorff arrives at a very different conclusion.[24] He rules that, though kosher (and especially Israeli) wines should be used for sacramental purposes, and though there may be some who might wish to be stringent because of the way some wines are processed, ultimately these wines should not be considered non-kosher. That is, Rabbi Dorff advocates the abandonment of the old *issur* (prohibition) of *stam yeynam*. The lines of argument that led him to this conclusion are numerous. But Rabbi Dorff's main contention is that the two-fold worry that served as the basis for

---

[23] Reconstructionism emerged from Conservative Judaism, in part, by insisting that this American influence be explicitly celebrated and elevated to a core value.

[24] Elliot Dorff, "The Use of All Wines," in *Proceedings of the Committee on Jewish Law and Standards of the Conservative Movement 1986–1990* (New York: The Rabbinical Assembly, 2001), pp. 203–226.

the ancient prohibition must be rejected. *Stam yeynam* was prohibited out of a concern that social interaction with non-Jews be prevented, so as to prevent intermarriage. In Rabbi Dorff's view, the ultimate goal of the *issur* is not attainable through these means. He denies that practicing such a prohibition will have any effect on the rate of intermarriage. More important, however, is his judgment about the intermediate goal of the *issur* — the inhibition of social interaction between Jews and non-Jews. On this Rabbi Dorff writes, "In keeping with our acceptance of the conditions of modernity, we in the Conservative movement would undoubtedly hold that, short of inter – marriage, Jews *should* have social and business contact with non-Jews."[25] Rabbi Dorff has substituted the old value of Jewish insularity with a new, American, value of Jewish integration in society.

While Conservative advocates are not bashful about accepting the proposition that Judaism must accommodate itself to the American scene, they insist that this is not a new invention of theirs; rather, Judaism's integrity has always depended on its adjustment to whatever might have been the context of the day. One attempt to root this value in traditional Jewish philosophical thought was made by Rabbi Louis Finkelstein in 1929. He approvingly cites Hasdai Crescas' analysis of the four-fold purpose of religion: "It endeavors to bring about perfection of human conduct, a knowledge of the truth, the physical enjoyment of life, and the happiness of the soul — spiritual happiness, as we should say in our modern terminology."[26] He then proceeds to try to evaluate how well contemporary Judaism meets these goals. He is satisfied with the contribution of modern Judaism to the spiritual happiness of the Jew, especially as it fosters intellectual fulfillment, ethical conduct and a relationship with the Divine. He writes, "The observant Jew still finds in prayer opportunity for communion with God; our ethics are still ideals the world is struggling to attain; and our understanding of reality is still most divinely true and most humanly effective."[27] However, he does find Judaism, as it has developed into modern times, lacking in one respect:

> The real difficulties that we face in our religious life center about our Judaism's underestimation of Crescas's fourth

---

[25] *Ibid.*, p. 217 (emphasis in the original text).

[26] Louis Finkelstein, "The Presidential Message: 'Traditional Law and Modern Life'," in *Proceedings of the Committee on Jewish Law and Standards of the Conservative Movement 1927–1970,* edited by David Golinkin (Jerusalem: The Rabbinical Assembly and The Institute of Applied Halakhah, 1997), Vol. I, p. 25. (See Hasdai Crescas, *Or Adonai,* II:6 (Jerusalem, 1963, p. 51ff).

[27] *Ibid.*, p. 27. This essay cannot attempt to examine the cogency of his assessment.

element in spiritual happiness, the satisfaction of physical needs and desires. In thinking of spiritual happiness we tend to forget, what Crescas is so careful to stress, the important part played in it by the satisfaction of natural impulses and desires. Spiritual happiness is the crown of human bliss, but the foundation is more earthly and material. Starving men do not readily rise into the full joy of Divine communion; "the shekhinah does not rest on one who is in sorrow," says the ancient rabbinic maxim.[28]

The desire to rectify this failing has influenced many discussions, proposals and rulings in the Conservative movement's struggle to define a modern traditionalist Judaism. And it is evident with regard to how Conservative authorities have dealt with many questions pertaining to *kashrut*. For example, aside from Rabbi Dorff's *teshuvah* on wines already mentioned, Conservative *halakhah* has been liberal in using the rabbinic concept of *davar ḥadash* (a new thing something originally non-kosher but now acceptable as kosher because it has been transformed to a degree beyond what is officially accepted in Orthodox circles). The Conservative movement has thereby decided that all cheeses made with rennet, as well as mono- and di-glycerides and pepsin are kosher, even without supervision.[29] This tendency toward leniency has been attacked by Orthodox critics, just as it has been defended by Conservative rabbis as simply being the result of independent halakhic analysis.[30] Occasionally the argument

---

[28] *Ibid.*, p. 28.

[29] See Isaac Klein, *A Guide to Jewish Religious Practice* (Supplement by Joel Roth) (New York: JTS, 1992), pp. 306–307, 525 (Roth). Klein's arguments are explained in detail in his *Responsa and Halakhic Studies* (Ktav, 1975), pp. 43–74. See, also, the responsa in *Proceedings of the Committee on Jewish Law and Standards of the Conservative Movement 1980–85* (New York: The Rabbinical Assembly, 1988), pp. 181–190, and *Responsa 1991–2000: The Committee on Jewish Law and Standards of the Conservative Movement,* edited by Kassel Abelson and David J. Fine (New York: The Rabbinical Assembly, 2000), pp. 98–100.

[30] See, as a recent example, the critique by Avi Shafran, "The Conservative Lie: Proclaiming Fealty to Jewish Law, Conservative Leaders Have Trampled It," *Moment* (February 2001). He writes: "The law of probability leads us to expect that there will be times when the halachic result will be more lenient than one might expect, and other times when it will be more demanding. Tellingly, though, and practically without exception, Conservative 'reinterpretations' of Jewish law have entailed permitting something previously forbidden ... That is a clear sign not of objectivity but of agenda, of a drastically limited interest in what the Torah wants from us and a strong resolve to use it as a mere tool to promote personal beliefs" (p. 54). Similarly, at a conference on halakhah at Hebrew Union College, March, 2001, an Orthodox participant challenged Elliot Dorff to name any decision in which Conservative authorities had opted for a more stringent, rather than lenient, approach. Dorff pointed to a recent decision

made since the Haskalah is reiterated:

> Unfortunately, the walls of the halakhic edifice have cracked and the building is collapsing. It is impossible for us to tolerate any further heaping on of stringencies. We must strengthen the halakhic edifice according to the ways of our Sages, of blessed memory, and with logical thinking, without dealing with worries and stringencies.[31]

This recognition of the pressure of modern times on the basic assumptions we use for halakhic deliberations has been expressed quite strikingly with regard to discussions about the determination of standards for any Conservative observance of *kashrut*. Explaining the tension experienced by any practicing Conservative Jew, Rabbi Gilbert Kollin posits that "we must bear in mind that Conservative Judaism, *on every level*, accepts social integration as a *sine qua non*."[32] Because this *modus vivendi* has been accepted, not only as a fact of life, but as a value, the compromise of the traditional halakhic system, which did not previously operate with social integration as a value, becomes necessary. Rabbi Kollin characterizes such compromises, not being based on a reformulation of *halakhah*, as "*ad hoc* adjustments regulated only by our conscience."[33] Rabbi Kollin then expresses great admiration for the commitment evinced by individuals who practice some kind of *kashrut* observance, however imperfect. In this he comes very close to Rabbi Kushner's description of *Kashrut* America. But Rabbi Kollin is not content to appreciate the existence of a range of personal choice; he insists on the necessity for a reformulation of *halakhah*. However, he does not offer one.[34]

A particularly clear instance of compromise can be found regarding the Conservative position on eating in non-kosher restaurants. Rabbi James M.

---

condemning the hoisting and shackling of animals prior to slaughter. One response to Shafran that addresses this question is by Samuel Fraint, "The Truth about Conservative Judaism," *Moment*, June 2001, especially pp. 56, 65. On these exchanges, see Shaul Magid, "Walking Softly on/with the Law: Apologetic Thinking and the Orthodox/Conservative Debate," in *Conservative Judaism* 54:1 (Fall 2001), pp. 29–52.

[31] Benjamin Kreitman, "*Ha-im Bereḥat Seḥiyah Kesherah Le-Miqvah*," *Proceedings of the Committee on Jewish Law and Standards of the Conservative Movement 1927–1970*, edited by David Golinkin (Jerusalem: The Rabbinical Assembly and The Institute of Applied Halakhah, 1997), Vol. III, p. 221 (Hebrew).

[32] Gilbert Kollin, "Kashrut in the Modern Age," in *Conservative Judaism* 20:1 (Fall, 1965), p. 56 (emphasis in the original text).

[33] *Ibid.*, p. 57.

[34] For an attempt to set forth a concept of halakhah and *kashrut* that would also allow for individual choice, see Hershel Matt, "Kashrut in Conservative Judaism," in *Conservative Judaism* 12:1 (Fall, 1957), pp. 34–38.

Lebeau writes:

> One of the more common problems that face us as we strive to maintain our observance of the dietary laws is the need, or desire, to eat outside our homes. Many of us travel frequently for business or pleasure.... May we eat in a non-Kosher restaurant and still observe *Kashrut*? This question has been debated by rabbis in the Rabbinical Assembly, the organization of Conservative rabbis, for over forty years. It seems that a majority of the rabbis in the Conservative Movement approve of eating dairy or parve foods in non-Kosher facilities.... One of the reasons that Conservative rabbis would generally permit this leniency is that they no longer accept the restriction against eating food prepared by non-Jews. Such a restriction was based on the fear that assimilation and intermarriage were necessarily caused by Jews frequenting non-Jewish establishments. In addition, many rabbis have carefully investigated the operation of restaurants and are able to offer guidance that allows Jews to eat non-meat products in them without violating Jewish law.... Let us state clearly, that this position results from the special needs that Jews face in our modern world. Many rabbis feel that if we did not have guidelines that allow Jews to observe dietary laws outside their homes (even in non-Kosher restaurants), we would be discouraging the overall observance of Kashrut.[35]

Rabbi Lebeau struggles with two sets of warring claims. The claims of strict adherence to traditional *kashrut* are at war with the community's refusal to follow them. In order to preserve basic adherence to the system, the system must be more flexible. In addition, in order to preserve the integration of the Jew into the modern world, it is necessary to make some adjustments in the system. Either way, the system as traditionally developed must change in the face of sociological factors. This sensitivity to social realities was most emphatically developed by the Reconstructionist movement.

---

[35] James M. Lebeau, *The Jewish Dietary Laws: Sanctify Life*, edited by Stephen Garfinkel (New York: United Synagogue of America, Department of Youth Activities: 1983), pp. 103–105. And see his further discussion, pp. 139–140.

Go See What the Folk are Doing[36]

As in so many other areas of Jewish living, Rabbi Mordecai M. Kaplan subjected the practice of *kashrut* to sustained examination and rethinking. Rabbi Kaplan considered *kashrut* as one of the folkways of the Jewish people. In this way, he advocated the overturning of the traditional concern to avoid transgression. In the traditional Jewis37

h legal system prohibitions outnumber "positive behests."[37] Folkways function, rather, as positive experiences, conducive to a meaningful life. By turning Jewish practice into a set of folkways, Rabbi Kaplan hoped to create a more positive lifestyle for the Jew. This would have important implications regarding *kashrut* observance:

> "Once these practices lose their character as laws and become folkways, Jews will be able to exercise better judgment as to the manner of their observance. There need not be the feeling of sin in case of occasional remissness, nor the self-complacency which results from scrupulous observance."[38]

Rabbi Kaplan's conception of *kashrut* presents itself as rational and practical. As Rabbi Richard Hirsh explains it, "Mordecai Kaplan's teaching that the ritual commandments are folkways designed to effect identification with the Jewish people led to an understanding that *kashrut* can be observed in some areas but not others, without inconsistency. As long as the level of observance supports and strengthens identification with the Jewish people, it is a functionally appropriate level of observance."[39]

Because *kashrut* was a folkway designed to promote Jewish peoplehood, Rabbi Kaplan was convinced that its utility for the Jewish people was limited to its practice in the Jewish home. The benefit from this approach was that there would no longer be any restriction on the Jew's involvement in the world through the artificial boundaries set up by *kashrut*. But Rabbi Kaplan was not able to eliminate all tension from the system since he also advocated the observance of *kashrut* as a way of "transforming the act of eating, as it were, into

---

[36] B. Berahot 45a

[37] *Judaism as a Civilization: Toward a Reconstruction of American-Jewish Life* (New York: Schocken Books, 1934, 1967), p. 439.

[38] *Ibid.* p. 441. (Italics in the original.) In a note to this passage, Rabbi Kaplan refers to a late 19th-century German work by A. Weiner for specific suggestions as to how to practice *kashrut*.

[39] "A Reconstructionist Exploration of Dietary Law: '*Kosher Consciousness*' and *Jewish Identity*," Online selections from the JRF quarterly—*Reconstructionism Today*, Summer 1998, www.jrf.org/rt/kosher.

a sacrament."[40] This would seem to argue for a personally oriented practice. Nevertheless, it was apparently of greater importance to him that the Jew be unencumbered while operating in the world than s/he cultivate the act of eating as a sacrament wherever s/he might be. For Rabbi Kaplan, the spiritual significance of *kashrut* was exhausted by its capability of "striking a spiritual note in the home atmosphere"[41] and not within the Jewish soul.

Reconstructionism has moved away from Kaplanian rationalism. A recent publication by the movement, entitled, *A Guide to Jewish Practice,* written by Rabbi David Teutsch and enhanced with glosses by various other rabbis, advances a number of basic values inherent in practicing *kashrut*: "Primary concerns underlying *kashrut* observance include identification with the Jewish people, creation of sensitivity to the ethical issues surrounding food, and cultivation of an attitude of gratitude and responsibility for the food we eat."[42] Additionally, contributors' glosses include concerns to promote *kedushah* and to "strengthen one's Jewish spiritual practice."[43] Suggestions are given for meditations prior to and after eating.

Kashrut is seen as a tool for heightening consciousness regarding one's identity as a Jew, the act of eating itself, and the act's ramifications as they connect to such areas as the food industry's labor policies or wastefulness and the prevalent cultural pressures affecting conspicuous consumption, self-image, health and body type. Acknowledging the close connections now common between the Reconstructionist and Renewal communities, many of these concerns are placed under the heading "eco-*kashrut*," explained in this way:

> A term coined by Reb Zalman Shachter-Shalomi in the mid-1970s, eco-kashrut was popularized by Arthur Waskow and the Shalom Center in the late 1980s. Today various Jewish and secular initiatives seek to further the connection by putting an "eco-hecksher" on those products which are least environmentally damaging. And eco-kashrut's scope is wider still: today's world "consumes" not only food but paper, energy, land, species, societies.[44]

---

[40] *Judaism as a Civilization*, p. 440.

[41] *Ibid.*, p. 441.

[42] David A. Teutsch, *A Guide to Jewish Practice: Introduction, Attitudes, Values and Beliefs*, Kashrut: *The Jewish Dietary Laws*, experimental edition produced by The Reconstructionist Rabbinical College in cooperation with The Reconstructionist Rabbinical Association (Wyncote, PA: RRC Press, 2000), p. 29.

[43] *Ibid.*

[44] *Ibid.*, p. 33. Gloss by Fred Dobb. A related concept is "ethical *kashrut*." For a Renewal perspective, see Arthur Waskow, *Down to Earth Judaism: Food, Money, Sex and the Rest of Life* (New York: Morrow, 1995).

This guide sets forth three categories of practices that can sustain and promote these values—vegetarianism, eco-*kashrut*, and traditional *kashrut*. It notes that these approaches are compatible with one another. It advocates informed choice on the part of each individual. Regarding traditional *kashrut*, its thorough overview makes the point, contra-Kaplan, that *kashrut* is traditionally relevant outside the home as well as in it; however, it acknowledges that many people compromise outside the home. It includes such traditional instruction as rules for soaking and salting meat. It follows Conservative opinion in allowing swordfish and accepting all hard cheese as kosher.

The value of social integration is central to Reconstructionism, to an even greater degree than in Conservative Judaism. Thus, with regard to wine, Rabbi Teutsch writes that the traditional prohibition was designed "to minimize contact between Jews and non-Jews. These concerns clash with our values. We now hold that all wine is simply wine *(stam yeynam)*."[45] Thus he appropriates a term that traditionally means prohibited and reads it as a term of permission. This was apparently not a strong enough statement for Rabbi Dan Ehrenkrantz, who added his rejection of the Conservative responsum allowing all wines: "The reasoning of the Conservative Law Committee maintains a respect for the traditional ruling that I do not share. I consider all wine kosher because I object in principle to interfering with social contact between Jews and non-Jews."[46]

On the other hand, the vegetarian approach is questioned by one contributor for potentially weakening Jewish identity. After Rabbi Teutsch observes that vegetarianism eliminates the need for different sets of dishes, Rabbi Sheila Weinberg writes:

> On the other hand, vegetarianism reduces the specialness of Jews. We are now as likely to bond with other vegetarians as with other Jews. Also by eliminating the separate dishes, pots and utensils and all that entails, there are fewer moments to remember the significance of *kashrut*, to use our eating practice as a call to awareness of our relationship to God, Torah and Israel.

But she concludes:

> We can, however, use our vegetarianism as a form of *kashrut* that connects us to universal values that are also Jewish values and still conforms with the traditions of our ancestors.[47]

---

[45] *Ibid.*, p. 47.
[46] *Ibid.* Ehrenkrantz seems to be unaware of Dorff's *teshuvah*, cited above.
[47] *Ibid.*, p. 32.

In this way, Rabbi Weinberg affirms the possibility that one may move beyond accommodation between two competing allegiances — to one's Jewishness, on one hand, and to social engagement, on the other — to a real synthesis. But this synthesis requires a high degree of conscious awareness and commitment.

"Just as Their Faces Differ, So Do Their Conceptions" [48]

What are the key issues, shared values and controversial claims that emerge from this short survey of denominational thinking on *kashrut*? There is a basic split between the Orthodox stream and all other streams. We have seen that the various non-Orthodox groups, while differing in nuance and emphasis, do indeed share certain general values, commitments, assumptions and perspectives. These become the basis for each group's handling of the specific questions surrounding *kashrut*. These can be described below:

Personal autonomy — All movements acknowledge that we live in a society that accepts the central notion of personal autonomy. When this is not taken for granted, but is challenged, the response is the renewed demand for society's members to have the right to choose, to be selective, to compromise or not to compromise as they wish. All movements recognize that their members are against accepting allegiance to any heteronomous system. The differences among the movements consist in their response to this accepted fact. Reform Judaism promotes this fact as a key value. Reconstructionism recognizes that any sense of commandedness must arise out of personal choices for individual behavior and communal involvement. Conservative Judaism tries to modify *halakhah* so as to persuade more Jews to accept it.

Issur ve-heter (prohibition and dispensation) — It follows that it is difficult for these movements to treat the idea of prohibited substances with total seriousness. Since the criterion for any action is determined by personal choice, there can be no inherently forbidden substances.[49] There are only warning

---

[48] J. Beraḥot 9;1. And see S. Lieberman, *Tosefta Ki-Fshutah, Zera'im*, Part I, p. 104, s.v. *lefi she-eyn*, who cites the Targum to Prov. 27:19 as: "Just as waters and faces differ, so do the hearts of human beings differ from each other."

[49] In the parlance of the yeshivot, all dispensation and prohibition, from the modern perspective, resides in the *gavra*, the person, rather than in the *heftza*, the object. From this perspective, for one to posit that an object itself is forbidden, one would have to be either a) committed to a legal system, or b) superstitious. Furthermore, even were one to accept the power of a legal system to prohibit an object, rendering it an "illegal substance," it would still be difficult to justify—as a legal operation—the notion that such substances could endow other, permitted substances with their prohibited character. For instance, one would probably not accept the idea that possession of one gram of cocaine mixed into 58 grams of powder is equivalent to the possession of 59 grams of

lights, which may be heeded or disregarded, depending on the circumstances and the individual. The issue will not be "Did this drop of milk render the food prohibited?" but rather, "Will I decide to eat this food at this moment, in this situation?" The decision becomes historicized: "In the past, a Jew might have forbidden this dish. Do I still want to do this?" The elements from which such a decision will be made will not consist of halakhic definitions of *issur ve-heter*, but will consist of assigning relative weights to values like Jewish identification, interpersonal obligations, a sense of personal comfort or discomfort.

Social integration — This value has been adopted by all non-Orthodox groups. Moreover, even though certain Orthodox groups may agree that social involvement is desirable, it is only the non-Orthodox groups that allow this value to be manifestly weighted against traditional halakhic values. In this sense, all non-Orthodox groups have knowingly and explicitly rejected a core value of *kashrut*: the maintenance of a segregated community. For Conservative thinkers this is either because it is no longer practicable, or because it is no longer desirable. Reform and Reconstructionism are even more emphatic in their positive acceptance of social integration.[50]

Community — *Kashrut* builds community. But the Orthodox and non – Orthodox streams approach the value of community from different angles. For the Orthodox, a strong community is conceived of as a collection of individuals united by their similarities of commitment and lifestyle. For the other denominations, a strong community is tested by its ability to include those who differ from each other or from the mainstream. This split is related to differing conceptions of Jewish identity.

Jewish identity — While traditional conceptions of Jewish identity emphasized a sense of uniqueness and hence required measures that would preserve and protect that uniqueness, there are increasing numbers of Jews who are more comfortable with notions of Jewish identity that derive from a sense of family and blessedness. Such notions do not imply the need for exclusiveness and insularity to the same degree as older notions. Conceived of as a product of individual choice, Jewish identity finds its expression in eclecticism. Once Jewish identity is conceived of as the product of a set of choices, it becomes important to respect the choices of others, however they may differ from one's own.

---

cocaine, since the cocaine has not become *batel be-shishim*, cancelled by sixty times the amount of permitted substance.

[50] Kaplan was contemptuous of the notion that the Jewish group should be protected through isolating practices. He wrote: "As for the fear that social intercourse between Jews and Gentiles may lead to the disintegration of Judaism, the reply is obvious: if Judaism is inherently so weak that it requires the artificial barriers of social aloofness fostered by dietary laws for its maintenance, the very need for maintaining it is gone." After the Holocaust, and given what we now know about the power of mass culture, it is difficult to agree that such a reply is still obvious.

At the same time, one's individual choices are enhanced through participation in community. But this community must be inclusive rather than exclusive. The ability to share becomes a central value.

Kashrut can be understood as being, among other things, the systematic attempt to create, with regard to food, a safe space for sharing. But this sharing is only possible when the definitions of *kashrut* are themselves shared. When they are not shared, the act of sharing becomes polluted by distrust and resentment.

Indeed, the Torah's first story of transgression of a dietary prohibition, the story of Eve and Adam's partaking of the forbidden fruit, is not only a story of transgression; it is also a story of sharing. Eve eats of the fruit and immediately shares it with Adam. Sadly, this generous impulse has tragic consequences. Of course, for traditional readers of the story it was easy to disregard this paradox. Such a reader would see her gesture not as generous, but as diabolical.[51] For the traditional halakhist, the impulse to share cannot be characterized as generous if what is shared is forbidden. But when the concepts of *issur ve-heter* are no longer central, and what determines the religious quality of an act is its *kavannah* — its intentional consciousness — the act of sharing takes on a stature independent of the stuff being shared. Then the clashing ideas of *kedushah* held by the Orthodox and non-Orthodox groups lead to excruciatingly different evaluations of events and imperatives.[52]

Kedushah — The Orthodox and non-Orthodox differ in their definitions of

---

[51] Rashi to Gen. 3:6, following Bereshit Rabbah 19:5, does not grant Eve a generous motivation. Rather, she seeks a partner to share her fate. See also Hizzekuni, ad. loc. But the kabbalists were more alive to the complexity of the situation. See *Sha'are Orah*, Ch. 10 (ed. Ben-Shelomo, II:127), who connects this episode with the portrait of the Woman of Valor, who bestows only goodness upon her husband. For Gikatilla, the sin of the primordial couple was the sin of impatience. Had they waited, they would have been able to share this fruit together. See also *Zohar* I:49b, which regards Eve's act as a paradigm of Divine union, albeit a flawed one.

It is worthwhile, in the context of this essay, to note how R. Naftali Zvi Yehudah Berlin explicates the above-cited midrash's explanation for Eve's success in persuading Adam to sin: "Now they have investigated in [Bereshit] Rabbah how Adam allowed himself to be seduced. And they answered that she squeezed grapes and gave it to him." This means that she explained to him that this is nothing more than *zei'ah be-'alma*— mere sweat, and not a food like the fruit. But, actually, regarding grapes the drink is the essence of the fruit, as is known." (*Harhev Davar*, ad. loc.)

[52] As we will presently point out, in a clash between the values of sharing food and maintaining *kashrut*, progressive groups often prefer the first value and Orthodox groups prefer the latter value. For a case of leniency in *kashrut* for the sake of enabling hospitality, see the permission to shorten the time for salting meat when guests are waiting or to prepare for Shabbat—*S.A.Y.D.* 69:6 and Rama. (Cited by Louis Jacobs, *A Tree of Life: Diversity, Flexibility, and Creativity in Jewish Law*, 2nd. ed. [Portland, OR: The Littman Library of Jewish Civilization, 2000], p. 39, n. 43.)

an essential component of holiness. For the Orthodox, *kedushah* entails the acceptance of limitations. To create a system of limitations is to create a system for the exercise of the human capacity for holiness. To abide by that system is to engage in holy living. Participating in that tradition one can express personal autonomy. The free choice of a life of *kedushah* results in the bending and transformation of one's will, rather than in its free expression. But for those who privilege personal autonomy, *kedushah* must be defined differently. Reform theory will emphasize the ethical aspects of *kedushah*.[53] A recent Conservative formulation downplays the necessity for self-sacrifice by emphasizing the positive quest for holiness. It translates the talmudic directive *kadesh et 'atzmekha ba-muttar lekha* (B. Yevamot 20a), traditionally understood as a call for self-control and abstinence[54] as "achieve holiness within the realm of the permitted," explaining that what is demanded is that one "go beyond obeying the letter of the law and refraining from what is forbidden by finding ways of sanctifying every moment of your life."[55] In this view, "To be holy is to rise to partake in some measure of the special qualities of God, the source of holiness. Holiness is the highest level of human behavior, human beings at their utmost."[56] Reconstructionist and Renewal approaches, instead of emphasizing separateness, tend to identify *kedushah* with the pursuit of higher consciousness, a consciousness that is integrative rather than analytical.[57]

Worry — It was suggested above that worry forms a constitutive element in the nature and development of our tradition, the Oral Law. It has been the fuel energizing the development of laws and customs and has inspired the search for deeper and more creative approaches to halakhic analysis. The denominations differ with regard to the religious value of worry and as to the focus of worthwhile worry.[58] The Orthodox worry about preventing sin; the non-Orthodox worry about inducing observance or inducing positive Jewish experiences. The place of worry as a motive force in religious life has been replaced by demands for higher awareness and consciousness of core values: justice, goodness, holiness, and the living of a fulfilling life. For the non-Orthodox, the problem with worry is that it has been turned from *ḥashash* (concern) into *ḥashad* (suspicion). This is seen as corrosive of the religious health of the individual and the com-

---

[53] See Gunther Plaut, *The Torah*, op. cit., p. 889ff.

[54] See above, at n. 20.

[55] *Etz Hayim: Torah and Commentary*, ed. David L. Lieber (New York: The Rabbinical Assembly/The United Synagogue of Conservative Judaism, 2001), p. 693.

[56] *Ibid.*

[57] See, e.g., in the Reconstructionist *Guide*, cited above, the comment by Myriam Klotz: "Holiness of the body as created in the Divine Image is a stance of integration as much as it is of separation" (p. 30).

[58] This essay is not the place to explore how this finds expression in the differing ways the denominations tend to learn Torah.

munity. From the Orthodox perspective, the relinquishing of worry promotes religious laziness and self-satisfaction. It prevents the ongoing creation of the Oral Torah because this traditional source of pressure has been jettisoned. We have seen that, with regard to relating to *kashrut*, Reform is stuck with accepting traditional definitions that will then put before its members to accept or disregard. The Conservative, accepting traditional *halakhah* as a base, has not formulated rules for systemic change.[59] Its changes are reactive to social pressure. Reconstructionism, in keeping with its name, has advanced certain alternative criteria for a system of *kashrut*, shifting the arena of worry into areas that can be perceived as those of concern to American liberals and spiritual seekers. It remains to be seen whether this will be a source of strength or weakness.

"We Shall Do and We Shall Listen"[60]— Elements of a Pluralistic Approach

The history of pluralism — ideological, religious, social and political — has yet to be written. There are many definitions of the term and discussions of the many issues connected to it.[61] Pluralism has attracted increased interest of late, embraced by some and anathematized by others. In general, non-Orthodox groups extol the ideal while most Orthodox bodies oppose its adoption into the Jewish communal agenda. However, many groups that seek to attract Jews of varied backgrounds and affiliations obviously must function pluralistically, and Orthodox leadership has been pronounced in them.

American Jewry has gone through a century of religious self-definition that has resulted in a denominational structure. As an illustration of that process, it might be pointed out that the Jewish Theological Seminary began as a pluralistic institution, only later redefining itself as the lead institution for the developing Conservative movement. Today many observers wonder whether this structure shows signs of loosening. The record is mixed. While the interdenominational Synagogue Council of America has folded, some interdenominational groups survive and new independent institutions and communities

---

[59] The influence of works such as Joel Roth's *The Halakhic Process* is questionable.

[60] Ex. 24:7.

[61] On pluralism, see the following selection of writings and their sources:

Elliot N. Dorff, "Pluralism," in *Frontiers of Jewish Thought*, ed. Steven T. Katz (Washington, DC: B'nai B'rith Books, 1992), pp. 213–233.

Reuven Kimelman, "Judaism and Pluralism," in *Modern Judaism* 7 (1987): 131–150. *Sh'ma* 29/561, April 1999.

Dan Dishon, *Tarbut Ha-Maḥaloket Be-Yisra'el: 'Iyyun Be-Mivḥar Mekorot* (Jerusalem/ Tel-Aviv: Schocken, 1984).

Michael Graetz, *Va-Yamodu Ba-'Omer* (Beer Sheva, 2001).

have arisen.[62] A striking example of the importance being given to pluralism as a compelling idea is the establishment at New York's Temple Emanuel, the most prominent Reform synagogue in the world: the Skirball Center for Adult Education aggressively markets itself as a pluralistic learning program. On the other hand, the one rabbinical and cantorial seminary dedicated to training its students through a pluralistic faculty and curriculum, the Academy for Jewish Religion, continues to struggle, despite significant recent growth.

In general, while there are many communities of individuals and many institutional contexts that are inclusive of Jewish religious diversity, the creation and development of a community consciously dedicated to developing a pluralistic way of Jewish living is still a desideratum. Even if the necessary support for such an enterprise could be garnered through consciousness-raising and fundraising in the Jewish community, one wonders how such a group could cohere. The problematic dynamic of worry is especially acute for any group dedicated to pluralism. On the one hand, a pluralistic group might be seen as a context that demands even greater suspicion and stringency, since it is clear that certain members of the group, in not sharing a common set of standards, cannot be trusted. On the other hand, it is precisely in such a group that, presumably, there is a mandate to find a set of behaviors that all can commit to so that all can be trusted.

What ingredients would be necessary for such a project to function? I offer the following suggestions and musings. One ingredient is "responsible discussion." This is expressed in Rabbi Elazar ben Azariah's exposition of the words of Kohelet:

> And he also opened by expounding: "The words of the sages are as goads, as well fastened nails, [composed in] (masters of) collections, given by one shepherd." (Eccles. 12:11) … Masters of collections— these are students of Sages who sit in groups and are busy with the Torah. These declare impure and those declare pure, these forbid and those permit, these disqualify and those accept. Lest a person say, "Since these declare impure and those declare pure, these forbid and those permit, these disqualify and those accept, how, now, can I learn Torah?" The Torah then states, "They were all given by one shepherd." One God gave them, one benefactor spoke them from the Blessed Lord of all that is created, as it says,

---

[62] These would include, among others, ḥavurot, non-denominational minyanim, synagogues that function across denominational labels, educational programs such as Pardes, CLAL, local community efforts at interdenominational cooperation, etc.

"The Almighty spoke all of these things" (Ex. 20:1). Therefore make your ear into a funnel and acquire a listening heart for the words of those who declare impure and those who declare pure, those who forbid and those who permit, those who disqualify and those who accept.[63]

While it is accepted that pluralism requires discussion among participants, this discussion should be more than a joint effort to understand a common text and more than the sharing of divergent viewpoints. A pluralistic community would affirm the need to actively engage in the critique of those viewpoints and the need for an acceptance of "responsibility," that is, the willingness to respond to critique. Response does not mean the automatic deflection of that critique. Rather, it means the taking of the critique to one's "listening heart" and the internal integration of the positive elements of that critique.[64]

To put this in homiletical terms, when the Israelites encamped around Mount Sinai to accept the Torah, they were, for a brief time, encamped "as one" ("and Israel encamped [va-yihan] there opposite the mountain" [Ex. 19:2]). Rashi quotes the Mekhilta, which noticed that the verb "encamped" is written in the singular, while the previous verbs in the verse are in the plural: "[They encamped] as one person, with one heart, though the rest of the encampments were with complaints and divisions." Now, it may be asked, given that this momentary show of unanimity was bound to dissipate, what good was it at all? If the giving of the Torah to Israel was predicated on their being unified, how could Israel retain possession of this Divine Gift forever, when the breakdown of its sense of unity was guaranteed from the start?

The answer must be that, thankfully, that sense of togetherness, though temporary, allowed Israel to utter a crucial pledge, by virtue of which we maintain our connection to Torah: We said, "na'aseh ve-nishma, we will do and we will listen." We committed ourselves to each other by saying na'aseh, we will each do what we think is right, ve-nishma, but we will also listen to hear what others are doing.

But the doing must be pushed even further. In addition, a pluralistic community requires the willingness to experiment. The experiment may be to engage in a religious practice foreign to one's own, such as praying a Reform service when one is used to an Orthodox one. This may be difficult enough. But a further step entails the willingness of the group to experiment together with solutions to the problem of pluralistic practice. This means the willingness to

---

[63] Num. Rab. 14:4 and parallels. The term "listening heart" is rendered "understanding heart" in B. Ḥag. 3b. In Tos. *Sotah* 7:12 the phrase reads: "Make your heart full of rooms — *ke-ḥadrei ḥadarim*—and put into it the words of those who ... etc."

[64] For a related point, see Shaul Magid's essay cited above, n. 19.

do something and then to consider how it worked. What was effective and what was not? What was gained and what was lost? And for whom? In the words of the Israelites at Mount Sinai, *na'aseh*, we will try it out, *ve-nishma*, and then we will listen for the result.

To do these things — to listen responsibly and to act experimentally — the pluralistic community requires of its members the willingness to make sacrifices and concessions. Such an attitude is necessary on practical grounds. But its significance reaches into the spiritual realm of holiness, as traditionally defined: *kadesh et 'atzmekha ba-muttar lekha* (B. Yevamot 20a). The injunction to be holy is the call to sacrifice for the sake of others even when one is convinced that one's position is correct and that were one to refuse to make that sacrifice, one would be operating well within one's rights.[65]

By the Sweat of Your Brow Shall You Eat Bread

This essay has attempted to begin a discussion that a pluralistic community might have regarding *kashrut*. Competing values and conceptions have been placed side by side. This is but a beginning of responsible discussion, an attempt to listen to contrasting viewpoints with a listening heart. One result of this discussion has been to posit that, when considered in terms of how the movements conceive of important Jewish values, a clear division exists — not between the denominations, but between Orthodoxy and all other movements. This discussion has attempted to walk between both these two camps. A response was offered to the concrete question of the use of a microwave oven in a pluralistic context. This was an example, however modest and timid, of experimentation. The solution required that liberal proponents of *kashrut* go quite a distance toward meeting the requirements of Orthodox practice. They were asked to accept practices and values that they find unnecessary or objectionable. Still, despite the traditional thrust of the proffered solution, it was noted that the solution advocated fell short of the requirements of many Orthodox authorities.

It is usually at this point that practical solutions and religious discussions break down. The question becomes whether there is any possibility of compromise by those who adhere to Orthodox standards. This is the challenge of the willingness to sacrifice. While sacrifice is difficult for any individual or group, there is an inherent asymmetry between progressive movements and the Orthodox with regard to the challenge of making compromises. The Reform and Reconstructionist movements, by placing decision-making powers in the hands of the individual, have relinquished any strong claim to an absolute standard of

---

[65] See above, at n. 19. And see the comments of the *Maggid Mishnah* on Rambam, *Hil. Shekhenim* 14:5, who ties the need for flexibility and social cooperation, including the relinquishing of one's entitlements, to the imperative to be holy.

behavior. The Conservative movement has elevated the practice of compromise to a high religious value. But the Orthodox perceive their situation differently. They see themselves as being subject to a Divinely ordained system of absolutes. How, then, from their own perspective, could they find room for compromise on religiously mandated standards?

One hesitates to instruct another group on how it should follow its own practices. But, in a pluralistic community one may be allowed at least the *hutz-pah* of making a suggestion. It has been pointed out that among progressive Jews, the rejection by one group or individual of an invitation to eat together is currently experienced as a hurtful act. Despite the insistence by Orthodox Jews that they have no choice in the matter, and that they are entitled to maintain the highest standards of *kashrut* as an expression of deep religious commitment, the refusal of Orthodox Jews to eat with other Jews who feel that they are keeping kosher is experienced as an act of rejection and is considered an act of personal and communal disrespect. Were this feeling taken seriously as an issue of *kevod ha-beri'ot* (human dignity) might it be possible to find a way to make compromises on an ad-hoc, local and temporary basis?

The tradition knows of the rule that "Human dignity is so important that it pushes aside a Torah prohibition."[66] The Talmud restricts the meaning of this sweeping declaration. But it allows the temporary suspension of rabbinic prohibitions for the sake of respecting the dignity of an individual or group. Talmudic cases include examples wherein the individual (or group) is allowed to continue acting in transgression of a law so as to prevent embarrassment. And cases include instances in which one individual or group may be engaged in an act permitted to them, and yet, for the sake of not offending the group, participation in that act is permitted even for another person for whom that act would be forbidden. Traditionally, these dispensations have not been welcomed with enthusiasm. Often, efforts were made to restrict them severely.[67] It would be up to those among the Orthodox community who wish to engage in the pluralistic experiment to examine whether such an expansion of this concept is acceptable and called for in this situation.

The question has been asked before. The Torah tells of a mysterious

---

[66] See B. Berahot 19a–b. I thank my students at AJR for helping me study this *sugya* and others related to this concept.

[67] On the subject of *kevod ha-beri'ot* see the important studies:
Nahum Rakover, *Gadol Kevod Ha-Beri'ot: Kevod Ha-Beri'ot ke-'Erekh 'Al* (Jerusalem: Sifir'at Ha-Mishpat Ha-'Ivri, 1999).
Yaakov Blidstein, "*Gadol Kevod Ha-Beri'ot—'Iyyunim be-Gilgulehah shel Halakhah,* (Jerusalem: Sh'naton Ha-Mishpat Ha-'Ivri 9–10 1982–3).
On the reluctance of halakhic authorities to apply this principle, see Blistein, pp. 141–149.

theophanic event that occurred after the revelation at Sinai:

> Moses and Aaron, Nadav and Avihu, and seventy of the
> elders of Israel ascended; and they saw the God of Israel; and
> under His feet there was a kind of paved work of sapphire
> stone, pure like the very heaven. And He did not send forth
> His hand upon the nobles of the people of Israel, and they
> saw God, and ate and drank. (Ex. 24:9–11)

The commentators are divided as to the literal and spiritual significance of
the elders' act of eating while apprehending God.[68] Was the verse to be taken
literally or metaphorically? Was their eating an act of religious celebration or
an act of crass rebellion? Rashi cites both views. He explains that he thinks the
elders were gross sinners. But he admits that the Targum translates differently.
The Targum renders the verse:

> And they saw the Glory of God, and they were overjoyed
> with their sacrifices that were accepted, as though they ate
> and drank.

Is it possible to conceive of the act of joining together for a meal as a religious
experience important enough to warrant the necessary sacrifice to make it possible? Could one feel that the acceptance of such sacrifice would be a source of
supreme joy? Our answers to these questions will help determine whether we
shall be able to eat together in holy communion.

The challenge of developing a pluralistic practice of *kashrut* consists in ef-
fecting a resolution of tensions deeply embedded in our tradition. It requires
a synthesis of forces that pull in opposite directions. These forces are those put
into play by the complex nature of the Torah's most central value, *kedushah*. It
is through this encompassing value that the Torah sought to reframe all the
competing values inherent in our ancient food taboos. What approach might
attempt to give proper expression to such a multivalent mitzvah? The forces of
inclusion and exclusion, of self-assertion and self-restraint, of satisfaction and
worry are all waiting to be harnessed through a pluralistic transformation.

We have learned that there are two properties to *zei'ah* (vapor or sweat). One
property is the quality of identity. Sweat is considered to have the identical
nature of the entity from which it emanates. It is the authentic product of that

---

[68] See *Vayikra Rab.* 20:10. Compare the traditional commentators such as Onkelos,
Saadiah, Rashi, Ibn Ezra, Rashbam, Ramban ad. loc. And see Maimonides, *Guide* I:5,
and *Zohar* 1:135a–b *(MH)*.

entity. The second property is the tendency for sweat to effect connections. As it rises or drips down, it brings about the intermixture of individual entities. The pursuit of a pluralistic agenda will require much effort and sweat. The intermingling of the sweat of diverse individuals can produce a new mixture, synthesizing the authentic uniqueness of each of our perspectives while bringing about a delicious sense of interconnectedness.

Conceived in this way, we may hope to turn the ancient curse, "By the sweat of your brow shall you eat bread together," into a blessing.

Magen Tzedek: A Memoir And Reflection

Morris Allen

> "I am grateful to God that in the official establishments
> and hotels kashrut is observed. But what hurts is the ques-
> tion why it is only required for butcher shops to be under
> religious supervision? Why not insist that banks, factories,
> and those who deal in real estate should require a hechsher
> and be operated according to religious law? When a drop of
> blood is found in an egg, we abhor the idea of eating the egg.
> But often there is more than one drop of blood in a dollar or
> a lira and we fail to remind people constantly of the teaching
> of our tradition.
>
> A.J Heschel, "Existence and Celebration"

Eating is a social act, especially for a Jew. In biblical times, after setting aside
the tithe, a person would say, "I have cleared out the consecrated portion from
the house, and I have given it to the Levite, the stranger, the fatherless, and
the widow, just as You commanded me." (Deut. 26:13) The rules governing our
eating include a ritual component as well as an ethical component. In following
these, we define our relationship to God, to our families, to the Jewish people,
and to all fellow members of the larger societies in which we live.

Issues of pluralism enter these considerations both privately and publicly. In
our private self-definitions, we open ourselves to competing claims of different
kinds of values and try to balance them and integrate them. On this plane, the
ritual demands of kashrut and the ethical demands of social justice both lay
claim on us, and we try to behave in a way that satisfies them both.

On the public level, we perceive especially today that the Jewish community
comprises various sub-communities. Through their definition and enforcement
of rules like kashrut, these sub-communities necessarily define their relation to
each other, in terms both of inclusion and exclusion. As will be clear from my
account below, the history of these interactions in recent times is mixed, with
positive as well as negative experiences to relate. On the positive side, the Jewish community is greatly indebted especially to the Orthodox Union and more
broadly to Orthodoxy in general for carrying the chief burden of the effort to
make kosher certified food a prominent feature of the American food marketplace. In so doing, it has also implicitly defined parameters that can define

an inclusive sphere of eating-space for American Jews across denominations. Also, as I attest from my own experience, until recent decades the enforcement of communal kashrut rules was often itself a pluralistic venture, with cooperative effort elicited by its Orthodox leaders from across the Jewish denominations. Also, looking at the broad picture, there are important voices in Orthodoxy who are important players in advancing pluralistic dialogue and cooperation among the branches of Judaism today.[1]

At the same time, there are circles, especially in ultra-Orthodoxy, where talk of pluralism is anathema. This would be a private issue, of little concern to us, were it not for the fact that their influence has become dominant in the kashrut industry and has the power to impede the course of pluralistically conceived endeavors in the general public Jewish sphere. As my account documents, the efforts to heighten awareness of ethical food-related issues among the Jewish and general community has been severely impeded by the organized opposition of these ultra-Orthodox players to allowing our efforts the space they need to operate. This vignette thus highlights the more general question of how the various parties in today's Jewish community stand in relation to each other, and what needs to be changed in that relationship in order for them to work cooperatively for the health and benefit of the Jewish community as a whole.

* * *

In 1995, I launched the "Chew by Choice" campaign, designed to encourage greater fidelity to the observance of the Jewish dietary laws—Kashrut. My campaign met with great success inside my own congregation and was featured prominently at an AVI CHAI conference held in Los Angeles in 1997. In truth, elevating the observance of Kashrut had long been a passion of mine and I carried with me a deep belief that increasing the observance of kashrut was critically important for Jewish life and continuity.

Kashrut, while a central element of Jewish life, has been transformed inside this country into a multi-billion dollar business. From the time in the 1920s when Heinz Foods agreed to place a "hechsher" on a can of Vegetarian Baked Beans and to certify them as Kosher until today, the growth of kosher certi-

---

[1] Editor's note: See elsewhere in this volume "Pluralism: Making a Passionate Orthodox Judaism More Meaningful" by Rabbi Asher Lopatin, president of Yeshivat Chovevei Torah, and the discussion of the writings of Donniel Hartman, Moshe Halbertal, and Avi Sagi (all affiliated with the Sholom Hartman Institute) in "Pluralism in the Talmudic Tradition".

fication has changed both the observance and the communal connection to kashrut. There were three major transformations in the 20th Century which fundamentally created a "Kashrut Industrial Complex". The first was the establishment of a national certifying agency. The emergence of the Orthodox Union as a major player in the food industry (especially from 1950 onward) cannot be overlooked—and for most of the 20th Century was greeted with joy by Jews across the religious spectrum. The ease of being able to enter a store and identify acceptable products for consumption, transformed the life of the kashrut-observant Jew. Today the top five major kosher certification agencies have contracts with over 10,000 food producers and certify over 1,000,000 different products.[2] And those are just the five major certifying agencies.

The second transformation has been the increasing polarization of Jewish communal life. In 1986, when I first arrived in the Twin Cities, I was invited by the Orthodox rabbinic head of the local Kashrut organization to sit on the board with him—proof (if such be needed) that orthodoxy is compatible in principle with pluralistic cooperation. Indeed, an older Conservative colleague was the vice-chair of the Kashrut council in the Twin Cities. With the retirement of this Orthodox colleague and his being replaced by a Ner Yisroel graduate, the Kashrut Council was transformed from a communal organization into a solely Orthodox organization that had little interest in the views or thoughts of the non-Orthodox community as it related to kashrut observance. This small scene was repeated on a grand scale across the continent. As a result of the non-Orthodox world's increasingly becoming non-existent in the discourse around kashrut, a parallel development occurred whereby increasing stringencies became the norm of kashrut observance. For example, glatt meat became the standard-and the use of the term glatt suddenly had nothing to do with its origins as it related to the lungs of a cow—but instead became a way to differentiate "real" kashrut observance from those who only "dabbled" in their practice.

This ultimately led to the third transformation of the kosher food industry in the 20th century—the near elimination of the local butcher shop. There were challenges and opportunities in applying industrial centralization to a distinctive product with its special requirements of kosher certification and fidelity to Jewish law. In the early 1990's, AgriProcessors began producing kosher meat and chicken in Postville, Iowa. While Stephen Bloom documented the change in the irenic town in his book published in 1999,[3] the real change

---

[2] Timothy Lytton, *Kosher: Private Regulation in the Age of Industrial Food*, Harvard University Press, 2013.

[3] Stephen Bloom, *Postville: A Clash of Cultures in Heartland America*, 1999.

was in the manner by which the kosher consumer gained access to tray-pack meat in grocery stores. Now, like non-kosher consumers who walked into a grocery store and bought their meat off the refrigerator shelf, kosher-observant Jews could enjoy the convenience of supermarket meat shopping, thanks to AgriProcessors. At the height of its production in 2006, AgriProcessors was slaughtering 60,000 chickens a day and 500 head of cattle a day—six days a week. This mass production of kosher food meant that for many local butchers it was no longer possible to compete. In the process of creating this extensive kosher meat production empire, Postville became both a company town and a place rife with abuse.

In the winter of 2006, I received a call from the local Lubavitch rabbi asking if I would support his desire to have a kosher meat section in a local grocery store. I responded that I would if we could have access to non-glatt meat once again. He replied that this was great, because his certification company actually did the non-glatt certification for AgriProcessors. In March of 2006, I made my first trip to Postville with him and the proprietors of the local grocery store we were going to use. After a tour of the plant and a protracted meeting with the owner of the company, it was decided that we would begin selling non-glatt meat as well as glatt meat in the local grocery store. For Pesach 2006, prices were brought down for kosher meat—for there was now both glatt and non-glatt meat on the shelf. For me, this fit into my desire to increase kashrut observance among the Jewish people. For the first time in years—people remarked that kosher meat prices were reasonable. All seemed good—until May 2006.

That May, the *Forward* published a detailed description of the labor practices at AgriProcessors. PETA had done an exposé of the animal welfare practices of Agri some three years earlier. The release of a highly controversial video of the treatment of an animal after it had been slaughtered, brought the condemnation of nearly 750 rabbis. (This led to Temple Grandin being called into the plant to reconfigure how the animals were treated.) The release of the *Forward* story passed with no comment. And things probably would have stood that way, except that I felt I was now complicit in the potential abuse of labor with my promotion of Agri's kosher non-glatt meat. I immediately called the local Lubavitch rabbi and asked if I could visit the plant and meet with the workers to verify the details of the story's claims. He assured me that he would go down and meet with them and report back to me. Upon his return, he reported that every individual with whom he met spoke highly of the owners and said they were treated with excellent care. I again asked for an opportunity to make an independent visit to the plant—and in August of 2006—

five of us spent three days in Postville. It is not necessary to detail every aspect of those three perilous days—which included being followed by paid observers from the plant, by threats being directed towards us, by our inability to have the plant owners allow us free access to their labor force. However, as a result of serious work and work with allies in the field, we had the opportunity to meet with over 75 employees, officials from the Iowa Department of Labor, religious leaders in the community, community organizers and a variety of other concerned citizens. Indeed, we discovered that there were serious violations of labor decency, that animal welfare standards continued to be lacking and that environmental infractions were rampant.

Prior to the High Holy Days in 2006, we sent a letter to AgriProcessors outlining three demands which we were making that we felt would go a long way to correcting the labor abuses at the plant. The first was to have an entire audit of the safety procedures and labor conditions—which would provide the plant 18 months to fix any negative findings. Secondly, all training of the employees needed to be in their vernacular. The vast majority of the work force was from Central and South America and their ability to understand directions in English was limited. Tragically, there was not at that time even one HR individual who spoke Spanish doing the training. Thirdly, a series of meetings should take place between the ownership of the plant and the workforce mediated by our representatives and with an agreement that no recriminations would occur for anything said. I am sad to say, the family that owned the plant refused those requests. In my own mind, I still believe that had they accepted those demands and begun a process of change, they would still be in business today.

As a result of that refusal, 11 years after I began my Kashrut campaign, I delivered an impassioned Yom Kippur speech demanding that Jews not settle for fulfillment of ritual law when our ethical precepts were being trampled. My new Kashrut program, then named Hechsher Tzedek and now known as Magen Tzedek, has attempted to address the unfortunate and non-defensible gap between the modern understanding of kashrut's ritual laws and our on-going engagement with our tradition's ethical precepts. Indeed, the back-story of Magen Tzedek shows how our tradition has become much more defined by ritual observance and much less interested in fulfilling the ethical vision of our people. The opening quote by Heschel underscores that already 50 years ago there was a realization that the historic tension between fulfillment of *mitzvot bein adam l'havero* (those demands that define how we interact with one another) and fulfillment of *mitzvot bein Adam l'makom* (our sense of how we fulfill ritual law) had shifted way to the side of the latter at the expense of the former. Magen Tzedek has sought to serve as a corrective to this loss of a serious and meaningful tension.

As part of our work, Rabbi Avram Reisner developed what is to this day the most serious and thorough textual analysis as to why the five major areas of our concern were consistent with the best of Jewish law and values. In his 2008 paper, "Magen Tzedek *Al Pi Din*," he introduced the notion that Judaism speaks clearly and unequivocally on the issues of wages and benefits, worker safety, corporate integrity, animal welfare and environmental concern. And in view of a now increasingly corporate Kashrut industry these concerns were as necessary to address as the ritual underpinnings of kashrut itself. Indeed, this embrace of such a tension is itself consistent with how we have historically understood Jewish life and law. Halakhic development has always involved a pull between competing values. This can be seen in the effort to strike a balance between the desires of the individual and the needs of the community; between support for the particularity of Judaism and the embrace of universalism; between acceptance of the status quo and the yearning for Messianic perfection. In more specific contexts, new stringencies meant to enhance ritual practice have been measured against *kvod ha'tzibbur* [dignity of the community]; restrictions on commercial interaction with non-Jews have abutted the value of *darkhei shalom* [social amity]. It is this dialectic context that makes Judaism the profound, nuanced religion that it is. The embrace of this dialectic, this tension between tradition and change, embodies Conservative Judaism and gives it meaning and value between the pillars of Reform and Orthodoxy. Magen Tzedek, too, shares this approach. For example, as they relate to wages, benefits and worker safety and training, our robust labor standards are in keeping with Judaism's rich history of protecting the well-being of workers. The Torah in particular takes pains to prohibit exploitation of employees by their employer. The Torah insists, for example, that employers pay employees on the day of their labor. Additionally, the standard's insistence on paying workers a living wage and its endorsement of the right to collective bargaining builds upon the conclusions of the most recent CJLS (Committee on Jewish Law and Standards) teshuva addressing labor rights, Rabbi Jill Jacobs' "Work, Workers and the Jewish Owner." Moreover, medieval and modern halakhists have found that Judaism endorses a variety of work-related benefits. As set forth in Rabbi Reisner's comprehensive work, "Magen Tzedek *Al Pi Din*," poskim have held that employees were entitled to paid sick leave, that an employer must pay the full wages of a worker limited by a disability, and that an employee is entitled to retirement benefits under Jewish law.

Indeed, in his closing section of "Magen Tzedek *Al Pi Din*," Rabbi Reisner articulated a vision for Magen Tzedek that actually articulates a vision for how we as Jews should be living our lives: He stated: (In quoting Proverbs) "This is the way of the righteous." It is not the standard of everyman. But as Mishnah Avot 5:10 suggests, what seems to some the standard of the average person, appears to others as too pinched and niggardly, and the gold standard is that of the way of the righteous.[4]

An example of application of this higher standard may be illustrated by the halakhic category of *tar'omet* [grievance short of a legally actionable offense]. When the majority of workers complain of "how it feels to have a religious Jewish owner treat us in such a way," then regardless of the specifics of the complaint, it behooves the employer to address the situation until the perception of fairness prevails.

In addition to insisting that kosher food manufacturers abide by the fullness of halakhic demands, it is a key goal of Magen Tzedek to provide convenient information for Jewish consumers who want to make ethically informed choices about their kosher eating. Like consumer ingredient and health information labeling, the hechsher of Magen Tzedek is one more step toward putting into action the goals that God and the Torah have set for us, and toward which we strive. But to obtain the information on which such certification is based, it is necessary to obtain the cooperation of the producer, and in practice at least the implicit consent of the other Jewish authorities certifying the ritual kashrut of the products. In trying to secure this cooperation, we ran into a barrier that raised for us in another form questions of pluralism involving relations of the denominations in the Jewish community.

For example, one kosher chicken plant was quite eager to embrace Magen Tzedek as their gold standard of ethical behavior. Actually, that company continues to this day to use our language in describing their "social justice commitments". And while they use our language, they continue to avoid undergoing a full audit to demonstrate their fidelity to their words. Why? Because their shochtim [butchers] have said they will walk off the floor if Magen Tzedek is allowed to place its emblem on their packaging. Note that the butchers were not being asked to embrace our ethical agenda. All that was asked was for them to abstain from interfering, to allow us to conduct our audit as a basis for our Magen Tzedek certification, which would be parallel

---

[4] "There are four qualities of human character. The first says, 'What is mine is mine, and what is yours is yours'—this is the intermediate quality, but some say it is the quality of Sodom [because such a person is not charitable toward the needy]....The third says, 'What is mine is yours and what is yours is yours—this is the righteous."

to—and not in conflict with—their continuing to certify the chickens as ritually kosher. But to do so would have implicitly granted us legitimacy.

Yet another issue was raised with a different party in the next step of this drama. When the impasse with the kosher butchers over doing an audit was relayed to the leadership of Magen Tzedek, a call was made to a major Jewish social justice organization that has been a leader in addressing the abuse of the tomato harvesters in Florida. When Magen Tzedek spoke to their professional leadership and asked if they would rally 300 rabbis outside this plant—the answer was "that plant is a union shop and we won't protest outside a union shop." Thus, between the impasse with the butchers over our right to audit and the insistence of the social justice organization to refrain from protesting a union shop, we were prevented from being able to certify a major kosher chicken producer in America. That story, repeated in a variety of variations over the years, has severely hampered Magen Tzedek in its effort to achieve its original goal: the ethical certification of kosher food producers.

And yet, it is clear that Judaism has always been a religion where ritual law and ethical law have defined the life of the common Jew. Pledged to this ideal, we continue to work in new ways to incorporate the ethical corrective alongside the equally important objective of ritual certification in the kosher food industry in America. Under the leadership of Rabbi Michael Siegel, we are currently laying the groundwork for the development of an app for Smart Phones. This app would allow consumers to see a score of a company that is producing kosher food as they peruse the shelves in a grocery store so they may make a buying decision based on which product has a more "ethical score" as it relates to workers, animals and the earth. A mere app falls short of our original objective of a certification printed on the package, which would be a public advertisement of the importance of ethical criteria for everyone's shopping decisions in the marketplace. Still, in the world in which we live, it would be available as a private alternative—dependent on the individual's initiative—to provide the Jewish consumer with an opportunity not only to observe the laws of kashrut, but to live a life of ethical vision as it relates to the food choices with which we are presented.

In our ideal conception, we still envisage a Jewish community in which the branches of Judaism respect each other enough to allow complementary efforts to achieve the manifold values of the Jewish tradition from their various perspectives. Pluralism as private virtue is achievable at any time, by those open to the many diverse teachings of Jewish teachers past and present. Pluralism as public policy of the major part of the Jewish community would be a much more powerful force for good and would take us forward in *tikkun olam*.

Some 44 years after his death, AJ Heschel remains the compelling Jewish thinker about our understanding of what it means to be a Jew today. He once wrote the following:

> The teaching of Judaism is the *theology of the common deed*. The Bible insists that God is *concerned with everydayness, with the trivialities of life*... in how we manage the commonplace. The prophet's field of concern is not the mysteries of heaven... but the blights of society, the affairs of the marketplace. He addresses himself to those who trample upon the needy, who increase the price of grain, use dishonest scales and sell the refuse of corn (Amos 8:4-6). The predominant feature of the biblical pattern of life is unassuming, unheroic, inconspicuous piety... "The wages of the hired servant shall not abide with thee..." (Lev. 19:13)... When you build a new house, you shall make a parapet for your roof" (Deut. 22:8)... The challenge we face is a test of our integrity. [5]

Those words are no less true today than when he first wrote them and they were no less true then then when the prophets themselves first uttered them. The ethical dimension of kashrut has now entered the discourse of Jewish life. In that regard Magen Tzedek has succeeded admirably, as we were the first folks to address the production of kosher food and the absence of serious fidelity to Jewish ethical demands. But the mission itself is not yet complete. That remains our challenge and our responsibility.

---

[5] Abraham Joshua Heschel, *The Insecurity of Freedom*, 102-104, emph. in orig.

Pluralism in Jewish Education

Documenting Core Values:
A Pluralism Audit in a Jewish Day School

Joel Alter

Many Jewish day schools recruit families and students from Jewishly diverse backgrounds, then market that diversity as a competitive advantage. Diversity in a school signals "we're like a happy family," in which everyone belongs. In truth, that diversity is often arrived at pragmatically, as a necessary choice to fill the seats. I do not mean that it is necessarily a grudging choice or that it masks some underlying conflict: the unity of the Jewish people is a deeply and broadly felt principle among school leaders. But how diversity plays out in the life of a school is different when it is arrived at pragmatically than when it emerges from an ideological stance.

A diverse student body that derives from the fiscal need to "put *tuchases* (bottoms) in seats" demands that school leaders make accommodations for everyone in the school. Typically, *tefillah* (prayer), *kashrut* (dietary laws), dress code, and the content and approach in Judaic studies classes are the primary contexts in which diversity is negotiated. A common version of a pragmatically diverse school is one sponsored by an Orthodox Jewish community that is too small in number to fill all the seats with the children of Orthodox families. In this example, Orthodox observance and outlook are the baseline in one or more respects of school life and program, while non-Orthodox practice and outlook are purposefully accommodated in a range of ways.

In intentionally diverse — or pluralistic — schools, diversity is not a set of accommodations; pluralism is the schools' central organizing premise. Pluralism, in this context, reflects and affirms the legitimacy of multiple expressions of Jewishness and Judaism. In a pluralistic school, the foundational ideas may read something like this:

> No one expression of Judaism has a monopoly on truth or legitimacy. Taken together, the many strands of Jewish expression weave the tapestry of Judaism. This is to be celebrated. It's important that our children be exposed to this diversity of Jewish expression; that they learn about different approaches and how to respect the people following them. Through that exposure, our students refine and strengthen their own unique expressions.

Such schools take form in the spirit of, "Let's see how broad a swath of the Jewish youth (and their families) we can bring together to learn and form a community. Our pluralistic understanding of Judaism echoes our celebration of diversity in society in general."

While it makes sense for a pluralistic school, which makes celebrating diversity a central value, to establish and maintain thoughtful structures and practices for negotiating differences, that is easier said than done. Jewish day schools, after all, teach toward commitment. Commitment is (typically) narrowing; pluralism is (typically) broadening. And there the challenge begins.

In 2010, when I served as *rav beit hasefer* (school rabbi) and assistant head of school at the pluralistic Jewish Community Day School (JCDS) in Watertown, Massachusetts, I was tasked with implementing a board mandate to conduct a pluralism audit. This was to be a thorough assessment of the state of pluralism in the school, which had, since its founding, considered pluralism as a cultural pillar. The pluralism audit was among the prescriptions of a strategic plan prepared a year earlier. If pluralism is essential to JCDS's identity, went the reasoning, then it requires the same amount of planning and assessment as the school's formal curriculum, enrollment goals and brick-and-mortar infrastructure.

If pluralism ought to permeate the school's operation and experience, then an audit should seek to comprehensively examine its presence wherever possible, in formal curriculum documents; pictures and materials on the walls; printed materials, such as the application packet; development materials, such as seasonal letters to prospective donors; and, of course, the school website. It should also examine the impact of pluralism on students through live observation of secular and Judaic classes, to describe well enough for analysis the transmission of openness and inquiry that underlie pluralistic modes of teaching and learning. Stakeholders with lived experience (e.g., current students, faculty members, alumni, parents of current and past students, etc.) of the school should be surveyed for their memories and perceptions.

Significantly, a pluralism audit (unlike the annual audits in a CFO's office) cannot simply grade the school for compliance. Compliance is relevant when there is a single, clear standard against which practice is measured. Pluralism, as an element of culture and an approach to living and learning together, must be assessed according to parameters that are variable and contextual. Thus, the first thing to measure through a pluralism audit is whether there is even a shared understanding of what pluralism means in the school community.

At its most basic level, a culture of pluralism clusters around a welcoming and caring spirit of live and let live, a comfort with—and celebration of—diversity. It implies recognition that everyone in the community has a respected place and the right to be him-, her-, and even their-self. This welcoming spirit, when applied in the context of a Jewish school, also embraces the range of Jewish identity, expression and observance among school families and their children.

Pluralism can also be understood as a way of living and learning together in a Jewish community. In this usage, pluralism is a prism, consciously used to mediate constituents' differences. The goal of pluralism, according to this understanding, is to sustain an intentionally diverse community that will learn and grow together. Such a community thrives best through students' (and their families') regular encounters with members who are different from them. Encountering difference increases one's self-understanding at least as much as it increases one's understanding of others. By this reasoning, an active culture of pluralism cultivates self-confidence and a non-defensive commitment to one's own position, even as one honors people who are passionate about their own, alternative commitments.

Critically, given the presumption of respect granted through the former understanding of pluralism (i.e., the ethos that I'm ok and so are you), the latter understanding (i.e., a way of living and learning together) calls on community members to navigate the tensions between preserving the integrity of their own values and preserving the integrity of others' values. This is the sensitive point where "mere" tolerance crosses over into pluralistic accommodation: Members may need to compromise certain personal priorities or beliefs to help ensure everyone in the community feels present, valued and welcome. At a minimum, a pluralistic community must grant full legitimacy to—and acceptance of—each person, regardless of whether certain members fundamentally disagree with each other. In this way, the community holds together.

The compromises required to establish and sustain a pluralistic community in a school highlight the inherent tensions between community and individual autonomy, value-based positions and "mere" preferences, competing cultural priorities, and sources of authority. They also highlight the shared values around which the school has coalesced and which make all the other compromises worthwhile. The discussions and negotiations around pluralism may be heady and they may be tense, but they are rarely boring. They can contribute powerfully to a culture of meaning in a school.

Like any core value a school may hold, pluralism is hard to practice. It will be set against other competing values (like unity) and constrained by pragmatic realities (like available teaching hours and faculty competencies). Pluralism in particular is hard to realize, both because it is not a single quantifiable thing and because it can always be cultivated in new, more sophisticated and subtle ways throughout the life of the school. Nonetheless, or perhaps even because pluralism is an imprecise target, a multi-modal mechanism like a pluralism audit offers a school the opportunity to examine a core value—a pillar of its mission—deeply.

Pursuing an exercise like the audit can feel indulgent because it is time intensive for staff and expends quite a lot of parents' and lay leaders' volunteer capital. The effort is worth it, however, because by investigating a school through a single lens, an audit can turn up valuable data that would otherwise pass unnoticed. By examining a core value in a sophisticated way, and with the involvement of the entire school community, a school can educate its stakeholders about its values. If conducted successfully, an audit will reignite stakeholders' enthusiasm for the school's mission and its as-yet unrealized potential. Lay and professional leadership may emerge with a clear mandate from parents and others about how to prioritize new and renewed efforts in cultivating and sustaining a pluralistic culture. My experience with the pluralism audit clarified for me and my school, the importance of reassuring the community members that their voices would be heard and that the pluralistic face of our *tefillah* program required consistent tending, for instance.

Most importantly, the pluralism audit highlighted for us at JCDS the importance of educating around a particular core value. The fact that this value was part of the school's vocabulary—in essence, was what the school believed and asserted about itself—did not guarantee that all the community members fully understood it. This was not surprising. But conducting the audit helped enlighten the community members and provide invaluable information for future prioritizing, teaching and programming.

Details of the JCDS audit are proprietary. This is key generalizable point of the audit I conducted, focusing on essential value at one school: The implementation of a school's core values merits periodic close examination. An audit of any one core value's lived expression in a school can be an exciting and motivating exercise in living the mission. And living their mission is what good schools do.

Building Community in a Pluralist High School

Susan I. Shevitz and Rahel Wasserfall

Context and Questions

The religious practice at an intentionally pluralistic Jewish high school in the United States that we are calling "Tikhon" entails prayer services in the morning and, for those who are interested, in the afternoon as well. In order to provide services that are appropriate to the full range of its students, Tikhon organizes dozens of options in the morning, though not all are during each trimester. These range from traditional services, in which males and females sit separately and men assume the leading liturgical roles, to discussions and yoga with meditation. Students choose the service that is of interest to them—and to some extent, since these are adolescents, with which their families are comfortable. By doing this, Tikhon legitimates the range of approaches to Judaism that Tikhon families hold and makes a statement about its understanding of pluralism.

Despite this effort to respect and support the multiplicity of approaches to prayer, conflicts that challenge students sometimes arise. A girl who believes that females should not be counted in a minyan (the quorum of ten needed to recite some of the prayers) and who goes with her friends to the most traditionally observant service held each morning, reflects on her experiences with prayer at Tikhon. The service is known as the meḥitsah (partition) minyan since the seating areas for the females and males are separated by a partition. She recalls a morning when the meḥitsah minyan did not have the ten males needed for a participant to say Kaddish (the prayer to remember a deceased relative):[1]

> I remember [what happened] earlier in the year, [with]
> my friend who couldn't say Kaddish because there wasn't a

---

[1] Minyan technically refers to the quorum of ten needed for the group to include several of the prayers; more generally, the term refers to the entire prayer group. In the meḥitsah minyan, males and females sit separately and only males are allowed to lead the prayers, read from Torah and assume other liturgical responsibilities. The egalitarian ("egal") minyan gives equal opportunity for males and females to participate in and lead the services and allows them to sit together during the services.

This research was supported by a generous grant from the Mandel Center for Studies in Jewish Education at Brandeis University.

minyan. So one girl from the [meḥitsah minyan] was actually willing to go to the egal minyan so that they could have a minyan [because a boy from the egal minyan came into the meḥitsah one and preserved the quorum] … so that the person in meḥitsah could say Kaddish. I don't know how you categorize that, like what's that called? But [the girl who left the meḥitsah minyan and went to the egalitarian one] honestly believed that she should not be counted in a minyan, but she went anyway for the sake of someone who had to say Kaddish. And that was just—people do make sacrifices.[2]

A boy who identifies himself as a Reform Jew quickly concurs: "You can keep your own beliefs, but at the same time help other people, acknowledge, accept and respect their beliefs."

This expresses the form of pluralism to which Tikhon aspires, as explained by the head of school's message on the school's website:

Jewish pluralism is a hallmark of our school. Our students represent a broad spectrum of religious, educational and cultural beliefs. Tikhon is a place where Conservative, Orthodox, Reconstructionist, Reform and secular Jews can come together as a caring community in which to learn and to grow. Here we celebrate the values we have in common as we explore the important ideological differences that make us distinct. The pluralism we preach is one of engagement through which we challenge each other in the process of understanding each other.

The tension between, in this statement's words, "the values we have in common" and "the important ideological differences that make us distinct" are visible in the students' discussion about the minyan decision. The student's ideological position is clear. Committed to praying in a meḥitsah minyan, she neither dismisses nor denigrates the other minyanim. Despite her commitment, she faces a dilemma. If she sticks with her beliefs and stays in her own minyan, another person is unable to say Kaddish, something this student agrees is important. This tension reveals a second key commitment: being part

---

[2] These and all following quotations from student and faculty are from written or recorded field notes.

of a wider community. The student expresses her resolution as a "sacrifice," neither taken lightly nor regretted.

This case uncovers the complex questions that are the focus of this chapter. They are generally below the surface at Tikhon and in other settings that value diversity: when is loyalty to one's own ideas and actions paramount, and when are the needs of others in the community taken into account when religious belief is at stake? How does Tikhon's emphasis on diversity affect its efforts to build a cohesive school community? With its focus on the differences among people, pluralism can be seen as a centrifugal force that helps individuals and sub-groups develop their unique viewpoints. The concept of community, on the other hand, is a centripetal force that brings people closer to shared understanding and values. If supporting individuals' diverse positions is essential to Tikhon's form of pluralism, what does it do to harness centripetal, community-building forces?

This chapter investigates how Tikhon deals with these questions in its educational practice, and analyses what the practices reveal about its understanding of pluralism. It argues that two dynamics are fundamental to Tikhon's efforts: first, the need to create an environment in which participants can risk the differentiation, debate, discussion, and openness to co-operation and change that are at the heart of Tikhon's understanding of community; and second, the need to create a psychological sense of community in which "difference" is central to the conception of community.

This inquiry is part of a larger project to study how pluralism is enacted and understood at Tikhon. During the 2005/6 school year the authors of this chapter followed the incoming class to see how they were socialized into the school's conception of pluralism. This observation took place in classes, at school events, and in committee meetings; in detailed interviews with thirty administrators and teachers; in focus groups with students; and through analyses of student work, curricula, school papers and magazines, the website, and other relevant sources of information. We believe that the approach and methods we found at Tikhon can be applied to other settings where the tension between the individual and the group is central to the educational approach.

Community, Diversity, and Pluralism at Tikhon

Founded in 1997, Tikhon draws students from a large metropolitan area. Students in the 2005/6 ninth-grade class that was followed come from families in thirty-five towns; thirty-seven percent of these families receive scholarships from the school that enable their children to attend. As an intentionally pluralistic school, Tikhon works hard to recruit students from across the spectrum of Jewish practice and beliefs, from secular at one end to Orthodox at the other, as well as students who are all—in the phrase heard frequently in the school—"serious about their Jewish lives." While all high schools face the problem of forging a disparate group of ninth-graders into a functioning class that identifies with the school's preferred values and norms, the problem of socializing new students in this school has an additional complication: the school's commitment to a particular type of pluralism.

Our analysis of pluralism is framed by the work of Walzer, who distinguishes between "tolerating" (the attitude) and "tolerance" (the practice),[3] on both the personal and the political level, and Stone, who defines pluralism as coexistence with difference that is born out of an appreciation for diversity, multiplicity and particularity; and a recognition that distinct traditions and opinions are nonetheless interdependent—that they share certain goals and common projects and therefore that social collaboration and legal interaction are both possible and necessary even between groups or individuals otherwise holding mutually exclusive, conflicting viewpoints, each deemed by the other to be in error.[4]

A senior student at Tikhon expressed this idea directly:

> During my time at Tikhon I have learned the importance and necessity for tolerance. It is a message ingrained in the very idea of Tikhon—a pluralistic day school tolerant of all forms of Jewish religious practice.

One way in which the types of pluralism enacted in Jewish educational settings may be distinguished is to see these efforts on a continuum of engagement with difference on which three points are identified: (1) demographic, (2) co-existence, and (3) generative pluralism. (Since this article was first written, we have differentiated between engaged pluralism and generative pluralism.) Tikhon goes beyond demographic and co-existence pluralism. While it actively seeks demographic diversity, and assumes that individuals and groups will learn to tolerate each other and co-exist with the different ideas and ideologies represented, it strives for what we call "generative pluralism" as its ideal model. The school's visionaries define pluralism as "the ability to understand, hold, and grapple with multiple, even contradictory interpretations

---

[3] Walzer, *On Toleration*, pp. xi–xiii.
[4] Stone, "Tolerance versus Pluralism," 107.

and perspectives.[5] They expect that students will learn to articulate their own ideas, engage with others' ideas, and think deeply, all towards the goals of strengthening their own positions, possibly changing them or even generating new approaches as a result of the interactions. Diversity of opinion does not necessarily exist only between different groups; it may also exist within any particular group, as it does among Tikhon students. In such cases, the challenge is that people who hold very different versions of a shared tradition and culture have to "tolerate, appreciate and work with others' interpretations."[6] Generating new ideas together with people who have different beliefs is the distinguishing characteristic of this type of pluralism. A Tikhon senior gives thoughtful voice to this idea:

> The Jews are a wandering people, both geographically itinerant and spiritually roving. A Jew can never stay in one state of mind for too long. We debate; we change our minds; we amend. Everything I've learned at Tikhon has bolstered this view . . . Tikhon allowed me to change my opinions and alter my beliefs in an environment where I can gracefully cede even my strongest certainties to new ideas.

An administrator at Tikhon illustrates one aspect of generative pluralism by relating how a very traditional student from the meḥitsah minyan challenged a young woman from the traditional but egalitarian minyan to explore why she was not putting on *tefillin* (phylacteries) even though she was wearing a talit (prayer shawl) and leading the service. She says that Tikhon asks people the question: "Within the context of your own Jewish construct, how can you be a stronger Jew?" We also see Tikhon's pluralism in the way in which it crafted a way to chant the opening section of birkat hamazon (grace after meals) that was acceptable to all students, from the most liberal to the most traditional.[7] Diversity at Tikhon, especially around significant Jewish ideas and practices, is the grist for the intellectual and religious mill associated with generative pluralism. It is a precondition for exploring and expanding beliefs and actions.

This stance is similar to the approach advocated by Diana Eck, one of

---

[5] Tikhon, "Self-Study," 47. See also Wasserfall and Shevitz, "The Language of Pluralism," for further discussion of how Tikhon understands this.

[6] Walzer, *On Toleration*, 65 (emphasis added).

[7] The more traditional students do not accept the legitimacy of a female leading the prayer, while other students believe that an egalitarian approach is the proper way.

the leading scholars of religious pluralism. Eck asserts that in contemporary American society, which is characterized by a religious diversity going far beyond the three monotheistic faiths that dominated just fifty years ago—Protestantism, Catholicism, and Judaism—pluralism entails "engagement, involvement and participation. It is the language of traffic, exchange, dialog and debate ... [that must be] claimed anew" as the context changes.[8]

Tikhon's pluralism focuses on pluralism within the Jewish community, largely avoiding situating it within general society. It relies heavily on cognitive approaches that are promoted through its formal and informal curricula by implicit norms and explicit instruction. It wants to enroll, in words heard repeatedly, "serious Jews" who will engage with ideas and texts. Teachers do not want "wishy-washy students," but enjoy encountering adolescents who can "push back." They claim this is not an "anything goes" approach but one that wants students to justify positions with information and textual references. As one teacher sees it, "You need to understand that your interpretations come from your religious beliefs and you must be willing to interpret your rules ...." Revealing assumptions and recognizing principles that one will not compromise are part of the Tikhon experience. The same teacher who emphasizes that people must "do things for the sake of the community" recognizes that "sometimes you have to keep your own principles."

Enacting Pluralism at School

To achieve engaged and generative pluralism Tikhon asks its students to take a risk; they are to relinquish certainty as they engage with people holding different ideas. This commitment is nowhere more apparent than in its "debate midrash." The phrase itself is a play on the Hebrew words "beit midrash"—the traditional term for the "house of study" which, in Tikhon's vocabulary, is also the large room in which the school community gathers for special events. The process leading to a debate midrash—as well as the event itself—demonstrates Tikhon's commitment to individuals' perspectives and group needs. One example follows.

> Several male students complained that Tikhon was becoming, in their words, "less Jewish." Administrators suggested that they bring their complaints and suggestions to the rabbis' committee that consists of the school's varied

---

[8] Eck, *A New Religious America*, 69.

rabbis: Reform, Conservative, traditional, Orthodox, and those who choose no denominational label. As the students entered the committee meeting, it was clear they were accustomed to speaking their minds. One charge followed another, infused with the emotion of aggrieved adolescents. Finally, some rabbis intervened, asking the complainants what they wanted to do about the situation. The students rattled off several ideas: the ninth graders should have more mandatory prayer; Tikhon should limit the number of students coming from public (state) schools; and males should have to wear kipot when they study the Judaic subjects. A debate midrash was called on the topic: "Should boys be required to wear kipot for 'limudei kodesh' [study of Jewish texts]?"

As the debate midrash began, a teacher stood in front of the large assembly of students and academic staff members. Groups were arranged in a U shape. People taking the pro position stood on one side of the room, those arguing con stood on the other, and the undecideds formed the base of the U. Those in the undecided group could not proffer their opinions until they moved to one side or the other. As speakers made their points, individual students and faculty changed sides, with the undecided joining the fray as they formed opinions. Any individual might change his or her mind and cross the room multiple times. The governing rules for the debate midrash were that people take turns in speaking and use respectful but strong language—they were not allowed to use "mushy" words. Below is a paraphrased excerpt of the debate midrash:

> Teacher 1 (pro): In the entire world you take your hat off as a sign of respect. For a Jew everybody needs to have their head covered: this is a sign of respect.
> Boy 1 (con; reads from a text he brought and says): It is only a custom, not a halakhah [rabbinic law].
> (Boy 2, pro, wearing a kipah, gets up and looks for a gemara [Talmud text] to refute this argument)
> Girl 1 (pro): It is a minhag [custom], but a symbol of learning and we should respect the learning.
> Boy 1 (con): It has become a symbol of observance; it is all about division, not about learning. I do not feel differ-

ently when I study and I should not be obliged to wear a kipah.

Teacher 2 (con): It bothers me emotionally to see somebody without a kipah learning but I am against making it a required practice because I see it as a very powerful symbolic act that somebody can study without a kipah. It means that the most secular person can have a claim on these texts. Kipah can also be divisive, kipah serugah [a knitted kipah, generally seen as a sign that the wearer is a modern Orthodox or right-wing Conservative Jew], where you wear it on your head ... or if you wear a hat ..., kipah defines and divides Jews.

At that moment Teacher 1 stands and moves to the con side with Teacher 2.

Many things are going on in this vignette. Students are comfortable airing their complaints to administrators and teachers who take them seriously and are willing to devote a precious resource, time, to exploring the topic through a "debate midrash." Students and teachers are expected, in the school's words, to be 'engaged' with the issue and each other. They develop arguments, citing texts and precedent, but they also speak personally, as did the boy who describes how he feels when he wears a kipah. A teacher changes his position even while acknowledging that he is not necessarily comfortable with the outcome—"it bothers me emotionally"—having been convinced that not requiring the kipah is the better option. The 'debate midrash' is a public display, not only of individuals' positions, but also of two other factors: how well a position can be argued and whether a participant will allow him- or herself to be persuaded enough to change positions. Participants change position only when they feel safe enough to risk publicly disclosing their ideas and changing their minds without fear of ostracism or ridicule.[9] Focusing on individuals' positions while maintaining the sense of safety are preconditions to the school's form of pluralism. They are also components of its community-building efforts.

The seriousness with which Tikhon takes the individual's perspectives, at

---

[9] The only time the researchers saw any ridicule was at the Purim celebration, where students poked fun at administrators, teachers, and a few other students. Although Purim is a topsy-turvy day, the faculty was aghast when a student was ridiculed, even if in jest.

least about religious matters, is seen in many aspects of school life. To give one example, there are thirty-seven different prayer experiences available over the course of a week, ranging from meḥitsah and traditional egalitarian minyanim to yoga or art and prayer, and from Reform to neo-Hasidic formats. And should a student not find one that meets her needs, she can approach an administrator to create another, as did the student who was "angry at God" and did not think any minyan addressed this adequately. Another student, believing that society's racial and ethnic diversity were not adequately acknowledged in the school, was empowered to find ways to address this in a study group.

An additional element of Tikhon's pluralism is that the issues must really matter to the students.[10] When this happens, they become a centripetal force that unites the students and teachers. Like the kipah question, issues often emerge from the students. At other times, Tikhon tries to stimulate enquiry around issues students might care about but rarely explore: beliefs about God, Judaism, religious practice, as well as social and political positions.[11] It creates programs that challenge students' self-understanding, such as showing a documentary, *Mixed Blessings*, about how four intermarried families deal with their religious differences. Enrolling students from intermarried families and others from families firmly committed to endogamy, the discussion about the film evoked deeply personal responses. In a small group debriefing, one student told of her father's boycott of his niece's marriage to a non-Jew. Another girl in the same session described how she feels pulled between her intermarried parents, one a fundamentalist Christian, the other an Orthodox Jew. In the administration's words, the purpose of these encounters is for students "to take [the presenting issue] seriously" and apply the ideas to their own lives. This process is fraught with risk, especially for adolescents, who are exquisitely sensitive to their place in the group even as they explore new behaviors and try on new ideas.

---

[10] Sociologist of religion Robert Wuthnow asserts that many manifestations of pluralism in America are shallow and avoid the hard questions about difference, pluralism, and society. He advocates a more "intentional" approach or what he calls "reflective pluralism," which acknowledges "how and why people are different and the same." See Wuthnow, *America and the Challenges of Religious Diversity*, on multiculturalism in the classroom.

[11] A weekly all-school assembly, called limud kelali, is one forum where a wide range of speakers come to introduce students to interesting, sometimes controversial, ideas.

Balancing Risk and Safety: Tikhon as a "Safe Enough Place"

Because Tikhon expects that students and teachers will risk self-disclosure and argument as well as openness to change, it needs to provide an environment in which all feel sufficiently safe to do this. Adapting Winnicott's well-known concept of the "good enough mother,"[12] we see Tikhon as trying to be a "safe enough" environment that stimulates differentiation and debate while also providing support and acceptance. Many teachers and administrators define the school and its pluralism as a safe place. Some mean by this that the school is a haven from the harsh divisiveness of Jewish life, while others describe how the school tries to create a safe environment for students to take the risks that are central components of Tikhon's brand of pluralism. The community does not shy away from controversy, even controversy that may be related to students' identities. Precisely because such controversies are relevant to students' lives, Tikhon believes that it is important to engage adolescents with them.

Tikhon tries to structure a "safe enough" environment in several ways. It works hard to develop personal trust and understanding among and between students and faculty. On the most obvious level, it has incorporated many established approaches to building a school community. The process starts with the orientation, where all the new students, from their different communities and backgrounds, interact with one another. Small advisory groups serve as places where concerns can be raised. There are dozens of informal learning programs outside the classroom that allow students and faculty to experience different facets of each other. The office of the director of student life is a hub of the concerns that the students bring. There are grade-wide and school-wide Shabbatonim, and weekly limud kelali assemblies that teach the entire school about interesting ideas, people, and projects. All these community-building activities run alongside a plethora of standard extracurricular activities, including many sports teams and clubs. The assumption is that individual connections build the necessary goodwill and trust among students with differing views that will serve as "money in the bank" when conflict, inevitably, occurs.

Vulnerable Student Groups

Even with these measures in place to help build a supportive community,

---

[12] Winnicott, *The Child, the Family.*

teachers and administrators still identify three groups of students they believe to be vulnerable: students with less Jewish knowledge than most, students with special educational needs, and those whose religious practices are more liberal or more traditional than the perceived norm.

Tikhon's largest single group of students comes from Conservative day schools, many of whom also attend Jewish camps and youth groups. They are described by some teachers as being on an axis of Jewish engagement.[13]

These students are deeply involved in Jewish practices at school: they sing special Sabbath songs at Shabbatonim, organize prayer services, and so on. Some teachers think that many students without this background are "at the periphery" and wonder whether they can be prepared before the event so that they can more fully participate. With Tikhon's strong emphasis on rabbinics, Tanakh (the Hebrew Bible), and Hebrew, as well as argument and debate, these students are at a disadvantage that is reinforced by how the school tracks the levels of students in Hebrew and other classes. Special needs students are also identified as vulnerable, since they have to work hard just to keep up with Tikhon's challenging curriculum. They are often at a disadvantage in an environment that stresses verbal and analytical skills, as are students whose strengths lie in other areas. Students, whether identified as having special needs or not, who are not comfortable or adept with Gann's focus on argumentation and analysis are also disadvantaged.

In addition, students who perceive their religious beliefs to be outside the center are sometimes concerned that their views will be minimized or, if an especially contentious issue is being discussed, in the words of a teacher, "bashed."[14] Tikhon challenges students who hold more and also less traditional beliefs. As we saw in the vignette about saying Kaddish, both liberal and traditional students sometimes consider compromising a principle in order to support others in their community. At other times, students feel pressure to fit

---

[13] The pattern of feeder schools in part explains the predominance of Conservative affiliated students. In Tikhon's region there are five K–8 (kindergarten to eighth grade) Conservative or community schools and a sixth, also K–8, is pluralist. There is also one Reform day school and a modern Orthodox K–12 school whose high school program was considered weak when Tikhon was founded. Many observers claim that Tikhon's opening motivated educational improvements there so that fewer of its students now want to leave after the eighth grade. The Reform presence, though small, is growing, and most of the Orthodox who have enrolled came from the pluralist school or schools that are further away.

[14] We saw some good-natured teasing but no instances of 'bashing' or belittling others for their religious beliefs; if this does happen it might take place outside the purview of researchers.

in—if not at school, then at events outside school. This might be in a setting as simple as a group gathered in a student's house on Sabbath afternoon or as exotic as somewhere in Europe during an Exploration Week trip with school-mates deciding what to have for dinner. Traditional students are also aware they learn less of the classical rabbinic texts than do students at Orthodox schools, and that, as seniors, they will study the documentary hypothesis regarding human authorship of the Bible. They face particular dilemmas around dress and behavior. In the words of one teacher, "It takes a special kind of Orthodox family to enroll their children here." The teachers are aware that these students sometimes feel under assault by the majority's more liberal thinking. Some students proudly identify as Orthodox and deeply appreciate being in this environment, and there are students who experiment with and embrace Orthodoxy as a result of Tikhon's pluralism.

Students from more liberal backgrounds likewise feel that they are asked to compromise, in their case to meet the needs of the more stringently observant students. They complain that the ideological seriousness of the liberal position is not always recognized. Students in Tikhon's wide middle range, the so-called Conservative axis, also face these issues, though not as acutely since they too are tugged by different commitments. Thus all Tikhon's students confront the question: When do I compromise, hold on to, or change my beliefs? Tikhon wants to make these questions discussable; it sees this as a characteristic of engaged, cognitive pluralism. And this can happen only when its students, especially those who are vulnerable, feel safe.

Teachers' Role in Enhancing Safety

Tikhon relies heavily on its faculty to create a "safe enough" environment in several ways. It assumes that the presence of teachers with diverse viewpoints and lifestyles is itself a powerful message. The range of faculty in terms of Jewish religious belief is immediately visible to anyone literate in the costumes of contemporary Jewry: men who wear hats alongside men who wear knitted, cloth, or no kipot; women whose heads are covered alongside others wearing jeans and sweaters. The rabbis' committee, composed of faculty and administrators from across the full spectrum of Jewish life, examine the school's religious and spiritual dimension. There are openly gay/lesbian teachers and non-Jewish faculty and staff. Students recognize this diversity, and many value the opportunity to study with someone whose religious views differ from their own. In interviews, several students mentioned an Orthodox teacher who is popular even though she presents content that seems strange to the less observant students.

They considered the teacher "brilliant ... she knows as much as any man or rabbi ... really cares about the subject, and is authentic." At the same time, Tikhon makes certain that students have access to role models who are more similar to their familiar ways of being Jewish.

Tikhon deliberately arranges for teachers with different points of view to work together, especially when exploring contentious topics such as intermarriage, attitudes towards the Muslim world, or sexuality. The mandatory "pluralism lab," taken by each ninth-grader for one term, is co-taught by two rabbis who represent different religious ideologies. Students see two authority figures respectfully disagree with each other and use information to bolster their positions. They model relationships based on respect and inquiry.

Not merely passive observers, teachers also stay actively alert to student discomfort. One teacher summarized the position of the teachers who make up the faculty's pluralism committee: "The school is obligated to make sure that once you're in this school you're protected, you're safe, you're respected. And you shouldn't feel pain. You shouldn't feel insecurity. There should be adult voices who can speak up, 'No, I think this is a legitimate position.'"

Many teachers take this responsibility seriously. After the documentary and debriefing about intermarriage, for example, several teachers sought out individual students who were upset. One boy felt marginalized because he is from an intermarried family; another was upset, a teacher recalled,

> "that the school would show a movie like that, that seemed to be non-judgmental about intermarriage." Before the ninth-grade Shabbaton, the teacher in charge of the new students instructed colleagues to "be very aware of kids at the fringes," and a secular Israeli teacher made a point of connecting with students who were not part of the axis of the more actively Jewish students. Several administrators and teachers described their offices as places where students who have concerns come to talk.

In particular, Tikhon works hard to maintain the Orthodox segment of its enrollment; it is widely believed that if it loses its Orthodox population, its community will be seriously compromised. Teachers—especially those teachers who are themselves Orthodox—go out of their way to support traditional students. Noting the liberal tendencies of most of the student body, they believe that when complex, controversial issues such as responses to homosexuality are brought up, "the real challenge [is] not to the liberal position but to tradition. Would the traditional voice speak up?" One traditional teacher talks about how careful he is to present a "nuanced view" that might otherwise be lacking. A graduate reported the importance of this teacher's efforts: "I dreaded going to the [whole school] meeting. It was going to be heavy and there would be tradition-bashing. I am struggling ... to hold on to my faith. That [the teacher, an Orthodox rabbi] took that position made it OK." Another graduate wrote that as a student he saw things "as black or white" and that an Orthodox teacher "reminded me, by using texts, [that] there are complexities. Not black and white. There can be texts that say homosexuality is wrong but others about how we have to treat people humanely."

While students from Reform backgrounds might seem to fit Tikhon's ethos more easily, we saw occasions when students or teachers had to remind people that "Reform is not less, it is other." There is the constant need at Tikhon to counter the Jewish community's hierarchical assumptions that Orthodox means most religious and Reform means least.

Relying on teachers' sensitivities to weave a safety net for students who may not feel comfortable is an ad hoc approach, and as the school grows it becomes harder for all teachers to be aware of the specific issues individual students face. Students might easily slip through the net, especially if the perception of one teacher is correct, in feeling that the less Jewishly knowledgeable students are "disenfranchised." It remains to be seen whether Tikhon will be able to rely on this close-knit support system as it grows.

An additional, but contested, way in which Tikhon attempts to make the school safe is by avoiding use of the standard denominational labels. Some teachers and administrators want students to work out their approaches to Jewish life on the basis of the principles and beliefs they hold, rather than by clinging to the names that indicate affiliation with a denomination or movement. These people argue that the key point is not loyalty to a movement, but determining one's own beliefs and being able to engage meaningfully with those who disagree. Other teachers and administrators are less comfortable with this approach, asserting that denominations and movements are the students' frames of reference; why pretend they are not there? The disagreement itself expresses Tikhon's pluralism, and since there is no need for a single policy or resolution, the "maḥloket"—legitimate difference of opinion—can be experienced as either confusing or empowering. It certainly reinforces the sense that different approaches, based in reasoned opinions, can co-exist in the school, and this helps students grow and work together productively.[15]

Characteristics of the Tikhon Community

We have seen how Tikhon creates its pluralism by maintaining a diverse student body and managing the risks involved in self-disclosure and argument with its "safe enough" environment. At the same time, Tikhon cultivates a sense of community, without which its pluralism would collapse into disconnected sub-groups doing "parallel play," so to speak. Simply enrolling a heterogeneous student body without helping it explore its diversity would produce mere demographic pluralism rather than the engaged, generative pluralism that Tikhon seeks. What, then, draws the students of different types together? What provides the centripetal force that fosters community? How does commitment to the community develop alongside Tikhon's efforts to support its diversity?

In thinking about how Tikhon creates community, we may usefully turn to Arnett's definition of community as a group built on shared memories and aspirations.[16] What is the history Tikhon's constituents share, as a people and as a school, and to what can they all aspire?

Part of the reason why this focus on community is so central is that Tikhon is a Jewish school. Judaism is a religion that is built on community experience and identity. A core assumption is that Jews are a people who share a common destiny; hence the requirement for praying in a minyan, the first-person-plural formulation of many prayers, and other manifestations of the prominence of the group. Valuing the group in this way is not easily compatible with the modern Western focus on the individual, and the tension between the needs of the individual and those of the group lies at the heart of many of Tikhon's dilemmas. As the mission statement says, Tikhon aspires to be "a sacred community within the Jewish people" and to form "a diverse and pluralistic community." It continues: "Our diversity is a strength. An atmosphere of mutual respect provides a welcome forum for grappling with fundamental religious questions and individual Jewish identities." The mission statement goes on to assert that the "school nurtures a Jewish community characterized by a shared tradition, a common dedication to social justice and a love of learning."

In visiting Tikhon, one feels, as if it is palpable, the sense of community. Students interact easily with faculty, administrators, and each other in and

---

[15] This analysis is based on Sarason, *The Psychological Sense of Community*, and Sergiovanni, *Building Community in Schools*.

[16] Winnicott, *The Child, the Family*.

out of the classroom. They seem at home in their space, using it respectfully yet fully. There are many informal areas where small groups of students catch up with each other, do schoolwork, or just hang out. Even during large events like school assemblies and fire drills, there is a sense of purpose, order, and belonging. Teachers often joke about Tikhon being their home, demanding as much of their time as it does of the students'. Seniors' statements in the graduation booklet often refer to "community"—a term they associate with wonderful group experiences, deep friendships, relationships with teachers, and other heartfelt memories that would be expected of high school seniors. But community holds other meanings as well. Typical statements include: "I have gained an understanding of how important it is for people to support each other." "Everybody has a different point of view …. I think our class is especially strong because we created a community in sincerity and honesty." "The community has been hungry for questions and open to different beliefs, and I have had the opportunity to observe both my own and my peers', and my evolving sense of curiosity." And within such an environment, another writes, "[I] learned patience and understanding of different people's ideas and views … while still being able to solidify my own beliefs and opinion."

Many of the ways Tikhon builds a sense of safety simultaneously foster commitment to the community: informal, experiential learning; close student-teacher relationships; opportunities for involvement; and being taken seriously. In addition, teachers and administrators openly describe how they do things differently "for the sake of" the Tikhon community—or, to use the formulation of the first student quoted in this chapter, how they "sacrifice" for the good of the whole. A Reform teacher, for example, explains to her classes how she adhered to a more stringent form of kashrut for the school barbecue than she would apply in her own home. An Orthodox teacher participates in Shabbatonim though he knows that many participants do things that he believes are prohibited on the Sabbath and that he would not want his children (who accompany him) to do. Sensitivity to the needs of others shapes faculty decisions. Students not only hear this; they see the debates and compromises in action and hear about the anxieties and satisfactions that this approach brings.

Stories repeated at Tikhon about occasions in the school's past convey these ideas. Sometimes they celebrate flexibility—as, for example, when the headmaster changed his mind on a highly charged issue about the ways in which the school could support students' struggles with their sexual identities. Another example relates to issues of Jewish identity: a student who is Jewish by patrilineal descent complained that he was not counted in the minyanim—

so Tikhon quickly added a liberal minyan in which he would be counted. This is consistent with the oft-repeated principle that if Tikhon admits students who are Jews by patrilineal descent and requires them to pray, it is obliged to provide a real prayer option for them if it is to remain true to its pluralistic mission. As a community, Tikhon must make space for all its members.

Other school stories reinforce the responsibility of the group to devise solutions to community dilemmas. We repeatedly heard from students, faculty, and administrators about how, in its first year, Tikhon prepared for its very first Shabbaton. To paraphrase these accounts, "It was three hours before Sabbath and they still didn't know how they would handle Sabbath observance and prayer. The headmaster put everyone in a room and said that they couldn't leave before they figured it out." They had to figure out acceptable ways for people with varied religious practices to live and celebrate together. Another story is told about prayer. Tikhon usually conducts multiple services so that everyone's ritual practices can be honored. After an emotional tour of Auschwitz, however, the students asked to pray together. Teachers recount with pride how students "grappled" with the issues and found a way that worked for traditional as well as non-traditional students, although one student chose to pray on her own rather than in the non-egalitarian minyan. The story epitomizes Tikhon's faith that its students will be sensitive to context and will leave room to maneuver where they can. These events, now part of the school's mythology, demonstrate that Tikhon "trusts the process," to borrow a term from social work. Sometimes it provides structured settings, such as the "debate midrash," to help its members decide what to do. At other times the arrangement is ad hoc. In both cases, Tikhon confers authority on the group to inform and sometimes make the decision, even though the group is working within a known framework, such as the expectation that there will be prayer or the need to respect Sabbath observance. The process assumes that through deliberation the group will successfully craft an approach that sufficiently meets everyone's needs.

When the process sidesteps the students, as with the occasional issues that are resolved at board level, the students react with chagrin, as the line from the student-written Purim shpiel (spoof) shows: "Pluralism rules, subject to changes based on our whims." This line captures two Tikhon realities: pluralism, with its appreciation for differences, does rule at Tikhon; and policies and practices do change, and it is not always clear how decisions are made. While the tacit assumption held by students, teachers and some others is that the final decision rests with the school head, himself an articulate and passionate advocate of pluralism, the process of determining what to do is often far more complex and nuanced than that.

Dealing with diversity in a community is not a challenge unique to Tikhon. Most other aspects of society, from government to families, confront the same task. Postmodern ideas about community suggest that under conditions of diversity communities must have two components: 'acceptance of otherness and cooperation within difference.'[17] Rather than imposing, however gently, the views of the dominant group and downplaying the needs of the others, people in the community are expected to cooperate with each other and find harmonious ways to deal with difference.[18]

In this sense, pluralism is the active engagement with people's differences. Tikhon is intentionally pluralist; it is organized in a way that supports and even favors this kind of engagement. It tries to be an environment in which students, faculty, and other staff explore their differences while feeling part of the collective. It aspires to be a community in which people are united by being different, by learning to respect others' positions, and by working with all sorts of Jews. Perhaps this is what is meant by the phrase so often heard at Tikhon: "We are serious Jews here." As long as students agree with this claim on some level, they belong at Tikhon, and Tikhon can expect them to explore what this means to themselves and others. The developmental need of adolescents to work out who they are while they try on identities and distinguish themselves by being distinctive is well served by Tikhon's brand of pluralism. The paradox is that diversity, often a centrifugal force, becomes the centripetal force. Diversity in Tikhon's pluralist environment unifies Tikhon's students, teachers, and administrators in a shared quest for self-definition, acceptance, challenge, debate, and generativity.

---

[17] Furman, "Postmodernism and Community," 57.

[18] See Beck, "Complexity and Coherence," and Furman, "Postmodernism and Community," for a full discussion of postmodern conceptions of community and their implications for education.

Bibliography

Arnett, R. C., *Communication and Community: Implications of Martin Buber's Dialogue,* (Carbondale, Ill., 1986).

Beck, L. G., "The Complexity and Coherence of Educational Communities: An Analysis of the Images that Reflect and Influence Scholarship and Practice", in G. C. Furman (ed.), School as Community: From Promise to Practice (Albany, NY, 2002), 23–49.

Eck, D. L., "The Challenge of Pluralism," Nieman Reports, 47/2 (1993), <http://www.pluralism.org/research/articles/cop.php?from=articles_index>.

—— *A New Religious America: How a "Christian Country" Has Become the World's Most Religiously Diverse Nation,* (San Francisco, 2002).

Furman, G. C., "Postmodernism and Community in Schools: Unraveling the Paradox," in G. C. Furman (ed.), School as Community: From Promise to Practice (Albany, NY, 2002), 51–75.

Hardy, H., "Taking Pluralism Seriously," Henry Hardy on Isaiah Berlin (Oxford, 2003), <http://berlin.wolf.ox.ac.uk/writings_on_ib/hhonib/taking_pluralism_seriously.html>.

Sarason, S. B., *The Psychological Sense of Community,* (San Francisco, 1974).

Sergiovanni, T. J., *Building Community in Schools* (San Francisco, 1994).

Shevitz, S. L., *Protocol for Investigating the Culture of Jewish Day Schools,* pilot draft (Boston, 2005). Shields, C. M., "Learning from Educators," in G. C. Furman (ed.), School as Community: From Promise to Practice (Albany, NY, 2002).

Sizer, T. R., *Horace's Hope: What Works for the American High School* (New York, 1996).

Stone, S., "Tolerance versus Pluralism in Judaism," *Journal of Human Rights,* 2/1 (2003), 105–19.

Tikhon, "Self-Study," unpublished document prepared for school accreditation process (2005).

Walzer, M., *On Toleration* (New Haven, 1997).

Wasserfall, R., and S. L. Shevitz, "The Language of Pluralism in a Jewish Day High School" working paper, Brandeis University, Waltham, Mass. (Sept. 2006).

Winnicott, D. W., *The Child, the Family and the Outside World* (Reading, Mass., 1987).

Wuthnow, R., *America and the Challenges of Religious Diversity* (Princeton, 2005).

CAJE into NewCAJE:
Pluralistically Educating the Educators

Cherie Koller-Fox

This article will examine the role of pluralism in two Jewish educational conferences—run by The Coalition for the Advancement of Jewish Education (CAJE) and NewCAJE (CAJE's successor). It will begin by giving a history of the organizations and their common philosophy of pluralism. It will then take a close look at the concept of pluralism as understood by conference participants. To research this topic, NewCAJE included two simple questions in its 2015 registration form. Over 400 Jewish educators answered questions about how they understood the importance of pluralism within the conference, how they understood the meaning of the word pluralism, and if and why it was important to them in the setting of a Jewish educational conference. One of the prime findings of this short study was that there was a multiplicity of definitions of the term pluralism, which also shed light on its importance to the individual as they understood the term. This article will also discuss other ways in which pluralism was modeled by the conferences.

The history of CAJE, NewCAJE and the ideal of pluralism

The predecessor organization to NewCAJE[1] was called CAJE—the Coalition for the Advancement of Jewish Education. It was birthed out of Network, a student youth movement aligned with the World Union of Jewish Students. In August of 1976, Network sponsored a conference for Jewish teachers—which was intended to be a place for sharing the many new techniques and ideas that were surfacing in the field of Jewish education at that time. This conference brought together 350 mostly younger educators at Brown University. When it ended, attendees formed a committee to plan another educational conference. The planning committee called the conference "The Conference on Alternatives in Jewish Education" or (CAJE).

From its earliest beginnings, CAJE was pluralistic—drawing its membership from every branch of Judaism. The founders[2] of CAJE, Jerry Benjamin and

---

[1] The acronym NewCAJE does not stand for anything in particular as of 2016.

[2] While Jerry and I were the catalysts who began the organization, it took many

I, believed pluralism was a core ideal for an organization of Jewish educators, holding that Jewish educators, no matter what or where or who they taught, had a great deal to share with each other.

Additionally, pluralism is also reflected in our personal backgrounds. Jerry's commitment to pluralism came from his freshman year in Israel. He saw modern Israel as pluralistic, its atheism as compelling to him as its struggle with religion. Upon his return, Jerry helped found a pluralistic havurah on the campus of Case-Western Reserve University. He also appreciated the Jewish political pluralism he discovered at The North American Jewish Students Network[3]. He became president of Network and brought to that position the Jewish values of his family—a *bubbe* who came from the shtetl and parents who were practicing conservative Jews. Network is where he formed his religious/political pluralistic ideology, which in turn helped to build the foundation of CAJE.

We both grew up in small Ohio cities[4] where the Jewish Center was a common meeting place for the children of the community no matter what synagogue their parents belonged to. In high school, I was very active in BBYO— a non-denominational youth group— and I went to Israel and Europe with them in 1963. The Israel trip was formative for me. It opened my eyes to the wider Jewish world and taught me there was so much more to Judaism and especially to Jewish peoplehood than the confines of my own synagogue or even my own community.

In the early 70's, I was involved with Havurat Shalom in Boston—an alternative model of a synagogue founded by graduate students and not aligned with any existing movement of Judaism. There, we experimented with alternative Jewish worship and living. Havurat Shalom offered a serious critique of synagogues and their overly formal and non-spiritual forms of davening and their hierarchical leadership. As a result of all these formative experiences, pluralism was a positive principle that resonated with me and which I brought to my early conversations about CAJE.

When the first Conference on Alternatives in Jewish Education was held at Brown University, we actively recruited educators from Orthodox and secular schools along with Conservative and Reform educators. We felt that as educa-

---

people on both the east and the west coast to found the organization that became CAJE. You can read more about the founding of CAJE in *Studies in Jewish Education VII: The Beginnings of Jewish Educational Institutions*, ed. Walter Ackerman, 1995.

[3] The North American Student Organization (NETWORK) was active from 1969 to 1978.

[4] I was raised in Akron, Ohio and Jerry in Canton, Ohio.

tors, we were all dealing with the same issues and were all teaching basically the same material. We didn't view denominationalism as a barrier not to be crossed, although previous to CAJE, educators had only met in denominational groupings.

Three anecdotes come to mind from these early conferences that illustrate the positive and negative experiences we confronted as we attempted to hold pluralistic conferences. First, one early conference drew a Chasid from a large, well-known Yeshiva. He had an interest in special needs education, a relatively new concept in the mid-1970's. Dressed in a long black coat and sporting *payot*[5], I saw him engaged in a serious conversation with a young woman wearing short shorts. Their talk was animated as they were both passionate about the subject of special education. In the United States at that time, CAJE was the only place such a discussion could have happened.

The second story I wish to share took place at the fourth conference, held in 1979 at Rutgers University. The conference model included a Shabbat in the middle because the organizers were committed to pluralism and wanted to push the concept and see how it played out over a Shabbat. Rules were developed to allow our diverse community to occupy the same space on Shabbat despite our different practices of Judaism. There were to be multiple *minyanim*[6]. To the organizers, pluralism did not mean that we all worshipped in the same room or in the same way. It meant that as a community, we could co-exist peacefully and could pray separately while celebrating, eating, socializing and learning together.

To realize this ideal, a differentiation was made between public space and private space. This allowed people to celebrate Shabbat according to their traditions in private space. Out of respect for others, however, all public spaces were to be *shomer shabbat*[7] so that no one would feel excluded from participating in public events. Private space also allowed the Reform community to worship with instruments and the Orthodox community to have a *mechitzah*[8]. There were to be study sessions on Shabbat but not classes as usual and there was to be no public writing or media. No one was allowed to live off campus and come in for Shabbat activities. With over 2,000 attendees, the celebration

[5] Side locks worn by some Hassidic Jewish men.

[6] Minyanim are prayer groups made up of ten people or more.

[7] *Shomer Shabbat* refers to observing all the commandments about the Sabbath as understood by orthodox Jews. Practically, it meant no driving in or out of campus, no musical instruments, no microphones, Shabbat elevators, an eruv (fence) that allowed carrying from one building to another, strict observance of candle-lighting times, etc.

[8] A *mechitzah* is a divider put up to separate men and women in prayer.

of Shabbat (planned by Rabbi Neal Kaunfer) showcased pluralism on a huge scale. There were seventeen *minyanim,* each with a full set of leaders and readers. They included an Orthodox service with a *mechitzah,* a women's minyan, a Conservative minyan, an egalitarian Conservative minyan, a meditation minyan, a yoga minyan, a Reform service with instruments, etc. All in all, these seventeen different prayer options were happening side by side in one location! On Friday afternoon, everyone dressed in white and as the *Kabbalat Shabbat*[9] services ended, all seventeen minyanim streamed into the dining hall and joined in singing the Shabbat table blessings together.[10]

My third example is about some of the moments when the ideal of pluralism failed. One year the Shabbat committee placed the Orthodox *minyan* in the room next to the Reform *minyan* and unfortunately, the instruments at the Reform service could be heard through the walls. That caused a great upset. There was also the time someone gave a session on David and Jonathan that implied that they were lovers and not just friends. After seeing the description of that session in the conference program, several Orthodox rabbis refused to allow their educators to attend future conferences. This type of criticism came from all sides. At the 1982 conference at Brandeis, a feminist group threatened to boycott the conference because we allowed a *mechitzah* minyan, which they saw as demeaning to women. Over the years, Reform Jews would complain about the kosher food at the conference, citing the fact that they were perfectly good Jews without keeping kosher; keeping kashrut laws at the conference seemed to them to be a put down of their Reform practice. Pluralism was challenged from many directions.

Even with all the challenges, CAJE continued to practice pluralism by opening the conference up to all those who worked on the transmission of Jewish education, belief, and culture. The conference was kosher and *shomer shabbat*[11] in public spaces so as to accommodate all participants. Because the conference often took place in the three weeks before *Tisha B'Av,*[12] alternative activities were provided—such as musical entertainment for some and non-music alternatives for others. It was always an important goal to celebrate

---

[9] Friday evening prayers welcoming the Sabbath.

[10] On a personal note, I thought that Shabbat at CAJE was the most beautiful thing I had ever seen. To me, the highlight of the CAJE week for the next 30 years was seeing a pluralistic vision of Judaism that I believe is an ideal for the American Jewish community.

[11] Sabbath observant.

[12] Tisha B'Av is a fast day that marks the destruction of the Temple in Jerusalem. It is a three-week mourning period that gets more stringent in the last 9 days. Not listening to live music is one of the stringencies of this period.

differences and promote the importance of respect for other people's ideas and practices because of an enduring belief in *k'lal yisrael*—the value of uniting the whole Jewish community.

Eventually, Shabbat came out of the center of the conference and became an add-on so people could opt in or out of it. This decision had nothing to do with pluralism; it was prompted more by participants desire to spend Shabbat with their families or because of financial concerns. While there had always been both a *mechitzah minyan* and an egalitarian *minyan* at the conference morning and evening, most participants did not attend either. Still, throughout its 34 years of existence, CAJE remained committed to pluralism and continued to attract participants from every corner of American Jewish life and practice.

In 2008, after a conference in Vermont that attracted 1,500 participants, CAJE went bankrupt.[13] Upon hearing of the bankruptcy, I consulted CAJE members through an online group and also gave a great deal of thought to future options. There are those who feel we should have let CAJE fall and see what another generation would have done to fill the hole its demise created; however, I felt that we knew both the people and the funders who could help us put the organization back together at which point we would hand it over to new leadership. After consulting with lawyers and putting together a small board including myself, Jerry Benjamin, the late Peter Stark, Ahouva Steinhaus and several others, we began the task of buying the intellectual property of CAJE from the bankruptcy court. In December of 2009, NewCAJE was born with a first conference that same year in Boston.

NewCAJE's commitment to pluralism is just as deep as its predecessors, but times have changed. Today, we also include a Shabbat before the conference formally begins; however, attendance at this program ranges from 60-125 compared to 400 conference attendees in the past. Still, we continue to experiment with how to celebrate Shabbat, balancing inclusiveness and respect for differences of practice. For example, we have adopted a *trichitzah*[14] to accommodate a communal Torah reading as well as three or four indi-

---

[13] The reasons for the bankruptcy are beyond the scope of this paper; however, it was related to the financial downturn in 2008 which made most synagogues unwilling to send teachers to the 2009 conference, the lack of an endowment cushion to pay debts incurred, and the lay leadership's unwillingness to continue the organization with volunteers only.

[14] A *"trichitzah"* is a concept I learned about from my daughter Leora Koller-Fox's experience at Brandeis in 2002. It was used at Purim to allow the whole community to celebrate together. It includes a *mechitza* between the men's and women's sections and another to mark a third section where men and women sit together.

vidual *minyanim*. Shabbat attendance will have to become larger before we can experiment with more pluralistic practices. The conference still attracts the spectrum of participants, but the numbers of Orthodox educators and day school educators are still lower than we would like. NewCAJE strives to be a welcoming place that respects the ideas and practices of all.

NewCAJE Pluralism Study

In 2015, when asked to write this article, I did a small study to determine if pluralism was as important to the participants of the conference as it is to its organizers. We asked 407 people two optional questions about pluralism on the conference application. Three hundred and fifty two responded to the first question and 184 took the time to answer the second question. The questions were:

- On a scale of 1-5 (5 being the highest/most) how important is the fact that NewCAJE is pluralistic to you?
- What specifically is important to you about pluralism at NewCAJE?

The rest of this article reflects the insights gained through this study. Before I speak about the results, here are the demographics of NewCAJE attendees who participated in this study. Participants came from 31 states, Washington, DC, Canada, Israel and Brazil. Forty percent of the participants are under the age of 50 and all the attendees represent 215 different schools and congregations. The clear majority are women. They work as classroom teachers, principals, clergy, musicians and artists, consultants and entrepreneurs.

Different Aspects of and Perspectives on Pluralism at NewCAJE

Let's begin by looking at the relative importance of the fact that the conference is pluralistic in the opinion of our participants. Here are the responses to the first question.

On a scale of 1-5, (5 the highest) how important is NewCAJE being pluralistic to you?

Scale of 1-5 (5 being the highest/most)	Of 352 total respondents
5	215
4	65
3	45
2	8
1	19

Almost 80% of Jewish educators at NewCAJE answered that pluralism was either a four or a five to them. We did not further define the meaning of the numbers but this is considered to be a universally understood 5-1 scale, with 5 being most important to 1 being least important. Here people place themselves on the scale according to their own understanding of their relative place on it.[15] This analytic was surprising, in part because we were previously unaware that a stated value of CAJE had become a shared value of our community, rather than being something imposed upon it.

The second question, "What specifically is important to you about pluralism at NewCAJE?" had 184 total responses. I will analyze these responses in the next section of this paper. It was not mandatory to answer either question, and the second one received about half of the responses of the first question. These questions were part of an application for conference attendance and we have to assume that many people were in a hurry to get their application finished and didn't have time for questions like these or couldn't articulate what was important to them. Still, 184 responses represent about half of the 407 applicants who could have answered the question, making this a very good sampling of opinion.

What is surprising here are the multiple definitions of pluralism that we received. I will take each of these definitions and explicate it, using illustrations and quotations from our research. It would seem important to understand how people think about pluralism and why it is important to them—at least within the context of an educational conference and community. Please note that all the quotations below are taken directly from our survey. Here are the responses in order of the most popular to the least popular.

---

[15] If I were interpreting this result, I would say that 5 equals most important and 4 very important.

Pluralism as inclusion

Diversity and inclusion are important values for many people today, perhaps most especially for the younger demographic in NewCAJE. These deeply held beliefs are perhaps why this was the definition that appealed to the largest group of respondents.

Those who defined pluralism as inclusion believe that there are categories of Jews who have been excluded by the Jewish community in the past—for example, Jews with disabilities, Jews with special needs, Jews of different sexual orientations, Jews of lower socio-economic classes, Jews who have chosen to intermarry, and Jews of color. The comments indicate that pluralism describes a world in which no Jew is excluded from the normative Jewish community or from a school.

Our community of educators includes people from all of these previously excluded groups and their allies. Here are some typical comments. "As a convert, I struggle with the lines separating us and hope that we can come to a time when we can just be Jewish."

One of the things people pointed to was NewCAJE's acceptance of all forms of Jewish worship, which is how they defined pluralism. The responses revealed an anger that people carry about feeling judged by others regarding their observance choices. As one person said: "I believe prayer is prayer, regardless of how it is said, what one wears or doesn't wear when they pray and or who one listens to or doesn't listen to. Worship is about God, not us."

Today it is important to reach out to previously disenfranchised Jews and welcome them warmly into the community. "Pluralism means bringing all Jews together." To some, this has become the most important definition of pluralism for the 21st Century, one based on community and the belief that "Every Jew is connected, no matter what!"

Pluralism as the ability to move between boundaries

As Sister Sledge sang in the 1970's, "We are family. I got all my sisters with me." But in the Jewish community, it is more the norm to gather in groups which share our Jewish practices and world view rather than with our whole Jewish family. This might be especially true for Jewish educators whose work centers them in a congregational school or in a day school or youth group sponsored by one of the movements in Judaism. NewCAJE is a place where there is an opportunity to both learn from and teach people who come from a Jewish practice quite different from their own. That experience can be thrilling. As one participant stated, "The experience of learning from and working with people from across denominations and experiencing the joying of moving beyond boundaries, is what makes pluralism at NewCAJE so special for me."

Others bring their concerns about Jewish life and Israel with them to the conference and feel that in the current climate it is especially important to recognize that Jews are part of one family. At NewCAJE, attendees can interact with Jews with whom they don't agree, and yet, they can learn educational techniques and content from them which they can apply to their own teaching.

Because of NewCAJE's diverse participant demographic, people at the conference can be very different from the Jews teachers normally encounter. This is a plus for many who realize that here their peers carry with them new and different ideas, many of which can be used to enrich the settings in which they teach. For example, as one respondent said, "The pluralism and the exchange of ideas and positions at NewCAJE is what allows us to grow and create new ideas." Many conference participants love to meet and learn from each other. They have a sense that there are ideas they are not familiar within sectors of Judaism that they might be able to incorporate into their own schools, if only they knew about them. They want to learn more about what each other has to offer.

The effects of this boundary crossing are clear when you go into an orthodox synagogue and hear the late Debbie Friedman's *Mi Sheberach* or Cantor Jeff Klepper's *Shalom Rav* melody. Debbie and Jeff are prominent writers of liturgical music from the Reform movement but their music has found its way into orthodox settings. Many in more liberal movements love to learn from Orthodox teachers of text. They happily adapt day school materials into their complementary school classrooms while day schools have realized the importance of family education which was the brainchild of the complementary schools. They have also embraced Tzedakah and social actions programs developed primarily in the Reform movement.

NewCAJE participants don't just accept this boundary crossing pluralism. They value it, as is seen in the following comments from respondents: "Respect for differences and the richness of varied forms of Jewish expression and practice give us the freedom to be authentic and sparks great learning and personal growth." "Interacting with all varieties of faith expands my experiences and horizons and makes me a better teacher and person."

Some people believe that we learn best from people who have different viewpoints than we do. If you talk only to those who share your world view, there is only so far you can go, but with the exchange of ideas from people of all segments of American Jewish life, you have cross-pollination. This was certainly the view of the respondent who wrote: "Pluralism and the exchange of ideas is what allow us to grow and create new ideas."

One of the negative results of the development of streams, or movements[16], of Judaism was that people drew lines and stopped seeing the whole of Judaism as a seamless collaborative team. Even where this idea breaks down, for example, around the concern of the Jewish community for Israel, it is unusual and newsworthy to see collaboration among Jewish communities of all different streams. This collaboration has always been a feature of a NewCAJE conference. This is clear in the dining room, where women wearing pants sit at tables with those wearing *sheitls*[17] and on Shabbat when people move from one prayer experience that is familiar to them, to one that is not. That collaborative spirit extends to the workshops as well. People do not go to a workshop based on the level of practice of the facilitator but solely on the content offered. When we start to de-emphasize our superficial differences and begin to learn from each other, the educational opportunities abound. The sharing of techniques and ideas is so strongly held in the NewCAJE community that several respondents had a spiritual take on the whole experience. As one participant said, "The more diversity, the more faces of the Holy One are revealed."

Pluralism as Klal Yisrael

Pluralism, when defined as *Klal Yisrael*, is an idea that encompasses the whole Jewish community without excluding any of its parts for any reason. Yosef Gorni, a sociologist, held that any definition of *Klal Yisrael* must be pluralistic. "Pluralistic Jews are individuals who possess multi-faceted and numerous identities in belief, culture and citizenship," he said.[18]

It is important here to draw a clear distinction between this topic and the earlier topic of inclusion. *Klal Yisrael* as understood by study respondents to mean the whole Jewish community/sacred cluster—meaning that no matter what our differences, Jews are one people—an *Am Olam* (a universal peo-

---

[16] Many people consider the term 'denomination' to refer more to Protestantism than to Judaism. Jews talk more of streams or movements because Jews still retain an ongoing believe in peoplehood which all Jews share. Many of the respondents I quoted do refer to the Orthodox, Conservative, Reform, secular, Reconstructionist and Renewal movements as denominations, which is a commonly used term in Judaism today. I left those references in the paper.

[17] Wigs worn by Orthodox women to cover their hair for the sake of modesty

[18] *Contemporary Jewries: Convergence and Divergence*, ed. Eliezer Ben Rafael, Yosef Gorni and Yaakov Ro'I, Brill Academic Publications, November 2002, page 19.

ple). Inclusion, on the other hand, posits that some groups in the community, while they might be included under the *Klal Yisrael* banner, might be considered more like second class citizens unless their realities are celebrated by the whole.

The subset of respondents who talked about *Klal Yisrael* mentioned the reasons why they prefer the pluralistic environment.[19] Some people reported that they held this belief because their personal reality seemed more pluralistic than not. For example, people who came to the conference from communities where the numbers of Jews have dwindled, have seen two movement-affiliated synagogues join together to form one new synagogue without a movement association. They were pleased to come to a conference that reflected this reality of their home communities hoping to learn how to teach in a pluralistic environment.

Others see *Klal Yisrael* as important because, in their mind, there is a paradigm shift away from denominationalism and toward pluralism. The make-up of the conference seemed to them to be forward-thinking. Here are two representative comments on that point: "The label 'just Jewish' seems to suit today's Jewish community better in some ways than the denominational label"; and "The denominational labels seem to provide a dividing line among Jews that doesn't necessarily delineate where our needs and approaches lie."

As educators, they were especially passionate about how to teach children to be Jewish. As one teacher said, "We are teaching children to be Jews, not to limit their choices of where or how they commit to that identity as adults." These respondents didn't feel there was a value in teaching children to be a Reform Jew or a Conservative one, but rather to identify as a Jew who could make those kinds of choices for themselves. They agreed that NewCAJE was unique in being a place at which all variations of Jews gathered together and learned from each other.

Others chose the value of *Klal Yisrael* as their definition of pluralism because they share a vision of the Jewish world that is more unified than divided. They said that they consider all Jews to be one people. One respondent put it simply: "Pluralism! That is the world we live in." Therefore, if that is the world you live in, then the conference mirrors the pluralism in the world rather than models it.

There seems to be a strong thread in this data suggesting that many people

---

[19] Most educational conferences are sponsored by denominations (see below), although certainly there are others that are pluralistic like the Network for Research in Jewish Education which began as an off-shoot of CAJE (one of many interest groups that formed there). Others such groups included, the Network of Small Cities, the Network of Family Educators etc.

who answered this question resonate more with a more post-denominational world view than with an exclusively denominational view. "I appreciate sharing ways that Jews are united instead of divided"; or "No denomination is more important than any other," was the view expressed by many. Some expressed an appreciation of all forms of Judaism, like this respondent who said: "All aspects of Judaism enrich each other".

One of the largest area of agreement among our respondents was the importance of community in Jewish life. As one said, "Everything is about community for me, so being inclusive is essential." The data indicated that when people come to NewCAJE each year, they appreciate the fact that the diverse community that gathers is all together—learning, playing, and praying. While they acknowledged that Jews have different perspectives, they agreed that our common bonds are more important. One person put it this way: "We are all working to maintain community and living the words of Torah." In this sense, the definition of pluralism simply means bringing all Jews together. This certainly is the mission of NewCAJE, because our organization realizes that all Jewish children and adults, regardless of their differences, need and deserve the opportunity to have the best Jewish education possible.

These responses led us to conclude that perhaps some people prefer the pluralistic nature of the NewCAJE conference to the denominational conferences such as ARJE (Association of Reform Jewish Educators), Torah Umesorah (National Society of [Orthodox] Hebrew Day Schools), JEA (Jewish Educators Assembly of the Conservative movement), or RENA (Reconstructionist Educators of North America); however, the research did not specifically ask for a comparison.

Pluralism as modelling NewCAJE's mission

Some people, as I have previously noted, found the pluralism of a NewCAJE conference to be inspirational, while others found it to be aspirational. It appealed to people who are looking for a new vision of Judaism. Some people described this feeling in terms of a healthier Jewish people. Others used aspirational verbs such "ought" or "should" or "must" to talk about the possibility or the intention of creating a different sort of Jewish world. As one respondent put it, "NewCAJE represents the inclusive nature that Judaism should represent."

There also were those who referred to NewCAJE as a place where the ideal of pluralism was modelled for them. "NewCAJE is a model of how all aspects of the Jewish community should function," said one respondent. Another said,

"As Jewish educators, we need to model the kind of respect that will inform the rest of the Jewish community." Along this same vein, there were people who idealized pluralism in the Jewish world and applauded NewCAJE for being on the leading edge of an important ideal. A couple respondents elaborated on this point. "The most formative experiences I've had are in programs and networks committed to pluralism such as NewCAJE. Pluralism is important in order to break down institutional and movement borders to create meaningful, down to earth, Judaism;" and "To me, pluralism means learning from others in our Jewish world and making bridges to others in different denominations. If we as Jews cannot work, learn, love and care together, we cannot expect the rest of the world to respect us." I would like to think that for many Jewish educators, pluralism has become an aspirational goal—one they learned at NewCAJE over the years and a model that they hope to incorporate whenever possible in their home communities.

Pluralism as a way to create safe space

The concept of a safe space is a complicated one.[20] It seems to have begun in the mid-1960's to describe the creation of a space where gay and lesbian individuals could be open and unafraid about their sexual orientation and in the women's movement to be a place where women could find other women searching for community. In any case, it is a term related to identity politics,[21] so it is no wonder it would come up strongly in a discussion about Jewish identity and pluralism. A current Jewish controversy about safe space concerns "Women of the Wall"—a group of women demanding a safe space to worship as they see fit at the *Kotel*[22]. It is a great example of the perceived and the actual power relationships between the Orthodox and the more liberal movements of Judaism.

This discussion needs some historical background to be understood. When Reform broke from normative Judaism after the French Revolution, it was seen as a move away from the norm and therefore "less" Judaism instead of "different" Judaism. Normative Judaism became Orthodoxy, in comparison,

---

[20] Fusion.net/story/231089/safe-space-history: "What is 'Safe Space'? A look at the Phrase's 50-year History," by Malcolm Harris. Accessed February 18, 2016.

[21] http://www.dictionary.com/browse/identity-politics: accessed September 8, 2016.

[22] This term refers to the "Wailing Wall" in Jerusalem. Currently, it is deemed a synagogue under the authority of an Orthodox rabbi. Both Orthodox women and liberal women have been fighting for their rights to pray there as they wish since 1988.

and thus claimed the authority of "authentic" Judaism. With that title came power. As liberal Judaism gained momentum and numbers, it became more confident of its authenticity, especially in the American setting. Perhaps it is utopian to think that we could ever find an equality of power among the different streams[23] of Judaism or even that all could accept that different streams that have equal merit. For example, in referencing the struggle at the *Kotel*, witness the response of MK Yaakov Litzman, the head of the powerful United Torah Judaism party, to an agreement the Israeli government made with Women of the Wall. He stated: "There is no desecration greater than that of women who come to desecrate the holiness of the Western Wall with all kinds of provocations such as carrying a Torah scroll and other things reserved by Jewish law only to men"[24].

Jews today, against the backdrop of public disputes over whose Judaism is more authentic, find themselves feeling judged by Jews who practice Judaism differently than they do. At NewCAJE, and at CAJE before it, there has always been a goal of providing "safe space" where Jews accept and do not judge each other. This has not always been easy and not always successful.

We have seen an evolution in this concept over the past 40 plus years. At first, we made it clear that all Jews were welcome into our tent, but that does not mean that they felt comfortable once they arrived. In time, and as we got to know each other, a genuine respect for all Jews and all forms of practice developed. When our respondents commented on this, "respect" was the most common word used. They talked about honoring the exchange of different ideas where all branches of Judaism are included and valued. One person put it so well, saying, "I find that pluralism allows for an open mind and an open heart to embrace everyone and I find that extremely important."

In recent years, there has been a demand from several groups not only to be respected but applauded for the life-style choices they have made and for their contributions to the Jewish community. Both intermarried educators and the LGBTQ community have asked the leadership to publicly celebrate the presence of these two communities at NewCAJE. Until recently, it was considered wrong to point out that someone was a convert; however, in recent years, attitudes about this have changed. For example, a new musician named Joe Buchanan appeared at NewCAJE. He sings about being a convert and says how proud he is to be one. His music is reaching an audience of converts

---

[23] I prefer the use of the word "streams" or movements to movements when referring to Judaism. See footnote 16.

[24] "Israeli Women Defy Custom, Say a Prayer for Equality," Tracy Wilkerson, LA Times, June 5, 2000.

who want to be acknowledged for the journey they have undertaken. His debut album "Unbroken" is filled with music that speaks "to the incredible beauty of finding a home after a lifetime of searching."[25] This is an example of celebrating differences that previously would not have been noted in that way.

NewCAJE has become a much safer space as it moves from inclusion to respect and from respect to the celebration of differences. In 2015, our conference application asked people to include their preferred pronoun and these were printed on their nametags. In 2016, some Orthodox participants were concerned that people wouldn't accept the decision not to have music in public spaces because the conference was held during the three weeks preceding *Tisha B'Av*.[26] A secular Jew worried that she wouldn't feel comfortable spending Shabbat with us. There is no question that tensions still arise around these issues; however, the idea is to create a community that discusses these conflicts openly and tries to resolve them for the sake of strengthening pluralism in our community. None of this is easy, but as one respondent put it, "There is room at the *tisch*[27] for all Jews to tell their Torah." In the end, the question must be whether we can understand and support each other. Can we be a truly unified community without being uniform in our approach to Judaism? The principle of "safe space" creates an opportunity to play this out at the conference each year.

There is one other aspect to safe space that might not be so apparent. There are those Jews who do not fit neatly into one branch or another of Judaism. We have liberal-observant Jews and modern Orthodox Jews as well as humanistic and secular Jews, to name a few people who straddle several boundaries. They reported that they feel most comfortable in a pluralistic setting that allows them to observe as they choose. No one at NewCAJE would question a Reform Jew coming to the Orthodox minyan or an Orthodox Jew walking into a session led by a woman scribe. For those and others, NewCAJE's pluralism creates a safe space for acceptance and emphasizes the connections among us rather than the divisions that are unsettling for many people who believe strongly in the importance of *kavod*[28] among all Jews.

---

[25] https://joebuchananmusic.com/press-kit/ September 8, 2016 by Joe Buchanan.

[26] The three weeks preceding the 9th of Av is a period of mourning in the Jewish calendar which comes with restrictions in the Orthodox community not observed in more liberal circles. One of these is the prohibition against live music.

[27] *Tisch* is the Yiddish word for table.

[28] *Kavod* is the Hebrew word for honor and respect.

Pluralism as an acceptable way to be curious about other practices

How do we know how other Jews pray and celebrate? We make assumptions based on our personal experience within our families and by observing and participating in congregations. We may have read books or magazines, watched a special on TV and of course, Facebook and other social media give us the opportunity to widen our perspective; however, our personal experiences still take place in a relatively small circle of family and friends.

Clearly there are many expressions of Jewish life in the United States. According to a US Government Census[29] done in 2001, there were 3,737 synagogues in the US. Eighty percent of these were in ten states: New York, California, Florida, New Jersey, Massachusetts, Pennsylvania, Illinois, Maryland, Texas and Ohio. Of these synagogues, 40 percent were Orthodox, 26 percent Reform and 23 percent Conservative. Other types of synagogues and minyans comprised only 3 percent. [30] The Pew Survey[31], done in 2013, reported similar numbers but a different breakdown with 35 percent Reform, 30 percent reporting no denomination, 18 percent Conservative and 10 percent Orthodox. Even if a person lives in one of the ten largest Jewish communities[32], it is not customary to visit other congregations even once for a service, let alone regularly. The same can be said for Passover Seders. According to the same Pew Study cited above, 70 percent of all American Jews attended a Seder.[33] Most Jews have attended their own family Seders or perhaps those of a few friends over the years—a small sampling in relation to the whole. People may express their opinions about rabbis, both good and bad, but most people don't know more than a handful of rabbis personally. There is a lot of potential variation in Jewish practice.

When I served as the rabbi of Congregation *Eitz Chayim* of Cambridge,

[29] http://www.jewishdatabank.org/studies/downloadFile. cfm?FileID=3022, "Census of US Synagogues," 2001, Jim Schwartz, Jeffrey Schechner, and Lawrence Kotler-Berkowitz, September 9, 2016.

[30] http://www.jweekly.com/article/full/18302/study-finds-orthodox-have-most-synagogues-in-u-s, "Study finds Orthodox have most synagogues in US," Joe Berkofsky, JTA, September 9, 2016.

[31] http://www.pewforum.org/2013/10/01/jewish-american-beliefs-attitudes-culture-survey/ "Portrait of American Jews," September 9, 2016.

[32] http://www.jewishvirtuallibrary.org/jsource/US-Israel/USjews-graph.html Greater NY, Los Angeles, Chicago, Dallas, Houston, Philadelphia, Washington DC, South Florida, Atlanta, Boston.

[33] http://www.pewresearch.org/fact-tank/2014/04/14/attending-a-seder-is-common-practice-for-american-jews/ "Attending a Seder is Common Practice for American Jews," Michael Lipka, September 10, 2016.

Massachusetts, we took our Bar/Bat Mitzvah classes on a comparative Judaism study trip on a Shabbat each year. The students and often their parents visited a reform congregation on Friday evening, an Orthodox one early on Shabbat morning, a Conservative one in time for the Torah reading and then to a nearby havurah[34], whose custom was to begin its service mid-morning. The third meal of Shabbat was celebrated with a Hassidic[35] community. Both the children and the adults were curious about other Jews and their practices. After a few years of our attending their community service, the Hassidic *rebbetzin* asked why we came each year. When she heard we were visiting synagogues, she also was curious about what it was like in these other congregations in her neighborhood that she had never visited. When we told her that each synagogue was filled with Jews celebrating the Sabbath, it was a revelation to her. Our students and their parents were also surprised to find things that they loved in all the services they visited even though they were different from the ones they were used to in our congregation.

Why wouldn't Jews be curious about other Jews and their practices? So when people come to NewCAJE and have the opportunity to room with and to learn from and to teach Jewish educators with different practices and beliefs, they naturally ask each other about which aspects of Judaism are important and meaningful to them. One orthodox educator in our survey said: "NewCAJE is a wonderful opportunity to get to know Jews from all backgrounds. We come together in our passion for Jewish education. I feel that every opportunity we have to gather together is sacred."

The word most people used to describe this curiosity was the word "learn." They wanted to learn from each other and felt that NewCAJE provided a unique opportunity to do so. They wanted to compare their experiences and open their minds to alternative viewpoints. They wanted to gain insight and they appreciated this exposure to differences. They were curious about other Jews and at NewCAJE they finally had access to *Klal Yisrael.* They wondered, "How are their needs different from mine? What are their expectations from Jewish education?" After all, teachers of Judaism are also students of Judaism, so it is natural for them to want to learn more about Judaism from people who

---

[34] Havurah refers to a small group of like-minded Jews who assemble for the purposes of facilitating Shabbat and holiday prayer services, sharing communal experiences such as lifecycle events, or Jewish learning.

[35] Hassidism is a Jewish mystical movement founded in the 18th century in eastern Europe by the Baal Shem Tov (Israel ben Eliezer) that reacted against Talmudic learning and maintained that God's presence was in all of one's surroundings and that one should serve God in one's every deed and word. The *Rebbetzin* is an honorific for the wife of the Rabbi.

they like and trust. This shows a pent-up need that Jews have to get out of the boxes in which modern American life has placed them. Do they want to just peek into these other worlds? Are they seekers? It is hard to know, but pluralism to this group of people provides an opportunity to be exposed to different streams and viewpoints and to learn from them all.

Pluralism as respect for who I am

As Rabbi Rebecca Sirbu said, "For too long, the Jewish community has been obsessed with defining people as 'in' or 'out' of the community."[36] As noted above, apparently some Jews feel their Judaism is being judged by others which make them feel unaccepted in certain environments. For some, New-CAJE is not one of those environments and that is why pluralism at New-CAJE is so important to them. Interestingly, this sense of being judged seems to be prevalent in the Jewish world as a whole. Apparently this is a feeling that many people have experienced.

The following comments made by respondents to the survey are particularly noteworthy:

- "As a woman who is Orthodox and feminist, it is highly important to me that NewCAJE is a place where new ideas can be explored, invited and developed in a warm and welcoming community of peers."
- "I consider myself a very liberal, observant Jew. I feel most comfortable in a pluralistic setting that allows me to observe as I choose, at the same time that it gives others the freedom to choose what fits them."
- "As a Reconstructionist Jew, I need to feel comfortable. Everyone needs to feel comfortable."
- "My Mom isn't Jewish but I am."

One observation about these responses is that they all challenge traditional categories. These are individuals who cross boundaries, so you could see why people within the boundaries might question them. How can you be Orthodox and feminist? How can you be very liberal and observant? What is Reconstructionism? How can you be Jewish and not technically Jewish or Jewish from an intermarried family? To them, being in a pluralistic environment such as NewCAJE means that they are in a place where all differences are expected and respected. As one respondent observed, "At NewCAJE we accept all different denominations and definitions of the Jewish faith without judging or being judged."

---

[36] Rabbi Rebecca Sirbu, *Contact Magazine*, Steinhardt Foundation for Jewish Life, 2015.

This feeling of being judged seems especially difficult for Reform Jews when they venture outside their Reform community. The streams of Judaism were created as a response to a changing world in Europe after the Emancipation, a new world in the Americas and the need to adapt Judaism to these changes. According to Rabbi Sirbu, "We are an ever-changing and growing people. No doubt that each of these historical transformations resulted in some loss, but it also helped us hone the skill that would carry us from era to era: resilience—taking the best of what has come before and building on that to respond to the needs of a new generation."[37] Reform Jewish educators are proud of their resilience and proud of their ability to be Jews and Americans. Yet when they interact with other Jews, they often feel looked down upon, as if their Judaism is not as good as others. NewCAJE for them is a place where, as some respondents noted, "Respect is given to Reform styles of worship and practice."

Thus, for some attendees of NewCAJE, pluralism is more of an environment or attitude more than a philosophy or an idea. They appreciate being in an environment where all Jews can self-define and feel equal and appreciated for who they are.

Pluralism as a category unique and beneficial to Jewish education

While NewCAJE is still engaged in formulating its mission and vision statements, it is likely that the official CAJE policy defining who is a teacher will not change. The CAJE definition of a Jewish teacher was "all those engaged in the transmission of Jewish education, religion and culture." Because of this definition, the conference attracts clergy, school principals, classroom teachers, entrepreneurs, informal educators, artists, musicians and storytellers, among other professions. In this broadly defined world there is obviously a continuum of beliefs about and loyalty to the various streams of Judaism. Statistics on who affiliates with what movement are not collected by NewCAJE. People may prefer to pray with those who have a similar style of prayer, but when it comes specifically to Jewish education, people seem to feel that categories like this are not particularly helpful to them. We do know that when participants choose sessions to attend at the conference, they have access to a session description and a biography of the presenter, which most of the time does not mention which stream of Judaism the presenter affiliates with.

Instead, they choose which session to attend by whether a subject interests

---

[37] *Ibid.*, footnote 31.

them and whether they feel it will be useful to them in their work. If the session was designed for an audience different than their own, they tend to adapt it to their situation if they want to use it.

Some people look to the conference to model pluralism, like this respondent who said, "As Jewish educators, we need to open our arms to one another." This seems to imply a belief that educators have important things to learn and share with each other. It also means that to them, being accepting is a Jewish value that they want to model in order to be better Jewish educators.

Another reason that pluralism is considered beneficial to Jewish educators is the sense that all Jews face the danger of Jewish survival. Therefore, as Jewish educators, we welcome all who want to join us in the common goal of strengthening the Jewish people. "I think it is critical that Jewish educators talk across communities of observance and practice. This is because non-affiliation is growing," said one concerned participant.

The final point here is that Jewish educators, in whatever setting they teach, are all involved in the same holy work. This is a strongly held feeling among NewCAJE attendees that may not be shared by all Jews. NewCAJE participants believe that Jewish educators are all involved in the enterprise of cultivating a love of learning in Jews of all ages. This love does not know affiliations or boundaries. As one respondent eloquently put it, "Since our common task—Jewish survival—does not have boundaries, neither should the marketplace that informs and fuels it."

Conclusion

One important conclusion emerged from our small research: that there are multiple definitions of what people mean when they use the word pluralism. In this paper, I have used a qualitative research model to inform my narrative of pluralism and the role it plays at NewCAJE. This small study was only illustrative of the larger points being made. Had the study been at the center of my thesis, I might have chosen to define pluralism in the question, but in this case, I am glad I did not. It was more important to understand what the respondents meant by pluralism than to impose my own definition on them. For me, it was fascinating to see how respondents put an emphasis on the different aspects of pluralism that were most important to them. From this I hope we have learned a more nuanced definition and understanding of the use of the word.

Unfortunately, we did not ask a question about pluralism in general and as a result, we cannot come to a conclusion about whether the respondents value pluralism in general, pluralism in Jewish education, or pluralism as a quirk that they appreciate at NewCAJE.

What impact, if any, as the conference had over its 40 plus years, in moving American Jewry toward a more pluralistic outlook of itself? This outcome has been easier to see in the United Kingdom where *Limmud*,[38] a conference that grew out of CAJE, has had an undeniable effect on a previously rigid communal structure. There was a time when the Orthodox rabbinate in England saw the conference as threatening Jewish life because it legitimized all forms of Jewish practice and many rabbis forbade "God-fearing Jews" to attend.[39] Today, Chief Rabbi Efraim Mirvis teaches at the conference along with close to 3,000 Jews from England and around the world who attend.

NewCAJE, like *Limmud*, is important in part because it brings Jews across the spectrum together as a community. It is a unique place where people can grapple with pressing issues of concern to the community and discuss and exchange ideas. It encourages cooperation among all educators and models it.

It is not easy to measure the impact of a pluralistic conference in the U.S., which has a large, diverse, and increasingly unorganized Jewish community. Change at NewCAJE seems to take place on an individual level more than on a communal one. Friendships are made and new understandings developed. I do recall, in the early CAJE days, the visual image of three rabbis from the same Midwest city who became fast friends after meeting at CAJE—one Hassidic, one Conservative and one Reform. Could their unusual friendship symbolize a change in the community as a whole? This is difficult to say.

In smaller cities in the US, more and more congregations are combining due to diminishing numbers. As a result, different practices have to coexist with each other in the sanctuary and in the school. Community day schools also abound. Many congregations have chosen to unaffiliate with the movements and as a result there is less support nationally for their schools around education. This may be a gap that NewCAJE can fill. Some rabbis are being trained in schools that see themselves as pluralistic.[40] Of course, we know that the previously citied Pew Study noted almost a third of Jews self-define as "no denomination." I doubt if any of this can be directly attributed to CAJE

---

[38] Limmud, a Hebrew word meaning learning, is a conference that has spread from England to 80 communities in 43 countries on 6 continents. It is similar to NewCAJE in its educational model and its volunteer structure but it encompasses the whole Jewish community whereas NewCAJE remains a professional conference of educators.

[39] *Lebens, Samuel (22 October 2013).* "Why Orthodox rabbis shouldn't boycott Limmud," *Haaretz*, September 11, 2016.

[40] AJR (The Academy for Jewish Religion New York), AJR-CA (in California), and Hebrew College Rabbinical School in Boston are among these.

or NewCAJE, but the conference did serve as a model of how Jewish community could be strengthened by pluralism. It did bring tens of thousands of individuals together during the 41 conferences it has sponsored.[41]

NewCAJE attracts educational leaders and front line personnel. Spending a week in a pluralistic environment year after year has likely taught them tolerance and respect for others who are as deeply committed to Jewish survival as they are. The networking, community building, friendships and sharing of ideas across all boundaries has created a more fluid educational world.

We know that teachers of all movements successfully teach in schools run by movements other than their own. We are aware that educational materials shared at the conference are being used across all boundaries. These changes have been incremental and individual. As seen in our study, the large majority of educators who come to NewCAJE believe in pluralism and feel passionately about it. This is one finding we can take from the question of whether pluralism is important to participants at NewCAJE. It is important because it has become important to participants over time.

Jewish educators do have a common bond that makes them more open to pluralism. The first thing that all Jewish educators share is the responsibility for teaching the next generation the richness of our heritage so that our people and our religion will survive. Whether Orthodox or Reform, we all teach the texts that are holy to us all. Some may teach more hours, some less. Some teach using traditional methods and others use new, innovative methods and technology; but in the end, Jewish peoplehood is important to us all. People at NewCAJE find a lot of common ground with each other. Innovations may be amended to fit local purposes and populations, but they are appreciated and shared.

---

[41] CAJE attendance averaged about 1500 people attending 34 conferences. NewCAJE has had 7 conferences of 400+ participants.

Where Denominations Lose Their Meaning

Beth Kissileff

As the lines between Jews of different denominations in the U.S. are becoming more rigid and stratified, many have begun to wonder if Jewish life is an all-or-nothing proposition. We have begun to ask ourselves some distressing questions: In order to study Judaism and its fundamental texts, must one live a religious life in a particular mode? Do alternative possibilities exist? Can a woman find a place to study Talmud wearing pants? Is there room for a man to study and teach bare-headed? Can religious people learn from their secular peers, or vice-versa?

Like everyone else, I have struggled with these questions; and I have often wondered if Israel might provide an answer: Since Judaism is the majority culture in the Jewish state, religious, secular, and those in between might have a sense of security that allows for individual and communal approaches to religion that don't exist elsewhere.

I'm not the only one. This past fall, delegations from the General Assembly of the Jewish Federations of North America visited ten different institutions of Jewish learning around Jerusalem hoping to find new ways to reach out to Jews of all lifestyles and denominations.

On a trip to Israel in January 2014, I hoped to examine some of these issues by visiting a variety of institutions in which secular and religious people study together. They promote the idea that Jewish texts and values belong to all Jews rather than one specific denomination, and can be understood and applied by both those who live a religious life and those who do not. I discovered that, while the process is often complicated and sometimes difficult, Israel is learning to strike a balance between secular and religious approaches to Judaism. Moreover, it is doing so not only in private institutions, but also in such public arenas such as the Knesset and Israeli television.

My experience with these issues goes back a long way. When I was studying at the Hebrew University of Jerusalem in 1990-91 prior to beginning a PhD program, I wanted to find a way to combine my academic study of the Bible and Midrash with a kind of learning that was more from the *kishkes*; I sought something that was also about inspiration and spirituality.

I tried a class on the weekly Torah portion at a Jerusalem girls' yeshiva, taught by a rabbi with an Ivy League PhD who was known for his love of modern art. But I was completely alienated when he said that getting a PhD was a waste of time for anyone.

I don't remember precisely how it happened, but I heard about a fledgling institution called Elul. As a result, I ended up studying one night a week with teachers Melilla Hellner-Eshed and Rotem Prager-Wagner. The topic was "images of Elijah the prophet," and we went through everything from biblical images of Elijah to rabbinic literature and mysticism to modern Hebrew poetry. The diversity of the texts we studied, the mix of students from different backgrounds, and the fact that I was the only English-speaker there was profoundly appealing to me. This eclectic and pluralistic approach to Jewish study was described in an article in *Eretz Acheret* magazine as "barefoot learning." Its purpose is to foster intentional learning, shorn of outside mediation—just the student meeting the text. This is meant to enable all students, secular and religious, to approach the text together, without the feeling that some have an advantage over others. One of the founders of Elul, Gera Tuvia, explained,

> People gave themselves the freedom to express their emotional responses to a text. The individual's direct contact with the text became an important element and this element bolstered the secular Jews' self-confidence: Your encounter with the text is not like learning a foreign language. You can approach the text and begin conversing with it; the text will teach you how to speak with it. You do not need a mediator. You can call this audacity, arrogance. Those who continued really learned, while those who did not continue were perhaps left with an illusion. For the religious Jews, this was an enormous, powerful liberation—the ability to rediscover texts that you think you are already familiar with, the ability to react in different ways, the ability not to love, the ability not to receive, et cetera.

One of the things I found so striking at Elul was that both secular and religious people had equal access to the text. Even though the religious students might have been more familiar with Talmud and Midrash, the secular students were able to bring a different perspective to them. Everyone agreed that we could learn from each other. This was a very different experience from the hierarchical atmosphere of university study. I felt this was a kind of learning that could only exist in Israel. I was fortunate to have experienced it, and wished it could be imported to the U.S.

Elul is still going strong. When I interviewed its new director, Shlomit Ravitzky Tur-Paz, during my latest trip, I asked about her vision for the institution. "The future of the Torah," she said, "is being able to understand that each one has his own choices and abilities." The daughter of Hebrew University professor of philosophy Aviezer Ravitzky, recipient of the 2001 Israel Prize, and Ruth Ravitzky, who edited a book on readings of Genesis by Israeli women, Tur-Paz grew up in a religious home. Yet she acknowledges that she can learn from secular people because there is value in different "worlds of knowledge," brought together by people with different backgrounds. This belief is reflected in Elul's dizzying variety of programs, which seek to integrate religious and secular Jews from all ethnic backgrounds.

Many of these programs are strikingly innovative and unusual. For example, Tur-Paz believes that a relationship with the arts is "something essential. We like people to see Jewish sources as inspiration for their creativity." This approach, she says, "enriches the Torah and the sources and it can bring new interpretations to the Torah"; which furthers the goal of making the Torah "wider and richer."

To that end, Elul has programs for storytellers and musicians as well as more conventional students. One of the most inventive is "Mekorock" (a portmanteau of "rock 'n' roll" and "mekor," the Hebrew word for "source"), a program for 15- to 18-year-old musicians in which they study texts and then write their own songs inspired by them. Major Israeli artists come to work with the students, such as Aya Korem, Idan Haviv, David Lavi, Ariel Horowitz (son of iconic singer Nomi Shemer), and the popular band Shotei Ha'nevuah. The musicians speak with the students about their own work and help organize a siyum—the traditional celebration of finishing a course of study—at the well-known rock venue Yellow Submarine.

Another arts-related program at Elul is the storytelling project. While I talk with Tur-Paz, the program is holding court in an adjacent room. I hear singing, then shouting. I ask my hosts what is going on and they shrug. The noise is "part of the training. They're rehearsing a story." After our interview concludes, Tur-Paz accompanies me to the classroom to see actors, teachers, and storytellers studying texts in order to adapt them into a theater piece for children. The idea is that children can be exposed not just to Little Red Riding Hood and Cinderella, but also stories from the Talmud, whose "issues are Jewish stories." Like the Mekorock project, the program is split between studying texts and discussing how to present their ideas to an audience. The teacher is clearly talented, circling the group, using her body to gesture at her mostly middle-aged students, leading them in the song "Leila, Leila," based on a poem by revered Israeli poet Nathan Alterman.

These programs are not limited to Elul's Jerusalem campus. There are 25 different groups meeting once a week to study subjects like the Bible, Talmud, emotions in Jewish sources, food in Jewish culture, various Hasidic rabbis and their world, and environmental issues in society.

The next day, I head to Kfar Adumim, outside Jerusalem, to visit the Ein Prat mechina (or preparatory) program. Established in 2001, Ein Prat consists of a 10-month first-year track, a six-month second-year track, and a Zionist midrasha that holds programs for visiting groups.

This particular afternoon is devoted to the issue of Jewish identity. Coincidentally, Shlomit Ravitzky Tur-Paz is the designated speaker. She tells the students about herself and her attitudes toward identity and pluralism. One of the things she shares is a joke: When one enters a mechina program as hiloni (secular), one comes out "datlash." I ask the young man next to me what datlash means. He tells me it stands for dati le'she'avar—"formerly religious." It takes me a while to figure it out, but I realize Tur-Paz is saying that the only difference between a hiloni and a datlash is that of consciousness of identity. A person with a hiloni background who spends a year at a mechina program will come out with an understanding of religion similar to those who grew up with it, even if neither is currently practicing.

After Tur-Paz speaks to the group, I watch Dr. David Nachman, head of the first-year track, in action. He gives the students an "identity quiz," with questions like "Are you a Jew? An Israeli? A human being? Is a Jew someone who fights anti-Semitism? Was born a Jew? Converted according to Jewish law? Someone who feels Jewish?" He also teaches them material prepared by the Israel Democracy Institute about Israel's Law of Return, Shabbat, and Jewish holidays.

Nachman's background is as eclectic as the material he teaches. Nachman is 44 years old and holds a PhD in Jewish law; he began his education studying at a field school in Kfar Etzion, moved on to a religious-Zionist yeshiva in Kiryat Shmona, served in the IDF, and took a variety of teaching jobs at both secular and religious institutions.

In his modest office, Nachman tells me a little about the history of the mechina movement. The mechinot, he says, were started in the town of Eli by rabbis concerned that students were "losing their kippot" during army service. They wanted to create a pre-army program that would strengthen their religious identity. After the assassination of Prime Minister Yitzhak Rabin in 1995, secular educators started to join in. They felt the need to bridge the gap between religious and secular Zionists by having students spend a year studying, volunteering, and asking big questions like "Who am I? Why do I serve in the army? What is it to be a Jew and to have a Jewish state?"

Ein Prat is highly selective. Only 50 students are accepted from hundreds of applicants. Half are male and half are female; a third are religious, a third secular, and a third somewhere in the middle. In potential students, Nachman is looking for a "gleam in the eye" and "boys and girls doing something in life—volunteering, going to youth group—interesting people, not boring," who will try to "push borders all the time." For example, the entire mechina is preparing to run a half-marathon in Jerusalem and has a project to get students to read the entirety of the Hebrew Bible—two chapters a day over the course of a year. The purpose of these activities? "We are trying to challenge them in all aspects of life."

Nachman also wants the students to grow as a group. For instance, they study the Sabbath through sources from the Bible to early Zionist thinker Ahad Ha'am to modern government reports in order to "decide how to do Shabbat together." There are rules for public places and for each individual caravan in which the students live. Nachman sees all this as "creating a new kind of Israeli Jewish identity above the question of how many mitzvot you keep," a "more holistic" view of religion.

Israelis are finding fascinating new ways to strike a balance between secular and religious approaches to Judaism.

Ultimately, he hopes that when his students and alumni go on to the army and university, they will "create a movement." He wants them to "speak a new language, sit together" and know the importance of "being responsible and doing good." His students, he says, "want to meet the other. The religious have a lot to learn from the secular, and the opposite also." On a personal level, he "can't imagine my life, my family without this" open-mindedness and interaction with all types of Jews. "My older boys are in yeshiva," he says. "I can allow it because they see what happens here, so they are not close-minded."

I spoke with a student named Noa Ganot, who echoed Nachman's ideals when she told me why she decided to come to Ein Prat. Her older brother had been in a mechina program, and though she heard him talk about "how amazing" it was, the "change in him" was even more powerful. "He matured," she said, "became more self-aware, aware of society and other people." I've talked to a number of parents whose children have attended mechinot. They all agree that the students take on a different level of responsibility after their first year.

Growing up in a religious home with no secular friends, Ganot knew nothing of the secular world. Though she always thought secularism was a "lack of religion," her experience at Ein Prat taught her this was false. "They have a framework," she said, and there is "a lot to it." She is grateful for the opportunity to get to know young people "from the whole country," and hear "different opinions" from the "crazy variety of people here…. I wish every teenager could do this."

But outside the cocoon of the mechina all is not rosy between religious and secular Israelis. Professor Yair Zakovitch, the Father Takeji Otsuki Professor of Bible Emeritus at Hebrew University, is a secular Jew committed to Jewish learning, but when I interviewed him, he expressed his worries about the future of secular Jewish culture. Young secular Israelis, he says, "take the state of Israel for granted," while his generation was suffused with the sense that Israel's existence is miraculous. There are times, he told me, when he looks out the window of his Mount Scopus classroom and sees the Temple Mount; then he stops teaching and tells his students, "Look out there. You are so lucky. You are studying the Biblical text in Hebrew in the place it was created. How many other people share this experience?"

Zakovitch started a program called Revivim, to encourage creativity in teachers of Bible on the high school level and thus promote more interest in the Bible among the younger generation. He speaks of the program as one that is "difficult to get into like the elite special forces units of the army," giving it prestige. Students learn to teach creatively and to cooperate with the art, music or literature teachers in their schools. He knows this program to train teachers is successful because it already has a second generation of students studying to be teachers; and there is a similar program at Tel Aviv University. This gives him hope, since he sees the competition as "very good" for both programs. "On the one hand," he says, "I am a pessimist and complain too much," since Revivim is a success and a book he co-wrote with Midrash professor Avigdor Shinan on the Bible has been a bestseller in Israel. Called *Lo Kach Katuv Ba'Tanach*, it was translated into English by his American wife Valerie as *From Gods to God: How the Bible debunked, suppressed, or changed ancient myths and legends.*

Yet Zakovitch also recounts a troubling recent experience. He and Avigdor Shinan, who is religious, often teach together; on this occasion, a religious man came up to Shinan, pointed his finger, and asked how he could possibly teach with a secular person. The pain in Zakovitch's voice speaks to the sadness he feels at Israeli society's lack of tolerance; he thinks the religious-secular divide is widening. What worries him most, he says, is that "many of my friends are religious," and there is a "difference between them and their children." While dialogue is possible with religious people of his generation, he worries that "my children will not be able to have a dialogue with their children."

Zakovitch's answer to this is also his life's work: getting secular Jews to read the Bible, "not to give up on it." He recounts a recent trip he took to Mount Gilboa, where he read David's lament over the deaths of Saul and Jonathan. To read the passage in the location where it took place brought tears to his eyes. "That's why I am so devoted," he says. He sees his "study of the Bible as an expression of my Zionism" and asks, "How can one be a Zionist without having this knowledge?"

To him, the desire to live in Israel is deeply connected to an understanding of Jewish culture. Zakovitch can't understand people who say they are "Israeli first and then Jewish." He quips, "Being Israeli without Jewish culture is hummus." He does love hummus, he hastens to add, but it is not "what keeps me here." It pains him to see so many Israelis leaving for the U.S. and even Berlin. "For anybody to leave," he says, "for a young Israeli to leave, is painful for me. We are still a young country; we have built this country, the generation of my parents; all of sudden these young people don't care anymore." He feels that the only choice Israelis have is "your Bible or your passport," and hopes that more study of the Bible and Jewish culture will help convince young Israelis to remain at home and connected to the country and its culture.

Despite Zakovitch's worries, there are many Israelis who are bringing their knowledge of the Bible and other Jewish texts into mainstream Israeli society. Dov Elbaum, for example, is a teacher and writer who was called a "hiloni rebbe" in a 2007 *Jerusalem Report* profile. The piece came out in conjunction with the publication of his spiritual autobiography, now translated as *Into the Fullness of the Void: A Spiritual Autobiography*. He tells me that he sees himself as a "spiritual leader, not a professor," because "when I teach Zohar," the central text of the Kabbalah, "I am so deeply involved."

The youngest of nine children raised in a Yiddish speaking ultra-Orthodox Jerusalem home, Elbaum is now a television writer and broadcaster. His Friday night program, *Welcoming Shabbat,* combines his two passions: "To speak and interview, and to speak about the Torah portion." He feels that he has been successful because "people who don't do anything accept Shabbat with my show.... Before my show nobody in secular Israel wrote about parshat hashavua (the traditional weekly Torah reading). All big platforms, Israeli internet, every big website, now has parshat hashavua."

When he left the religion of his youth, Elbaum wanted to find a way to bridge secular and religious culture. He is now "very proud" of his show, because he feels it has accomplished precisely that. And like Zakovitch, he is convinced that "Israel cannot exist without Jewish texts. It is the base of Israel, the foundation of our being here."

Another teacher of rabbinic ideas is not just able to reach people, but also create laws inspired by Jewish texts. Member of Knesset Ruth Calderon holds a PhD in Talmud studies from Hebrew University, helped start Elul with Melilla Hellner-Eshed, and then moved on to found Alma, a pluralistic seminary in Tel Aviv. Her first book to be translated into English is the accessible *A Bride for One Night*. Swept into the Knesset with Yair Lapid's Yesh Atid party, Calderon told me that, in all her work, "I work for the same boss, the same project. The Master of the Universe is my boss. My project is the identity of Israel as a Jewish and democratic state, and making Israel more Jewish in a pluralistic and democratic and Jewish way."

Calderon says that "I feel I am in some ways a translator" of traditional Jewish texts into the language of everyday life. She sees the Talmud as "living Torah, something that is "existential, a way to learn to know how to be a good person and mother, how to love and how to read." In the Knesset, she believes her mission is "to study text and to use authority as a politician" to express the "beautiful values in the text like the sabbatical year"—the biblical injunction to return land to its original owners and forgive debts every seven years. She is now trying to translate the text about the sabbatical year into practical legislation that will take 10,000 families out of debt through a year-long process in which creditors, the government, and the families themselves will each pay a third of the money owed.

Throughout my visit, I've been amazed at the variety of ways traditional Jewish texts are being reinterpreted and remade by these teachers and institutions. The day before I leave, I meet with a currently secular writer, who grew up in a religious home steeped in Jewish learning, at one of my favorite Jerusalem cafés. Like me, he occupies an in-between space, neither entirely secular nor religious; the fiction and poetry he writes is very much informed by values and texts from both the Jewish world and from international literary influences, some of which he has translated into Hebrew. He sees himself not as an Israeli writer but a Hebrew and Jewish writer. I am surprised when, like so many other Israelis, he does not ask me if I am secular or religious, but whether I've ever thought about living in Israel.

I tell him about the fascinating developments I've seen in my reporting on this trip, how there seem to be so many spaces for different approaches to Judaism: The Knesset with its Talmudically educated lawmakers and weekly Torah study classes, the Hebrew University Bible classroom, the television studios of Channel One, the mechinot programs around the country, the pluralistic study houses. None of this exists in the U.S. or anywhere outside of Israel. "I have thought about it," I finally say. "I'm still thinking. And I like what I see."

American Jews today tend to be most concerned with very basic issues—continuity, endurance, maintaining their longstanding institutions. Israeli Jews have different concerns. Beyond the existential issues of the country's continued survival, the question of identity is of profound significance to the modern Jewish state. In the years ahead, the possibility of spaces where religious ideas are thought about and probed without obligations to a particular religious practice will become more and more crucial to Israel's future as a Jewish and democratic state. And Israel's struggle with the issue may ultimately help American Jewry find its own way to a new and more unified sense of Jewish identity and culture.

Jews and Others in Today's World

Dilemmas of Judaism and Democracy in Israel

Reuven Hammer

Looking back over the history of the State of Israel since its creation, we can see that so much has happened, for both good and bad. We have had too many wars, terrorist attacks, and false starts at peace. We had the assassination of a Prime Minister because of his stance regarding peace. We have made peace with two neighboring states, Egypt and Jordan, have seen the fall of the Soviet Union, the mass aliyah from that country and several mass aliyot from Ethiopia.

Yet the basic conflicts within Israeli society have not changed greatly. We are still conflicted over the questions of peace and territories. Social problems are ubiquitous within Israel. And many of the great challenges of the creation of a modern, pluralistic, democratic, and civil society within a Jewish context have yet to be addressed seriously.

Nevertheless, we must never give up hope; Israel is too important for that. The creation of the Jewish State may have been the most important event in modern Jewish history, truly the culmination of the vision of Theodore Herzl who described it in his seminal work, *The Jewish State*. Yet it is still an unfinished creation, whose future has yet to be determined.

In many ways, Herzl's book was the modern parallel to the Torah of Moses, who likewise, was faced with a situation of a people living in exile, without a land. Both men had to do the political work which would allow our people to go free, and also to prepare and communicate the vision of life in their new land. Moses's ideas concerning the ideal society were embedded in the Torah. They served as the basis for the codes of law that were included in that book. As I indicated in my book, *The Torah Revolution*, his ideas were revolutionary for their time. He rejected the way most nations were governed, building instead on enlightened concepts of government, religion and human rights. Moses wanted a nation in which the gap between the rich and poor would be almost totally eliminated; all would share the land equally: national rulers and the priests would all have clear limitations to their power and authority; and non-Israelites could live among and receive equal justice with the prevailing Israelite population.

The reality of Israelite rule, which came about after Moses's death, may have preserved many of those ideals, but it never completely realized them. If it had, we would not have needed the prophets to castigate Israelite kings and nobles for oppressing the poor and the stranger, and for grabbing land and power.

Much the same situation occurred in Herzl's day. He saw how the puta-tively enlightened nations continued to hate Jews, even after the emancipa-tion and enlightenment, and he envisioned a better way for Jews to live: a Jewish-ruled nation in which Jews would comprise the majority, and where Jewish life would flourish freely in creative ways. He shared his view of a utopian society, where the power of religious authorities was confined to the synagogue, where Jews and non-Jews lived together in peaceful harmony, and where government acted with equity, justice and honesty.

The modern state of Israel has fulfilled Herzl's vision as incompletely as the ancient nation fulfilled Moses's. Today, the state-sanctioned rabbinate exerts the power of its monopoly over *all* Jewish marriages, divorces and conversions, eclipsing any vestige of religious freedom. Religious pluralism has never been recognized by the State of Israel. Though many streams of Judaism are prac-ticed within its borders, none but Orthodoxy has official standing. The gaps between rich and poor and between Ashkenazim and Sefardim have become chasms. Ethiopians face discrimination at every turn. Arabs and Jews co-exist with increasing unease. And, above all, lasting peace with the neighbors has yet to be achieved.

A major difference between the nation crafted from Moses's vision and the state created by Herzl's is that the modern Jewish State is conceived as a secular entity, with all that that entails. The State of Israel's formation as "a Jewish state in the Land of Israel," in the words of Israel's Declaration of Independence, created a situation unprecedented in Jewish history of the past two millennia: a Jewish polity added a new dimension that is not to be found where Jews are simply part of a general population in a non-Jewish country.

From the destruction of the Temple and of Jerusalem in 70 C.E. to now, Judaism had been the religion of a people living in exile, a minority ruled by others. Its spiritual leaders were rabbis, and its self-governing regulations were based on such rabbinic works as the Mishnah and the Talmud. The Jew-ish polity of Israel's millennia in exile developed no philosophy or regulations realistically addressing problems of this modern sovereignty: controlling a territory; ruling as a majority while ensuring the rights of minorities; or cre-ating laws for the governance of secular Jews and non-Jews. In exile, those tomes of Jewish law addressing kingship, warfare, and governance did so ex-clusively for a theoretical, wished-for sovereignty.

Once the Jewish settlement in Palestine, known in Hebrew as the *yishuv*, became the State of Israel in 1948, the ethical problems of sovereignty arose. In what ways would this modern state be connected to the Jewish people? What rights would be acknowledged for non-Jews? Would they be full citizens? Could they vote, own land and serve in official capacities? For the first time, a totally secular, sovereign political entity was established by the Jewish people, with a democratically-elected parliamentary system in which all the citizens, Jewish and otherwise, were to be granted equal civil rights. The state, in the words of the Declaration of Independence, was to "uphold the full social and political equality of all its citizens, without distinction of race, creed or sex." It guaranteed all Arab inhabitants "full and equal citizenship and due representation in all its bodies and institutions." The Israeli Declaration settled these questions—in theory, at least—by those statements.

In practice, however, there remained difficulties for many years. Until 1966, Arab sectors remained under military rule in accord with Israel's Defense Emergency Regulations. Even if administered with a light hand, this treatment placed these communities in a lower status than Jewish ones, and constrained their residents' freedom of movement.[1] Arabs were also exempted from military service, thus drawing a major distinction between Jewish and Arab citizens, which even if benevolent in its original intention had negative consequences. Discrimination in land purchase was illegal, yet land owned by the Jewish National Fund had been designated for Jewish settlement, with no interference, and was unavailable for purchase by Arabs. Much like minorities in many countries, Arabs frequently felt—and often were—discriminated against in ways not controlled governmentally but socially, influenced in part by religious beliefs that differentiate between Jews and non-Jews. Attempts were made to alleviate this.

"Israel is a Jewish and democratic state" has become a well-accepted mantra, proclaimed in two Basic Laws promulgated by the Knesset in 1992 and proposed in 2011 as the central part of a controversial oath to be taken by non-Jews becoming Israeli citizens. Although the phrase appears nowhere in the Declaration of Independence, it can be said to stem from that document, which both "declares the establishment of a Jewish State," speaks of the government as being "an elected body," and guarantees liberty, justice, and full social and political equality for all its citizens.

These descriptors, Jewish and democratic, contain an inner contradiction. The tension informs much of the political debate in Israel, and has never been resolved. If truly democratic, is Israel to be a state of and for all of its citizens, religion notwithstanding? If so, then how is Israel to be a Jewish state? If Jewish, how can it be authentically democratic? Judaism, after all, is a religious-legal system based not on the equal power of all citizens, but rather on the

---

[1] Howard M. Sachar, *A History of Israel* (New York: Alfred A. Knoff, 1976), pp. 384 *ff.*

authority of rabbis bound by Torah-based Jewish law. Perhaps "Jewish and democratic" means that compromises must be reached between these two sets of values, but then, can the state ever be truly be both Jewish *and* democratic?

The Israel Democracy Institute published a volume of essays by prominent leaders of all sectors devoted to defining "the identity and character of the State of Israel through scrutiny of the expression 'a Jewish and democratic state.'"[2] The variety of opinions expressed therein includes those who deny the idea of a Jewish state, preferring "the state of the Jews",[3] those who see problems with the very term "Jewish and democratic",[4] those who state clearly that "we put our emphasis on 'a Jewish state,' and if 'a democratic state' runs counter to this," they will do everything possible to "underscore the Jewish nature of the state",[5] and, the direct opposite of this, those who see democracy as the prime value, since "democracy today is legitimate in its own right ... and does not require the legitimacy of the Torah handed down by Moses."[6]

Many Orthodox contributors attempted to demonstrate that the very basis for democracy is found in Jewish doctrines, such as the concept that humans are created in the image of God,[7] that Judaism is opposed to totalitarianism, and that "the democratic concept of government is the closest among all the forms of government to being a suitable solution from a religious Jewish perspective."[8]

One of the most articulate contributors to the symposium was Prof. Aviezer Ravitsky. He viewed the tension as being not between Jewish identity and democracy (as some of the symposium participants had proposed), but between Judaism and democracy.[9] Ravitsky emphasized the fact that the new Jewish state "is an extraordinary historical phenomenon, never before envisioned in Jewish literature," which "took the sources by surprise."[10] He saw in this both a problem and an opportunity for creativity. Judaism teaches that "Divine au-

---

[2] Joseph E. David, ed., *The State of Israel: Between Judaism and Democracy*, Jerusalem,: Israel Democracy Institute, 2003), p. 9.

[3] Anita Shapira, *ibid.*, p. 19; Menachem Brinker, *ibid.*, p. 88, Asa Kasher, *ibid.*, p. 124, Haim Cohn, *ibid.*, p. 187.

[4] Ruth Gavison, *ibid.*, p. 343

[5] Rabbi Israel Meir Lau, *ibid.*, p. 38.

[6] Yaakov Katz, *ibid.*, p. 80.

[7] Rabbi Aharon Lichtenstein, *ibid.*, p. 106.

[8] Yoel Ben-Nun, *ibid.*, p. 148.

[9] *Ibid.*, page 264. See also his listing on various articles on the subject in note 20, page 280.

[10] *Ibid.*, p. 271.

thority has ceded political authority to human beings,"[11] and what is required now is to seek "to fuse two ethical worlds that have left their stamp" upon us as Jews and as modern people.[12]

The democratic nature of the state is also difficult to define. Democracy generally means a government elected by the citizens, with each citizen of age having an equal vote. By this criterion Israel is undoubtedly democratic. There are, however, certain problems in this regard as well. Because of the fact that representatives are elected through party lists by proportional representation, no specific representative is ever personally elected by constituents.[13] Some parties are more democratic in their selection process than others. Ultra-Orthodox parties have lists that are basically selected by the rabbinic authority or authorities, and no women are permitted to be selected. Because of the complex party system, reigning governments result inevitably from coalitions, through which minority parties, generally—but not exclusively—religious parties, gain greater influence than their numbers alone would indicate. Because the government could crumble without them, small-party coalition members have disproportionately great influence on policies and legislation. Furthermore, although Arab parties theoretically could be part of a coalition, in fact they have never been so, although individual Arab members of major Zionist parties have participated as government ministers.

Israel is a Jewish state, though its citizenry is not exclusively Jewish; its laws are democratically determined by officials elected by all citizens, Jews, Arabs, and others. What, then, is the status of Jewish Law – *halakhah* – in Israel? At the nation's birth, Jewish Law as such was specifically *not* to become the law of the state: not only because there were non-Jewish citizens, but also because the majority of Jewish citizens then living within its borders were opposed to being governed by religious laws as interpreted by religious authorities. Indeed, the role of Jewish Law within the State of Israel has constituted one of the basic sources of conflict within Israel since its founding.

One major problem is that within the vast corpus of Jewish sources there exist concepts that would no longer be considered ethically acceptable. There are prohibitions, for example, concerning selling land to non-Jews. An extreme example is the fact that in 2010, a Hebrew volume was published entitled *Torat Hamelekh (The Laws of the King)*,[14] written by two well-known

---

[11] *Ibid.*, p. 272.

[12] *Ibid.*, p. 279.

[13] An exception to this rule was the direct election of the Prime Minister from 1996 to 2001.

[14] Rabbis Yitzhak Shapira and Yosef Elitzur, *Torat Hamelekh* ("The King's Torah,

rabbis of the extremist right wing, which stated that Jewish Law's prohibition against murder applied only to Jews, spoke derogatorily about non-Jews, and permitted the killing of non-Jewish babies since "it is clear that they will grow to harm us." The authors, and others who endorsed the book, were investigated by the Israeli government. Many prominent rabbis contended that the views expressed in the book represented a distortion of Jewish law. Many non-Orthodox Israelis denounced it as well. Major controversy arose, however, since there were many rabbinical authorities who contended that the government should not investigate the authors and certainly not arrest them, since they were simply quoting Jewish Law. Indeed, for many Israeli citizens from the ultra-Orthodox sectors, the tension between secularism and religion is such that their recognition of the state and its authority is partial at best: it is a reality not to be ignored, but also not the desideratum, which for them would be a theocratic state governed by and bound by Jewish law.[15]

The tension between maverick religious leaders and the state came to a boil during the evacuation of Jewish settlers and settlements in the Gaza Strip, when army troops, many of whom were Orthodox,[16] were sent to enforce the evacuation. When rabbinical authorities, including teachers of some of these same soldiers, ruled that the evacuation was a violation of Jewish law, Orthodox soldiers were faced with the dilemma of obeying the state or obeying their rabbis, to them, in essence, obeying the Torah. Some asked to be excused from this duty, and the army seemed to go out of its way to avoid a conflict.[17] The settlers themselves and their civilian supporters, however, opposed the army, sometimes violently, when being evacuated.

The founders of the state, led by David Ben Gurion, attempted to maintain unity and avoid a culture clash by agreeing to the maintenance of the status quo in religious matters. Whatever was the accepted practice at the founding of the state in 1948 would remain in place: secular Jews would not nullify any existing religious practices, and religious Jews would not demand any new Israeli laws to enforce religious practices. For example, since there was public transportation in Haifa on the Sabbath at that time, it would continue,

---

Part One: Laws of Life and Death between Israel and the Nations", Yitzhar: Od Yosef Chai Yeshiva, 2010). See also *The Forward* and Daniel Estrin, "The King's Torah: A Rabbinic Text or a Call to Terror?" *Haaretz*, January 22, 2010.

[15] See Charles S; Liebman, ed., *Conflict and Accommodation between Jews in Israel* (Jerusalem, Keter, 1990).

[16] Orthodox: that is, religious-Zionist, graduates of the "national religious" Israeli schools and political heirs of the Mizrachi movement and National Religious Party.

[17] "Army Chief Condemns Rabbis' Call", Associated Press, October 20, 2004, http://cjonline.com/stories/102004/pag_rabbis.shtml

but since there was none in Tel Aviv or Jerusalem, none would be permitted. Although there was a general effort to adhere to this agreement, it did not prevent attempts by either bloc to gain ground. Indeed, one could say that the status quo has been more honored in the breach than in the observance, with each side castigating the other for attempting to make changes.[18]

One of the major points of contention is the Sabbath, which is the national day of rest. Issues concerning the opening of stores and businesses on the Sabbath, the employment of Jews, and the opening of cultural and entertainment places, remain very much in question. Attempts, so far unsuccessful, by the Israel Democracy Institute and others to formulate and legislate a constitution for Israel have all had to wrestle with the role of religion in marriage and divorce, and the observance of the Sabbath. A document prepared by Prof. Ruth Gavison and Rabbi Yaakov Medan proposed a compromise, but it has not found wide support from either side.[19]

Following the creation of the State, subsequent legislation granted certain powers to religious authorities, establishing a Chief Rabbinate that has exclusive jurisdiction among Jewish citizens over such matters as marriage and divorce. The same powers were granted to religious authorities of other religions as well. This followed the pattern that had existed since the days of Turkish rule, thus continuing the status quo. Israel has no civil marriage. It is the secular State, however, that grants this authority to religious authorities, and that theoretically could nullify it. In effect, then, the Chief Rabbinate is exercising civil—state—authority in their rulings regarding the personal status of Israeli Jews, even though they are basing their determinations on Jewish religious law, not Israeli civil law.

In a similar vein, Ben Gurion granted an exemption from army service to ultra-Orthodox yeshivah students. Ben Gurion assumed that this would apply to a very small number of people.[20] As the number of such students has multiplied many times over, so that today a sizable number of young men do not serve, it has become a major source of friction in society. In 1999, by which time there were over 30,000 yeshivah students exempted from army service, a law proposed by Justice Tzvi Tal was passed, aimed at finding a way

---

[18] *Ibid.*, pp. 376ff.

[19] See Yoav Artsieli, *The Gavison-Medan Covenant: Main Points and Principles*, Jerusalem: Israel Democracy Institute, 2004; http://en.idi.org.il/media/1353278/GavisonMedanCompact-MainPrinciples.pdf.

[20] See Dr. Moshe Sokolow, "Yeshiva Students and Military Service," Ramat Gan: Lookstein Center for Jewish Education, 2014, http://lookstein.org/resources/giyus.pdf.

to encourage more to serve voluntarily, but so far few have done so. The Tal law was also intended to find a way to bring more ultra-Orthodox men into the work force. The ultra-Orthodox ethos that it is praiseworthy for males to spend their lives in Torah study and not engage in work was resulting in a burden on the families of these students and on taxpayers who subsidized their study. The government is now wrestling with this problem since the Israeli Supreme Court declared the Tal law illegal in 2012.[21]

The Jewish nature of the state was expressed, as well, through the "Law of Return," passed by the Knesset on July 5, 1950. It stated unequivocally that "Every Jew has the right to come to this country as an *oleh* (immigrant)." The question immediately arose: Who is a Jew? The government's position, that anyone who declared him/herself to be a Jew and did not practice any other religion was to be accepted as a Jew for this purpose, did not resolve debate, especially in Orthodox circles.

Because of the decisions of the court, conversions by recognized non-Orthodox Jewish groups in the Diaspora may be (and usually are) accepted by the Ministry of Interior for purposes of aliyah and citizenship. In a strange twist, today there are often more problems in Orthodox conversions from the Diaspora, since the Chief Rabbinate in Israel has attempted—rather successfully—to make itself the universal authority of the Orthodox political bloc in Israel. They are consulted as to which Orthodox conversions are accepted and have a very strict and brief list of which Batei Din and which rabbis they accept. How long American Orthodox rabbis will take that sitting down remains a good question. It has been remarked that if you want to make aliyah as a convert, you're better off converted with the Rabbinical Assembly than with an unrecognized Orthodox rabbi.

The court also, in the case brought by the Masorti (Conservative) kibbutz Hanaton in 1995, eventually required the Interior Ministry to register Israeli converts to Judaism, converted in Israel by a Masorti rabbinical *beit din*, as Jews.[22] What remains undecided is whether or not these same Israeli converts can become Israeli citizens under the Law of Return. Under the present inter-

---

[21] See https://en.wikipedia.org/wiki/Tal_committee. On the ethos of total devotion to Torah study to the exclusion of livelihood, see the mythic portrayal of the Levites in Maimonides *Hilkhot Shemittah Veyovel* 13:12–13, cited in Sokolow, p. 6; also the example of Simeon ben Yochai in Abraham Joshua Heschel, *Heavenly Torah* (New York: Continuum, 2006), pp. 155–159.

[22] For a description of the case, originally brought in February, 1995, see Anti-Defamation League, "Israel: Religion and the Secular State", January 27, 1999, http://archive.adl.org/israel/jerusalemjournal/jerusalemjournal-990126-1.html#.V-Mv-U5MrKRt.

pretation of the Law of Return, the answer is no. As of this writing in 2016, this case is awaiting consideration by the Supreme Court. More accurately, the case is in suspended status, under an agreement for Orthodox and non-Orthodox religious representatives to sit and talk about long-term solutions to the problems of conversions in Israel, while suspending both court cases and political action. It is essentially a repeat of the process that led to the 1998 Neeman Committee Report.[23] The current agreement runs out very soon, and I doubt if it will be renewed. Based on my long years of experience in these matters as a representative of the Israeli Masorti movement, I personally do not believe that the current negotiations will yield any significant change. Only a structural change in the relation of religious and secular authority in Israel can achieve that.

In Israeli society, larger than that concerning the Masorti Movement's conversions, is the problem regarding conversion of approximately 300,000 non-Jews from the former Soviet Union (FSU) who are already citizens of Israel, and to their non-Jewish, native-born Israeli children, many of whom see no difference between themselves and Jewish Israelis.

The problem of converting non-Jews from the FSU and their children remains a ever-shifting mess in 2016. First the Joint Institute, with both a civilian and a military wing, was set up by the government to resolve the issues. Then, the scandalous and anti-halakhic decision, made in May 2008, of the High Rabbinical Court of the Chief Rabbinate, revoked all conversions performed under the supervision of Rabbi Haim Druckman, head of the government's Conversion Authority. That move rendered the Joint Institute virtually impotent. Then, after long hesitations, Rabbi Amar followed Ovadia Yosef and apparently reversed the court's revocation of those conversions.[24]

The Joint Institute's military wing has become especially controversial, since it functions with some independence from the Chief Rabbinate, upon which it does depend for final approvals. Members of their *batei din*, religious courts, tend to be much less stringent than in those in the civilian sphere: they are not ultra-Orthodox or subject to ultra-Orthodox pressures. A committee appointed by Amar recommended that the Nativ courses (given in the Israeli Defense Forces to potential converts serving in the army) be discontinued because there are teachers in the program who are not Orthodox.[25] As of this

[23] See http://www.jewishvirtuallibrary.org/jsource/Judaism/conversion_law.html.

[24] The Israeli Supreme Court upheld Rabbi Druckman's conversions in 2012. See "Rabbi Druckman's Conversions Upheld," Israel International News, April 25, 2012, http://www.israelnationalnews.com/News/News.aspx/155138.

[25] See "Rabbi Amar Failing to Protect Converts, Says Army Official," *Haaretz*,

writing in 2016, there are still state-sanctioned rabbis who refuse to register those converted under the Nativ program for marriage. The common resolution has not been to fire these defiant rabbis, but to instruct rejected converts to register to wed in localities with more compliant rabbis.

One clearer solution could be to provide for the possibility of marriage outside of the framework of the Chief Rabbinate. This could be authorized by civil partnerships, with or without religious solemnization by rabbis of any denomination. Another, at least partial, solution might be to permit alternative Orthodox courts to perform conversions and authorize marriages, outside of the Chief Rabbinate's control, that would be recognized by the state. There are enough modern Orthodox rabbis in Israel who understand the situation and the halakha to build this alternative systems, though they would need courage to stand up against the current state rabbinic monopoly. These solutions are not mutually exclusive and both entail breaking the Chief Rabbinate's monopoly on marriages.

The Chief Rabbinate has thus far failed to adequately address one of the great social challenges of our time. Hundreds of thousands of new *olim* came to Israel. Many if not most of them are anxious to be integrated here as Jews; many indeed already consider themselves Jews. Instead of welcoming these eager souls and providing ready access in reasonable conversion, the Chief Rabbinate has denied the potential, and put stumbling blocks in their way.

This failure may prove to be a historic blunder, salvageable only by a government willing to apply solutions at the risk of earning the Chief Rabbinate's ire. The government would have to transcend political considerations, acknowledge the failure, and seek new solutions from every quarter. Some in Israeli society believe that the future of the Jewish people demands no less; others despair, sure that that this will not happen any time soon. Many believe that the inaction is tragic for Jews everywhere.

Are there solutions to these deep ethical-political dilemmas plaguing Israeli government and society? Some see the drafting of a constitution as the next step, a constitution that, according to the Declaration of Independence, was mandated to be completed by October 1, 1948. This constitution, advocates hope, would delineate once and for all the nature of this Jewish *and* democratic state. The process would require painful compromises: religious leaders would have to agree that the government and the laws are built on secular, democratic foundations, while the secular and non-Jewish population would have to agree that Israel's Jewish identity would be reflected in the

March 11, 2011.

national calendar and symbols, and in the states' embrace (but not imposition)of Jewish tradition and religion.[26]

To paraphrase Herzl, if we will it, we can attain the society envisioned by Herzl and enshrined in the Israeli Declaration of Independence. We must overcome the difficulties; there is so much yet to do in order to lower the obstacles. Israelis must never lose that founding vision and never give up striving to attain it. The positives still outweigh the negatives in Israel, the central locale for Jewish life, and the only place where Jews are in the majority. This modern young state is an unfinished creation, whose future has yet to be determined. Hopeful and courageous Israelis, working together, can influence that future by forging links between "Jewish and democratic" that are sustainable in Israel's diverse immigrant-based society.

---

[26] See, for example, Dahlia Scheindlin, "The Problem is Constitutional," *Haaretz*, August 6, 2010.

Texting Across the Arab-Jewish Divide: Of Taxis, Terror, and Tikkun[1]

Shira Pasternak Be'eri

Part I: For the Sin We Have Committed by Race-Based Fear

It should have been a simple taxi ride.

In the midst of the war in Gaza, I needed to get to a mid-morning medical appointment. Though time was tight, I didn't want to trouble my son for a ride. Busy on the computer, he and his friends were enjoying their summer vacation, despite the dings from their phones that punctuated the hours, alerting them to the rockets raining down on other parts of the country.

Thankfully, my son had introduced me to GetTaxi, an Israeli app that enables you to order a cab through your smartphone. Just enter your address, your destination and push a button, and a GPS system locates the taxis in your area, offers your trip to anyone available and closes the deal with the first driver to accept.

Standing at the curb, I watched as the program scanned my neighborhood and locked in my ride. The taxi would arrive in three minutes. Running late, I smiled with relief.

But then I saw the driver's name, usually an advantage of the system. My blood ran cold. It was an Arab name.

What should I do?

Some three weeks after the murders of Gil-Ad, Naftali, Eyal, and Mohammed, tensions were running high between Jews and Arabs in Jerusalem. Just days before, I had received an email warning that an Arab taxi driver with a gun had tried to kidnap a woman in the German Colony, not far from where I live. The same cautionary tale had appeared repeatedly in my Facebook feed for days.

The admonitions about personal safety fell on receptive ears, since many years ago I was attacked by an Arab man who left me battered and bruised in

---

[1] This article was originally published as a pair of blog posts by *The Times of Israel*, October 2 and November 30, 2014, http://blogs.timesofisrael.com/for-the-sin-i-have-committed-by-racism-and-fear/ and http://blogs.timesofisrael.com/of-taxis-terror-and-tikkun/.

my Jerusalem home. It took years until I could take taxis alone, because that involves being in close quarters with an unfamiliar man. It is still not easy for me, especially when the driver is an Arab. That's what trauma does to you.

So here I am, in the midst of a war, with racially motivated attacks by both Jews and Arabs disrupting the routine of life in the Holy City, and three minutes in which to decide whether to get into a cab with an Arab driver.

I phone my husband. No answer. I burst into a cold sweat. He is no doubt in a meeting. The app says I have two and a half minutes. I send my husband a text:

> Ordered taxi from GetTaxi. On its way. Arab driver. If anything happens to me, his name is XXX XXXX.

Two minutes to go. The cab is getting closer. What should I do? Cancel the cab, pull my son away from his friends and tell him he has to drive me? Conquer my fear and get in the taxi nonetheless?

I text my husband again, in the hope that if I disappear, the message will enable the police to find me:

> His license number is XXXXXXX. I'm only writing this because an Arab taxi driver tried to kidnap a woman at gunpoint on Emek Refaim this week.

I'm terrified, but I do not want to give in to the fear. How can I deprive someone of their livelihood through no fault of their own? And what does it mean about the possibility of co-existence if I won't get into a cab just because the driver is an Arab?

A minute and a half left. I could cancel the ride but I will be late for my appointment. And I can't stand the fact that I'm being motivated by fear.

One minute. Perhaps I should let the taxi arrive, give the driver some money for his time and say that I'm terribly sorry but I have to cancel. But how could I look him in the eye knowing that I'm canceling just because of his nationality?

Half a minute to go. The taxi is just a block and a half away. "Don't do unto others . . ." falls by the wayside. I press the cancel button. The app warns me that if I do this often, I will be blocked from using the service, but I don't care. I finalize the request and run into my apartment.

I cancel. I couldn't take the anxiety. I'm really unhappy with myself for having done this.

And that's when my phone starts ringing. Repeatedly. From an unfamiliar number. Horrified, I realize that when you book a cab through GetTaxi, the driver not only has your address but your phone number too; you can't simply slip away anonymously. I ignore the call. What could I possibly say?

Instead, I pick up my landline and call an ordinary taxi company, one that has always sent Jewish drivers. I hear the dispatcher's familiar "six, seven minutes" and know it will be ten. When the cab arrives, the Hebrew news is on the radio. We ride without speaking, as I mentally beat myself up for giving in to my fear.

Several hours later, I receive a text message in Hebrew.

> May God give you what you deserve. For playing with
> people's livelihood. How disgusting.

There is no question who it is from. It's from the same number that called me repeatedly after I canceled the taxi.

I'm terrified. There's now an Arab man with a grudge who has my phone number and knows where I live. A friend recommends that I file a police report because the text message was threatening. I choose to see it as an expression of frustration rather than a threat. In the climate of fear, perhaps I was not the only passenger that day who canceled upon seeing the driver's name. Maybe that is why he was available.

It took many days until I started feeling safe again. In the meantime, I tried to assuage my guilt. I contemplated convoluted ways of making reparation. I considered texting an apology to the number that was still on my phone. But fear was a wall in the way.

Eventually I pushed the episode aside. But now, as the High Holidays approach and I review my behavior toward others during the past year, the memory has again surfaced. Questions of power and powerlessness, aggressors and victims, morality and self-preservation concern me, both on a personal and on a national level.

So this Yom Kippur, while engaged in my personal soul-searching, I will remember the day I stiffed a cab driver for no reason other than the fact that he was "other." I will remember how the events of the summer led me to deprive someone of his livelihood. I will think of the things, big and small, that we do as individuals and as nations when we act under the influence of trauma.

For the sin we have committed by acting callously.

For the sin we have committed by passing judgment.

For the sin we have committed by groundless hatred.

For the sin I have committed by race-based fear.

Part II: Texting Across the Jewish-Arab Divide

Three months after the war in Gaza, as my city of Jerusalem is consumed by the fire of hatred, it is time for a tale with a glimmer of hope for redemption.

In the days leading up to Yom Kippur, I published a blog post in *The Times of Israel* in which I described my feelings of guilt for canceling a taxi at the last minute during the Gaza War, after GetTaxi, the app I had used to order it, let me know that the driver was an Arab. Through a series of text messages, my unsettling account, which could be read on many levels, gave a glimpse into how trauma affects decision-making and culminated with a confessional that included my contrition for the new sin of "race-based fear."

When I published my post, I thought I was presenting food for thought about power and powerlessness, aggressors and victims, and the tension between morality and self-preservation, whether on an individual or national level. And some of my readers understood. I was particularly touched when a friend whose husband died while preventing a suicide bomber from entering his kibbutz shared my post; it was moving that she, of all people, understood my ambivalence and identified with what I was trying to say.

The discussion on social media, however, largely focused on whether I was right or wrong to cancel the ride and whether there was any cause for penitence. What surprised me most was how many people thought that I had not done anything wrong. Some saw the question purely as an issue of consumerism; I was entitled to cancel my order, and I did. Others pointed out that I had only wasted a few minutes of the driver's time and he probably picked up another fare soon after. But the most common response was that I was right to cancel because I was protecting myself and there was no reason to feel bad. Indeed, an ominous text message that I received after canceling the ride seemed to indicate that the taxi driver was not a nice person.

My conscience, however, was still not clear. During the days that followed, I found myself engaged in on-line discussions with people I didn't know— complete strangers on *The Times of Israel* website and friends of my family and friends on Facebook—who encouraged me to apologize and perhaps find a way to compensate the driver for his lost fare. Eventually, they convinced me that the road to peace is paved by individuals and that an apology could be a bridge to repair, even if only for one person and his family.

And so it came to pass that just before lighting candles on the concluding holiday of Sukkot, at the time that Jewish tradition sees as the last opportunity to repent before fates are sealed for the coming year, I mustered up my courage, dug into my phone records, and reached across the Arab-Jewish divide, sending the following Hebrew text message:

> Hello. I owe you an apology. During the summer, I ordered a taxi using GetTaxi and when I saw your name, I canceled the order because I was scared. At the time, there were rumors of attempted kidnappings of Jewish women by Arab taxi drivers in Jerusalem. I was on my way to the hospital for treatment and was afraid to travel with you by myself. I hope you picked up another fare quickly and I am sorry that I wasted your time. I pray that the relations between our two peoples in Jerusalem and in all of Israel will improve such that we don't judge each other and are able to live together without fear and with respect on both sides.

When the holiday was over, I turned on my telephone and found the following reply from the person my fears made me see as a potential terrorist, the driver who had sent a nasty text message to the person who had canceled his fare:

> "Wow. Your message was very moving. First of all, I accept your apology. And I understand you. Secondly, I have no words to respond to your moving message except to say amen to your wish that peace and respect between our two people will come. I do not know you, but I like you and respect you already. Happy holiday."

As I reached the end of the text, the world around me melted away, dissolved by tears of disbelief, relief, and hope. Because I need to believe that there is the possibility of coexistence and reconciliation. I need to believe that we can see past our individual and collective traumas. I need to believe that there is the possibility of repair.

Today, as extra layers of trauma are added on all sides and the possibility of coexistence seems to be an ever more distant dream, as Arab taxi drivers are increasingly being rejected by Jewish passengers, and as Jews live in fear of vehicular terror of all kinds, I take solace in the knowledge that somewhere there's an Arab taxi driver who knows that a Jewish woman reached out and apologized, and I find comfort in my record of what he wrote in turn.

Would that we could all find ways to enable the voices of humanity and compassion to be heard above the clatter of hatred and conflict, in order to build bridges — however small they may be — across the Arab-Jewish divide.

With special thanks to Ari Epstein, Melissa Bartick, Sam Bridgham, Billy Mallard, and Greg Smith, whom I have never met, for the role they played in making the world a slightly better place.

From Burma to Brooklyn and Back Again: How Mindfulness Captivated Jewish Spirituality

Michael Friedman

In 1957, Eliezer Livneh wrote an article for the summer issue of *Judaism* entitled "Judaism and the Religions of the Far East." Livneh argued that, due to a lack of historical contact, any resemblance between Judaism, Hinduism, Buddhism, and Taoism would speak to "the fundamental sameness of the spiritual imagination in the human species, which addresses itself to the same questions, and the same answers, regardless of geographical and physical circumstances."[1] Livneh then cited Shabbat as an example of this phenomenon, suggesting that the Sabbath "can readily be expressed in terms of Buddhist wisdom" insofar as the "disciples of Buddha emphasize the spirit of 'Sabbath' on the weekday."[2] In this convergence, Livneh saw "the great wisdom shared by different revelations."[3]

The past fifty years of contact between Jews and Eastern religious traditions have rendered Livneh's first contention obsolete: There is no longer a world—and perhaps, according to some, there never was—in which Judaism and the "religions of the Far East" stand in isolation.[4] By contrast, Livneh's closing observation was unwittingly prophetic, as the number of Jews drawn to Buddhist contemplative practice today stands in the hundreds of thousands, and many of those Jews' spiritual journeys have brought mindfulness to Judaism in turn.

Jewish-Buddhist syncretism, often referred to as the "JuBu" phenomenon, has been widely documented and appears to be an important marker of American Jewish spirituality. Though "official" numbers vary, conservative estimates hold that Jews comprise 16.5% of the Western Buddhist population, whereas more liberal claims suggest that close to one million of the three million Buddhist practitioners in the United States are Jewish.[5] Beyond these raw numbers,

---

[1] Eliezer Livneh, "Judaism and the Religions of the Far East," Judaism 6.3 (1957): 225.

[2] Livneh, 234.

[3] Livneh, 235.

[4] Nathan Katz has been the most outspoken proponent of the argument for historical contact between Jews and Buddhists. See, for instance, his article "Buddhist-Jewish Relations Throughout the Ages and in the Future," *The Journal of Indo-Judaic Studies* 10 (2009): 7-23.

[5] Yonatan Gez, "The Phenomenon of Jewish Buddhists in Light of the History of

listing prominent Buddhist teachers of Jewish descent has become something of a sport in scholarship on JuBus: Typical lists boast Zen teachers Norman Fischer, Bernie Glassman, Natalie Goldberg, and Philip Kapleau; Theravada teachers Bhikkhu Bodhi, Sylvia Boorstein, Ruth Denison, Joseph Goldstein, Jack Kornfield, and Sharon Salzberg; and Tibetan teachers Harvey Aronson, Alexander Berzin, Thubten Chodron, Surya Das, Georges Dreyfus, and John Makransky.[6] Moreover, Shambhala Publications, the leading publishing house for Western Buddhist books, was founded by two Jews, Sam Bercholz and Michael Fagan, in Berkeley in the late 1960s.[7] Clearly, Buddhism seems to hold an attraction for liberal Jewry, and this chapter will explore the nature of that encounter and its impact on Jewish spirituality.

A few preliminary remarks

At the outset, it is important to define two key terms, namely what is understood by "Buddhism" and by "JuBu." Regarding the former, while any definition of a religious tradition will surely frustrate its adherents as being either inaccurate or incomplete, it is nevertheless helpful in interreligious contexts to offer a working definition. The closest translation in Sanskrit and Pali (two of the earliest Buddhist languages) to the Western term "Buddhism" is *buddhavacana*, which refers to the "word of the Buddha," or "those teachings accepted as having been either spoken by the Buddha or spoken with his sanction."[8] This translation thus situates the teachings of the historical Buddha, Prince Siddhartha Gautama, at the core of Buddhism itself. Such teachings include the Buddha's first sermon, in which he taught the "Four Noble Truths" that life is characterized by suffering, that the cause of suffering is craving, that liberation from suffering is possible, and that the means to

---

Jewish Suffering," *Nova Religio: The Journal of Alternative and Emergent Religions* 15.1 (2011): 51. James Coleman, "The New Buddhism: Some Empirical Findings," in *American Buddhism: Methods and Findings in Recent Scholarship*, ed. Duncan Ryuken Williams et al. (Surrey: Curzon Press, 1999), 94. Harold Kasimow, "Mount Sinai and Mount Fuji: The American Fascination with Buddhism," *Dharma World Magazine* January–March (2007). Brenda Shoshana, *Jewish Dharma: A Guide to the Practice of Judaism and Zen* (New York: Perseus Books Groups, 2008), 2.

  [6]Kasimow. Katz, 12. Jay Michaelson, *Evolving Dharma: Meditation, Buddhism, and the Next Generation of Enlightenment* (Berkeley: Evolver Editions, 2013), 14.

  [7]Ira Rifkin, "The Jewish-Buddhist Encounter," *MyJewishLearning*, http://www.myjewishlearning.com/article/the-jewish-buddhist-encounter/.

  [8]"Buddhavacana," in *The Princeton Dictionary of Buddhism*, ed. Robert Buswell Jr. et al. (Princeton: Princeton University Press, 2014): 155.

liberation is the "Eightfold Path." Following the Path enhances one's conduct, concentration, and wisdom, such that suffering turns to joy and one recognizes the true nature of reality.[9] However, this definition of Buddhism as the "word of the Buddha" privileges a highly textualized, philosophized vision of Buddhism that lends itself readily to the oft-heard question, "Is Buddhism a philosophy or a religion?"[10] In contrast to this dry, philosophical reading of Buddhism, the *buddhavacana* has, in fact, spread dynamically throughout Asia, and there are today three main forms of Buddhism, namely: Theravada Buddhism, which predominates in India and Southeast Asia; Mahayana Buddhism, which has flowered throughout East Asia; and Vajrayana Buddhism, which has taken root in India and Tibet. Each of these traditions emphasizes different aspects of Buddhist thought and practice, often attended by stunning iconography and elaborate ritual. The JuBu population has had particular exposure to Burmese Theravada, the Zen sub-school of Mahayana, and Tibetan Vajrayana.

The term "JuBu" is significantly more recent, but likewise fraught and complex. Nathan Katz offers a rather basic but helpful distinction between Jews who adopt Buddhist practice and sever ties with Jewish life, whom he terms "Buddhists of Jewish background," and Jews who adopt Buddhist practice while affirming their Jewishness, or "JuBus."[11] More rigorous typologies of the Western encounter with Buddhism have been put forth by Wendy Cadge— who differentiates between "ascribed" or inherited, and "achieved" or chosen, identities—and Thomas Tweed, who distinguishes between "sympathizers ... who have some sympathy for a religion but do not embrace it exclusively or fully" and "night-stand Buddhists...who might place a how-to-book on Buddhist meditation on the nightstand...and read it before they fall to sleep, and then rise the next morning to practice, however imperfectly or ambivalently, what they had learned the night before."[12] As grassroots syncretism becomes

---

[9] For a standard primer on Buddhism and Buddhist thought, see Rupert Gethin, *The Foundations of Buddhism* (Oxford: Oxford University Press, 1998).

[10] This definition is emblematic of the moniker "Protestant Buddhism," which refers to the manner in which Orientalist European scholars crafted Buddhism in the likeness of an anti-ritualistic, highly-textualized Protestant Christianity. For more information on this, see Stephen Prothero, "Henry Steel Olcott and 'Protestant Buddhism," *Journal of the American Academy of Religion* 63.2 (1995): 281-302.

[11] Katz, 12.

[12] Wendy Cadge, *Heartwood: The First Generation of Theravada Buddhism in America* (Chicago: The University of Chicago Press, 2005), 157. One of Cadge's fieldwork sites was the Cambridge Insight Meditation Center, where several members were Jewish. Cadge relates that Jews were statistically sig-

ever more common in the Jewish community, scholars will need increasingly refined systems for classifying what they observe. For this overview, however, Katz's straightforward typology seems to be the most appropriate schema.

Whence the appeal

Without question, the issue of appeal has garnered the greatest attention from observers of the JuBu phenomenon: Why has Buddhism been so attractive to the post-war American Jewish community? Scholars have offered any number of interpretations, some focusing on Judaism's failures and others on Buddhism's strengths. For instance, several such observers suggest that contemporary Jews find belief in a "traditional supernatural Jewish concept of God" to be an overwhelming impediment to religious observance.[13] Others assert that Jews simply feel "disengaged and detached" from their religious identity because Jewish communal teachers and leaders have failed to furnish Jewish life with sufficient "spiritual dimension."[14] According to one analysis, this spiritual impoverishment is the direct consequence of the post-Holocaust Jewish community's obsession with practicality and survivalism.[15] Rodger Kamenetz, poet and author of *The Jew in the Lotus: A Poet's Rediscovery of Jewish Identity in Buddhist India*, has captured this picture quite vividly:

> The Jews who are turned off to all spirituality, and the JUBUs and other Jews who have left the burnt house of Judaism for other traditions, are responding, then, to a real crisis. The materialism of much of Jewish life today, the lack of spirituality in our synagogue life, and the failure to communicate Judaism as a spiritual path have led, and will lead, many Jews to look elsewhere.[16]

---

nificant in reporting "both ascribed and achieved components of religious identity," 166. Thomas Tweed, "Night-Stand Buddhists and Other Creatures: Sympathizers, Adherents, and the Study of Religion," in *American Buddhism: Methods and Findings in Recent Scholarship*, ed. Duncan Ryuken Williams et al. (Surrey: Curzon Press, 1999), 74-75.

[13] Kasimow. Rifkin.

[14] Nicole Libin, "The Choosing People: Constructing Jewish Buddhist Identity in America" (PhD diss., University of Calgary, 2009), 123. Kasimow.

[15] Anne Vallely, "Jewish Redemption by Way of the Buddha: A Post-Modern Tale of Exile and Return," *Jewish Culture and History* 8.3 (2012): 26.

[16] Rodger Kamenetz, *The Jew in the Lotus: A Poet's Rediscovery of Jewish Identity in Buddhist India* (New York: HarperOne, 1994), 282.

At best, these assertions only explain Jews' flight from their own "burnt house." Why, specifically, did so many Jews turn for wisdom to Bodh Ghaya, Lhasa, and Kyoto?

The typical response to this question has been to line Buddhism's perceived strengths up against Judaism's apparent deficiencies. Critics maintain that where Judaism is unacceptably theist, Buddhism is non-theist; where Judaism is disengaging, Buddhism is accessible and instantly spiritual; where Judaism is obsessed with survivalism, Buddhism offers to explain and to end one's suffering.[17] Most importantly, however, the sociological evidence suggests that Buddhism enables JuBus to avoid guilt over their religious "switch."[18] As historian Alan Levenson suggested rather bluntly, "Confrontations with Christianity and Islam demanded betrayal as the price of leaving the Jewish fold. Eastern religions make no such demand."[19] Buddhism, at least as articulated by Westerners, offers an accessible and helpful spiritual path that is not weighted down by theological baggage or the sociocultural impact of conversion.

Despite the seemingly broad appeal of Buddhism for the Jewish community at large, the response has not been uniformly positive. Condemnations have come largely, though not exclusively, from Orthodox sectors and often assert that Buddhism is idolatrous. For instance, Emanuel Feldman, during his tenure as editor of *Tradition: The Journal of Orthodox Jewish Thought*, took aim at JuBus' alleged idolatry in a piece entitled "'Buddha is Not As Bad...': The Floundering of American Jewry," remarking incredulously that "Not a few Jews have been known to experiment with Buddhism (which, according to many halakhic authorities, is out-and-out *avoda zara*), but in the eyes of masses of wavering American Jews, Buddha somehow seems not as bad as Jesus."[20] A second approach was deployed in a 2012 responsum from the

---

[17] Regarding Buddhism's non-theism, see Kasimow; Rifkin; and Sheila Weinberg, "Many Voices in One Mind," *The Reconstructionist* Fall (1994): 54. Regarding Buddhism's accessibility and spirituality, see Rifkin; Kamenetz, 149; and Weinberg, 55. Regarding Buddhism's explanation of suffering, see Kasimow; Rifkin; and Sandra Lubarsky, "Advice to Job from a Buddhist Friend," *Shofar: An Interdisciplinary Journal of Jewish Studies* 3 (1999): 61-62.

[18] Gez, 56. Rosie Rosenzweig, *A Jewish Mother in Shangri-La* (Boston: Shambhala Publications, Inc., 1998), 166.

[19] Alan Levenson, "Syncretism and Surrogacy in Modern Times: Two Models of Assimilation," *Shofar: An Interdisciplinary Journal of Jewish Studies* 30.1 (2011): 24.

[20] Emanuel Feldman, "'Buddha Is Not As Bad...': The Floundering of American Jewry," *Tradition* 32.1 (1997): 2. This claim has been echoed elsewhere, such as the article by Rifkin on the popular site *MyJewishLearning.com*, mentioned above.

Central Conference of American Rabbis about welcoming a Jewish couple who practice Buddhism into the synagogue and enrolling their child in the religious school. The CCAR's response held that because Buddhist traditions "denigrate [the world's] importance," there is a fundamental and irreconcilable conflict between Judaism's "world-affirming view" and "a world-denying Buddhism."[21] The most sustained critique to date came not from institutional organizations but was put forth in Akiva Tatz's and David Gottlieb's *Letters to a Buddhist Jew*. In his book, Rabbi Tatz offers many arguments against Jewish-Buddhist syncretism, but the most pervasive holds that Jews attracted to Buddhism "have no experience of genuine Torah" and are simply drawn to the exotic: "Some men will always be attracted to other men's wives."[22] Typical formulations of the latter two responses—that Buddhism is nihilistic and that JuBus are Jewishly illiterate—are unsettling in the unsubstantiated nature of their claims. In the citations mentioned here, for instance, no reference is made to Buddhist sources or sociological data of any kind.[23] As for the specific question of idolatry, as Nathan Katz has suggested vis-à-vis Hindu-Jewish dialogue, "...how could we know whether Hinduism is idolatrous a priori? Wouldn't that understanding only emerge out of dialogue, not prior to it?"[24] Nevertheless, such criticisms and allegations are an ongoing reality of the Jewish-Buddhist encounter.

---

[21]"CCAR Responsa: Practicing Judaism and Buddhism," *Central Conference of American Rabbis*, http://ccarnet.org/responsa/tfn-no-5752-3-123-126/. The view that Buddhism is nihilistic is a relic of early scholarship on Buddhism, which has long since been corrected. However, this assertion appears not only here, but also in an article from *Aish.com* which incorrectly asserts that Buddhism sees the world as "ultimately purposeless": Sara Rigler, "Buddhism, Judaism, and the Great Cheerio Fiasco," *Aish*, http://www.aish.com/sp/so/48893617.html.

[22]Akiva Tatz and David Gottlieb, *Letters to a Buddhist Jew* (Southfield, MI: Targum Press, Inc., 2004), 7, 32.

[23]Exception could be made for *Letters to a Buddhist Jew* on this score, as David Gottlieb was previously ordained as a Zen priest. However, the book itself does not present a balanced perspective; the glossary at the end, for instance, includes no Buddhist terminology.

[24]Nathan Katz, "The State of the Art of Hindu-Jewish Dialogue," in *Indo-Judaic Studies in the Twenty-First Century: A View from the Margin*, ed. Nathan Katz (New York: Palgrave Macmillan, 2007), 118.

The history of the phenomenon

To date, the majority of discourse on the JuBu phenomenon has focused on the preceding points: namely, just how widespread the JuBu phenomenon is, and why Buddhism has held such great appeal for the Jewish community. This chapter will now attempt to draw those data points into a coherent historical narrative and to consider the JuBu phenomenon's impact on the contemporary Jewish community, both in terms of reviving Jewish spirituality and advancing the question of pluralism in religious life.

Broadly speaking, the Jewish-Buddhist encounter has unfolded in three stages. In the first stage, individuals of Jewish background became interested in Buddhism through travel or teachers and decided to share what they had learned. As mentioned above, there are three main lineages of Buddhism which have been popularized in the West, particularly Zen Buddhism through the figure of D.T. Suzuki, Tibetan Buddhism through Chogyam Trungpa Rinpoche and His Holiness the Dalai Lama, and Theravada Buddhism through several figures, both Western and Eastern.[25] Of these, Theravada Buddhism, with its practice of *vipassana*, or insight meditation, and its focus on mindfulness, has penetrated Western culture most deeply. According to scholar-practitioner Jay Michaelson, *vipassana* meditation has appealed to Westerners because its target is wisdom rather than devotion, rendering it "compatible with secularism, atheism, and also with religions such as Judaism, because it has relatively little emphasis on worship, ritual and faith in the religious sense of the words."[26] It is worth noting that *vipassana* meditation as it is known in the West is a modern construct, having been adapted from earlier practices by Buddhist modernizers such as Mahasi Sayadaw and U Ba Khin in Burma, Ajahn Chah in Thailand, and S.N. Goenka in India.[27] In the West, *vipassana* meditation has even become a stand-in for Buddhism itself, particularly as interest in mindfulness has exploded across the American cultural landscape.[28]

---

[25] There are, of course, other influences, such as the modernizing trends of Vietnamese monk Thich Nhat Hanh, but these traditions present the broad strokes.

[26] Jay Michaelson, *Everything is God: The Radical Path of Nondual Judaism* (Boston: Trumpeter Books, 2009), 82.

[27] For an excellent history of these developments, see Erik Braun, *The Birth of Insight: Meditation, Modern Buddhism, and the Burmese Monk Ledi Sayadaw* (Chicago: The University of Chicago Press, 2013).

[28] For a recent monograph on the growth of mindfulness meditation, see Jeff Wilson, *Mindful America: The Mutual Transformation of Buddhist Meditation and American Culture* (Oxford: Oxford University Press, 2014).

Wendy Cadge traces the beginnings of a permanent Theravada presence in the United States to the mid-1960s, when in the wake of the Hart-Celler Act, Buddhists from Sri Lanka, Burma, and Thailand began traveling in earnest to the United States, and the Washington Buddhist Vihara purchased its first property in Washington D.C.[29] In the 1970s, Jack Kornfield and Joseph Goldstein returned from Peace Corps tours in Thailand, and Sharon Salzberg from studies in India, after having trained in meditation with several of the aforementioned Theravada modernizers.[30] In 1975, Kornfield, Goldstein, and Salzberg formed the Insight Meditation Center, which eventually established itself as the Insight Meditation Society in Barre, Massachusetts.[31] As Kornfield describes this period:

> We had no idea that mindfulness would blossom into a huge national movement. [...] We simply wanted to serve in a wise, supportive and integrated way the community of people we knew who were practicing. It blossomed and flowered far beyond anything we imagined. [...] Even though we had no idea it would become this great kind of force in the society, from the very beginning those of us who had practiced initially in India, Thailand, Burma and elsewhere knew we had found something marvelous.[32]

Though Kornfield, Goldstein, Salzberg and others grew up in Jewish households, their teachings at IMS were squarely in the Buddhist tradition. And yet, as the numbers above have borne out, Jews flocked to insight meditation in droves.

Formal responses to this groundswell of Jewish interest in Buddhism and Eastern religions appeared by the end of the 1970s. In 1978, Aryeh Kaplan published his *Meditation and the Bible*, which he followed seven years later with *Jewish Meditation: A Practical Guide*. In his introduction to *Jewish Meditation*, Kaplan singled out Eastern religions as a particular cause for concern:

> Jews are by nature a spiritual people, and many Jews actively

---

[29] Cadge 19, 25.

[30] "Biography," http://www.jackkornfield.com/about-bio/.

[31] Michaelson, *Evolving Dharma*, 14.

[32] "Tending the Garden of the Dharma for 25 Years: An Interview with Jack Kornfield," www.jackkornfield.com/tending-garden-dharma-25-years-interview-jack-kornfield/.

seek spiritual meaning in life, often on a mystical level. [...] Today, many American Jews have become involved in Eastern religions. It is estimated that as many as 75 percent of the devotees in some ashrams are Jewish, and large percentages follow disciplines such as Transcendental Meditation. When I speak to these Jews and ask them why they are exploring other religions instead of their own, they answer that they know of nothing deep or spiritually satisfying in Judaism. When I tell them that there is a strong tradition of meditation and mysticism, not only in Judaism, but in mainstream Judaism, they look at me askance. Until Jews become aware of the spiritual richness of their own tradition, it is understandable that they will search in other pastures.[33]

The concern that Jewish spiritual seekers were turning elsewhere was voiced not only by scholars such as Kaplan, but by community leaders as well. In July 1979, none other than the Lubavitcher Rebbe spoke out against "the dangers that Eastern cults and their form of meditation posed for many Jews" and "the need for professionals to offer meditation without idolatrous trappings," warning that many "ordinarily healthy people wanted to meditate and would go to Eastern cults if not offered an alternative."[34] It is thus unsurprising, though nevertheless remarkable, that the Chabad website now boasts nearly 1000 entries touching on meditation and mindfulness. As we will see, however, the sentiment that Eastern religions are threatening to Jewish communal life continues to appear in the discourse of contemporary Jewish organizations.

In the second stage of contemporary Jewish-Buddhist encounter, many JuBus decided that they wished either to maintain their Judaism in tandem with their Buddhist practice, or to deploy their Buddhist practice in service of their Jewish life. Two essential examples of this stage are meditation teacher Sylvia Boorstein, who studied with Kornfield, Goldstein, and Salzberg, and Rabbi Alan Lew, who was ordained as a monk in the Zen tradition. Boorstein, who famously wrote *That's Funny, You Don't Look Buddhist: On Being a Faithful Jew and a Passionate Buddhist*, was born in 1936 to a traditionally observant household and became involved with Buddhist meditation through a mindfulness retreat in 1977. Boorstein records that the great revelation of her first retreat

---

[33] Aryeh Kaplan, *Jewish Meditation: A Practical Guide* (New York: Schocken Books, 1985), viii.

[34] Yehoshua Landes, "The Inside Story of the Founding of Jewish Meditation," *B'Or Ha'Torah* 23 (2014-2015): 181.

was "to hear, presented as the *main* subject for consideration, the fact that life *is* difficult."[35] In the years to follow, Boorstein trained under this first generation of JuBu meditation teachers—Jack Kornfield, Sharon Salzberg, and Joseph Goldstein—and began teaching *vipassana* herself in 1985 with the founding of Spirit Rock Meditation Center in California.[36] However, Boorstein reports that she also experienced a spontaneous impulse to take up, once again, "religious practice as a Jew."[37] As she describes the experience:

> I began, over the next several years, to read scripture, now as an adult. By and by, I synchronized myself with what I knew was the *parshah* (weekly Torah reading), and sometime later I joined a Conservative congregation, the nearest one to my home where I now attend services regularly. I became, once again, *kashrut* observant. It just all happened. Really, it came from being *mindful*, from paying attention to what I needed to do next, to what felt meaningful.[38]

In contrast to Boorstein, who practices both Judaism and Buddhism, another well-known figure in Jewish-Buddhist encounter is rabbi and author Alan Lew, who turned his years of Buddhist training to the service of Jewish spirituality. In a short memoir entitled "Becoming Who You Always Were: The Story of a Zen Rabbi," Lew reports finding himself at a Zendo in Berkeley, California, which led to ten years of meditative discipline as a monk in the Soto Zen tradition.[39] Lew recounts realizing that "a highly disproportionate amount of my own unconscious material is Jewish...a kind of Jewish background noise, a Jewish static as it were, constantly whirring around in the background of my life."[40] Confronted in this way, Lew took up Sabbath observance, kashrut, daily prayer, and Torah study. In a beautiful passage, Lew reports realizing the value his Zen practice might hold for his re-awakened Jewish life:

---

[35] Sylvia Boorstein, "It's a No-Karma Event," in *Beside Still Waters: Jews, Christians, and the Way of the Buddha*, ed. by Harold Kasimow et al. (Boston: Wisdom Publications, 2003), 25.

[36] "Biography," http://www.sylviaboorstein.com/about.html.

[37] Boorstein, 26.

[38] Boorstein, 26.

[39] Alan Lew, "Becoming Who You Always Were: The Story of a Zen Rabbi," in *Beside Still Waters: Jews, Christians, and the Way of the Buddha*, ed. by Harold Kasimow et al. (Boston: Wisdom Publications, 2003), 50-51.

[40] Lew, 53.

I think the first thing I was aware of taking with me as I moved from Zen to Judaism was a sense of the value of disciplined spiritual practice. In America, spirituality has come to be a kind of leisure activity, something we do on weekends and at retreats, a supplement to life, like exercise or cultural enrichment. But what my ten years as a Zen student had taught me beyond the shadow of a doubt was that if a spiritual practice is to transform us—if it is to have real meaning in our lives—it must be practiced every day, and it must be practiced with discipline.[41]

A second pulpit landed Lew in San Francisco, where he was soon approached by JuBus who described themselves as "haunted" by their Jewishness, as well as by Jews who felt that spirituality was missing from their lives.[42] Both groups hoped that Lew's background would enable him to help them. The end result of these conversations was Lew's co-founding, with Norman Fischer, of Makor Or: A Center for Jewish Meditation.[43] There, Lew deployed his Buddhist training not on its own terms, but rather, in support of vibrant Jewish life.

Figures like Boorstein and Lew bridged the gap between the second stage of Jewish-Buddhist encounter and our contemporary situation, in which efforts to harmonize Judaism with Buddhist practice and the desire to compete against Buddhism have both waned. Rather, a new synthesis has emerged under the rubric of "Jewish mindfulness," which appears to be a re-packaging of Buddhist wisdom intended to revive Jewish spirituality. Hence, one finds local groups, such as Nishmat Hayyim at Temple Beth Zion in Brookline, Massachusetts, which describes itself as "a resource for Jewish contemplative practices in the Boston area and throughout New England."[44] Similarly, at the Adas Israel congregation in Washington D.C., one can visit the Jewish Mindfulness Center of Washington. There are also national organizations engaged in this work, such as the Awakened Heart Project for Contemplative Judaism, the Institute for Jewish Spirituality, Metivta: A Center for Contemplative Judaism, and Or HaLev: Center for Jewish Spirituality. Such programming

---

[41] Lew, 55.

[42] Lew, 55-57.

[43] Lew, 59.

[44] "Nishmat Hayyim: Jewish Meditation," *Temple Beth Zion*, https://www.tbz-brookline.org/shabbat-and-holidays/nishmat-hayyim.

has even penetrated rabbinical education, as in the case of the "Spirituality Initiative" at Hebrew Union College, which "aims to bring mindfulness and contemplative practices to the educational experience of those training to become rabbis, cantors, and educators at our New York campus."[45]

At a glance, this sampling—and indeed, this list provides just a few examples of a larger phenomenon—reveals widespread Jewish efforts at cultivating contemplative, mindful, spiritual practices, but a closer look reveals somewhat more. First, a significant portion of these organizations is strongly indebted to Buddhism. The Jewish Mindfulness Center of Washington, for instance, offers mindfulness meditation, while standard programming includes teachers such as Sylvia Boorstein herself.[46] Nishmat Hayyim offers a "mindfulness practice group" which features "Jewish, Buddhist and other mindfulness texts," as well as teachings by Norman Fischer and the founding rabbi's own *metta* (Pali for "kindness") meditation, a practice popularized by *vipassana* teacher S.N. Goenka in the 1980s.[47] One of the most prominent organizations, the Institute for Jewish Spirituality, reports that they are "incorporating the Four Noble Truths and Eight-fold Path" into their Jewish Mindfulness Teacher Training in order to "provide a systematic presentation of the dharma and Buddhist path from which we will approach Jewish life, the Jewish year, Torah and key texts, and other Jewish teachings."[48]

At the same time, however, these organizations describe their practices in a Jewish key, often downplaying Buddhist and otherwise non-Jewish language. The Awakened Heart Project states that its mission is to "promote Jewish contemplative techniques that develop a *heart of wisdom and compassion*," which is a characteristically Buddhist phrase, and features teachings by Alan Lew and Sylvia Boorstein, but makes no explicit references to Buddhism on its website.[49] The Institute for Jewish Spirituality describes their use of hatha yoga

---

[45]The Spirituality Initiative," *Hebrew Union College*, http://huc.edu/campus-life/new-york/spirituality-initiative.

[46]"Jewish Mindfulness Center of Washington @ Adas Israel," *Adas Israel Congregation*, http://adasisrael.org/jmcw/. Jennie Litvack, "Widening the Tent with Jewish Mindfulness," *The Wexner Foundation Blog*, October 29, 2014, http://www.wexner-foundation.org/blog/widening-the-tent-with-jewish-mindfulness.

[47]"Reb Moshe's Metta Practice," Temple Beth Zion, https://www.tbzbrookline.org/shabbat-and-holidays/nishmat-hayyim/reb-moshes-metta-practice/.

[48]"Institute for Jewish Spirituality," *The Frederick P. Lenz Foundation for American Buddhism*, http://fredericklenzfoundation.org/institute-jewish-spirituality.

[49]"Welcome," *The Awakened Heart Project for Contemplative Judaism*, http://www.awakenedheartproject.org. For instance, Tibetan teacher Dzogchen Ponlop Rinpoche has referred to "wisdom joined with compassion" as the "true essence" of the Buddha's teachings in his book *Rebel Buddha: A Guide to A Revolution of* Mind (Boston: Shamb-

in exclusively Jewish language: "During all yoga sessions, basic postures are taught within a Jewish framework, utilizing Jewish term and references. In so doing, the experience of developing a yoga practice can be 'felt' Jewishly."[50] In fact, with the exception of Nishmat Hayyim, none of the organizations mentioned here reference Buddhism in their own materials.[51]

Lastly, several of these organizations portray themselves as explicitly doing outreach to Jews drawn to Eastern spirituality. The impetus for the Jewish Mindfulness Center of Washington arose directly from such a vision:

> We all had the personal experience of wanting more spirituality from our Judaism than our traditional synagogue was providing. And we all noticed that despite the heavy investment in "engagement" and "outreach" by Jewish institutions, many Jews in the DC metro area had given up on looking for spirituality in Jewish settings, choosing instead to help fill Buddhist meditation halls and yoga studios to capacity. We envisioned a different approach—a center dedicated to Jewish mindfulness and contemplative practices that would provide Jews in the DC area a way to access a sense of the spiritual.[52]

Similarly, Or HaLev reports being "committed to reaching out to a generation of young Jews who are not served by current offerings and the many tens of thousands who have departed Judaism because they have not found the meaningful spiritual practice they were seeking."[53]

It is surely too soon to say how these organizations will impact Jewish spirituality in the long run, but they clearly represent the most recent iteration of Jewish-Buddhist encounter in a manner that appears to be garnering attention and gathering support. To the extent that they prove successful, they are shaping Jewish spirituality in terms of mindfulness and contemplation in ways that are highly indebted to Buddhism, but which seem to see that in-

---

hala Publications, Inc., 2010),

[50] "Embodied Practices," *Institute for Jewish Spirituality*, http://www.jewishspirituality.org/our-spiritual-practices/embodied-practices.

[51] The reference above to Buddhist frameworks for IJS trainings was found not on their own website, but on a grant entry from the Lenz Foundation.

[52] Litvack.

[53] "Vision," *Or HaLev: Center for Jewish Spirituality and Meditation*, http://orhalev.org/vision/.

debtedness as a potential problem. However, there is a current of pragmatism running through the whole venture as well, which aspires to deploy mindfulness as a powerful technique for strengthening the Jewish community.

Implications and further questions

As for the question of pluralism, the Jewish-Buddhist encounter provides a fascinating test case in two key ways. First, JuBus represent an extraordinary range of commitments: As discussed in this chapter, there are Buddhists of Jewish background, Jews who practice Buddhism alongside Judaism, Jews who deploy Buddhist spiritual techniques in the service of their Judaism, and Jews who have adopted simple mindfulness practices as part of their spiritual seeking. Each of these is an example of pluralistic meaning-making at work. However, the JuBu phenomenon is also instructive for what it is *not*, as few of the examples above fit accepted definitions of pluralism. Diana Eck's classic formulation, for instance, posits five key elements:

> First, pluralism is not the sheer fact of plurality alone, but is active engagement with plurality. [...] Second, pluralism is not simply tolerance, but also the seeking of understanding. [...] Third, pluralism is not simply relativism, but assumes real commitment. [...] Fourth, pluralism is not syncretism, but is based on respect for differences. [...] Fifth, pluralism is based on interreligious dialogue.[54]

For a pluralism defined by engagement with diversity, seeking of understanding, encounter of commitments, respect for difference, and dialogue, JuBus provide a curious case study.

To begin, one might agree with the arguments that the Jewish-Buddhist encounter exhibits active engagement with plurality and the seeking of understanding. The JuBus mentioned here and many others are indeed seeking to understand a religious tradition that is not their own and are doing so in a manner that is both absorbing and sustained. However, when we arrive at Eck's three other factors, the issue becomes more complicated. Regarding the assumption of real commitment, while some JuBus have certainly explored Buddhism as a religion in its own right, others have assumed that Buddhism is a philosophy rather than a religion, so that it occupies an interstitial space

---

[54]Diana Eck, *Encountering God: A Spiritual Journey from Bozeman to Banaras* (Boston: Beacon Press, 2003), 191-197.

where religious commitments are moot. From a pluralistic standpoint, these types of statements are troubling, as they approach what Eck has referred to as "a valueless relativism—an undiscriminating twilight in which 'all cats are gray,' all perspectives equally viable, and as a result, equally uncompelling."[55] Does the Jewish-Buddhist encounter genuinely qualify as pluralism when the other religion in question has been commodified in this way? Does the argument that Buddhism is "hot-swappable" rob Buddhism of its meaning and particularity?

Eck's criterion of "respect for differences" is similarly problematic in Jewish-Buddhist encounter. While JuBus typically have great respect for Buddhism as it is commonly taught in the West, such as the *vipassana* meditation techniques that emerged from the work of Buddhist modernizers, many shy away from more visibly exotic practices, such as the Tibetan *gcod/chö* ritual, in which a practitioner visualizes butchering her own body and offering the pieces to demons and spirits as a ritualized severing of her attachments. From a Buddhist perspective, both *metta* meditation and the *chö* ritual are powerful means of cultivating compassion and generosity, so is it problematic that the JuBu community has elected to adopt only one as its own? Is there an implicit judgment, or a denial of pluralism, at work in adopting only the similar and familiar?[56] Or do JuBus eschew similarly "exotic" practices in Judaism, and so this pattern constitutes, rather, a broader trend in modern religious life?

Finally, Eck posits that genuine pluralism must be "based on interreligious dialogue." However, the Jewish-Buddhist encounter has been a largely one-sided affair. There is ample evidence of Jews seeking out Buddhist teachings and practices, but there is almost no evidence of Buddhists asking Jews for the same. The notable exception, of course, would be the historical dialogue in Dharamsala, India, between His Holiness the Dalai Lama and Jewish rabbis and scholars, as recorded in Rodger Kamenetz's *The Jew in the Lotus*. For the most part, however, Jews have primarily been students of Buddhist teachers and texts and recipients of their wisdom, as well as subsequent adaptations of that wisdom.

The JuBu phenomenon therefore presents a peculiar problem for the theorist of religion. Its manifestations are clearly pluralist, but it also defies es-

---

[55] Eck, 193.

[56] We might hope for a response from the Buddhist community here, but surprisingly little has been written on the subject. One exception is the aforementioned teacher Dzogchen Ponlop Rinpoche, who argues that Buddhists must offer a "culturally stripped-down vision of the Buddhist spiritual journey" in order to "connect these ancient teachings on wisdom with our contemporary sensibilities," *Rebel Buddha*, 5-6.

tablished categories of analysis. In doing so, it forces the Jewish community to consider a number of significant questions, such as where to draw the line between cultural exchange and cultural appropriation, how to better partner with the Buddhist community in advancing both spiritual and humanitarian causes, and—looking forward—what the widespread secularization of mindfulness might mean for the future of contemplative Jewish spirituality. Lastly, scholar Barbara Holdrege, in writing on her comparative work with Hinduism and Judaism, has argued that "comparative studies of Hindu and Jewish traditions can provide the basis for developing alternative epistemologies to the Protestant-based paradigms that have served to perpetuate the ideals of Enlightenment discourse and colonialist projects."[57] In a similar way, the JuBu phenomenon, taken seriously as a topic for study in interreligious encounter, might offer new models for interpreting spirituality and religious life.

---

[57] Barbara Holdrege, "Beyond Hegemony: Hinduisms, Judaisms, and the Politics of Comparison," in *Indo-Judaic Studies in the Twenty-First Century: A View from the Margin*, ed. Nathan Katz (New York: Palgrave Macmillan, 2007), 87.

Affiliation with and Abandonment of Judaism as Acts of Spiritual Migration

A Theological Essay

Yehoyada Amir[1]

"Do not entreat me to leave you, to return from following you, for where you go I will go; and where you lodge I will lodge; your people shall be my people, and your God my God. Where you die, I will die, and there will I be buried. The Lord do so to me, and more also, if aught but death part you and me." (Ruth 1:16–17)

Introduction

For many generations traditional Judaism has considered itself a non-missionizing religion, which does not take the initiative to proselytize and does not encourage this process. This is not the place to enter into the temperamental debate concerning the extent to which this self-depiction agrees with historical events in various periods. In any case, it is easy to see that it has had profound influence on Jewish discourse, at least starting with the Middle Ages. This applies to traditional halakhic and ideological discussions of the question of conversion to Judaism and issues concerning the relation to proselytes and their status, as well as the way that the phenomenon of joining Judaism or the Jewish people is perceived today in various groups. Non-Jews are not expected to observe any but the Noahide laws, and the Talmud even voices the opinion that a gentile who observes the Jewish Sabbath is subject to capital punishment.[2] But those who decide to affiliate with Judaism are clearly regarded as joining themselves to God's inheritance and are freed of their previous mode of existence.[3]

---

[1] Translated by Leonard Levin

[2] Babylonian Talmud (BT) *Sanhedrin* 58b.

[3] See Maimonides, *Mishneh Torah*, "Laws of Kings," 10:11–12: "A gentile who engages in Torah [study] is subject to the death penalty; he should engage only in [studying] the seven Noahide laws. Similarly, a gentile who observes Sabbath-rest, even on a weekday, if he treats it like the Sabbath, is subject to the death-penalty, and all the more so if he appropriated practice of a Jewish holiday. The general rule: one does not permit them to invent a religion and to intentionally appropriate mitzvot, but such a one should either choose to be a full convert to Judaism accepting all the mitzvot, or

The traditional attitude to those who embrace Judaism is quite variable. On the one hand, Rabbi Helbo's saying, "Proselytes are as difficult for Israel as a scab"[4] has enjoyed central attention and is quoted innumerable times, even though in fact it is a marginal individual view, with no actual legal standing. On the other hand, mainstream rabbinic sayings praise converts and see in conversion to Judaism a positive and praiseworthy process. Characteristic of this tendency are the words of Tractate *Gerim*:

> Beloved are proselytes, for Scripture applies the same terms to them as to Israel. God is said to love Israel, and God is said to love the proselyte (*ger*). Israelites are called God's servants, and the proselytes are called God's servants. Israel enjoys God's favor, and the proselytes enjoy God's favor. God guards Israel, and God guards the proselyte. Israel ministers to God, and the proselytes minister to God.[5]

We should point out that here, as in many other places, the rabbis (playing on the dual significance of the term *ger*) apply biblical verses addressing the status of the resident alien to the case of converts, while purposely ignoring the far-reaching significance of mixing such diverse categories. They did so in order to give unequivocal anchoring to the principle of absolute equality of converts to born Jews. In the same spirit, Maimonides emphasizes (in his account of the development of the Oral Torah in his formative introduction to the *Mishneh Torah*) that a whole series of prominent sages, central pillars of the Jewish tradition, were proselytes or descended from proselytes.[6] One may say that the abundance of sources expressing an extremely positive attitude to

---

else stand pat with [the Noahide] law, neither adding to it nor diminishing from it. If a gentile engages in Torah, rests on the Sabbath, or adds a mitzvah, one flogs him and fines him and informs him that he is legally liable to the death penalty, but one does not put him to death."

[4] For example, BT *Yevamot* 17b, which is the primary Talmudic source dealing with conversion and the laws connected with it. Rabbi Helbo was a third-generation Amora of Eretz Israel who came from Babylonia.

[5] Tractate *Gerim* 1:2, citing biblical prooftexts for each example.

[6] "Shemaiah and Avtalyon were proselytes ... Rabbi Akiva b. Joseph's father was a proselyte ... R. Meir was the son of a proselyte." (Maimonides, *Mishneh Torah*, Jerusalem: Mossad Ha-Rav Kuk, 1972, Vol. 2, pp. 6–7) See also the Baraita in the Babylonian Talmud (*Gittin* 57b): "Nebuzaradan was a proselyte. Haman's descendants learned Torah in Bnei Berak; Sisera's descendants were teachers of children in Jerusalem; Sennacherib's descendants taught Torah to the masses. Who were the last-named? Shemaiah and Avtalyon."

proselytes could be read largely as a protracted leadership effort of the sages and legal authorities to counter the problematic and vulnerable status of converts within Jewish communities in various periods.

In any case, the positive principled attitude toward proselytes expressed in the majority of Talmudic sayings and post-Talmudic legal sources provides no grounds for inferring openness toward or positive valuation of non-Jews, their religiosity or way of life. On the contrary, they seek to place confidence in the power of the primary decision of the proselytes to forsake the worthless ways that characterized their previous existence and to cleave to the service of God. This is expressed in a whole series of laws. We examine, for example, the assumption in Tractate *Gerim* concerning the ideological starting-point of the process of conversion: "Whoever wishes to convert, should not be accepted immediately, but they should ask him, 'Why do you want to convert?'...If he says, 'I am not worthy to place my neck under the yoke of Him who spoke and brought the world into being, Blessed be He,' they accept him immediately."[7] The assumption behind these words is clear. Up to this point, the prospective convert was not under God's yoke, for only Israel are God's servants, and only if he converts will he become a member of the congregation of worshippers of God. This is the only motivation for conversion to be declared as legitimate by halakha,[8] although it is clear from reading these sources that in practice many converts were motivated by a much broader spectrum of interests.[9] This conception, with respect to the complete transformation that the proselyte undergoes from worthless gentile ways to worship of God, dictates the demands

---

[7] Tractate *Gerim* 1:1.

[8] Ibid. 1:3: "Whoever converts for a woman [i.e. for the sake of marriage], for love, or out of fear is not a [valid] proselyte. Thus Rabbi Judah and Rabbi Nehemiah said: 'Those who were converted in the days of Mordecai and Esther are not [valid] proselytes, as it says, "Many of the people of the land professed to be Jews [*mityahadim*], for the fear of the Jews had fallen upon them" (Esther 8:17).' Anyone who does not convert for the sake of Heaven is not a proselyte."

[9] See, for example, *Genesis Rabbati Vayishlah* (p. 149): "It was taught: There are four kinds of proselytes: the one who converts for love, from fear, for economic reasons, or out of righteous motives. These are all indicated in the Torah according to their deeds. The convert for love—how so? If he loved an Israelite woman and came to convert in order to marry her, the Torah compares him to a dog...The convert from fear—how so? These are the converts of Mordecai and Esther, who came to convert only from fear, and are compared to cattle...The convert from economic motives—how so? He saw the poor of Israel who are properly fed and came to convert for the sake of the economic perquisites, and therefore he is compared to a poor man...The convert from righteous motives is one who has converted for Heaven's sake, therefore the Torah compares him to a citizen..."

with respect to the attitude one should have toward him after he converts:

> Our rabbis taught: "You shall not wrong one another"
> (Lev. 25:17)—this refers to demeaning someone in speech.
> How so? If one was a penitent, one should not say to him,
> "Remember your former deeds." If he was the child of pros-
> elytes, one should not say to him, "Remember your parents'
> ways." If he was a proselyte and came to study Torah, one
> should not say to him, "Shall the mouth that ate *treyf* and
> forbidden animals study Torah that was spoken from God's
> mouth?"[10]

The proselyte is considered here as similar to the penitent who has left a life of sin behind. He is assumed to regard his parents' lifestyle in the same light as the penitent should regard his life prior to his transformation. His lifestyle prior to conversion is compared by this source to the sinner's transgressions, even though by every traditional normative standard there was nothing wrong with a non-Jew's eating *treyf*. His being accepted into the community of Israel and Torah means a full-as-possible erasure of this shadowy past and its memory. "A proselyte who is converted is like a newborn babe."[11] It should be noted that the rabbis deal very little with the decisive question, what were the spiritual, psychological, social and cultural elements that brought him in the first place, as a non-Jew, to the decision to convert to Judaism? What were the "holy sparks" in his soul and in his non-Jewish environment that induced him to recognize the value and truth of Jewish life?

If there is a wide range of views on the attitude to the proselyte, a more sharply defined attitude prevails toward one who has left Judaism. One who changes his religion and leaves Judaism is a *meshumad* (apostate), i.e., one who has destroyed himself.[12] Indeed, in principle a Jew who changes his religion remains legally a Jew—that is, an Israelite apostate—but he is regarded as guilty of a heinous sin, one that (according to some sources) should be avoided on pain of martyrdom. He is considered the lowest of the low, far below the born gentile on the self-congratulating Jewish scale of values. The apostate is

---

[10] BT *Bava Metzia'* 58b.

[11] BT *Yevamot* 97b and elsewhere.

[12] It is not clear whether the term originated from this etymology, but it is quite clear that this is the connotation it has carried over the generations. For this reason, over time the Christian censor forbade its use, and the more neutral term *mumar* ("changed") was substituted for it.

regarded as a dangerous enemy, a traitor and despicable. It was customary to sit *shiva* for him when his apostasy became known, out of the understanding that with the act of apostasy, his life had ended for all purposes.[13] Consistent with this view, halakhic sources rule that when the apostate actually dies, his family should not mourn but rather rejoice, because an enemy of God has perished from the world.[14] The sense of hostility toward apostates is one of the most deeply rooted in Jewish group psychology to this day, among religious and secular Jews, in both Orthodox and liberal communities.[15]

Praise of converts and condemnation of apostates was certainly not unique to Judaism. Indeed, these attitudes were picked up even by those lay members who are more or less distant from religion and from the lifestyles that it prescribes. Christianity, as a frankly missionary religion, and Islam, as a religion laying claim to universal truth and political hegemony, developed even more extreme ideas and behaviors. If Jewish authorities debated whether and in what sense a Jewish apostate was still a Jew, Christianity and Islam often condemned those who sought to leave them to actual death. If Judaism was ambivalent toward those who embraced it, the other religions saw—and to a large extent still see—the act of embracing their religion as a clear criterion for salvation, superiority, and for approaching the fulfillment of their religious calling. Nevertheless, one should note the gap between the official theological position and the suspicions, restrictions, and reservations that were frequently the lot of new converts to these faiths.

At the root of this picture stands a fundamental characteristic of monotheism in all its forms. By its very nature the monotheistic position tends to confer legitimacy only on one religious way, or at the very least regards only

---

[13] See, for example, the attestation concerning Rabbenu Gershom Light of the Exile who did so for his son who was baptized (*Or Zarua* § 458).

[14] Tractate *Semaḥot* 3:5: "As for apostates (*meshumadim* and *mumarim*), not only should one not mourn their deaths, but their relatives should rejoice and wear white and eat in celebration that an enemy of the Holy One has died." In the ultra-Orthodox world, many observe this practice for those who have left for modern culture.

[15] This sentiment was expressed by the well-known Israeli thinker Yeshayahu Leibowitz. Quite a few times in the Israeli media he labeled the atomic spy Mordechai Vanunu as "the scum of humanity"—not because he was a traitor to his country, which in many cases can be an honorable thing, but because he betrayed Judaism by converting to Christianity. Thus, converting to Christianity was no way, in his view, a transition to another way of serving God, but total abandonment of living properly before God. This abandonment was in Leibowitz's eyes far more problematic than the decision of a secular Jew who chooses not to observe the mitzvot and to cut himself off from everything symbolizing religious life before God, in the manner that Vanunu lived, as far as we know, before his conversion.

one way as fully legitimate and complete. In the eyes of the monotheistic believer, other religions are necessarily forms of unbelief, or at least inferior and
imperfect religious ways.[16] From this follows the unequivocal attitude toward
conversion to the faith as a praiseworthy act of repentance; regarding cleaving to the faith and refusal to leave it as the supreme expression of fidelity to
God, even to the point of martyrdom, which attests to the superior truth of
this religion; and regarding leaving the faith as flagrant betrayal of God and
His truth. We should note that what applies to the external boundary lines
between the religions applies to a large extent also to the internal boundary
lines between various sects within a religious group (such as between Shi'ites
and Sunnis in Islam, between Catholics and Protestants in Christianity, and
between various Orthodox sects, non-Orthodox movements, and secularists
in Judaism). This paradigm would thus appear as a necessary, ironclad principle of monotheistic religions and of the cultures based on them, a paradigm
that is ubiquitous and unchangeable.

   In the following, I will seek to refute this apparently absolute and self-
evident proposition. I will propose an alternate way of thinking about the
issue of embracing a religious community or deciding to leave one community
in favor of another. At the center will stand, of course, the question of embracing Judaism and the Jewish people, as well as the question of leaving Judaism
and the Jewish people. But the application of the criteria that I propose will
be broader. I will rest my words on philosophical and theological supports, as
well as on reflective observations concerning the human reality of this topic, which arises between the lines even of the classic halakhic discussion, of
which a cursory survey is offered here.[17]

Cultural and Religious Belonging as a Particular "Landscape"

   At the foundation of the perspective presented here stands the conception
of religious and cultural affiliation that distinguishes religious communities
and peoples as a "landscape." It is a particular expression, one of many, distinguishing the group and differentiating it from other groups. The special

---

[16] One can find a position like this in Islam's principled attitude to the "people
of the Book" or in the distinction made in much of the Jewish halakhic discussion
between Christianity, regarded by most of the medieval authorities as idolatrous, and
Islam, which is not so regarded.

[17] For a broad discussion of the legal and ideological issues that arise from the
halakhic literature, see Zvi Zohar and Avi Sagi, *Transforming Identity: The Ritual
Transition from Gentile to Jew—Structure and Meaning*, New York: Continuum, 2007.

quality of belonging to a specific religion plays a decisive part in the formation of individuals and sub-groups of every such community on the planes of
spirit, society, language and experience. Belonging to a specific landscape—
whether spiritual or geographic—from birth and from the most primal stages
of identity-formation is indeed particularistic. It marks the similarity of those
who grew out of the same landscape, as well as the differences between them
and those who grew out of different landscapes. But in itself it is a universal characteristic of human existence. For every person, family, congregation,
community, or people, the landscape or sub-terrain that marks them takes
part in shaping them, conditioning their point of view on the world and serving as a point of origin for their life's journey and the legacy that they are
likely to bequeath to coming generations. The uniqueness imposed by a specific landscape, the proximity or distance between various landscapes, and
the commonality among human landscapes as such—these are among the
foundations of development of human culture generally, of specific human
cultures, and no less of religious communities and their expressions.

Every person carries with her—from birth, from gender, from upbringing,
from the choices she makes, from her life experience, from parental language
and education—components of a particular identity that shape her life and
the point of view from which she will interpret the world and make her decisions. This is the case for every individual, and for every community, tribe,
congregation or people. These components of identity are of primal importance and decisive force, positive and negative, whether they operate on the
level of conscious knowledge and volition or on the subconscious levels of the
personality. The particular identity, which has grown up out of a specific landscape, is likely to acquire great significance in questions of ethical conduct.
Related to this is one's consciousness of special responsibility to one's com-
patriots and coreligionists, as well as to the fate of one's religious community,
state and culture. One's particular identity and the landscape that gave rise
to it also acquire great significance in matters of cultural and artistic creation.
This is most prominent in the genres of poetry, fiction, theater and cinema,
but applies also in painting, sculpture, music and dance. It is clear that this
identity also plays a significant role—for better or worse—in the horizon of
development of every individual, group and community. This is the case by
virtue of the components of their self-concept, as well as their conceptions of
and attitudes toward those around them, members of their own group as well
as of other groups. Thus the developmental horizon of the medieval Jew was
determined by his status as a member of a pariah group, as well as by the cultural and religious formation that belonging to this group conferred on him.

Similarly, the developmental horizon of members of the community of Israeli Palestinians is determined by the way in which Israeli society defines and restricts the status of that community, as well as by their national, linguistic and religious identity, be it Muslim or Christian.

This state of affairs in itself is independent of any ideology or theoretical orientation. It is the given situation out of which individuals, communities and peoples grow. The question that we should raise concerning it, a question that will bring us closer to the issue of transition from one religious affiliation to another, is that of the value that should be placed on the various components of this picture.

What is subject to choice, education, and theoretical and cultural awareness is the extent to which a person roots herself in the particular identity out of which and into which she grows, conferring positive and generative meaning to this identity. No less than this, there may dawn the awareness that this particular identity is only one of many, and that around her—sometimes even within her—other identities exist, other groups live, other languages and literatures develop, other different and varied perspectives function. To be rooted in a particular landscape is a very proper and natural aspiration, and the curricula that different societies have developed for educating and acculturating their members are designed to a large extent to foster and ground this sense. But when in the course of this development the individual is blocked from seeing other kinds of landscapes—and thus acquires the conception that only this specific landscape has value and legitimacy—then this attachment becomes diseased, degenerate and dangerous. This exclusivity of attachment is the fundamental difference between open/liberal and fascistic/racist manifestations of modern nationalism. Herein lies the test of every multiculturalism and pluralism that is based on being deeply anchored in a particular identity and a sincere sense of responsibility to it. The ability to reconcile the universalistic and particularistic is the yardstick for the ability to enrich cultures through contact with other cultures, to base cooperation on recognizing the riches that difference can generate. Only by virtue of it can one base responsibility to universal humanity on the best of one's particular identity, while basing the appreciation of the existence of one's specific group on the value of human life as such.[18]

First and foremost, such a perspective is based on—and reinforces—the recognition by the individual and the community of the value of other par-

---

[18] See Yehoyada Amir, "The General-Human and the Particular-Jewish Dimensions of the Holocaust: A Philosophical-Educational Reflection", *Dapim: Studies on the Holocaust*, 27, 3 (2013), pp. 157–73.

ticularisms, those that exist in their immediate surroundings, as well as those to which one is exposed only thanks to the flow of information, ideas and discourse of the "global village." This is likely to lead one to the realization that precisely as a result of one's standing amid a variety of identities that one is aware of, one has a deeper appreciation of the unique qualities of one's own personal and group identity. Such a perspective inoculates one from malignant exclusivism, and at the same time from the delusion that the choice standing before one is a choice between a rich but narrow particular identity and a bland universal cosmopolitan identity embracing all humanity. On the contrary, the human species is composed of terrestrial families. Outside one's particular identity there is not a uniform general human identity—as those assimilationist European Jews who longed to be liberated from the Jewish ghetto and enter the gates of a pan-human Europe imagined—but rather a wide variety of other particular identities, comprising together what can be viewed as a universal human ensemble.

If this perspective can be perceived as reasonable and proper and enjoy broad enough consensus on the general cultural plane, still, on the religious plane it is faced with a series of challenges that we alluded to earlier. Its adoption would demand a series of theological decisions, as such a procedure would entail conflict with many of the traditional normative assertions of the various religions.

Theologically, such a cosmopolitan outlook must rest on the assumption that God is able to reveal God's self to various groups of humanity, to "choose" various peoples, to impart to humanity an infrastructure of commandment and "truth" out of which various religions can grow. Along those lines, when a specific religion—our interest here is primarily the Jewish tradition—is possessed of the consciousness that it expresses truly the service to God and God's truth, this outlook can indeed be well supported and may fertilize and deepen its believers' religious life. Moreover, without a strong grasp of this consciousness, religion would lose its meaning and become a ritual devoid of content or mere folklore. On the other hand, when a religion attributes this character to itself exclusively, when it announces that it has the one divine truth and the only valid divine commandment—this is a false presumption bordering on idolatry. For whoever holds to such a claim is asserting de facto that God is not the God of humanity, in all its ways and religions, but rather only their own God. It should be noted that the distance between this conception and the classic idolatrous conception according to which our gods take an interest only in us, and rule only our inheritance, is much smaller than one would like to assume. Moreover, this conception presumes to leave God the possibility to maintain only one communications channel, to reveal God's self only in the way that this specific tradition understands God's revelation, to express God's self only through one human particularism—the one that sees itself as the chosen people, or the one that sees itself as the sole kernel of redeemed humanity. One should emphasize that this presumption implies far-reaching denial of the all-embracing omnipotence of the God of heaven and earth, Creator of the world and humankind.

One should not infer from this that a specific religious tradition—Jewish, Christian, Muslim, or other—possesses only relative value, or that all of this is human invention and no more. For if the canonical forms of the various religions were designed as responses to the word of God addressed to human beings—and we may understand the concept of "word of God" however we choose—then they are both divine and human. Each of them is the attempt of a faith community to articulate its stance before God, expressing it in language, garb, narrative, commandments and life regimen—in short, a religious culture—renewed and elaborated over the course of generations. It is a specific "landscape"; it is a unique and valid mode of human existence before God. Within its circles this landscape is apt to acquire absolute meaning, or perhaps better: meaning aspiring to the absolute inasmuch as it is within human power to bear this aspiration and realize it. In a broader perspective, encompassing other religions and nations, periods and creations, "no religion is an island" as Abraham Joshua Heschel put it.[19] Such a perspective would reveal that no landscape is "the truth" but the portion of certain human beings in the divine truth, as Franz Rosenzweig said.[20] Around this landscape one finds other terrains, other landscapes, other portions in truth, religious qualities that touch each other, or are parallel to each other, or even opposite to each other.

All this still does not eliminate the question of false worship, or the command to struggle against it and uproot it from our midst. The fact that truth can be revealed in various forms and various modes of expression does not imply that there is no such thing as falsehood. The recognition that good and justice have a variety of manifestations does not negate the recognition that injustice and wickedness also exist, and it is incumbent on us to bring near

---

[19] Abraham Joshua Heschel, "No Religion is an Island," in *Moral Grandeur and Spiritual Audacity: Essays*, ed. By Susannah Heschel (New York: Farrar, Strauss and Giroux, 1996), 235–6.

[20] See Yehoyada Amir, *Da'at Ma'aminah: Iyyunim bemishnato shel Franz Rosenzweig* (Tel Aviv: Am Oved, 2004), 256–65.

the day in which "the mouth of iniquity will be shut."[21] The many-faceted experience of beauty, enriched by its different expressions in various cultures and nations, does not dull the sting of ugliness and the obligation to distance oneself from ugliness and whatever brings about ugliness.[22] This is the imperative to mend the world, to be a partner in completing the work of creation. This is the continuing struggle to bring about redemption. But the frontier lines of this struggle are not to be drawn between one religion and another, and certainly not between my religion and all other religions. False worship extends its tentacles into my religion as well, into my community and my culture. Fundamentalism, racism, injustice, misanthropy, hubris, violence and exploitation—all these are not foreign to my Jewish existence, just as they are not foreign to the existence of other cultures and religions. Their danger for my very existence is greater and more severe especially when they appear within my people, my country, my religion and culture; and when they do, it is all the more imperative for me to fight them and vanquish them. On the other hand, much of what exists in other religions, near and far, from East to West, is a way to seek truth, an attempt to live a proper life before God, by fearing God and loving humankind.

This broad outlook has implications for all areas of religious and cultural life. As for the imperatives of religion and its normative and theological judgments, it implies that they are human no less than they are divine. The eternal dimension in them does not cancel out the temporal, transitory dimension. On the one hand, they are all a true attempt to carry out what the Jewish prayer formulates when it says, "You distinguished mankind from the beginning and recognized him to stand before You."[23] Yet this does not contradict the fact that they are a cultural expression rooted in time, in place, in a worldview and in social constructs. On the particular plane, religious fidelity requires deep surrender of oneself to the yoke of a sacred tradition, drawing on the experience of past generations and presenting them before God. Yet it means no less perpetual readiness to examine, to correct, to update, and to depart from fallible elements that once seemed sacred and eternal. Thus, for example, all the products of religious creativity—theology, religious law, liturgy, and more—are stamped with the sign of gender. The religions relevant for our discussion were fashioned mainly by men who lived in patriarchal societies and held patriarchal outlooks. If we—women and men alike—seek to cure ourselves of this patriarchalism and to live in an egalitarian society

---

[21] From the Amidah for the High Holy Days.
[22] Tosefta, *Ḥullin*, 2, 24
[23] From the Amidah for Yom Kippur *Ne'ilah*.

respecting everyone created in the divine image—women and men, hetero-sexuals and LGBTQ individuals—it is incumbent on us to change a whole series of matters embedded in our religion.

Migration from One Landscape to Another

One could articulate at length the implications that follow from this con-ception of religious affiliation as landscape. For the purpose of the present discussion, it is important to clarify its far-reaching implications as to the meaning of continued fidelity to the religion in which a person grew up, and no less to the meaning of a person's decision to make a spiritual migration, to attach oneself to another religion, to become rooted in its particular landscape and to make it a portion of one's life and identity.

The natural first choice for a person is to root oneself in the circles of the particular identity from which and in which one grew up, to express oneself creatively in the language and culture that were stamped on one's personality, to take part in its development and its struggles. To be sure, this may include also the aspiration to bring into the circles of this identity materials, creative products, and insights whose parentage is from other places. But success in realizing this aspiration is contingent in large measure on the ability to absorb these external elements in the interior of one's identity and cultural language, until they are perceived as a natural part of it and become a component of the landscape characterizing it. It is no less understood that responsibly rooting oneself in the landscape of a particular identity requires also critical observa-tion, readiness to struggle against phenomena of falsehood, ugliness, deca-dence and corruption that are liable to spread in it. Moreover, as my pain over the distortions and failures of my "family" grow, I feel more that it is indeed mine; the readiness to rebuke, to correct, to try and to heal is an important yardstick of my devotion and dedication to my family.

But there are also situations and moments in which one finds oneself—out of conscious and reasoned choice, or on account of the circumstances of one's life, or out of a combination of these two—migrating from the physical and cultural landscape in which one was born and into which one was educated, and adopting another landscape. "A man is nothing but the mold of his home-land's landscape," said the Israeli poet Saul Tchernichovsky. [24] But his biog-raphy tells the story in a more complex manner: he was born in the Russian Empire (today Ukraine), migrated more than once within Europe, and in the

---

[24] Saul Tshernichovsky, poem, "Ha-adam eino ela...", http://benyehuda.org/tchernichowsky/haadam_eino_ela.html.

end, followed his flame of Zionist persuasion and adopted the physical and emotional landscape of Eretz Israel. He believed strongly that in doing so he was able to root himself properly in the Jewish national culture. This biography, characteristic for many creative spirits of the Zionist renaissance in Eretz Israel, confers special meaning on Tchernichovsky's utterance. Though it speaks of that which the child's ear perceives when "still fresh," of that which one sees before "being fed-up from seeing," it does not describe an established reality but expresses yearning for creating a reality. It does not point to a mere natural rootedness in a piece of landscape but rather gives expression to a life decision, though rooted in the physical and spiritual landscape of one's childhood, to re-root oneself in a landscape that from then on will become the mold that will shape one's life. What does this all mean?

We begin with a short inquiry concerning geographic migration. It is likely to have many causes: economic, security, cultural, family and spiritual. A person may be driven from her house or remain in it at peril to her life; a person may feel that what was her home is no longer right or proper for her; a person might yearn for the spiritual or material treasures of the land to which she is going. It seems that in all these instances, there must be a substantial cause—a cause that has the power to decide the course of one's life—in order for a person to pick up the staff of wandering and accept the hardships of migration and the fate of the immigrant. But the degree of weight of this factor, its power and the meaning of the force that motivates this step could be judged and appreciated only by the migrant herself. Millions of Jews migrated toward the end of the nineteenth century and the beginning of the twentieth century from Eastern Europe westward, especially to North America; millions of Jews came to Eretz Israel in the various waves of aliyah; tens of millions of human beings would migrate or attempt to migrate during these years from lands of oppression, war and hunger to the developed world of plenty. More recently, hundreds of thousands of Israelis have migrated from Israel to Europe and North America. Each of these waves—of Jews and other ethnicities—had its own quality, specific circumstances, unique fate. What they all had in common was being uprooted from one piece of landscape and transplanted into another piece of landscape, as well as the complex process of developing relations toward what was left behind and toward the new place that was adopted as home. In many cases the life of the migrant is marked by a feeling of belonging—real, hoped-for, or nostalgic—to both pieces of landscape, the one from which the migrant was uprooted and the one to which he arrives. It is often accompanied by the difficulty of rooting oneself completely in the chosen landscape, or the awareness that this process of taking root is for him the fruit of a conscious voluntary effort and not necessarily a "natural" result of the circumstances of life.

In light of what has been said so far, I will seek to examine a few aspects of the transition from one religion to another as a spiritual migration. Of course, only such a migration made out of conscious, voluntary choice, completely or largely free, is relevant to our inquiry. Such a spiritual migration is apt to be accompanied by geographical migration—as its cause or result—as in the cases of converts who choose to make aliyah to Eretz Israel in order to realize their Jewish identity in a way that seems more complete to them; or of immigrants to Israel who choose to convert to Judaism in order to realize more fully their choice to live in a society which is mostly and mainly Jewish. It can aim at realizing a biographical or genealogical element of one's identity, as in the case of many Poles who have a Jewish component in their family of origin, who have turned to convert in recent years, especially with Reform rabbis and rabbinic courts. Conversion as spiritual migration is often bound—here, too, as cause or effect—with social migration. It was so, for example, in many cases of Jews who were baptized into Christianity in Europe in the late nineteenth and early twentieth century, whether because they wanted thereby to enter the circles of "general" Christian society, or because they wanted to give full expression to the integration that they had earned. Understanding conversion as voluntary migration is expressed in the terminology adopted by liberal Jewish discourse in North America, which distinguishes between "Jews by birth" and "Jews by choice." It is clear that in both these cases, even that of Jews by birth, giving meaning to Jewish identity has in it a clear element of choice.

As with geographic migration, spiritual migration may also spring from different motivations. One of these can be deep religious conviction, the faith that religious truth is to be found in the paths of the other religion, and with it the proper potential for serving God. In this case, the migration itself depends on the sense that the previous landscape is less worthy—that the rejected religion is less true and is not a satisfactory expression of service to God. We recall that this is the one motivation that Jewish law singles out as a proper basis for conversion. This is also the basis for the sense of hostility and rejection that halakha and Jewish social practice expressed toward those who left Judaism in favor of another religion. However, in many instances this would not be the only or primary motive; and occasionally this motive would be entirely absent. It was entirely possible that a person would feel that he could express what Aaron David Gordon called "the religious sensitivity," that is, the primal religious element implanted in our being and our experience,[25] in one religion or another to the same extent, inasmuch as the difference between the particular garbs (or, in our image, between the pieces of landscape) did not add or detract in this regard. One would then be speaking of entirely other motives: family, cultural, economic, social, emotional. Viewing change of religion as a spiritual migration allows for full recognition and full acceptance of motives such as these, which religious law would have to disparage. For migration is not essentially a matter of forsaking falsehood for the sake of truth, evil for the sake of good, the ugly for the sake of the beautiful. Religions, unlike most countries of today's world, are not only "lands of migration" in actuality, but also frameworks obligated to receive willingly those who migrate to them in all innocence. Indeed, when migration is performed in all innocence, when a proper effort is made to root oneself in the new landscape and to adopt it, when the progression of one's identity influences the life of the migrant and her conduct—when all this happens, then as time goes by it does not make much difference why the decision to migrate took place originally. Surely it is not the right of the society to inquire into the motives of one who joined it or chose to leave it.

Notably, the conception of changing religion as a spiritual migration does not entirely negate a judgmental approach. Even in geographic migration, it is possible that migration in one direction can be perceived as "ascent" [*aliyah*]—as biblical, rabbinic, and Zionist perspectives regard migration to Eretz Israel; and accordingly, going in the opposite direction would be regarded as "descent" [*yeridah*].[26] It would appear that one cannot erase completely the tendency to feel pride when others join their destiny to ours and to see in their joining us confirmation of our vitality and strength or the truth of our way— or, conversely, the tendency to have difficulty in developing a tolerant attitude toward those who leave for another religion, or all the more, in fully accepting this step as a proper and legitimate expression of their life's path. Nevertheless, it is clear that adopting this approach would be a decisive contribution toward

---

[25] For elaboration, see: Yehoyada Amir, *Prophecy and Halakhah: Towards Non-Orthodox Religious Praxis in (Eretz) Israel* (New York: Tikvah Center Working Paper 06/12, New York: New York University School of Law, 2013), pp. 28–39 [online version: http://www.nyutikvah.org/pubs/1112/amir.html] .

[26] In the Genesis narrative, God instructs Jacob, "Do not fear to *go down* to Egypt, for I will make of you a great nation there. I will *go down* with you to Egypt and *bring you back up*" (Gen. 46:2–4). See also: Ezra 1:3. For the rabbinic view, see the end of Mishnah *Ketubot*: "A man may compel his family to *go up* to Eretz Israel but may not compel them to leave it. A man may compel his family to *go up* to Jerusalem, but may not compel them to leave it" (Mishnah *Ketubot* 13:11). See also: BT *Kiddushin* 69a.

moderating the judgmental aspect and accepting the legitimacy of such processes. Seeing change of religion as migration can provide a significant influence on engendering healthier and more fitting reflection on the full parallel between the process of embracing Judaism and leaving it, and on the obligation to base one's attitude to these parallel processes on the same criteria.

Throughout the generations, the Jewish people were generally more familiar with the case of individuals who left Judaism and embraced one of the two dominant religions of the lands where Jews lived. Despite the emphasis that was given in Jewish consciousness to imposed conversions and the readiness to die for the sanctification of God's name, demographic data point clearly to the fact that most of those who left Judaism did so without compulsion, and certainly without direct violent compulsion. This was a painful, bitter and disturbing component of Jewish existence. It is easy to understand and appreciate the degree of revulsion it engendered, especially in those times when Jews were a small minority, discriminated against and often persecuted. Now the tendency is reversed. Lately there is a growing awareness of the fact that the phenomenon of embracing the Jewish people and Judaism has increased greatly; and that leaving Judaism in favor of another religion is a rather rare and marginal phenomenon. This is the case not only in the majority Jewish society in Israel, but also in North American society, in which—according to some recent sociological studies—the status of Judaism has risen greatly.[27] In this reality, it is vital to undertake a critical examination of the traditional Jewish attitude toward conversion out of Judaism, and to question how legitimate and fruitful it is for us. Understanding change of religion as a kind of migration will assist us greatly in this self-examination.

As we saw, the halakha sees conversion to Judaism as a kind of rebirth. The proselyte loses at an instant his former family ties as well as his cultural and religious ties. Thus, the convert to Judaism is considered as a son or daughter of Abraham and Sarah, rather than of the convert's biological parents. For this reason, according to tradition converts are not supposed to mourn their biological relatives who have died, even if the latter have also converted, for in the process of rebirth that conversion entails, the mother who converts ceases to be the mother of her children, and the child who converts ceases to be the children of his or her parents.[28]

---

[27] See, for instance, Charles Silberman, *A Certain People: American Jews and Their Lives Today* (New York: Simon & Schuster, 1985) and Sylvia Barack Fishman, *Double or Nothing? Jewish Families and Mixed Marriage* (Waltham, MA: Brandeis University Press, 2004).

[28] *Shulḥan Arukh, Yoreh De'ah* § 269:1. But see next note.

However, halakhic discourse knew that reality is much more complicated than this. The *Shulḥan Arukh*, from which we have cited this law, in addressing the permission of the proselyte to marry close blood-relatives, is quick to interject that "the Sages forbade this, so that [the converts] should not say, 'we have passed from a more stringent regimen of sanctity to a more lenient regimen in this regard.'"[29] This reasoning can gain meaning only if we assume that it expresses, if only indirectly, the recognition that this neat depiction of "rebirth," erasing the past as if it did not exist, does not withstand the test of psychological and spiritual reality. The mother and sister did not stop being one's mother and sister, and marriage to them is unthinkable to anyone who takes the prohibitions of incest as a guiding light. As we said earlier, the Sages' need to praise the proselytes repeatedly and to demand a positive attitude toward them proves that this description does not withstand the test of social reality either. In the eyes of society, the proselyte is not a newborn babe. His life experiences, his cultural formation, his emotional world and family ties have not been erased, nor has the complex process that brought him as a non-Jew to the decision to embrace Judaism.

This state of affairs enjoys full recognition and full expression in the proposed approach, which sees in conversion a spiritual migration, and which frees us from regarding every change of religion as forsaking falsehood and attaching oneself to the truth. Indeed, unlike geographic migration, which often has a place for double citizenship, there is traditionally no provision for spiritual migration to include this syncretistic possibility. This follows first

---

[29] *Ibid.* Translator's note: It is possible to explain both the leniency with regard to mourning and the stringency with regard to marrying on the basis of social realia. Given the intergroup hostility prevalent in the ancient and medieval social worlds, it could often happen that a person who converted to Judaism incurred the severe censure of his or her parents and was in a real sense cut off from them interpersonally and spiritually. To require observation of the forms of mourning under these circumstances would have imposed on the convert a severe inner conflict. To assuage this, and to encourage the convert to have a sense of a fresh start, the fiction of "being reborn" was invented. This had, however, the undesirable result of allowing, by this logic, for the proselyte to marry close kin, in violation of the rules of incest that applied not only to Jews but also to Noahides. To avert this consequence, the rabbis immediately imposed a secondary ban on such unions. It should be pointed out that the halakhic *permission* for the convert to waive mourning his/her biological parents does not *require* this waiving. Indeed, where a loving relationship with one's parents prevails, such mourning is not only permissible but right and proper. And even where a problematic relationship exists, the psychological need to acknowledge one's connection to the deceased still has its valid claims, which ought to be addressed constructively—so mourning is generally appropriate.

and foremost from the preconception that religious fidelity should by its nature be all-embracing, unlike the obligation of civic loyalty, which is always circumscribed by the limits imposed by law. It seems that the various "immigration authorities" that see themselves in charge of spiritual migration to Judaism, Orthodox and non-Orthodox alike, are bound to the principle that a person cannot hold two religions at the same time. The secular Jewish public in Israel and in the Diaspora also seems to accept the principle that to be a Jew, one must "not be a member of another religion," a principle enshrined in the Law of Return of the State of Israel. Syncretism and conversion (i.e., conversion to Judaism, but the same seems to apply also to conversion out of Judaism)—are irreconcilable opposites.

Nevertheless, there is no place for the demand that the immigrant should "forget" the previous landscape and erase her memories of the land from which she emigrated. There is also no reason to demand from her not to feel nostalgia for the landscape that she left, its qualities and its beauty. Indeed, choosing a new landscape requires an effort to adopt it, and is rooted in the feeling that the new landscape is sufficient to fill the immigrant's life-world in an adequate and proper fashion. However, carrying with her the memories from the land that she left, the longing for a language that is no longer the language of the society in which she lives, nostalgia for tastes and odors, is in many cases a substantial part of her life. The landscape that she left behind becomes the landscape of her past, but it does not necessarily disappear. One is not obligated to see it as a land of horrors, far from worship of God, from which the immigrant slogged her way to get to the "Holy Land" and to the true and proper worship of God. What she learned there is still a part of her intellectual world; what she experienced there is still part of her spiritual journey; the spiritual, social and intellectual substrate with which she arrived, as a non-Jew, to the decision to convert, is still the substrate of her current Jewish existence. The traditional expectation that the past will be erased is inappropriate to us, all the more the expectation that the proselyte should cut himself off from his or her family. It is proper for converts to continue to love their relatives, to honor their parents, to be loyal children to the past generations of their families, even if they do this in another context, while standing on a terrain that is apt to be strange and foreign to those past generations. In place of the prohibition against reminding the proselyte of the deeds of his forebears and his own past, one should say that it is a more serious case of "wrongful speech" to ignore the proselyte's past, his spiritual richness, his family background and his full journey. Ignoring these is both morally wrong and false.[30] For the fiction that the past has been erased as if it never was, will eventually explode in the face of the convert and of the surrounding society.

The same applies to one who has emigrated from us and gone to another religion. The act of converting-out does not erase him from the book of Jewish life, even though he chose not to live as a Jew, and even though he is no longer a part of the community of Israel in its full and usual sense. His fate and his journey are to be found within the continuum of life journeys available to Jews, for better or worse. On occasion the very act of converting-out is a part of the distinct and unique Jewish reality. Such, for example was the journey of Archbishop Jean-Marie Lustiger, born Aaron Lustiger, whose life was saved during the Holocaust by a French Catholic family, and who embraced their faith until he eventually became one of the leaders of the Catholic Church. In his eyes, as an immigrant loyal to his new spiritual homeland—Christianity—there was nothing in his Jewish identity that contradicted this loyalty. In his eyes, it was even proper that at his funeral they would offer psalms in Hebrew and say Kaddish. Indeed, both the halakha and mainstream Christianity would have difficulties accepting this request. Nevertheless, he and his Jewish relatives knew full well that it was the right thing to follow this personal and unique path. Similarly, one should not ignore the Jewishness of Edith Stein, who converted to Christianity out of deep faith and was murdered in Auschwitz as a Jew.[31] A century earlier lived the great German-Jewish poet Heinrich Heine, whose struggle over his Jewish identity was complex and fruitful, before his conversion to Christianity and even more so after it.[32] What holds true of these famous cases of spiritual individuals should hold true in principle also regarding ordinary people, whose struggles of identity and faith led them

---

[30] The Hebrew term used by the rabbis (BT *Bava Mezi'a* 58b; see note 9 above) is *hona'a*. In rabbinic Hebrew it means "wrong;" modern Hebrew understands it as fraud and cheating.

[31] This question was at the center of the controversy that was stirred up around commemorating her as a Catholic saint in the Carmelite monastery that was built near Auschwitz. The argument of the Jewish organizations, which had a good deal of merit, was that this was a deliberate attempt to deny and cover up the fact that Stein, who never denied her Jewishness, was killed as a Jew, not as a Catholic martyr.

[32] See Na'ama Rokem, *Shavui shenifdeh: ofanei hitkabluto shel Heinrich Heine be'ivrit* (The redeemed captive: the ways of Heinrich Heine's acceptance in Hebrew) in *Zehuyot: Ktav et l'tarbut ul'zehut yehudit* (5774/2014), 27–53. (In English, see Naama Rokem, *Prosaic Conditions: Heinrich Heine and the Spaces of Zionist Literature*, Evanston: Northwestern University Press, 2013). Translator's note: The Jewish dimension of Heine's legacy has been explored by many of his biographers and translators, among them Max Brod, Frederic Ewen, Lewis Browne, Moses Hadas, Israel Tabak, and Ernst Pawel.

to leave Judaism in favor of another religion—namely, whether they remained "Jewish" in the last analysis should be decided on a case by case basis.

Conclusion

The rabbis saw in the embracing of the Israelite people by Ruth the Moabitess, great-grandmother of King David, a firm basis for the conception of conversion that they developed. Of course, in order to do so they had to deploy powerful and far-reaching midrashic modes of interpretation that took great liberties with the plain sense of the text. The narrative of this book contains no hint or trace of a judicial or ritual act of conversion, but only the private declaration of a widow cleaving to her mother-in-law, that henceforth she would adopt her land and identity. In general, apparently one should agree with the prevailing opinion among biblical scholars, who see the purpose of the book as articulating an alternative to divorcing non-Jewish wives at the time of Ezra during the return to Jerusalem [in the beginning of Second Temple times, around 450 BCE]. This interpretation stands in utter contradiction to the image of Ruth as a convert, in the sense that rabbinic tradition developed it. Even more important for our purpose is the motivation for affiliation with Jewish society that arises from Ruth's words to Naomi, which are quoted at the beginning of this essay. Ruth's words express a purpose entirely different from that which the rabbis would develop later. They do indeed include a religious element ("your God is my God"; "The Lord do so to me and more also"), but in essence they express a totally different motivation from the one that the rabbis intended when they spoke of conversion "for the sake of Heaven." Ruth seeks to join the society from which Naomi came and to migrate to Bethlehem to which her mother-in-law is returning, as an expression of the completion and deepening of the loving connection between them. Of course, the rabbis sense this clearly and make a great effort to divert the words from their presumed meaning and adapt them to their own conception of conversion.[33]

---

[33] Thus, for example, the authors of *Midrash Ruth Rabbah* sense the enormous difficulty of reconciling their own understanding of conversion with the opening words of this speech: "Do not entreat me to leave you, to return from following you." The midrash takes these words entirely out of context and puts in Ruth's mouth the following words: "'It is my intention to convert in any case, but I would rather do so through you and not through another.' When Naomi heard these words she started enumerating the rules of conversion to her" (*Ruth Rabbah* 2:22). It is worth noting that precisely the interpretation of the words "Your people shall be my people and your God my God" suggests a recognition of the complex relation between Ruth's affilia-

The proposal laid out in this essay seeks to a large extent to turn the course of development back to the central outlook of this biblical source, but not in all respects. The intention is not to abolish the conception that spiritual migration into Judaism requires—communally, politically, nationally—"immigration authorities," that is to say, conversion courts that should be operated by the whole range of Jewish communities.[34] But it is vital that we free ourselves and our conversion-courts of the need to impose an ideological model that has guided, at least on the surface, the halakhic tradition and social consciousness until now. It is no longer adequate to express the complex reality that brings women and men to decide to give up the spiritual and religious landscape in which they grew up and to adopt another landscape for themselves, to exchange the literary and communal language into which they were born for another religious language. Adoption of this approach will allow both con-gregations—the one that was left behind and the one that was adopted—to accept the act of migration with understanding and love, without injecting into their relation with the other religion the poison of delegitimation.

Furthermore, those who adopt a new landscape and make it their own are indeed called on to display loyalty to this landscape and its qualities, but this loyalty should operate by the same rules as the loyalty displayed by those for whom this has been their landscape since birth. All parts of the landscape, the whole variety of its phenomena, all its navigation channels are open to them. Jews by choice are as free in their Jewishness as Jews from birth. They have the right to find their place in any part of the Jewish landscape that fits them. Conceiving conversion as an act of migration should put an end to the terrible distortion that some, in Israel and in the Diaspora Orthodoxy, seek

---

tion as an act of migration according to the plain sense of the narrative and the need to confer on it a meaning in keeping with the rabbis' conception: "*Your people shall be my people*—to abolish my idolatrous worship, *and your God shall be my God*—to reward me for my action." The abolition of idolatry, referring to cutting herself off from the Moabite gods, is represented here precisely as an act of affiliation to the people. The religious expression "Your God shall be my God" is associated by the midrash with the life that Ruth envisions after the completion of her migration. (For this connec-tion, see also Ruth 2:12, where Boaz says to Ruth: "The Lord recompense your work, and a full reward be given to you from the Lord God of Israel, under whose wings you are come to take shelter.")

[34] From an Israeli viewpoint it must be noted that one needs to broaden this range substantially and award univocal recognition to courts representing non-Orthodox as well as secular versions of Jewish commitment. Nonetheless, this struggle should not overturn the understanding that the development of Judaism for the last two thousand years absolutely requires the existence of an apparatus that performs and authorizes conversions.

to impose, as if only one way of Jewish life can be the legitimate portion of converts. Conceiving conversion as spiritual migration carries with it the demand and expectation of seriousness, depth, and honesty. But it cannot carry with it the demand or expectation of adopting this or that portion of the Jewish landscape, much less disqualification of other portions of that landscape. The rootedness required of the immigrant can wear different garments, can be performed in different communities within the tapestry of the new "land," and can even contribute to the creation of new communities within it.

Finally, one more observation, reflecting my Israeli point-of-view from which I offer this essay. What I say here is based, as was said, on philosophical and theological considerations as well as on insights into the reality of changing religion and the spiritual dynamics of our day. There are great differences among different societies in which Jews live, and the spiritual migrations to and from Judaism take place in their context. Nevertheless, in relation to all of them it is fully evident that the classic paradigm of ideas that shaped the halakhic tradition in Judaism—towards proselytes as well as toward apostate Jews—has lost its relevance. Of course it is possible to continue operating, more or less, as if it were still valid; but to do so is not helpful either to the development of the tradition or to establishing a proper relation to this important phenomenon in our lives. As was said, these observations are correct as applying to the broadest spectrum of phenomena of embracing Judaism and the Jewish people, as well as of leaving Judaism and the Jewish people. But they are especially vital as they apply to the Israeli reality, a reality in which the primary effort toward conversion and the primary longing for conversion are rooted in geographic-social migrations, generating a deep need for their completion through spiritual migration. It seems that in this reality it is especially proper that we return to the words of Tractate *Gerim*, from which we have already quoted several times: "Dear is the land of Israel which prepares people for conversion. Whoever in Eretz Israel says, 'I am a proselyte,' should be accepted immediately, whereas in Diaspora he is not accepted unless he has witnesses with him."[35] It is possible that in Jewish communities in Diaspora it is proper to examine cautiously when and under what conditions one should confer Jewish "citizenship" on those who seek to immigrate to the Jewish landscape. In Israel, whose landscape is mostly Jewish to begin with, and in the Zionist context whose essence is the "ingathering of the exiles" [*kibbutz galuyot*] and establishing them as a majority Jewish population, it is imperative that we accept prospective proselytes "immediately"; that we prepare the ways

---

[35] Tractate *Gerim* 4:5.

and the hearts, and that we understand that this spiritual migration is—just like the physical migration to Israel—an act of *aliyah*, of ascent.

Teachings

Reflections on Gathering in Grief for Hope and Healing

2014 Israel/Gaza Conflict and Beyond

Katy Z. Allen

After the violence began between Gaza and Israel in the summer of 2014, I felt such pain about the situation, and I didn't know what to do with those feelings. I was upset about many aspects and impacts of the conflict, and I was immobilized.

Then one day something shifted in me, and I suddenly found the strength I had been lacking. I began to realize that there is one thing we all share, and that is our intense grief – grief for those who have been killed, grief at the shattering of any hope that might have been building, despair that the future will ever brighten, and so much more. And it occurred to me that our grief could bring us together. I have led grief workshops in other contexts – facilitating and holding the expression of intense emotions in others are skills that I have. I realized that this was a way that I could do something, here was a way I could make a difference in people's lives.

I reached out to my Muslim friend, Chaplain Shareda Hosein, whom I know and respect from the chaplaincy world. When we spoke, she told me that when she read my email, she felt as though an aching prayer in her heart had been answered.

Shareda and I worked hard to design an environment for deep listening, which we wanted at the core of the program. The two of us clicked – the process was simple, for the planning simply flowed forth without hindrance. We contacted Open Spirit Center, A Place of Hope, Health, and Harmony, in Framingham, MA, where both Shareda and I had previously lead workshops, and they eagerly agreed to host the event.

Once Shareda and I knew what we wanted to do, we asked other faith leaders to help us facilitate the gathering. We invited six in total, knowing that it would be too powerful for just the two of us to hold, and wanting to include our Christian friends. When the evening arrived, we had no idea how many people to expect, but at least there would be the six of us: Rev. Debbie Clark of Edwards Church and Open Spirit Center; Rev. Fred Moser, then of Church of the Holy Spirit in Wayland; Nabeel Kudairi of the Islamic Council of New England; Rabbinic Pastor Matia Angelou, chaplain at that time of Newton-

Wellesley Hospital and continuing with Care Dimensions Hospice; Chaplain Shareda Hosein of the Islamic Society of Boston Cultural Center and the Association of Muslim Chaplains; and myself, a staff chaplain at Brigham and Women's Hospital at that time and rabbi of Ma'yan Tikvah – A Wellspring of Hope.

When the evening came, people started arriving early. One woman told me that she wanted to get a parking space, and she feared the parking lot would fill up! Slowly people trickled in, in ones and twos and threes. Before long, the parking lot *did* fill, and we kept adding chairs to our circle.

Debbie welcomed everyone to Open Spirit, and we stated that we were not gathering to solve anything or to blame anyone, but to share what was on our hearts and to hear what was on the hearts of others. We acknowledged that what we had gathered to do was difficult, and that we needed both to be gentle on ourselves and also to hold ourselves to the ground rules we agreed upon.

We began by using ritual to create a sense of safe and sacred space. In the center of our circle we placed a large glass bowl of water. Shareda spoke about the importance of water in Muslim tradition for ritual cleansing, and then about gratitude. Matia gave each person a beach rock to hold, inviting them to squeeze it tightly if they found themselves triggered by something someone said. Fred spoke about deep listening from the perspective of Christian tradition.

Nabeel invited people to pair off and to practice deep listening by introducing themselves to their neighbor and then sharing about something for which they felt grateful. The previously quiet room was suddenly abuzz with voices as people got to know each other. We then took the time to allow each person to introduce his or her partner and to tell what they felt grateful for. A number of people mentioned their gratitude for being present in this gathering. We went around the circle in order, and by the time each person had spoken, the space inside our circle was being framed and held by gratitude. The sense of the sacred was immanent.

We turned then to grief. I spoke about the mosaic of grief: our grief in response to a personal loss is made up of many aspects and many emotions; it is not a single feeling, but a multitude of responses to our days, our environment, and our situation. When we are dealing with communal tragedy, it takes all of us together, with all of our myriad emotions, to create the mosaic of our grief.

We gave people sheets of colored paper. Debbie asked everyone to write down their feelings and place their papers on the floor. Gradually the floor became covered by paper "tiles" as we created the mosaic of our grief. As people finished, we spread out the papers and invited everyone to walk around and read all the comments.

After we had returned to our seats—then, and only then—we invited people to speak their grief. The circle of 39 people held all of our intense emotions. It was strong enough and solid enough to do so.

When we had finished speaking, we held our shared emotions in silence.

I spoke about post-trauma *growth* and the fact that researchers have found that after a trauma, most people eventually work through it and grow. Our losses can, and do, transform us. We affirmed our dark emotions with a reading from *Healing Through the Dark Emotions*, by Miriam Greenspan.

We then shifted directions and invited people to speak about hope and faith and trust. Quickly, the positive connections began to flow and to fill the circle, entering into the spaces in the mosaic between the paper tiles of grief and fear and despair.

We took time for prayers from our heart: prayers for peace, prayers for the people of Israel and Gaza, prayers of hope and healing and faith.

The last words from one of the participants were, "We may have come in fear, but we needn't have. This worked. For me, it worked."

We stood and stretched, with our arms and hands taking blessing into our circle and ourselves, letting it go outward, into the universe. And we concluded with Matia leading us in the song, "Peace Will Come", by Tom Paxton, which ends with the words "Peace will come, and let it begin with me."

Since this event took place, Open Spirit has hosted several events for healing, peace, and courage in the face of our world's violence. Using "Gathering in Grief" as a foundation, circles inviting prayers, readings, songs and stories have brought people together to share their emotions and to find strength. As Open Spirit continues to assert its place in the community as a multifaith center focusing on hope, healing, and harmony, the connections among people of different backgrounds strengthen, and new faces keep joining the conversations.

We cannot change the situation in Israel and Gaza. We *can* support those with whom we identify with our words and dollars, and we *can* support those we know who live there. We cannot create peace in the Middle East, or in other hot spots.

We will never all agree with each other, and it is fruitless to expect or hope that we will. We each have different perspectives, different loyalties, and different—and amazing—personalities.

But despite our differences, we do have common ground: in our grief, in our hopes for a better world and in our determination to do whatever we can. And on a very basic level, we all share and depend upon the same, wondrous,

Earth. Our planet, with all its own wounds, is our only home; we all turn to it, directly and indirectly, to meet our needs. By acknowledging this common ground, we can create a little bit of peace at home and in our communities, but only when we are ready to begin with ourselves. We are able, when we open our hearts, to listen and hear each other, and to respect one another.

As our world grows ever smaller the violence feels closer and closer, and more and more personal. The demand for strength and resiliency within ourselves and within our communities, and even more so, across communal boundaries, grows ever stronger. It falls on each of us to seek partners in the work of healing, to build a web of connections. For together, we can create sacred spaces in which all can feel safe to articulate and begin healing the pain, despair, and fear.

In the words of Rabbi Abraham Joshua Heschel, "There are three ways to mourn, the first is to cry, the second is to grow silent, and the third is to transform sorrow into song." When we mourn together, cry together, and sit silently together, the transformation of our collective sorrow into song is so much more powerful than when do the work alone. As Rabbi Tarfon famously reminds us, it is not our responsibility to finish the work, but neither are we free to desist from it. All of us must do the painful work of grieving, and the rewards of doing it together are great.

Judaism as Ongoing Spiritual Evolution

Three Sermons

Kaya Stern-Kaufman

The recent news from the Middle East is unbearably painful and tragic. We have been witnessing the radicalization of the Middle East region and the strengthening of tribal mentality. There is a return to a literal and fundamentalist understanding of the Koran, one that sanctions the rape of women and young girls, and the murder of innocent men.

This trend toward fundamentalism is, however, not limited to the Muslim world. Within the Haredi/ultra-Orthodox and settler communities there are some who also hold similar radical views, and who call for the death of Arabs. They, too, draw their support from ancient, sacred texts.

It is true that when our Torah is read literally, without the benefit of commentary, without 2,000 years of rabbinic response and modification of the laws, the horrors we have recently witnessed in Israel become possible. The murder of Shira Banki, a young woman who attended the Gay Pride Parade in Jerusalem, by an ultra-Orthodox man, was a tragic outcome of such thinking and a true desecration of the Torah. The burning of a Jerusalem church in June, a sacred site for Christians, believed to be where Jesus performed the miracle of the loaves and fishes, was evidently perpetrated by religious Jews. The church was spray-painted with the words: *u'ma'avir gillulim min ha-aretz*. These are the words recited in the Aleinu prayer at every Jewish prayer service, meaning: "May idolaters be removed from the earth."

There is no question that certain Torah texts and traditional prayers can be used to fuel hatred and violence. However, there has been a long and persistent response through the efforts of our greatest teachers over millennia to follow the heart, and reinterpret those profoundly disturbing, inhumane texts that appear in Torah.

One classic example of this kind of spiritual evolution comes from this week's Torah portion, *Ki Teitzei*, in which a rebellious child is condemned to death. The text reads:

> If a man has a stubborn and rebellious son, who will not
> obey the voice of his father, or the voice of his mother, and

who, when they have chastened him, will not listen to them;
Then shall his father and his mother lay hold of him, and
bring him out to the elders of his city, and to the gate of his
place; And they shall say to the elders of his city, "This, our
son, is stubborn and rebellious, he will not obey our voice;
he is a glutton and a drunkard." And all the men of his city
shall stone him to death. (Deut. 21:18-21)

In response, the later oral tradition rejects this possibility by creating so
many onerous conditions to be met that it would, in fact, be impossible to
carry out the prescribed penalty. At times the rabbis go to absurd lengths
to prevent the death penalty, despite the Torah's clear ruling. In the Talmud, Rabbi Yehudah states that in order to accuse a wayward son, the mother
would have to be identical to the father in voice, appearance, and height. And
what is the reason for this condition? Because the Torah text says "he does not
listen to *our* voice." That implies that the voices of the two parents must be
equal; and once there is a requirement for the voices to be equal, their appearance and height must also be equal. This would, of course, be impossible. In
fact, the Talmud records that there never was a case of a wayward son being
stoned to death.

Similarly, in this week's portion, the Torah states:

"If a girl who is a virgin is betrothed and a man finds her
in the city, and lies with her; you shall bring them both out
to the gate of that city, and you shall stone them with stones
that they die; the girl, because she did not cry out."

Torah explains that since there were no witnesses to her crying out, there
is an assumption that this was consensual and she was unfaithful to her betrothed. Nevertheless, the rabbis during the Talmudic period create such a
web of conditions for the adjudication of such a case, that it becomes logisti-
cally impossible to issue the death penalty to such a woman.

We cannot change the text of the Torah. We cannot omit disturbing sections, for they are a record of our history, a record of the development of
morality; but we must continue the rabbinic process of interpretation and
evolution.

So as not to give you a skewed view of this week's Torah portion, I want to
make it clear that the majority of the text appears to support the creation of
a compassionate society. Repeatedly, the reader is commanded to care for the

widow, the orphan, and the stranger; to preserve the dignity of the poor; to behave with honesty and integrity; and to minimize the suffering of animals.

In a recent interview, Rabbi Arthur Green stressed the profound need for us to reclaim Judaism from the religious far right, who themselves betray the rabbinic tradition of compassionate interpretation of the law. He recounts the Talmudic debate between Rabbi Akiva and Ben Azzai concerning the most fundamental and underlying principle of the entire Torah. Many of us are familiar with Rabbi Akiva's response—*v'ahavat l'eiakha kamokha*–You shall love your neighbor as yourself. But Ben Azzai argued that there was an even more fundamental principle expressed in the Torah: that all human beings are created in the image of the Divine. In fact, the entire project of the rabbinic period was to uphold this value through the reinterpretation of Torah texts. This has been an ongoing project and we must continue—for the sake of the soul of the Jewish people, and even more so—for the future of humanity. Rabbi Green stated, "Any mitzvah that doesn't increase the sense of *tzelem elohim* must be re-examined." That is, any commandment that does not increase the sense that all human beings are created in the image of Divine, must be re-examined.

Torah has much to teach as a reflection of our past, but also as the foundation of an ever-evolving moral code. As Judaism unfolds, rooted in the teachings of loving one's neighbor and recognition of the Divine aspect in all human beings, we should strive to bear witness to the process.

As this *parashah* closes, we read these familiar and perplexing statements:

> Remember what Amalek did to you by the way, when you came forth out of Egypt; how he met you by the way, and struck at your rear, all who were feeble behind you, when you were faint and weary; and he did not fear God. Therefore it shall be, when the Lord your God has given you rest from all your enemies around, in the land which the Lord your God gives you for an inheritance to possess, that you shall blot out the remembrance of Amalek from under heaven; you shall not forget it. (Deut. 25:17-19)

These statements seem to present a paradox; remember what Amalek did and also blot out the remembrance of Amalek. Taken within the larger context of this portion, it appears to say: Remember what Amalek did to you so that *you* do not become like Amalek and abuse those who are powerless. Remember how your weak and feeble ones were attacked. Now that you are about to enter the land and become an empowered people with your own government and army, remember what it felt like to be powerless and abused. Blot out the memory of Amalek from under the heaven. Blot out any potential for you to become Amalek.

Create a just and compassionate society for all who dwell with you, just as this portion states several times: Always remember that you were once a stranger in Egypt.

May we continue the work to reclaim Judaism as a path for the development of a just and peaceful world. And may we be daring enough to support our ongoing spiritual evolution so that *tzelem elohim*–the divinity in all human beings–is recognized and cherished.

Contemporary Relevance of Ancient Sacred Space

Parshat Terumah begins with the command to build a Tabernacle. God commands Moses to instruct the people to build the Tabernacle so that God's presence may dwell among the people. "Have them make me a sanctuary and I will dwell among them." This verse from Exodus 25:8 appears to say that the purpose of the Tabernacle is to create a place for the indwelling of God among the people. The transcendent God who has at this point bcome accessible to the people only through the overwhelming experience of Sinai–a vertical experience of the Divine–commands the people to build a horizontal space as a channel for God's immanent presence. However, the text does not explicitly reveal *why* God initiates this new form of relationship.

The medieval commentators Rashi and Nachmanides each take a different view as to God's ultimate motivation for the construction of the Tabernacle. Their debate echoes and further elucidates the ancient Talmudic debate between the schools of Rabbi Ishmael and Rabbi Akiva regarding when the actual tabernacle decrees were given.

We see that parshat Terumah comes immediately after the giving of the laws at Sinai, found in parshat Mishpatim. The blueprints for the structure and all its vessels are given, but the Tabernacle is not erected until after the Golden Calf episode in parshat Ki Tissa, which occurs many chapters later. The historic debate between the schools of R. Ishmael and R. Akiva–and later between Rashi and Ramban–center on whether the Tabernacle decrees were given after the Golden Calf episode or before. Each point of view has specific theological implications.

Rashi contends that the building of a *mishkan* (Tabernacle) became a necessity only after the construction of the Golden Calf, because of the sin of the

Golden Calf. One cannot separate the need for the *mishkan* from the Golden Calf episode. Although the descriptions of this building project are presented in the Torah prior to the narrative of the Golden Calf, Rashi resolves this difficulty by quoting the rabbinic principle established by the school of Rabbi Ishmael: "There is no order of precedence or succession in the Torah–*ein mukdam u'm'uchar batorah.*" Events in the Torah are not necessarily presented in chronological order. With that premise, Rashi proposes that God never intended for the people to worship through sacrificial service in the *mishkan* or even at the Temple in Jerusalem. Rather, God intended for each person to experience the presence of the *shekhinah* directly, personally, as occurred at Mt. Sinai. There was to be no need for prescribed actions, for a sacrificial system, in a designated location. However, the sin of the Golden Calf expressed a human need to have a physical expression for a relationship with this divine non-physical being. The people were not able to make the paradigm leap from the concretized images of the divine in Egypt to this disembodied God of Heaven who turns nature upside down at will. Therefore, Rashi explains, God responded to their need by initiating the creation of a designated space with a prescribed service that would allow the people to express their spiritual needs. Both the service and the structure would provide form in the midst of the wilderness, order in the midst of chaos.

Maimonides takes up this line of thought as well in his *Guide to the Perplexed* by asserting that the people had become habituated to animal sacrifice as a method of worship. God recognizes this and provides a vehicle–the *mishkan*–for the people to redirect their need for sacrificial service toward God rather than toward idols. Maimonides states, "Here, God led the people about, away from the direct road which He originally intended, because He feared they might meet on the way with hardships too great for their ordinary strength; He took them by another road in order to obtain thereby His original object ... to spread a knowledge of Him and cause them to reject idolatry." Following the sin of the Golden Calf, God redresses his original plan in order to accommodate human weakness and the desire for animal sacrifice. The Tabernacle and, later the Temple, would serve this need while directing the people to the recognition of the One God. The *mishkan* and Temple would also serve as vehicles for expiation of sin, which was first needed after the Golden Calf incident.

Whereas Rashi and Maimonides attach the significance of the *mishkan* to the Golden Calf, Nachmanides, a kabbalist, argues along the lines of the school of R. Akiva: that the essence of the Tabernacle was to extend the momentous experience of Sinai into a daily-accessible experience. The *mish-*

kan, as described by Torah, creates a place for the *shekhinah* to dwell, so that the relationship established between the people and God at Mt. Sinai could continue to be manifest. The presence of the Tabernacle within the Israelite camp was intended to bring down to earth, literally, a continuity of revelation and relationship experienced first on Mt. Sinai. The Tabernacle was meant to deepen the relationship between God and the people and should not be viewed as a remedy for spiritual failure and an addiction to animal sacrifice. It is for this reason that the directives to build the Tabernacle were given directly after the revelation at Sinai.

The twentieth century Bible scholar Umberto Cassuto states similarly:

> "The nexus between Israel and the Tabernacle is a perpetual extension of the bond that was forged at Sinai between the people and their God. The children of Israel, dwelling in tribal order at every encampment, are able to see, from every side, the Tabernacle standing in the midst of their camp, and the visible presence of the sanctuary proves to them just as the glory of the Lord dwelt on Mt. Sinai, so he dwells in their midst wherever they wander in the wilderness."

Each view expresses different principles about the function of worship. The Maimonidean view explains worship in the Tabernacle within the historical and psychological context of the times. He sees it within an evolutionary process. Communal worship expresses the idea that organized, dedicated service to the One God can refocus the human tendency to fall into misguided forms of worship. Viewed through today's lens, we might say that the establishment of a sacred community, focused on the Divine Center of All, tempers and balances the needs of the ego. It stands as a buffer to the very human tendency to focus on the self, and elevates wealth and power as supreme objectives. A holy community functions as a grounding anchor, reminding us of our place in the web of life, in the society we wish to create and of our relationship with our Creator. Like the Israelite encampment around the Tabernacle, such a community puts God at the center; ideally this central focus may then be reflected in the relationships among the people.

Nachmanides/Ramban the kabbalist, on the other hand, focuses on the relationship between the people and the Divine that serves both parties. Following in the footsteps of the Akivan school, he describes a compassionate God who desires connection with the people. The *mishkan* serves as a conduit for attracting the presence of God and maintaining that relationship within the Israelite community. Sinai, the peak revelatory experience between God and the people, took place once in the life of the nation. The Tabernacle expresses God's desire for an ongoing, portable relationship with an immanent God who travels with the people. It requires and demands dedication and maintenance by the people. Through the manipulation of the mundane world into a sacred space, a channel for the indwelling of the Divine is created.

Given the painful history of our people, Nachmanides' theology, and much of the kabbalistic enterprise of his period, serves as a comfort to a persecuted people. The *shekhinah* is always with us and accessible despite our travail. The *mishkan*, and later the Temple, express God's desire for an ongoing relationship with the Jewish people. Following the destruction of the second Temple, this idea flourishes through countless *midrashim* that depict the *shekhinah* accompanying the people into exile, weeping for them and longing for reunification.

Theology clearly changes with history, as the emotional and spiritual needs of the people change through time. Similarly the function of sacred space and the nature of worship change as well. What remains constant are the values of a community that recognizes God at the center, a community that places *harachamana*—the source of compassion and love at the center.

Whether we follow Maimonides or Nachmanides, our sacred spaces are meant to magnify and channel this awareness so that we can create a truly exalted community. And yet our sacred spaces—our synagogues and churches—are failing. They no longer adequately communicate the relevance of the sacred and no longer draw people to worship. I have frequently heard from youth and others that the theology these sacred spaces represent has become irrelevant to them. It behooves us to deeply explore and understand what people feel to be the pressing spiritual needs of our day. How might we begin to consider a theology that serves the spiritual needs of people today, of our children and grandchildren? I fear for what appears to be a growing cynicism that threatens the hearts of the next generation.

And so I ask these three questions:

What are the spiritual needs of our day?

How does our theology need to change?

And following this idea, how might our worship need to change to convey relevancy and the urgency of our times?

Finally, let us look at the very first vessel that is described and decreed to be built, after the *terumah*—the donations—are collected. This is the *aron hakodesh*—The holy ark (Ex. 26:10-22). We might assume that the primacy of this command reveals something important about the mission of the *mishkan*. Atop the holy ark sit two cherubim facing one another and, according to the text, the space between the cherubim is the place from which God will communicate through Moshe to the people.

Within the space that is created between these two individualities lies the possibility for a holy conversation. Duality, implicit in the physical world and represented by the two cherubim, is bridged through relationship, through sacred communication in the empty space between them. Additionally, the Talmud relates that in the Temple, the curtains around the Holy of Holies would be pulled back on the Holy Days and the ark would be visible to the people. And what did the people see of the cherubim at these times? "They would be embracing one another [carnally]" (Babylonian Talmud, Yoma 54a). Such an image expresses the holiness of two coming together as one.

Similarly, a sacred community must allow for the tension of polarities to exist in dynamic and loving relationship. Moreover, it should facilitate such encounters. Such a community creates a culture of inclusion but not sameness. It encourages deep listening and creates the safety for honest sharing.

May we create a culture such as this among the Jewish people: a sense of expanded community that attracts our youth, our spiritual seekers, our marginalized, our disheartened; a culture that places the highest value on humility, compassion and justice; a community which therefore cannot help but be a magnet for the indwelling of the Divine.

Tisha B'Av: Overcoming Baseless Hatred

For many Jews, *Tisha b'Av* (the ninth day of the month of Av) is an unwelcome interlude in the midst of summer pleasures and respite. As American Jews living in freedom, safety, and material comfort, it is difficult to connect with a day designed to immerse us in a collective experience of mourning and grief—one that spans all of Jewish history—across time and space alike. On *Tisha b'Av* we mourn the destruction of two Temples of which we have no personal memory and, for most Jews, no true desire to rebuild. We recall other Jewish tragedies that have occurred on this date, such as the expulsion from England in 1290 and the expulsion from Spain in 1492. We remember also the mass deportation of Jews from the Warsaw ghetto to Treblinka which began on the eve of *Tisha b'Av*. On this day we enter into a period of mourning for events that span nearly 2,500 years of persecution, exile, expulsion, and slaughter. Time and space are collapsed as we connect with our ancestors. Their tragedies are our tragedies

Yet, for most post-modern Jews, *Tisha b'Av* is seen as an observance that reinforces a collective identity of victimization. For many, if not most, American Jews, *Tisha b'Av* has been rejected because of its identification with perpetual victimhood.

Nevertheless, history provides a lens for understanding the present moment and establishing the vision we strive for. The arc of Jewish history tells a story that has implications for every human being. It reveals essential information for the healing of this fractured world, still seething with baseless hatred and violence. Jewish history tells the story of a people labeled as 'other' and persecuted on this basis. While persecution is not unique to Jewish history, its consistency throughout the western world and across multiple historic periods provides us with a powerful lens for viewing certain aspects of human nature.

What relevance does *Tisha b'Av* hold for us today? It demonstrates and confirms the awesome dangers of demonizing others. Recent Jewish history attests to the truly horrific implications of such attitudes.

Current world events reveal how easy is the tendency to demonize the "other". Tragically, we have too many current examples within our own communities and on the world stage. It is our responsibility not only to look outward, but to look inward at how we may be contributing to this malady. How do we think about those who are different from ourselves? How do we generalize about Palestinians, Muslims, our Christian neighbors, Jews of different denominations, and Jews of no religion?

Traditional Jewish teachings about *Tisha B'Av* assert that while we have been victims, we also share in the responsibility for exiling God's presence from the world. The Talmud teaches that the Second Temple was destroyed due to *sinat chinam*–baseless hatred–within the Jewish community. While Jewish tradition has taught that the destruction and exile were acts of Divine retribution, for most people today, the concept that God metes out reward and punishment for our actions no longer resonates. Yet there is an important truth that lies within this teaching. Baseless hatred within a community destroys relationships and eventually causes the destruction of the community itself. In this sense, the Divine Presence is exiled.

Many Jews and others often ask the question: where was God during the Holocaust? To that question one might answer: God was in the hearts of the rescuers; those who did not allow the propaganda of their time and the pressure of external authority to expel God from their hearts. Dr. Eva Fogelman, in her book "Conscience and Courage," describes the qualities of those who resisted Nazi propaganda and coercion and risked their lives to rescue Jews.

She interviewed hundreds of rescuers and describes their motivations. She concludes that the majority possessed a strong sense of morality and learned from an early age to think for themselves and to tolerate—if not embrace—those considered different from themselves.

Maintaining an awareness of the divine spark that resides within everyone must be an essential goal for our communities, our families, and our systems of education. Our tradition teaches that every human being is created *b'tzelem elohim*—in the image of God. Let us reconsider *Tisha b'Av* as an opportunity to build something new from the ashes of the past: a world wherein we embrace our common humanity while affirming the value of our diversity. And may we begin within our own communities.

God and Gender

Dorothy Goldberg

I am often asked to do weddings near my home in Connecticut; it is one of the aspects of my work that I love dearly. Tonight's sermon is based on an experience I had last year at one of these weddings, an experience that caused me to question many assumptions, including one that I made about myself—that I had seen a broad range of human experience in my time as a member of the clergy. This experience stretched me both personally and theologically.

I got a call from my friend Laura, with whom I had celebrated an adult bat mitzvah in 1998. Laura is a Jew by choice and wanted to go further in her Jewish studies. I was new to congregational life and, raised in a secular family, had had little Hebrew school training and no bat mitzvah. My husband and I became good friends with Laura and her husband Robert, both teachers. Their two sons, Max and Jason, were the same age as our children, Rebecca and Adam.

Over the years we lost touch a bit as our children grew up and I went to seminary and then became the cantor at another congregation. We stayed friends though we rarely got together.

So it was with great delight that I received Laura's call and her request for me to officiate at the wedding of her older son, Jason. Jason and his fiancée began to meet with me on a regular basis as we prepared for the wedding.

All of this was quite normal. Here's the part that was new to me. Jason's younger brother Max now lived by the name Mel (a gender nonspecific name) and no longer identitied as male. What had happened over the years we'd lost touch was a long, and sometimes difficult, story.

Growing up, Max had always identified more with girls than with boys, choosing traditionally girls' toys, clothes and company. As generally tolerant parents who trusted Max to find his own way, Max's parents did not impose culturally masculine norms on him. Nonetheless Max felt increasingly alienated from his peers as he moved into adolescence, particularly as they all seemed to feel more secure than he did in their male or female categories. It drove Max to increased isolation and alienation from himself and within his family. Eventually, Max and his parents entered psychotherapy together which helped Max clarify his identity.

After some deep soul searching, Max told his parents that he knew he didn't feel like a boy and wondered whether he would feel more comfortably himself if he tried living as a female. Although he tried living within a female identity for many months, over time he found that this solution didn't feel right either. In time, Max changed his name to the gender-neutral name Mel, adopted the gender-neutral pronoun they/them, and came to identify as "genderqueer," a person who does not identify as either end of the male/female binary, but whose gender identity falls outside of these categories. Mel finished college, married his male partner, and now would be attending his brother Jason's wedding.

Mel's understanding of how binary categories of gender fail to encompass the gender identities of some people came to have an influence on the entire family. So when Jason and his fiancée came to see me, they spoke about wanting to craft a ceremony that removed all gendered language. No longer would they be "bride and groom" but "beloveds" or the "loving couple." This transition turned out to be much easier than I expected; in fact, in many ways, it enhanced the service. Mel came with their spouse, wearing a flowing silk suit and scarf, and looked happy and relaxed.

This experience got me thinking about the theological aspects of gender. How could a religious view possibly help in a situation like this? Could Mel and their spouse feel comfortable in a congregation and with the concept of God?

The answer, I realized, is a resounding "yes." In fact, God's gender is quite fluid in our tradition. As a being without a physical body, God should, of course, be gender neutral. God is portrayed as a physical body in the chol ha-moed portion from Exodus, where God succumbs to Moses's pleas to come down and show Godself. God passes by Moses in a cleft in the rock, and shields Moses's face so that he can only see God's back, not God's face. Anyone who would look God in the face, it is written, would die. Yet even from this physical appearance of God, we have no idea whether this physically manifested God is male, female or something altogether different. The problem here is that the Hebrew language is not gender neutral; it designates every object, sentient or not, as male or female. A God whose origins come from a deeply paternalistic society will, of course, be designated as male by its language.

Let's consider some of our traditionally male names for God: Elohim, Adonai and El Shaddai. Elohim is plural means "Gods" in Hebrew. Various scholars attribute this to God's use of the "royal we," but others suggest that Elohim may originally have come out of Sumerian and other older cultures where Elohim would have meant a pantheon of many Gods. Surely, some of these would have been female. The whole idea of a God with a plural name begs the question: Are we talking about male and female aspects of God? We just don't know.

The tetragrammaton, yud/heh/vav/heh, probably represents a variant of a phrase translated as, "I will be what I will be." No gender implied, this name is about infinite possibility. It is our use of the substitute word for yud/hey/vav/hey—Adonai, or my Lord—that labels God as male.

Then there is the thundering El Shaddai, translated usually as, "Almighty

God," said to be a man who wrestles with Jacob and then changes his name to Israel. This name is used often in both Jewish and Christian evangelical circles, and is usually translated as, "God of destructive power." The Hebrew root, shin-dalet-dalet, means to destroy, to annihilate. However, as my female biblical Hebrew teacher at Yale Divinity School pointed out, the word "shad" also means breast, and El Shaddai could also be translated as, "God of my breasts." Other scholars point out that this name is often associated with a commandment to be fruitful:

> "May God Almighty (El Shaddai) bless you and make you fruitful and increase your numbers . . ." (Gen. 28:3).
> "I am God Almighty (El Shaddai): be fruitful and increase in number" (Gen. 35:11).
> "By the Almighty (El Shaddai) who will bless you with blessings of heaven above, blessings of the deep that lies beneath, blessings of the breasts (shadayim) and of the womb (racham)" (Gen. 49:25).

In Kabbalistic writings, God is said to have many names and aspects, some of them overtly female. Take Shechinah, for instance, which comes from the Hebrew root for "dwell" or "reside." According to the medieval Kabbalists, Shechinah is the comforting, close manifestation of God who stands with us when we are in peril. Tradition has it that Shechinah stands at the head of a person who is ill — and guards us all in the shadow of her wings.

In a Dvar Torah from The Women's Torah Commentary on Parashat Vaera, in the thick of the Passover story, Dr. Sharon Koren writes about this manifestation of God:

"The signs and wonders (or "plagues") described in Parshat Vaera must have been extremely frightening for both the Egyptians who suffered and the Israelites who bore witness to God's might for the first time. Thirteenth-century Kabbalists believed that when the Children of Israel braved the agonies of slavery and the ten displays of divine might that devastated Egypt, they did not do so alone. Rather, the Israelites knew that the **Shechinah**, the preeminent feminine aspect of God, dwelled alongside them in Egypt. Medieval **Kabbalists** often portrayed the feminine Shechinah as a loving mother who suffers along with her children Israel in exile. She toils with her children while they are slaves in Egypt and protects them in the wilderness after they are liberated."

I would take this analysis even further. Look at the meta-story. The Israelite people, as a whole and under great pressure, pass through a narrow watery channel and are expelled into a wilderness in which they cannot feed themselves. God rains down a white, opaque liquid that is described as sweet-tasting, which feeds the population until it is fully grown as a people and able to enter a land capable of supporting them. That is a pretty accurate description of a mother birthing, breastfeeding and raising her babies!

Let's return to my original story about Mel and their (the singular their) struggles to find their gender identity. What can we learn theologically from examining the many faces of God? This is a difficult idea and one that I have struggled with; as we meet people who are more fluid than firm in their identification with gender, many of us feel quite awkward. It's not easy to look this one straight in the face.

We learn that God Godself defies all gender stereotypes and categorization. How much closer to God, then, is a person who also defies gender stereotypes and categorization? Perhaps it is Mel who is closest of us all to the image of God; Mel whose soul is less tethered to the hormonal demands of the body and more connected with what is divine in them. So, instead of making Mel feel effectively homeless in their own body, we could embrace Mel — and others like Mel — for their closeness to our non-, or multi-, or differently-gendered divine being. We could get closer to the aspects of ourselves that don't conform to our born gender. And we can look at each human being — even one who confuses us — and remember that this person, too, is created in the image of God and YHVH, and El Shaddai, and Elohim, and Shechinah.

Kavanah Before Shofar-Blowing

Trisha Arlin

A Prayer for Praying Before Blowing the Shofar

This was written as a kavanah for the Women of the Wall on Rosh Hashanah 5774

> From Rabbi Arthur Waskow: 'There are three notes on the shofar — Tekiah (Awake!); Teruah (Open your heart!); and Shevarim (Sob with all who suffer!).

Let us blow the shofar
So that everyone can hear:
Awake!
Open Your Heart!
Sob with all who suffer!
We pray for all who thus pray.

However you may gather
Only with your own kind,
Only with your own gender,
Only in mixed company.
After a kosher meal,
After a BLT,
In a minyan,
On your own.

In your holy language, whatever it may be:
All the languages we yearn in.

At your holy sites
In a church,
In a temple,
In a shul,
In a mosque,
In a forest,

In a foxhole,
On a mountain,
At a wall.

However you may be heard
Singing,
Speaking,
Reciting,
Whispering,
Moaning,
Silently,
Blowing a shofar.

However you may hold yourself
Eyes open,
Eyes closed,
Kneeling,
Sitting,
Standing,
Shuckeling,
Spinning.

For whatever reason
With your heart, wishing for the health of a loved one,
With your mouth, reciting liturgy for the continuation of community,
With your body, dancing for spiritual transcendence,
With your feet, acting for a socially just world.

Because when you pray
Whether in obligatory fulfillment of a commandment
Or in mindful awareness of every moment,
Whether in deepest faith or faithful doubt,
When you pray you are kadosh.

And we honor you
Even if you do not honor us.
Please remember,
You may speak to God,
But you do not speak FOR God.

So let us blow the shofar now
So that everyone can hear
That on this holy day
We pray for all who pray,
Even those who would stop us from our prayer.
We pray with a loud, joyful noise
So that we may be heard
Through all the walls,
Because this is a holy conversation.

Awake!

Open Your Heart!

Sob with all who suffer!

Amen.

NOTES ON CONTRIBUTORS

Katy Z. Allen is rabbi of Ma'yan Tikvah: A Wellspring of Hope, facilitator of the One Earth Collaborative (*www.oneearth.today*), and president of the Jewish Climate Action Network (*www.jewishclimate.org*). She posts on www. mayantikvah.blogspot.com.

Morris Allen has served as the first rabbi of Beth Jacob Congregation in Mendota Heights, MN, since 1986. The congregation has grown into a vibrant, vital and affirming community. Rabbi Allen continues his work to establish ethical norms for the production of kosher food and is credited with changing the discourse around kashrut. He is married to Dr. Phyllis Gorin, and they are the parents of three adult children.

Bruce Alpert is rabbi of Beth Israel Synagogue in Wallingford, CT. He also serves as chair of the Board of Trustees of the Academy for Jewish Religion. Prior to his ordination, he was president of Pentron Clinical, a developer and manufacturer of dental restorative materials.

Rabbi Joel Alter earned a BA in Jewish History from Columbia University, and an MA in Jewish Education and rabbinic ordination from JTS. Over 16 years Joel served pluralistic day schools in Washington, DC, Baltimore, and Boston as a teacher, assistant head of school, and *rav beit hasefer*. Since 2012, Joel has served as Director of Admissions for the Rabbinical and Cantorial Schools of JTS.

Yehoyada Amir is a theologian, scholar of Jewish thought and Reform rabbi. He is a professor of Jewish Thought at Hebrew Union College – Jewish Institute of Religion in Jerusalem and the president of MARAM (The Israel Council of Reform Rabbis). He is a board member of Rabbis for Human Rights.

Trisha Arlin—liturgist, AJR student, teacher, freelance writer—is online at OpenSiddur.org, Ritualwell.org and Trisha Arlin: Words of Prayer & Intention (www.triganza.blogspot.com). Her book, *Place Yourself*, is to be published by Dimus Parrhesia Press. For residencies, readings, writing, tutoring and workshops: trisha.arlin@gmail.com. @trishaarlin.

Shira Pasternak Be'eri is a Jerusalem-based editor. She is the website coordinator of the Mandel Foundation-Israel and the former editor of the Israel Democracy Institute's English website. Shira has a BA in Judaic Studies from Touro College and studied Communications at Hebrew University. She blogs at the *Times of Israel*.

Richard L. Claman has written and lectured, for the past 20 years, on various issues in contemporary Jewish philosophy, especially value pluralism, Rawlsian justice, the transition to modernity, and the importance of a Jewish democratic Israel. His "day job" is as head of business litigation at a New York City law firm.

Michael Friedman is a Wexner Graduate Fellow in Jewish Studies and a doctoral candidate in the Department of Theology at Georgetown University. His research focuses on the turn to spirituality in contemporary American Judaism, with attention to developments such as Jewish-Buddhist dialogue and the growth of Jewish mindfulness practices.

Cantor Dorothy Goldberg (AJR '05) has served Reform and Conservative congregations in Connecticut, New Jersey and Puerto Rico. She has also worked as a hospice chaplain and has a special interest in end-of-life issues. Dorothy is a member of the Association of Rabbis and Cantors (ARC) and the American Conference of Cantors (ACC).

David Greenstein, PhD (AJR '96, NYU, '03)) served AJR as faculty member (1997-2009), president and *rosh ha-yeshivah* (2001 – 2002), rabbi-in-residence (2004-2006), and *rosh ha-yeshivah* (2006 – 2009). He is presently the rabbi of Congregation Shomrei Emunah in Montclair, NJ. Summers, he teaches at the Conservative Yeshivah in Jerusalem and Neve Schechter in Tel Aviv. He is the author of *Roads to Utopia: The Walking Stories of the Zohar*, Stanford University Press, 2014.

Reuven Hammer, a former president of the International Rabbinical Assembly, served as dean and professor of Rabbinic Literature at the Jerusalem Campus of the Jewish Theological Seminary. He is one of the founders of the Masorti Movement in Israel and the founding director of the Schechter Rabbinical School. A prolific writer, his column appears regularly in the Jerusalem Post. Two of his books, *Sifre, A Taanaitic Commentary on Deuteronomy* and *Entering the High Holy Days*, were awarded the National Jewish Book Council prize as the best book of scholarship for the year. His most recent book is *Akiva: Life, Legend, Legacy* (JPS).

Heidi Hoover is the rabbi of Temple Beth Emeth v'Ohr Progressive Shaari Zedek in Brooklyn, NY. She was ordained in 2011 by the Academy for Jewish Religion (New York) and holds a Masters in Jewish Studies from Gratz College. She is a fellow of and blogger for Rabbis Without Borders.

Beth Kissileff is the editor of the anthology *Reading Genesis: Beginnings* and the author of the novel *Questioning Return*. Her journalism and fiction appears frequently in a variety of publications. She has taught at Carleton College, the University of Minnesota, Smith College and Mount Holyoke College. She lives in Pittsburgh with her family.

Cherie Koller-Fox received rabbinic ordination from AJR. She is rabbi emeritus at Congregation Eitz Chayim in Cambridge MA, where she served for 25 years. She is a trained chaplain working at hospitals and nursing homes. She currently is the president of NewCAJE, of which she is a founder, and was also a founder and past president of CAJE.

Leonard Levin (Rabbi, Ph.D. from Jewish Theological Seminary) teaches Jewish philosophy at the Academy for Jewish Religion. He is the author of *Why God Is Subject to Murphy's Law: Dialogues on God and Judaism,* and has translated many works on Jewish thought. Selections of his current writing can be found at https://ajrsem.academia.edu/LennyLevin.

Rabbi Asher Lopatin is the president of Yeshivat Chovevei Torah Rabbinical School, an Orthodox rabbinical school that teaches an inclusive, open and welcoming Torah. Previously, he was the spiritual leader of Anshe Sholom B'nai Israel Congregation, a Modern Orthodox synagogue in Chicago, for 18 years. He received his ordination from Rav Ahron Soloveichik and Yeshivas Brisk in Chicago, and from Yeshiva University, as a Wexner Graduate Fellow. A Rhodes Scholar with an M.Phil. in Medieval Arabic Thought from Oxford University, Rabbi Lopatin is the author of numerous scholarly and popular articles.

Alan Mittleman is the Aaron Rabinowitz and Simon H. Rifkind Professor of Jewish Philosophy at the Jewish Theological Seminary. His most recent book is *Human Nature and Jewish Thought: Judaism's Case for Why Persons Matter* (Princeton University Press, 2015). He is currently writing a book entitled *Holiness and Violence in Judaism: A Moral Philosophical Investigation,* under contract with Princeton University Press.

Dr. Ora Horn Prouser is executive vice president and academic dean at the Academy for Jewish Religion. She has worked with educational institutions to develop Bible curricula and pedagogy. Her book, *Esau's Blessing: How the Bible Embraces Those with Special Needs,* was recognized as a National Jewish Book Council finalist.

Dr. Ruth N. Sandberg is professor of Rabbinics and Director of the Jewish-Christian Studies program at Gratz College. She authored *Rabbinic Views of Qohelet* and *Development and Discontinuity in Jewish Law* and contributed a chapter to *The Words of the Wise are Like Goads: Engaging Qoheleth in the 21st Century.*

Eliezer Schweid is an Israel Prize laureate (1994) and Professor Emeritus of Jewish Thought at the Hebrew University, where he taught for four decades. He is the author of over forty books and hundreds of articles covering every aspect of Jewish thought from ancient to modern times. As public educator and intellectual, he has provided a rich, original interpretation of the legacy of cultural Zionism for Israel and world Jewry today.

Susan Shevitz, EdD is associate professor emerita, Brandeis University, where she taught in and directed the Hornstein Professional Leadership Program. She is completing a book about the conceptualization and enactment of pluralism that proposes principles for sustaining pluralism in schools and community organizations. She also teaches and consults widely on leadership and evaluation.

Rabbi Rebecca W. Sirbu is the Director of Rabbis Without Borders at CLAL – The National Jewish Center for Learning and Leadership. Rabbi Sirbu was named as one of the "Most Inspirational Rabbis in America" by *The Forward*. She is a consultant for synagogues, organizations, and individuals on leadership development, building creative capacity, actualizing ideas, and how to work across religious and cultural borders. She is an expert voice on social media, and a speaker and writer on a variety of issues related to religion in America today. She is published in several books: *I am Here: The Untold Stories of Everyday People, Faithfully Feminist: Jewish, Christian, and Muslim Women on Why They Stay*, and *The Sacred Calling: Forty Years of Women in the Rabbinate*, and is a regular contributor to eJewish Philanthropy, among other publications. She manages and writes for the Rabbis Without Borders blog on myjewishlearing.com. A Phi Beta Kappa graduate of Vassar College, she holds a master's degree and ordination from The Jewish Theological Seminary of America. She tweets at @rabbirebecca and @rwbclal.

Rabba Kaya Stern-Kaufman, MSW is the spiritual leader of Congregation Agudat Achim, Leominster, MA. She is founder of Rimon Resource Center for Jewish Spirituality and the S. Berkshire Community Hevra Kadisha. Recognized by *The Forward* as one of "America's Most Inspiring Rabbis," Rabba Kaya has taught throughout the northeast and abroad.

Rahel Wasserfall is the Director of Evaluation and Training at CEDAR and Resident Scholar at the Women's Studies Research Center at Brandeis University. An anthropologist with a PhD from Hebrew University, Jerusalem, she has wide experience on three continents, and has published on the anthropology of gender, pluralism and qualitative methods. She is the editor of *Women and Water: Menstruation in Jewish Life and Law* (UPNE, 1999) and is currently working on the book: *Eating Together with Difference*.

Pluralism and the Academy for Jewish Religion

The concept of pluralism – embracing Jews from across the religious spectrum – may be the wave of the future in the Jewish community, but at the Academy for Jewish Religion (AJR), we have been living pluralism for the past sixty years. In 1956, at the height of denominationalism, AJR's founders realized that the future of the Jewish People was in acceptance and inclusiveness, cherishing and learning from the other. For sixty years, AJR has led the Jewish community in the pluralistic training of rabbis, cantors and, more recently, graduate students.

The Academy for Jewish Religion ordains rabbis and cantors, and trains Jewish leaders, to combine their mastery of the intellectual and spiritual richness of our tradition with openness to its application in the pluralistic, contemporary Jewish community and awareness of living in the presence of God. Its graduates and students fill movement-affiliated and unaffiliated pulpits, and serve as religious leaders, chaplains, teachers, and organizational innovators in North America and around the world. AJR's pluralistic education provides them the tools to connect meaningfully with Jews, and others, in what many call a post-denominational period.

AJR rabbis and cantors:

Lead dynamic, spiritually uplifting, religious services using the liturgical rubrics and musical legacies of all denominations;

Provide skillful, compassionate counseling;

Utilize traditional and contemporary sources to teach Torah in lively, meaningful, and intellectually engaging manner;

Incorporate spiritual practices, meditative techniques and sacred arts into their personal and communal prayer experiences;

Officiate at moving, beautiful Jewish life cycle ceremonies;

Guide congregations and organizations in their creation of supportive, spiritual, religious communities; and

Embrace all Jews and their families regardless of religious affiliation, personal practice, sexual identity or gender identity

Students earning Master's degrees in Jewish Studies learn to apply their knowledge and skills within the same context of openness and divine presence as those being ordained.

CPSIA information can be obtained
at www.ICGtesting.com
Printed in the USA
BVHW051109310721
612915BV00006B/837

9 781934 730607